Development Prospects
of Pakistan

SCANDINAVIAN UNIVERSITY BOOKS

Universitetsforlaget, Oslo/Bergen/Tromsö
Munksgaard, Copenhagen
Svenska Bokförlaget, Stockholm

OLE DAVID KOHT NORBYE

Development Prospects of Pakistan

UNIVERSITETSFORLAGET

BERGEN/OSLO/TROMSÖ

© UNIVERSITETSFORLAGET 1968

Distribution offices:

NORWAY
Blindern, Oslo 3

UNITED KINGDOM
16 Pall Mall, London S. W. 1

UNITED STATES
Box 142, Boston, Mass. 02113

Printed in Norway by E. Sem A.s, Halden

Foreword

Pakistan is one of the most populous underdeveloped countries in the world. With more than 115 million people and an average annual level of *per caput* income equivalent to less than $75, it represents a most dramatic challenge to human endeavour. National determination and international support have combined to make Pakistan one of the few post-war success stories in the race between economic advance and population growth. This success, however, is tenuous rather than assured, within reach rather than realized.

In the 1950s, *per caput* real income in West Pakistan rose by no more than the equivalent of 60 US cents per year, while in East Pakistan the already unbelievably low level of *per caput* income actually declined. During these years the basic physical infrastructure was built up, as were social and educational services, and improvements were made in national and local administration.

In the 1960s, economic growth has so far been very rapid in both provinces — even more rapid than the target set for the Second Plan period 1960—65. Although the growth of population has accelerated to almost 3 per cent per year, average *per caput* real income has increased at nearly the same rate. Moreover, in sharp contrast to the 1950s, the economy of East Pakistan has in recent years developed as rapidly as the economy of West Pakistan. And, finally, there is evidence that these satisfactory developments are now accelerating rather than slowing down. Pakistan's own plans and projections are based on continued emphasis on economic growth and realistic acceptance of the costs of development.

Pakistan has received assistance of increasing importance from foreign countries. Over the last ten years the total value of foreign assistance (loans and grants) has increased nearly tenfold to about $ 550 million in 1965, or over 6 per cent of the total GNP in that year. At the same time, internal savings have increased to nearly 10 per cent of the GNP in 1965, an effort which has required a sustained marginal rate of savings of well over 20 per cent during the Second Plan period (1960—65).

Structural change has been an essential feature of the growth process as is evidenced by the changes in rates of savings and investment, in employment patterns and urbanization, in the relative contributions to the national product of the various sectors of the economy, in consumption patterns, etc. Most striking are the structural changes in foreign trade patterns. In 1951—52 only 1 per cent of total export receipts was represented by manufactured goods, in 1964—65 the share was 29 per cent. Over the same period the share of agricultural products declined from nearly 90 per cent to 53 per cent of total exports. Similarly, the import pattern has been radically changed. The share in imports of capital goods and raw material for the domestic capital goods industries har increased from little over one-quarter of total imports in 1951 to nearly two-thirds of all imports in 1964—65, the share of consumer goods imports having dropped correspondingly.

The orientation of this study of the economy of Pakistan — as of other studies included in the research programme of which the present work forms a part — has been to identify, evaluate, and describe the nature of the structural changes that are associated with economic growth in a developing country. We have tried to do so by an analysis which encompasses the whole economy: patterns of production and consumption, of saving and investment, of employment and migrations, of trade and finance, etc. We then subject the foreign trade sector to particular scrutiny, both from the point of view of internal consistency with the other elements of structural change in the economy and in order to evaluate the implications for foreign assistance and foreign market developments.

This study of the Pakistan economy is based on a very thorough compilation and analysis of existing data on the current structure of the economy, on developments over the last ten or fifteen years and on plans, programmes, and projections for the future. Since the objective has been to analyse structural change, we found it necessary to carry projections and analyses quite far into the future; 1985 was chosen as the terminal year. It should be clear, of course, that we do not present these projections of structural change so far into the future as a prognosis of developments that will necessarily be realized. The picture of the future of the Pakistan economy which is drawn in this study is, we submit, well founded and realistic in its main characteristics, but it is based on assumptions with regard to policy and external developments which may or may not be realized. It is neither a perspective plan for the Pakistan economy — since it is not the result of an exercise in policy formulation by responsible planning authorities — nor a set of 'most likely' projections of how the economy may evolve. The value of this study, such as it is, lies mainly in the application of a methodology by which the inter-relationships between the many and various elements of structural change and economic growth are brought out. From this point of view the main results are summarized in the input-output Tables for each of the years 1960, 1965, 1970, 1975, 1980, and 1985, given in Appendix I. These Tables, which present a detailed sector breakdown, represent the result of intensive work on individual industries and activities and on inter-relationships between them. It is a significant characteristic of these Tables that the structure of the economy and the input-output coefficients change from one year to another.

The results of the study of Pakistan as presented here represent only a summary of the research findings. A stencilled version of this study included two volumes of appendixes which contained a large number of detailed Tables*. It is possible that some formulations in the text published here may be thought arbitrary or insufficiently supported by evidence and by analysis. In fact most estimates and projections published in this text are substantiated and backed up in considerable detail in the unpublished tabular appendixes as well as in the text which originally accompanied these detailed Tables.**

The analysis of the Pakistan economy presented in this volume forms part of a series of studies on the long range outlook for balance of payments relations between developed and developing countries, as well as analyses of the longer term development patterns of a number of individual Asian and African countries, with particular emphasis on their external economies. This research is conducted under the auspices of the Chr. Michelsen Institute with financial support initially from the Rockefeller Foundation and the Norwegian Research Council for Science and the Humanities, later also from the Ford Foundation and the Norwegian Agency for International Development.

This study has been prepared by Mr. O. D. Koht Norbye, a Norwegian economist with experience from the Organisation for European Economic Co-operation (OEEC, later OECD) in Paris

* [0].
** This text was not reproduced in [0], partly for reasons of economy and avoidance of repetition, partly because the text would have needed revision to account for changes introduced in the figures at a later stage. The text is, however, available in a limited number of copies from the Chr. Michelsen Institute.

and from the Harvard University Advisory Group to the Planning Commission in Karachi where Mr. Norbye worked for more than two years from early 1959. Since July, 1961, Mr. Norbye has been a senior member of the research group in development economics at the Chr. Michelsen Institute. From October 1965, Mr. Norbye had leave from the Institute to act as economic advisor to the Government of Kenya.

Just Faaland
Director of Research

Acknowledgements

This study would probably never have been started, had it not been for the Harvard University Pakistan Advisory Group to which I belonged during the period 1959 to 1961 as advisor to the Planning Commission in Karachi. This advisory group and its present parent organization, the Harvard University Development Advisory Service, has shown great interest in my research, has provided me with up to date documentation on Pakistan, and at the end of 1963 invited me for a stay of several weeks in Pakistan to discuss a preliminary draft with interested officials and others. That trip enabled me to obtain valuable additional information and to check many of my preliminary conclusions. It is, of course, impossible to list all those persons, members of the Harvard team, Pakistan officials, and others, from whom I have got inspiration, ideas, and information, but their contribution is most gratefully acknowledged.

Since the approach adopted in this study is in many respects experimental, I have been compelled to carry out practically all the detailed calculations and various statistical adjustments myself; only occasionally was I able to make effective use of assistants for the tedious work involved in cross-checking, preparation of estimates, and the establishment of the input-output tables. However, Miss Sarah Karslake, Mr. Mark F. Cherniavsky, and Miss Sarah O'Connelly all worked patiently on many of the Tables at various stages and prepared elements for the input-output Tables.

The typing work of the earlier versions of this study was particularly difficult and boring since it included not only all the Tables which were presented in the unpublished annexes, but also lengthy, detailed footnotes. Miss Sue Dalgleish, Miss Angela Richardson, Miss Betty Balfré, Miss Sarah O'Connelly, and Mrs. Joan Chartroule did most of the typing for the earlier drafts; Mrs. Aslaug Blom and Miss Vivian Wakabayashi did most of the typing for the present version.*

* [0].

I have received most useful oral and written comments on earlier versions of this study from Professor Ray Vernon and Dr. Gustav F. Papanek of the Harvard University Development Advisory Service, from Dr. Richard V. Gilbert, Mr. Wouter Timms, Mr. Asbjørn Bergan, Mr. Per Tveit, and Professor Oddvar Aresvik of the Harvard team in Pakistan, from Mr. Ghulam Mohammad of the Pakistan Institute of Development Economics, from Mr. Jo W. Saxe of the OECD, and most extensively from Mr. Just Faaland of the Chr. Michelsen Institute. Mr. Faaland also scrutinized the entire manuscript for the present version and made a number of suggestions for improvements. The responsibility for the analysis and the presentation is, of course, mine.

My thanks go also to my present employers, the Ford Foundation and the Ministry of Economic Planning and Development in Kenya, who let me have one month's extra leave in August, 1966, so that I could write Chapter 14 and thereby finish this study.

Ole David Koht Norbye

Contents

1. Purpose and Background

The purpose of the present study is ambitious, namely to trace out a possible pattern of development of the economy of one of the largest, poorest, and in many respects most complicated developing countries in the world. Pakistan has now more than 100 million people and is with Japan and Indonesia one of the countries which can claim to be the fifth largest nation of the world. Its national income per head is only around 75 U.S. dollars (1967) which puts it in the class of the very poor countries, in company with several other large Asian and African nations. Its economic structure is a mixture of traditional activities, which dominate the economy, and very modern and efficient units in manufacturing, energy, and transport which give Pakistan the image of being a truly developing country. The country consists of two major regions, more than 1,000 miles apart, which differ fundamentally in natural resources, in degree of development, and in other characteristics. An analysis of the growth of the economy of Pakistan must therefore take into account not only the dualism of the traditional and the modern sectors, but also the dualism of two widely different regions.

This study has the specific purpose of broadening our knowledge of the pattern of international trade of developing countries in a future which is not too distant for meaningful projections, but at the same time is distant enough to imply significant changes in this pattern from what it is now. It is an integrated part of a research programme which aims at analysing the future role of the developing countries in world trade. Such an analysis requires a study of the future import demand by the developing countries, both the level and the structure of demand, and of their export potential, again with stress on the possible structure of their future exports. Both the level and the structure of imports and of exports are closely linked with the internal structure of the developing economies. While bearing in mind that economic projections over a period of 20 to 25 years must become very uncertain, the need to obtain a fairly detailed picture of the foreign trade prospects of a developing country leads logically to an effort to project structural changes of a developing economy in considerable detail over such a period of time.

It is its specific purpose which has made this study possible, since it has permitted the author to spend most of the last four years on scrutinizing available material on Pakistan, making detailed projections for all major sectors of its economy, bringing all data together in the form of comprehensive input-output Tables, and undertaking several rounds of adjustments in order to make all data internally consistent.

Although the data on the possible future trade pattern of Pakistan and its need for foreign 'aid' during the next twenty years are some of the most important findings of this study, and also should be interesting from a practical and political point of view, they represent nevertheless only one part of the results. The picture of the internal structural changes in a developing economy is in itself, at least in the opinion of the author, of even greater practical interest. From a purely analytical point of view the data on the internal structural changes are less subject to errors than those on the foreign balance which inevitably must represent differences between domestic supplies and demand and therefore are also subject to wider margins of errors. But the cob-web of mutually dependent data on the internal structure of a developing economy is a necessary precondition for long-term planning. The need for long term, or 'perspective', planning is gradually being recognized, particularly in Pakistan, as an indispensable part of the planning process in a developing country. In a highly industrialized country the economic structure is diversified and so are the resources for future growth. In an underdeveloped country the economic structure is inflexible because most of the resources needed for the modernization of the economy are scarce. Steps must therefore be taken today in order to plan changes which will take place in a fairly distant future. This is most evident in the case of education, since today's pupils in the lower schools will be called upon to fill posts as managers, highly trained specialists, and skilled workers some twenty years from now. It is equally true for the planning of the modern part of the economy, such as modern industries, power supplies, and transport network. Pilot units which appear to be dead losses today are needed to prepare for large scale units which will prove to be viable cornerstones of the economy a couple of decades hence.

If it were not for the fact that the author has been and still is firmly convinced that detailed studies of the internal structure of a developing country will prove to be indispensable for its future planning effort, he would never have had the courage to carry this study through. The foreign trade aspect of the analysis does not merit the same detailed approach, although the end result is probably better if more attention is given to some pertinent details. The analysis of internal structural changes must, in contrast, be based on rigorous efforts to make all figures internally consistent.

My interest in this kind of analysis was very much strengthened during my stay as adviser to the Planning Commission in Pakistan for two years, during the preparation of the Second Five-Year Plan and its implementation. My special field was industrial development, and I discovered very soon that industrial planning based on imminent needs (or export prospects) and cost-benefit analysis of individual projects meant that the time-horizon was far too narrow. Moreover, the fact that no systematic analysis of inter-industry relations was available ('input-output Tables') meant that even data on the domestic demand in the imminent future were missing. During my stay in Pakistan I was therefore led to make efforts to analyse the input-output structure, at least of the manufacturing industries, and to make some crude projections of the long-term structural changes of the economy. But it was only after I became able to devote full time efforts to these studies that it was possible to carry them out in depth.

In the meantime perspective planning has been taken up by the Planning Commission in Pakistan. The idea was launched in a very crude form during the preparation of the Second Five-Year Plan when some broad targets for 1985 were suggested.[1] In recent years internally consistent models have been built up, input-output analysis has been brought into use, and the Third Five Year Plan contains the tentative, main results of this perspective planning. Hitherto, however, the Planning Commission has not completed its research into the pattern of Pakistan's economy in the same detail as shown in this study.

This analysis of the changing pattern of a developing economy has been pursued in order to find out whether *new lessons* can be drawn which cannot equally well be drawn from empirical studies of developing economies in the past. A lot of factors suggest that historical data are not relevant to the developing countries. Technology has changed; and, what may prove to be even more important, the science of economics has made great strides, and it is now possible to envisage planned growth based on sound scientific methods. One result of this progress in economics is that it is also possible to envisage high and fairly steady growth rates over a prolonged period. In the past, economic crises and wars influenced economic growth to such an extent that there are no historical examples of economies which have grown at a rate of 5 to 7 per cent per year over a period of a quarter of a century. Today a developing country has to plan for such targets if it wants to escape from the claws of poverty within a reasonable span of time. Another new element which is worth mentioning is the stress on a balanced economic growth which not only emphasizes that all sectors of the economy must take part in the growth process but also that all population groups shall to a reasonable degree benefit from the gains of economic development.

In conducting this study I have not aimed at setting up a hypothetical growth model for an undefined developing economy. On the contrary, all data are as far as possible closely linked to the existing and potential human and natural conditions in Pakistan. This attempt to make a case study of a developing country on the basis of a multitude of given facts, made it necessary to examine very closely a large amount of existing information on Pakistan in order to get a reasonably true picture of the state of Pakistan in the chosen base period: 1 July 1959 to 30 June 1960. Eventually, I was led into a cobweb of scattered information, difficult to compare on different types of schools, scope for further irrigation and double cropping in agricultural areas, the structure of the road transport industry, and the number of handloom weavers — to mention a few typical examples. As the study progressed, it became apparent that only a rigorously consistent classification of all available data could lead to satisfactory results. In the end the statistical work became far more ambitious than originally envisaged, and all data suitable for such presentation were brought together in the input-output Tables which are included as Appendix I.

While the study has thus gained in rigour, it has become somewhat less up-to-date. The standard of economic analysis in Pakistan has continued to improve during the last four years, and statistical sources have been improved. New data have become available; where possible, these have been taken into account. But on one important point it has not been possible to follow the latest developments in Pakistan. The planned growth for the Second Five-Year Plan upon which this study is based was, after revisions, set at 22 per cent, whereas the most recent information suggests that the growth in fact reached 29 per cent. This encouraging performance makes some of the basic figures in this study out of date, but it does not in any way upset the pattern of projections for the period 1965 to 1985. The basic problems remain the same. The long term prospects of agriculture depend on natural conditions, possible investments, and, not least, the adaptability of the peasant. Some years of promising progress in agriculture do not prove that progress will accelerate during the next couple of decades. The recent Indian setbacks in agriculture should be taken as a healthy reminder that a breakthrough in agriculture is hard to achieve even if progress is promising for a while. The growth of modern manufacturing industries is easier to plan, but it depends on the enterprising spirit of private businessmen and of the government itself as well as on the ability of the government to help provide the necessary infrastructure, that is, adequate supplies of personnel, literate workers, good transport, and safe and cheap supplies of gas and electricity. The problem of the extent to which growth of the service trades will help fulfil growth targets and provide jobs is essential in planning, and is a major subject of this study.

With all its shortcomings this study should give a reasonably realistic picture of the immense changes which will have to take place in the economic structure of a country which manages to achieve a high rate of economic growth. The emphasis is on the purely economic factors, and, amongst these, first of all the 'real' factors such as production, consumption, investments, exports, imports, and employment. The financial, fiscal, and monetary structure has been treated in a cursory manner only. Factors essential to the implementation of planning like administration and organization, entrepreneurship, and social and cultural barriers to development have been touched upon only to the extent that they clearly relate to the rate of growth of some specific sector of the economy. Thus the behaviour of the average peasant is the most important factor which determines the growth in agriculture. Main emphasis has been laid on the growth of education since the skill of the labour force determines the growth potential for most economic activities. In projecting the future pattern of personal consumption, assumptions had to be made about the speed at which the population in Pakistan will change their consumption pattern if they have the economic opportunity to do so.

The stress on the real economic factors does not mean that the author neglects the essential importance of political, social, financial, and monetary factors on the growth of an economy. It merely means that it is explicitly assumed that the government and the people of Pakistan will be able to follow policies and take attitudes which allow the economy to grow at approximately the rate and the pattern which is outlined here.

For two reasons this study should not be considered as an exercise in long-term planning. Firstly, as already pointed out, it does not supplement the growth and investment targets with financial targets which, for example, would show necessary changes in taxation and likely movements in relative prices. Nor does it deal with the human aspect of plan implementation — use of scarce administrative resources, means of persuading farmers and artisans to change their methods, and so on. Secondly, it does not include any evaluation of how to allocate scarce foreign exchange resources. The reason for this is simply, as will be pointed out later, that it is assumed throughout this study that foreign aid will be made available to cover the projected balance of payments deficit. This assumption does not imply that *all* resources have been considered as available without limits. On the contrary, the scarcity of land, of well-trained manpower, or of mineral and forest resources are factors which have been taken fully into consideration in determining the growth potential of any single industry. But even in these cases, no efforts have been made to find the optimum allocation of such scarce, domestic resources. For example, the use of land between different crops has not been studied with that aspect in mind, but merely to decide whether there is enough land to produce crops which will be needed. When the answer is no, I have made an arbitrary choice in order to determine which products will have to be imported since I have neither the technical competence nor the time to aim at finding the optimum solution to this crucial planning problem.

The growth pattern given in this paper is one which appears fairly likely on the basis of present knowledge of the economic potential of Pakistan. My personal judgement — which is based on two years' experience as adviser to the Planning Commission of the government of Pakistan — has had a major influence on the chosen growth pattern. Although it is based on extensive knowledge of the economic structure of Pakistan, and although in my capacity as adviser I had access to a considerable amount of unpublished material, my personal interpretation of the facts will necessarily have had a strong influence on my conclusions. Clearly, the growth pattern which I have arrived at is nothing but an illustration of one possible growth pattern which in my view corresponds to the possibilities and needs of Pakistan.

It is necessary to stress that this study does not represent the blueprint of a long-term plan but merely a picture of a possible development pattern. It is justifiable to argue that the projected pattern is *likely* because it is closely linked with very plausible projections of the *pattern of demand*, and it is all too probable that the pattern of growth of a developing country will be more influenced by demand pressures than by an attempted optimum allocation of resources.

The present study should permit some interesting conclusions about the future foreign trade needs of a developing country of the size of Pakistan. For smaller countries, whether isolated or members of free trade areas or customs unions, the trade pattern will certainly be quite different. It should also be remembered that the study on Pakistan is based on the natural resources which exist in that country, and that for this reason alone the findings of this study cannot be expected to have universal validity.

2. Problems and Analytical Framework

A. *Significant progress over a long span of time*

A study of the influence of the modernization of the economies of the economically backward countries on world trade and on the economies of the now highly industrialized countries implies the assumption that the developing countries actually will achieve rapid and stable growth so that changes in their economic structure will have a profound influence on world trade. In addition, it must cover a sufficiently long period so that the expected changes will be large enough to permit a meaningful analysis of the resulting problems.

For these reasons the working hypothesis is that the developing countries will attain growth rates corresponding to the ambitious growth targets which are now being set by the most determined amongst them. The projections have been carried forward to 1985. Nobody can expect that the world economy in 1985 will look anything like what would result from a long series of country studies like the present one on Pakistan. Some developing countries may fail to develop while others may do even better than projected. Technological developments may make havoc of many of the assumptions about growth and development for individual economic sectors. In spite of such uncertainties a series of country studies would nevertheless suggest major structural changes which will take place in the world economy. Maybe these changes will not be as strong and as fast as, for example, this study of Pakistan implies, but this might mean that in broad terms the changes will take a longer time than the assumptions behind this particular study suggest.[1]

B. *The growth of the Gross Domestic Product as a guide*

Most countries state their economic goals in terms of desired growth rates for their Gross Domestic (alternatively National) Products. It is quite legitimate to state the goals in this manner, but this does not mean that national planners will disregard other targets and consider the achievement of a postulated rate of growth of the GDP as the ultimate and sacrosanct goal.

The responsible authorities in the different countries are faced with the problem of allocating scarce resources (human and natural resources, man-made capital, financial means, and foreign exchange supplies) in such a manner that both short-term needs and long-term aspirations are met in the best possible manner. If these allocations are made within the framework of a national plan, it is possible to state that the GDP is likely to grow at such or such a rate within a given period of time. Under the restraint of scarce resources — foreign and domestic — the growth target for the national income cannot be fixed initially, but only after thorough consideration of all relevant facts. Most developing countries will find that shortage of foreign exchange limits their growth potential so severely that they will have to deviate from this pattern of planning by considering foreign exchange as a flexible resource. They will therefore make their plans on the assumption that foreign aid will be forthcoming. A country which puts forward a realistic development plan and determined policies for its implementation can hope that the richer countries will underwrite its efforts by capital export in one or several forms. This means that the national development target expressed in terms of the growth rate of the GDP will become a firmer guideline than suggested in the beginning of this section. Even in such a case, the developing country will have to plan the allocation of resources between different uses. The plan figures for the GDP are *results* of such detailed plans.

The 'national income' is in itself an inadequate measure of the economic well-being of a country. International comparisons can at their best only be very approximative. First of all the figures expressed in national currencies have to be converted into a common unit, for example US dollars, usually by means of the ruling exchange rates. These exchange rates will only accidentally correspond to the ratio of the price levels in the two countries under comparison. Several attempts have been made to overcome this difficulty by measuring the purchasing power ratio between the currencies of two countries.[2] Such comparisons will never lead to one single answer, but two, depending on whether the structure of the national income or the use of national resources in the one country or the other is used as weights for the prices. By using statistical averages of some kind or another, this difficulty can be met, but such averages are not as meaningful as either of the two sets of bilateral comparisons. Comparisons of the levels of the national incomes in a series of countries are even more dubious than between pairs of two countries.

Quite apart from the problem of differences in the purchasing power of the money, comparisons between rich and poor coun-

tries or even between poor countries involve another basic difficulty. The standard methods of national accounting include in
the national income all economic activities which give rise to
the earning of a money income (except criminal activities). In
addition a figure is included for main subsistence activities such
as the production of food for own use (usually for the farmers
only). This means that in a highly urbanized country the *costs*
of urban living are included as a part of national income (i. e.,
urban transport costs, the processing, transport, and distribution
costs of food, etc.). In a poor country in which most of the people
belong to a subsistence agriculture, such costs to a large extent
do not exist. This statistical difficulty can be avoided by inflating the value of the subsistence product to include fictitious
processing, transport, and distribution costs, or in other words, by
measuring the subsistence end products at the same prices as
similar products in the urban sector.[3] Such adjustments are seldom made when the national income of two countries is being
compared.

In principle, the total national income of a country should
measure its total economic strength. If the proper adjustments
are made, it is possible to make fairly adequate comparisons between the economic strength of two countries. But in most con-
texts it is far more meaningful to compare the national income
per caput between two countries, again if the relevant adjustments are made. A country with low national income *per caput*
has very few resources left for purposes other than the mere
struggle for survival of its people. Nevertheless, a poor country
with a large population may mobilize more resources for research,
cultural activities, defence, etc., than a poor country with a small
population. In this context the absolute size of the national income is relevant.

The national income per head, if properly adjusted, is a significant measure of the *potential* economic strength of several countries. But it is not a measure of the relative levels of the standard
of living in different countries. Even if personal consumption
per head (or the sum of personal and government consumption
per head) is used as a measure, it does not adequately describe the
differences in the standards of living of the peoples of different
nations. The obvious reason for this is that the income may be
distributed in such a manner that the relative income levels of
the great majority of the people of different countries may differ
very significantly from the relative levels of the average national
income or consumption per head in the same countries.

This study is not concerned with income differentials between
countries, but with the effects of the growth of the national in-

come over time in low income countries. However, the statistical problems are closely related to those which appear in international comparisons. Significant changes in the structure of the national income mean that there will be two measures for the rate of growth depending on whether the price structure in the initial or in the final year is used as weight.[4] Furthermore, the modernization of the economy also leads to urbanization, and a significant part of the increased national income will consist of income from activities which represent costs of urbanization. Finally, the growth of national income and of consumption *per caput* do not represent a corresponding increase in the welfare of the people, unless it can be shown that the benefits of the growth are distributed in such a manner that welfare and national income or consumption, in fact, rise at approximately the same rate. There exists no entirely satisfactory measure of the welfare of the people, but it is at least possible to make some crude estimates of how economic progress influences the standard of living of a population.

The national planners have to determine the use of additional resources in order to ensure a satisfactory growth in the welfare of the people. The target for the national income does not give any answer to this. Not only that, but the planners must explicitly, or in most cases they will do it implicitly, base their decisions on a 'preference function' which determines the desirable balance between immediate and future gains for the people.

In spite of all the inherent weaknesses in the use of national income as a measure of economic growth, its projected growth has been used as the main yardstick in this study, for the simple reason that it is the best and first of all the most convenient yardstick available for the global development of an economy.

'National income' is the easiest term to use in the description of economic progress. In a statistical analysis it is more convenient to use a related concept, namely the Gross Domestic Product.[5]

The key concept used in this study is the *Gross Domestic Product at factor cost*. Gross is used in preference to net because the calculation of depreciation allowances is bound to be arbitrary. Similarly, it is more straightforward to deal with gross investments instead of net investments. It is necessary to use the concept 'domestic' since it is impossible to determine *'ex ante'* how large the net foreign indebtedness and therefore factor income payments to abroad will be. Finally, the development of the GDP *at factor cost* is directly linked with the development of the national income which by definition is expressed at factor cost.

The use of the Gross Domestic Product at factor cost involves one major difficulty, however. The allocation of the available domestic resources between different uses is expressed at market prices.[6] In order to project the use of resources correctly, it is therefore necessary to calculate the Gross Domestic Product at market prices. For the final reconciliation of the data in this study, this correct approach was used, but in the intervening stages it was necessary to rely on the GDP at factor cost because it was impossible to calculate in advance how the GDP at market prices would develop in relation to the GDP at factor cost. Even on the assumption of constant tax rates the ratio between the GDP at market prices and at factor cost cannot be calculated before the structure of the GDP is known, since the amount of indirect taxes depends on the production and turnover of taxable goods and services.

C. *Which growth rate will the planners aim at?*

For an underdeveloped country whose national income per head only permits the great majority of its citizens to exist at a subsistence level, the achievement of a growth rate which embodies the prospect of raising the standard of living to tolerable levels in the course of a generation is an imperative policy target. In Asia, several of the world's largest countries in population are so poor that in terms of national product per head of population they only produce something between 50 and 100 dollars a year. If it were possible to imagine that the national income per head could be doubled without altering the present structure of personal income distribution, of the settlement of population, or of the composition of production between large categories af activities, we could state that such a development would effectively eliminate real misery and distress. But we know that a substantial growth of national income per head cannot take place without a modernization of the economy which entails industrialization as well as urbanization. Unfortunately, a higher national income *per caput*, even though it leads to higher *per caput* consumption in a formal sense and strengthens the economy of the country, does not necessarily lead to higher economic welfare.

The practical conclusion to be drawn from this very short summary of a well-known paradox of the development problem is that very poor underdeveloped countries must set themselves very high targets for their production growth. If not, they will fall between two stools. A high, but insufficient, development effort will in itself create so many demands on the increased national product — notably expenditure linked with urbanization, industrialization, and education — that very little, if anything, is left to provide a better standard of living for the masses.

In the great majority of the poorest underdeveloped countries, the governments and enlightened public opinion are determined to do something to improve the material standard of the citizens, and therefore to strive for the achievement of a growth rate which promises real progress for the majority. The question is, how courageously should this problem be faced, what kind of growth rate should be aimed at?

During the preparation of the Second Five-Year Plan, the Pakistan Planning Commission raised for the first time questions about the growth rat during subsequent plan periods. For the Second Plan period — mid-1960 to mid-1965 — national income was planned to increase by 20 per cent; and as the population increase at the time of planning was assumed to be 9 per cent, income *per caput* should increase by 10 per cent. At this rate it would take about 35 years before national income per head was doubled. As the national income per head in Pakistan was only a little above 50 dollars, such a growth rate was obviously unsatisfactory. Thirty-five years from now the country would still be unable to provide adequate living conditions for the masses. In the provisional outline of the Second Five Year Plan a much more ambitious longer-term target was indicated: 'it is proposed to double the pre-First-Plan level of national income in the Fourth Plan period, and to quadruple it in the Sixth Plan period. Adherence to this growth pattern necessitates a rate of growth of 20 per cent during the Second Plan period, rising to 25 per cent during the Third Plan period, and 30 per cent during the Fourth and Fifth Plan periods.'[7]

No target was suggested for the Sixth Plan period; but if the national income were to be quadrupled over thirty years, it would have to grow by 43.5 per cent during the last five years of this period (see Table 1, page 17).

Much of the analytical work in the present study was made under the assumption that these tentative targets suggested by the planners themselves in 1960 would eventually become firm targets (with the exception, however, that the growth rate during the Sixth Plan period would reach 'only' 35 per cent). Since then, however, the Planning Commission and the Government of Pakistan have raised their sights considerably. At the same time the detailed analysis of the growth prospects made within the framework of this study showed that under favourable conditions economic growth in Pakistan most certainly can be far faster than thought possible only six or seven years ago. This optimism seems to be justified by recent achievements which are illustrated by the fact that national income rose by 29 per cent instead of 20 per cent as stated in the Second Five Year Plan.[8] It should be

underlined already at this stage that although the recent achievements result from a determined development effort on the part
of the government and the people in Pakistan, they have been
made possible through an increased inflow of foreign aid. Continued rapid growth will depend on a steady inflow of such aid
and probably for a long while also on increasing absolute levels

Table 1. *Growth targets and recent achievements*
Growth of population and national income

	1950	1955	1960	1965	1970	1975	1980	1985
Rate of growth of population								
A. 1960 = 100								
Planning Commission I	n.a.	92	100	109	120	132	145	160
Planning Commission II			100	114	131	150	168	183
Planning Commission III	80	89	100	112	127	145	165	184
Planning Commission IV	80	89	100	113	129	148	169	187
Assumption in this study			100	113	129	148	169	193
B. Per five-year period ending in year indicated								
Planning Commission I		n.a.	9	9	10	10	10	10
Planning Commission II				14	15	15	12	9
Planning Commission III		11	12	12	14	14	14	12
Planning Commission IV		11	13	13	14	15	14	11
This study		n.a.	n.a.	13	14	14	14	14
Rate of growth of 'national income'								
A. 1960 = 100								
Planning Commission I	n.a.	91	100	120	150	195	254	344/363
Planning Commission II	n.a.	n.a.	100	122	159	209	291	402
Planning Commission III	79	88	100	126	163	218	300	416
Planning Commission IV	78	89	100	129	178	254	367	530
Assumptions used in this study			100	122	159	214	300	435
B. Per five-year period ending in year indicated								
Planning Commission I			10	20	25	30	30	35/43.5
Planning Commission II			n.a.	22	30	32	39	38
Planning Commission III		11	14	26	30	33	37	39
Planning Commission IV		14	13	29	38	43	44	44
Assumptions used in this study		–	–	22	30	35	40	45

Sources: Planning Commission I, [1], p. 2, para. 7, for population during the
periods 1955 to 1965. For later periods the author assumed an increase of approximately 2 per cent per year since the source did not express its assumptions.
For data on national income, *ibid*, p. 2, para. 6.
    Planning Commission II, [3], Table 1, page 10.
    Planning Commission III, [4], pp. 1, 18, and 20.
    Planning Commission IV, [5], pp. 1, and 19.

of aid. Thus even though an accelerated growth rate undoubtedly is possible, certain conditions as regards internal policies as well as external aid must be fulfilled. It is the purpose of this study to throw some light on these conditions. At this stage we will limit ourselves to a general statement of the problem.

The growth targets suggested, or, more recently, stated, as firm long-term goals by the Planning Commission are summarized in Table 1, which also contains the population estimates which are essential for understanding Pakistan's economic problems. The Table includes for comparison the revised growth assumptions upon which most of the detailed estimates of this study have been based.

The figures given for the expected rate of growth of the population are of importance for the understanding of the targets which have been set for the growth of the national income. The Population Census of 1961 showed that the reported population had increased by 24 per cent between 1951 and 1961. Before the results were known, the authorities responsible for the population statistics had used estimates of the annual rate of growth of population of only 1.4 per cent per year. In the Planning Commission the opinion was held that this figure was too low and that the annual growth rate was at least 1.8 per cent, and that a 2 per cent rate of growth might be likely during the next couple of decades. The observed growth rate between 1951 and 1961 proved to be above 2.2 per cent per year. However, part of the apparent growth reflected only the fact that the coverage in the 1961 Census probably was better than in the preceding one. But a closer analysis of the Census results revealed that there certainly was considerable under-reporting in the 1961 Census as well, and that the growth rate in the beginning of the 1960s was probably well above 2 per cent per year. Extensive health programmes, such as the malaria eradication programme, contribute to reducing the death rate and thus to raise the rate of growth.[9] The Government of Pakistan is launching a series of steps to promote family planning and in the long run this should reduce the birth rate enough to offset the fall in the death rate. In 1963 when the first perspective plan was prepared by the Planning Commission, the Commission expected that the rate of growth of population would start to fall considerably as early as 1975 onwards. Now it only expects that this effect will take place after 1980. For this study it has been assumed that the results of family planning will only be sufficient to offset the fall in the death rate throughout the period under review. This is *not* a pessimistic assumption as regards the efficacy of family planning, since it is likely that the death rate will fall very considerably during the next 20 years, and the assumed fall in the birth rate as a result of family planning is therefore very considerable.

The prospects of an annual growth of population close to 3 per cent per year forced the planners in Pakistan to raise their targets for growth of production. In itself a high rate of population growth leads to faster growth of output in many sectors. At the same time rapid population growth undoubtedly reduces the ability of a country to undertake investments to strengthen its economy since a significant part of resources available for investments will have to be used to cater for the needs of the growing population. If the efforts which are needed to promote faster economic growth are to have a noticeable effect on the living conditions of the common man during the next twenty to thirty years, the rate of growth of the national income must exceed considerably the rate of growth of the population.

A government which will not admit defeat in advance in the struggle against poverty is forced to set growth targets which contain hopes for real improvements in living conditions.

Ambitious targets are not of much use if they remain paper targets. Fortunately the higher targets chosen by the Planning Commission are not merely based on the political need to inspire hope in the population but also on recent achievements. The target for the Second Five-Year Plan (1960 to 1965) was originally to raise the national income by 20 per cent — in 1962 the target was raised to 22 per cent and in the spring of 1965 the result of the Plan appeared to become 29 per cent growth. The achievements are so promising that the final version of the Third Five Year Plan raised the income target to 38 per cent which is considerably above the 30 per cent increase which for some time had been the official figure.

The assumptions about the growth of the national income which have been used in this study are based on the ideas prevailing in Pakistan in late 1963. But as is shown in the Table, the author used more ambitious assumptions for the period 1970 to 1975 (the Fourth Plan period) and particularly for the period 1980 to 1985 (the Sixth Plan period) than the Pakistan authorities. In the course of this study it became apparent, however, that a 45 per cent growth target for the period 1980 to 1985 will be very hard to achieve.[10]

D. *The savings assumptions*

A high and rising rate of growth of the national income depends, of course, almost inevitably on a high and perhaps also rising level of investments in relation to the national income. Whereas short-term growth can take place through better utilization of existing capacity, long-term growth requires investments in additional production facilities. It is credible, but not certain, that the capital-output ratio in many developing countries over some years may be falling, and in that case the rate of growth might be rising without a corresponding rise in the investment ratio. If this is so, the tasks facing the developing nations and the countries which assist them are substantially lighter, but unfortunately there is also evidence which suggests that the capital-output ratio may be rising rather than falling.

The present situation in most underdeveloped countries, and Pakistan is no exception, is that the level of domestic saving is too low to finance anything but a very slow growth of the national income. Regardless of what happens to the capital-output ratio, a developing country which sets for itself ambitious growth targets must plan to raise the ratio of domestic savings to the national income unless it resigns itself to beg its richer brethren to finance its development efforts indefinitely. The second basic target which a developing country will set itself is therefore a goal for domestic savings, expressed as a percentage of the national income. The main reason that the ratio of domestic savings to national income is low in a developing country is the poverty of the country — people who live at a subsistence level have nothing to save, and the saving efforts of those who are better off cannot compensate for the lacking ability to save of the great majority. A poor country cannot raise its rate of saving out of a *stationary* income to any significant extent. Its only possibility is to save as much as possible out of its additional income. This is feasible for several reasons. Additional income may automatically create additional savings. This is the case when idle labour is mobilized to undertake investment works without any significant increase in the consumption by the labourers. Additional income may accrue to persons or organizations which will save a large part of it voluntarily. This is notably the case when the modernization of the economy results in high profits in the enterprise sector, and a large proportion of these profits are then plowed back into business in the form of expansion or new ventures. Finally the government may levy heavy taxes on the additional income and use the proceeds for investment purposes. Against this background it is realistic for a developing country to express its savings targets in the form of a target for the 'marginal rate of savings'. The crude measure of the marginal rate of savings is the ratio between the increase in total domestic savings to the increase in national income.[11]

The marginal rate of savings is in itself not a satisfactory measure of the saving effort, but the concept can be used without harm in a situation in which national income is planned to grow much faster than population.[12]

Under certain assumptions it is not only feasible but quite likely that a developing country which grows at a fairly slow rate nevertheless will show a marginal rate of savings higher than the average rate of savings, and consequently a 'marginal rate of savings out of income *per caput*' which may exceed one (or may be negative, in cases where income *per caput* falls). This will be the case when the growth of the economy is almost exclusively caused by rapid growth in the modern, predominantly urban sector. Such growth will most probably lead to high profits and often to increased savings. In this situation the rural economy will stagnate, and rural income *per caput* will fall, but this fall will mainly affect the rural standard of living and not the level of savings. Such assumptions are, however, contrary to the underlying assumption in this study, which is that planned growth will

Table 2. *Assumptions about the rate of domestic savings*

	1950	1955	1960	1965	1970	1975	1980	1985
*Domestic savings in % of GDP**								
Planning Commission II	n.a.	n.a.	n.a.	9.0	13.1	16.1	20.9	24.6
Planning Commission III.....	5.8	7.2	6.0	9.5	12.6	16.2	20.0	22.8
Planning Commission IV	4.6	6.8	5.9	10.3	13.6	16.9	20.2	21.8
Assumptions used in this study	n.a.	n.a.	6.7	8.8	13.0	16.9	21.5	25.7
Marginal rate of savings, in 5–year period ending in year indicated								
Planning Commission I	–	–	–	15	20	25	25	20
Planning Commission II	–	–	–	18.5	27	28	33	33
Planning Commission III.....	–	18	–3	23/21	23	26	30	31
Planning Commission IV	–	23	–1	22/22	22	25	28	25
Assumptions used in this study	–	–	–	18.5	27	28	33	35
Marginal rate of savings, from income per caput†								
Planning Commission III.....	–	–	–	36	36	38	38	35
Planning Commission IV	–	–	–	31	28	31	32	28
Assumptions used in this study	–	–	–	38	42	39	42	42

* Not available in Planning Commission I. †Not available in Planning Commission I–II.

Sources: Planning Commission I, unpublished staff paper (from 1959); Planning Commission II, [3], p. 10; Planning Commission III, [4], pp. 7, 20, and 21; Planning Commission IV, [5], pp. 7, 19, and 22. Note that in the two newest estimates made by the Planning Commission, the figures for the marginal rate of savings during the period 1950 to 1965 are in 1959/60 prices whereas for the later periods 1964/65 prices have been used. Two sets of figures are given for the period 1960 to 1965.

not only be achieved through the expansion of the modern sector of the economy, but also through progress in the traditional sector. As higher output of food in traditional agriculture will certainly lead to higher food consumption per head, it follows that consumption *per caput* will rise and thus that the marginal rate of savings out of income *per caput* must be well below one. The marginal rate of savings out of the total income, in spite of its shortcomings, is a good measure because it relates the increase in savings to the increase in income which can be mobilized for savings. But it is necessary to consider the marginal rate of savings out of income *per caput* as well, in order to verify how much of the increased income might be available for additional savings.

The savings assumption, or targets, which have been set by the Planning Commission at various stages of planning and those which are used is this study are presented in Table 2.

Table 2 shows how the Planning Commission has altered its assumptions as regards the possible marginal rate of savings. The assumptions used in 1959 were fairly modest; in 1963 the savings targets were raised considerably, but these targets have again been considerably reduced during 1964 and the spring of 1965.

The assumptions used in this study were based on the targets set by the Pakistanis themselves in 1963, and they even exceed these targets for the Sixth Plan period. They are consequently far more ambitious than the present targets set by the Planning Commission. However, it is shown in Chapter 13 of this study (on the financial flows) that these ambitious savings targets are not unduly ambitious from the point of view of income flows which can be mobilised for saving.[13] Other limits to the capacity to save are discussed in chapter 3.

E. *The capital-output ratio*

The targets for savings set by the Planning Commission during the last five-six years all aim at reducing and eventually eliminating the need for foreign aid. This means that gross domestic savings must grow faster than gross domestic investments and eventually catch up with the investment.[14] The first crude 'perspective plan' suggested in 1959 was based on the assumption that the marginal rate of savings shown for Planning Commission I in Table 2 would be sufficient to eliminate the need for foreign aid during the Sixth Plan Period (1980—85). This would only be possible, however, if the incremental capital-output ratio during the Third to Sixth Plan periods were lower than during the Second Plan period, and if net investments remained constant in relation to gross investments.[15]

With the elaboration of a perspective plan, the Planning Commission has followed up the pioneering work of Dr. Haq and has set out its assumptions on the capital-output ratio in considerable detail. These assumptions and their implicit impact on the need for foreign aid are presented in Table 3.

Table 3 reveals the fundamental changes in assumptions which have taken place in Pakistan during the last couple of years. In 1963, when the work on the perspective plan was started, the Planning Commission assumed that the capital-output ratio would be very high, but that it would tend to fall somewhat. In spite of this the Commission set itself the target that foreign

Table 3. *Assumed capital-output ratios and their influence on the ratio of gross investments to the Gross National Product and the need for foreign assistance*

	Years or Plan periods ending in years:						
	1955	1960	1965	1970	1975	1980	1985
A. *Figures referring to Plan periods*							
Time-lag between investment and output (years)							
Planning Commission II	n.a.	n.a.	3.5	3.0	2.8	2.6	2.5
Planning Commission III*. . . and IV							
Capital-output ratio							
Planning Commission II	n.a.	n.a.	3.0	3.1	3.1	3.2	3.2
Planning Commission III. . . .	n.a.	n.a.	n.a.	3.5	3.5	3.6	3.7
Planning Commission IV	n.a.	n.a.	2.8	2.9	2.9	2.9	3.0
B. *Figures referring to years at the end of the plan periods*							
Gross investment in % of GNP							
Planning Commission II	n.a.	n.a.	15.8	20.0	24.0	24.5	24.6
Planning Commission III. . . .	8.4	10.8	15.6	18.6	19.9	22.2	23.9
Planning Commission IV. . . .	n.a.	n.a.	18.4	20.2	21.4	22.1	22.9
Foreign assistance in % of GNP							
Planning Commission II	n.a.	n.a.	6.8	6.9	7.9	3.6	0
Planning Commission III. . . .	1.3	4.7	6.3	6.0	3.7	2.2	1.1
Planning Commission IV	1.1	5.0	8.1	6.6	4.5	1.9	1.1
Foreign assistance (Rs Mill.)							
Planning Commission II	n.a.	n.a.	(2,800)	(3,700)	(5,600)	(3,550)	(0)
Planning Commission III. . . .	350	1,500	2,750	3,400	2,900	2,500	1,600
Planning Commission IV	300	1,580	3,690	4,185	4,000	2,500	2,000

* The time lag has not been specified in Planning Commissions III and IV, but the capital-output ratios have been raised to account for the lag.

Sources: Planning Commission II, [3], p. 10; Planning Commission III, [4], pp. 4, 18, and 20; Planning Commission IV, [5], pp. 19 and 8.

assistance should become superfluous in 1985. The Plan outline published in the late summer of 1964 (Alternative III) operated with somewhat lower capital-output ratios than the guidelines for the Plan (published in 1963, Alternative II). However, the savings target was also reduced, so that the country would still depend on foreign aid in 1985. The final version of the Plan (Alternative IV) contains very much lower figures for the capital-output ratio, but as the growth targets were raised in relation to those in the outline, the investment effort remained about the same, and the need for foreign aid was assumed to be higher during most years of the perspective plan than in the outline. The lower figures for the capital-output ratio which are now being used are justified by the fine performance of the economy of the country during the Second Five-Year Plan — a performance which suggests that considerable growth can be achieved in certain important sectors without large investments.

The authors of the Third Five-Year Plan stress that the estimates for the twenty-year period 1965 to 1985 are tentative and that detailed work is proceeding on these estimates.[16] It is known, however, that the Planning Commission has prepared multi-sector planning models in order to check the estimates given in the Third Plan. The staff of the Commission must have had reasons for reducing the previous estimates of the capital-output ratio.

Long-term planning based on a crude estimate of the capital-output ratio is bound to be very uncertain. If, for example, the capital-output ratio during the Sixth Plan period should turn out to be 3.3 instead of 3.0 as now assumed by the Planning Commission, the need for external resources would be increased from Rs 2,000 million to Rs. 6,300 million (if savings remained constant) or from 1.1 to 3.4 per cent of the GNP.

In this study no assumption has been made for the global capital-output ratio. The basic assumptions concern the rate of growth of the Gross Domestic Product and the marginal rate of savings. The size of the capital-output ratio and the future need for inflow of foreign capital are two of the main subjects of enquiry of the study itself, and the findings are presented in Chapters 9 to 11.

F. *Doubts about the validity of the chosen assumptions*

There are strong reasons for questioning some of the assumptions set out above on which Pakistan's 'Perspective Plan' was based.

First, is it realistic to assume that 22 per cent of the additional national income will be saved during the Third Plan period, and that this marginal rate of saving will reach 25 per cent during the Fourth and 28 per cent during the Fifth Plan periods? We will not analyze this question in all its implications in this paper. But the validity of the assumed rate of marginal saving will be dealt with from certain points of view in the analysis which follows. The main aspect which will not be elaborated in this analysis is the distribution of additional income among the several categories of income-earners, and its possible influence on the rate of saving.[17] The results of the present study suggest that a high marginal rate of savings is possible.

Second, is it realistic to assume that the capital-output ratio will remain fairly low and not grow much higher than observations from recent years seem to indicate? It can be shown that if the capital-output ratio is only slightly higher than a ratio which entails a shrinking import surplus, there will be no tendency towards a smaller import surplus. This question is studied in connection with the pattern of economic development which is required to achieve the postulated growth rates, and the answer is that it is doubtful whether the capital-output ratio can fall significantly.

Third, is it realistic to assume that the effects of increased domestic savings are such that increased investments can effectively be financed? If domestic savings increase more than investment, the foreign balance should by definition become more favourable. This means that increased savings will both restrict the increase in imports and encourage the growth of exports so that they will rise more rapidly than imports. This will indeed often be the case in a highly industrialized and diversified economy. But in an underdeveloped economy both imports and exports are often linked to factors which are affected only to a very limited extent by what happens to domestic saving. For example, imports will tend to rise with the growth of the national product, and, even more important, increased investment expenditure will lead to increased import of capital equipment, technical services, etc. On the other hand, exports often depend to a great extent on market conditions abroad, and also often on crop results at home. In other words, favourable changes in the foreign balance will not automatically result from higher domestic saving but are primarily influenced by investments and specific efforts which aim at reducing imports and/or increasing exports. Similarly, higher domestic saving will not automatically provide the facilities for an increased investment effort without relying extensively on imported capital equipment and technical services. This point was recognized by the authorities in Pakistan when they prepared the Second Five-Year Plan. Shortage of foreign exchange was considered to set a limit to the amount of domestic saving which could be usefully mobilized. Under these circumstances it is justifiable to question whether it is feasible for the foreign deficit to shrink from 44 per cent of investment in 1964/65 to less than 5 per cent in 1984/85. This cannot be discussed in purely theoretical terms. The study of the structural pattern of Pakistan's future development will aim at throwing some light on the problem through an analysis of the possibilities of expanding exports, replacing imports, and building up a domestic capital-goods industry.

G. *A study of structural changes in Pakistan's economy during the period 1960/85*

It is possible to design a multi-sector growth model which shows a number of conditions that have to be fulfilled if an underdeveloped country like Pakistan is to be able to accelerate its growth rate and at the same time reduce its dependence on foreign contributions. Such a model might include an input-output matrix with changing technical coefficients. The foreign-trade part of the model might be built on a changing classification of imports between competitive and non-competitive imports. The model might also include a fairly detailed investment model and, as far as savings are concerned, some device which would illustrate how the required rate of marginal saving could be obtained, through taxation and through voluntary saving by various broad categories of income earners.

To design such a model a number of difficult problems have to be resolved: considerable additional research into the economic structure of Pakistan would have to be done to establish existing structural relationships, and there would have to be considerable research into the economic potentialities of Pakistan to decide when and how the various structural relationships would change. Furthermore, some of the changes which would have to be built into the model are of such a character that they would involve discontinuous changes in the coefficients in the model. It would be useful if a start could be made on resolving the many problems connected with the setting-up of a sufficiently detailed growth model for Pakistan. Such a model would be a valuable tool for increasingly precise economic planning. If properly designed, it could be utilized as a decision model to assess the implications of crucial economic policy decisions.

It will undoubtedly take considerable time to set up a realistic and comprehensive growth model, and this is why I have tried to present something much cruder, and less ambitious. The presentation in the following pages does not constitute a theoretically self-contained model.

It provides, however, 'elements of a growth model'. Among these elements there are several of the most important relationships which have to be included in a complete model, such as the consumption function, the investment required to reach certain growth targets, and the resulting impact on the foreign balance.

The aim of the analysis which follows is to outline the structural changes which will most probably have to take place if a certain rate of growth is to be achieved. The overall growth rate itself is therefore, for analytical purposes, regarded as a given factor which determines the structural changes. In actual fact, of course, the growth rate is a *result* of structural changes and their impact on the economy.

H. *The growth of each component of the Gross Domestic Product*

The Gross Domestic Product is, by definition, the sum of the value added contributed by the different domestic economic sectors. For our analysis we assume that the Gross Domestic Product will increase at the rate shown for the national income in Table 1. The rate of growth of the value added contributed by the individual sectors of the economy has to be in conformity with the postulated growth rate for the total Gross Domestic Product. But *initially* we will calculate the growth of the output of each sector on the basis of factors which will, in fact, determine their development. If the sum of the value added by the individual sectors is different from the predetermined result, adjustments have to be made for the contribution of those sectors in which such adjustments seem logically possible. (The most obvious example is the contribution of the construction industry to the Gross Domestic Product, which can be adjusted considerably without altering a whole series of underlying assumptions, but the indirect effects on trade, transportation, building-material industries, etc., must, of course, also be taken into account.)

The factors which determine the growth of each individual sector of the economy are: intermediate and final demand for the output of the sector, (final demand for consumption, for investment, and for export), the available natural resources, and the technical factors limiting the growth potential. *Demand* is assumed to be a factor limiting expansion in a number of activities. Demand from private consumers can, as we shall see, be expressed in the form of income elasticities. Demand from a government may be quite flexible as regards certain products, notably investment goods and services from the construction industry, but fairly rigid as far as it affects other sectors. Investment demand may also be a limiting factor — e. g., it will certainly set a limit to the possible expansion of the cement industry. Export demand falls into two categories. For 'traditional' products of which Pakistan is an important exporter on the world market, foreign demand is a definite limiting factor. For other products, notably manufactured products, for which Pakistan may remain a small supplier on an international scale, export demand is assumed to be fairly flexible. The limiting factor in such cases is the ability of an industrial sector in Pakistan to produce a competitive product. This is dependent on the technical factor. We will apply a 'rule of thumb' in this respect. Except for industries which are developed primarily for export, we will assume that an increasing proportion of the total output can be exported, say 1 per cent more or less on a pilot basis at the end of one plan period, 5 per cent at the end of the next plan period, 10 per cent five years later, etc.

In many sectors the *productive capacity* is primarily limited by technical skill. In certain activities the proportional rise in production can be very steep because productive units can be set up and run by foreign technicians for an initial period of time, e. g., chemical industries, oil exploitation, etc. Others, notably the engineering industries, are highly dependent on indigenous skill. In general we will assume that production in such industries cannot be more than doubled during a plan period. Progress in activities like forestry and mining are definitely limited by the natural resources, whereas it is more a matter of judgement how fast yield per acre can be raised in agriculture.

If the products of the individual sectors add up to less than the target for the national product, it is possible to 'stretch' the assumptions as regards technical progress, utilization of natural resources, and export possibilities, but the most important adjustment factor will remain the creation of national income through public works. If, on the other hand, the products of the individual sectors add up to more than the target for the national product, it is, of course, easy to reduce the assumed level of production in those sectors in which optimistic assumptions have been made as regards the rate of increase.

I. *Some special methodological questions*

Some further clarification of the principles which have been followed is needed in order to enable the reader to offer constructive criticism.

(1) *To what extent has full coverage of domestic-demand ('self-sufficiency') been used to determine targets for production? This differs from industry to industry.*

(i) Certain industries already cover a high proportion of domestic demand. How quickly full coverage can be obtained depends on the investment costs involved and on the priority assigned to the product, as well as on the feasibility of increasing production quickly enough to catch up with demand during, say, a five-year period. A couple of examples will illustrate this point. The sugar industry is by now well established in Pakistan, but it covers, according to expert opinion, only about 40 per cent of Pakistan's need for refined sugar. The investment costs involved in expanding the industry by 150 per cent are so substantial that the government decided to expand the industry by only 50 per cent during the Second Five-Year Plan. The fact that refined sugar has a relatively low priority, because of the existence of domestic substitutes (village-produced sugar), was a major factor behind the decision to postpone full satisfaction of demand to a later plan period. Food-grain self-sufficiency is another case in point. One method of achieving this target is to improve more land, through irrigation or through reclamation of water-logged land. However, investment costs are very high (and cost estimates often exceeded) so that to obtain food-grain self-sufficiency rapidly by such means would require a very high proportion of development expenditure for this single target. Consequently somewhat lower targets for land improvement have been assumed in the analysis below.

(ii) There are other industries which for the moment cover only a very insignificant part of domestic demand. Very often the shortage or complete absence of technical skills prevents production from being expanded sufficiently to cover domestic demand (e. g., many capital goods industries). These are clear-cut cases in which the technical factor determines the rate of growth, relatively independent of demand.

(iii) In other industries the feasibility of profitable production is closely related to the level of demand. In these cases, domestic demand will have to be covered by imports until the potential demand has reached a level at which sufficiently large-scale production becomes possible. A special problem should be mentioned in this connection. In Pakistan imports of consumer goods are severely restricted, to the extent that in 1959/60 they probably made up less than 2 per cent of total private consumption, if food-grain imports are excluded. But the potential demand for imported consumer goods which are at present not available, or rationed, or obtainable only at very high prices, is obviously much higher than the imports indicate. This has to be taken into account in assessing the scope for domestic production.

(2) *How has the growth rate, within the limits set by demand,*

been determined for industries which are already established? How have technical progress and availability of natural resources been assessed? Several factors have been taken into consideration.

(i) Some industries, notably agriculture and small-scale manufacturing and handicrafts, consist of a great number of small producers. Progress in such industries is dependent on how fast these very numerous producers are willing and able to expand and improve production of already known goods or to introduce production of unknown goods. The requisite for progress in such activities is comprehensive educational efforts, which spread technical knowledge as well as an understanding of the benefits of modern production methods to the greatest possible number of the small producers. Nobody can predict with any assurance how long it will take to achieve these educational targets and how rapid progress will become as soon as there is a 'breakthrough' in influencing the activities of the millions. I have been forced to use very simple assumptions, such as an average rate of increase in yield per acre of about 15 per cent per five-year period, or ability of certain sectors of the small industries and handicrafts to participate in the industrial expansion at competitive terms.

(ii) Other industries are predominantly organized in larger units, and the problem of management may be easier to solve because the number of people to be trained is fairly limited and training within industry is possible through participation of foreign experts in management during an initial period. Nevertheless, many industries require considerable skill and technical qualifications from a substantial number of people, and progress will depend on the rate of training and of learning through experience of skilled workers, of foremen and other people in lower management, and of technical personnel in all grades. To some extent it is possible to assess the scope for progress on the basis of the number of trained persons turned out by various educational institutions. But on-the-job training can be of such importance in many industries that to assess potential progress on the basis of the number of people who have been given a formal education would only give highly misleading results. My assumption has been that in 'process-controlled' industries — notably chemical industries — the scope for rapid progress is considerable, since there it is possible to recruit a nucleus of staff from abroad, and to replace them after a few years by locally trained staff who get their final training on the job. There are numerous examples of this method of training staff in Pakistan and in other underdeveloped countries. Industries which employ a large number of skilled workers and which need a substantial number of well-trained supervisors and technicians can only expand far less rapidly. In my opinion it is nevertheless not unduly optimistic to assume that even in such industries production can easily be doubled during a five-year period, if determined efforts are made to provide basic technical training and to promote such industries. In short, I have assumed that from a technical and organizational point of view, production in industrial sectors with predominantly larger units can be at least doubled during each five-year plan period during the 25-year period studied here. Inadequate demand and difficult access to essential raw materials are two limiting factors in many industries (under the general assumption that *financial* resources for investment can always be found).

(iii) Limited natural resources will obviously restrict progress in primary industries. But natural resources are in themselves, from an economic point of view, *not* a given, unalterable quantity. This holds true for land and it also holds true for mineral resources. Land can be made usable through irrigation, drainage, reclamation of flooded land, etc., and mineral resources can be discovered. Through investment in land improvement and in geological research the natural resource endowment can be improved. Similarly the off-shore fishing potential can be effectively increased through research. The output from given natural resources can be substantially increased through better production methods. Strictly speaking this does not mean that a country has acquired more natural resources, but that in countries which exploit their natural resources with primitive techniques, there is considerable scope for the expansion of primary production. In assessing the potential growth of primary production in Pakistan, I have made the following assumptions:

Agriculture — some further increase of arable land will take place, but due to shortage of water in West Pakistan, it will *not* be possible, with present-day techniques, to convert most of the deserts into fields. On the other hand, I have assumed that yield per acre can be increased by about 15 per cent per five-year period during the 25 years under review. Furthermore, I have assumed that considerable areas of semi-arid and other types of land 'not available for cultivation' can be used much more effectively than at present as pastures for livestock.

Forestry — there is clearly considerable scope for much better utilization of existing forests, both through better exploitation of existing forests and through scientific forest management and reforestation. Further progress is obviously dependent on reforestation of large areas. The prospects for such reforestation are not yet well known, but they do not have any significant influence on the potential output of forests during the period under review.

Fisheries — there is no doubt that fishing resources in the Bay of Bengal as well as in the Arabian Sea are such that the catch can be increased more than enough to satisfy domestic demand and still leave a considerable surplus for export. There are also immense possibilities for raising more fish in ponds, canals, and other inland waters. During the period under review I have assumed that natural resources will not set any limit to the expansion of fisheries.

Mining — today Pakistan is considered to be poor in mineral resources. West Pakistan has ample resources of limestone, gypsum, and certain other non-metallic minerals. East Pakistan is poor in all mineral resources, and it has even been difficult hitherto to find the right clays and sands for the manufacture of finer ceramics and glass. The most promising recent discoveries have been the large natural gas fields in both provinces. Searching for mineral oil continues in both provinces. I have assumed that this will finally meet with success, and that the country will become self-sufficient in mineral oil and be able to use natural gas as the most important source of energy apart from oil. I have furthermore assumed that geological surveying and prospecting will assure the supply of most non-metallic minerals, though mainly in the western regions. I believe that coal will become increasingly unimportant as a source of energy and that the domestic coal-mining industry will be able to supply enough coal for most uses, although it may be doubtful whether metallurgical coke can be supplied in sufficient quantities, at least during the earlier plan periods, i. e., before techniques have been found to use indigenous coal for making such coke. Finally, the availability of metallic ores is somewhat of a problem. It is doubtful whether suitable iron ore can be found to supply a domestic iron and steel industry, at least not before the off-take of ore becomes large enough to pay for very expensive means of transport to haul the ore from almost inaccessible mountain areas.

Secondary industries — A word is needed about the effect of natural resources on the development of certain secondary industries. An ample supply of raw materials derived from domestic natural resources will evidently encourage the growth of processing industries. The result of this is twofold: it will provide a basis for export production, and it will encourage domestic use at the expense of substitutes which have to be imported or can only be produced domestically at high cost. Consequently I have assumed that the availability of raw materials, such as cotton, jute, hides and skins, to mention a few examples, will continue to stimulate jute and cotton manufacturing, tanning and leather-goods manufacturing. The implied assumption is that the switch over to the use of substitutes for these products will be significantly delayed in Pakistan itself, although on the export markets Pakistan will have to meet the full pressure of competition from substitutes. Scarce or non-existent domestic supplies of certain raw materials will, however, delay or prevent the growth of certain secondary industries, notably those which are based on bulky raw materials. It is not possible to give a clear-cut answer as to whether some heavily raw-material-oriented industries will be developed sufficiently to cover domestic demand or not. Since Pakistan will probably suffer from foreign-exchange difficulties, it is likely that industries which save foreign exchange will be established and expanded even where this may entail the import of bulky raw materials and higher prices than for imported goods. Thus I consider it very likely that a domestic steel industry will be established even if both ore, scrap, and coke may have to be imported. In this study, however, I have assumed that the raw material will, on the whole, be supplied from domestic resources. Of course, allowance has been made for the import of certain special raw materials, for which substitutes cannot be found (like sulphur, phosphates, several metallic ores and metals, etc.). The paper industry should be mentioned as a typical example of this approach. The forests will probably not be able to provide enough timber for the rapidly expanding production of pulp; I have nevertheless assumed that the use of other raw materials — certain grasses, straw, etc. — will enable the paper industry to be based on domestically produced pulp. Allowance has been made for some import of pulp for mixing purposes.

(3) *How have limited investment resources been taken into account in determining the growth potential of the different economic activities?*

The approach has been to regard financial resources for investment as unlimited, so that shortage of domestic finance will be remedied by capital import and the necessary capital euqipment and technical assistance imported. As the whole purpose of the analysis is to show the impact on the foreign balance of a certain growth rate and pattern of growth rate, it follows that investment resources needed to achieve the given growth rate and pattern must be assumed to be available. This approach does not mean that I have entirely disregarded the investment costs in choosing the pattern of growth. But it has nevertheless been the pattern of demand and the technical, organizational, and economic feasibility of expansion which in this study have been the determinants of the pattern of growth, rather than the desire to achieve a certain rate with a minimum amount of capital. This follows from an underlying assumption that the development will take place in a mixed economy in which the broad pattern of development is centrally planned but in which the consumer has considerable scope for free choice both as regards choice between consumption and saving and between alternative patterns of consumption. It is also assumed that private enterprise will play an important role in the development. Such assumptions probably imply that the rate of saving will be lower than under a more firmly planned economy, and that the pattern of investment will require more use of foreign exchange than one which aims at a maximum use of potential domestic saving.

(4) *Which assumptions have been made as regards the choice between autarky or extensive reliance on foreign trade? Two significant facts, one economic and one political, have been taken into account in determining the pattern of growth in this respect.*

(i) For the time being it looks as if Pakistan has limited possibilities for expanding its exports rapidly. All students of the economy of Pakistan seem to agree on this. Since Pakistan now has more than 100 million inhabitants, there is also considerable scope for large-scale production of a great number of manufactured products — the low average income *per caput* notwithstanding. Thus Pakistan may be forced to, and also has the possibilities for, an extensive degree of autarky.

(ii) For many underdeveloped countries it would certainly be advantageous to aim at regional economic co-operation, in order to benefit from some degree of international division of labour. For Pakistan any effective regional co-operation would have to include India; and as long as the political relations between the two nations remain strained, such economic co-operation on a large scale is unthinkable.

In spite of these two important facts which favour a high degree of autarky, the main assumption has been that exports will be expanded rapidly and that domestic production will not replace imports if domestic production costs exceed import prices considerably. It is, of course, not possible to predict with accuracy how prices will develop, neither internationally nor in Pakistan. But there are a number of products which probably cannot be produced at a reasonable cost in Pakistan during the next couple of decades, and it has been assumed that such products will continue to be imported.

3. Methods of Projection

In the previous chapter the problem which is posed in this study and some of the basic assumptions were outlined. This chapter will describe the methods whereby the basic assumptions about growth, savings, and adequate inflow of foreign capital are translated into projections for the development of the various sectors of the economy, and the influence this development will have on investments and on foreign transactions. In the course of this exercise it will also become necessary to adjust the basic assumptions to the results of the detailed projections. It is theoretically possible to construct a model which ensures that the basic assumptions are fulfilled. It is an open uqestion whether it is *practically* possible to bring the original assumptions in line with the detailed findings without undue manipulation of presumably realistic assumptions behind the detailed projections. The basic assumptions represent a *working hypothesis*. In this study of Pakistan the detailed assumptions are meant to be as realistic as possible in that they should represent realistic assessments of the potential performance of the various productive sectors and the potential behaviour of the people as consumers. To the extent that there appears to be a conflict between the basic assumptions which are used as a working hypothesis and the global figures obtained on the basis of 'realistic, detailed assumptions', it is fair to conclude that the basic assumptions are unrealistic. This conclusion cannot be final. After all, the detailed assumptions which are contained in this study are all based on my personal judgements. Since these judgements have a fundamental influence on the final outcome, care has been taken to set out the detailed assumptions clearly. It is up to the reader to evaluate, on the basis of the details given throughout this study, whether I have been unduly pessimistic or clearly over-optimistic in my judgements. The present chapter shows the framework within which the detailed assumptions, or judgements, have been injected into this study.

A. *Base year and time periods*

As the work on the present study was already started in 1961, the last year of the First Five-Year Plan period (1955/60) which served as the base year for the Second Five-Year Plan was taken as base year for this study as well.[1] Projections have been made for the last years of five plan periods — from the Second Plan (1960/65) to the Sixth Plan (1980/85). The 'plan period' and the 'last year of a plan period' are, therefore, the two basic time units which have been used. Figures for growth refer to plan periods; the static description of the economy is based on the last years of the plan periods. Occasionally some estimates had to be based on figures for other than the last years of the plan periods, and in most of these cases it was assumed that the annual growth during a given plan period would be constant, i. e., the growth per five-year period was translated into average growth per year, at a compound rate. In the analytical sections annual growth rates have been preferred to the five-year growth rates, but it should be kept in mind that the statistical work is based on five-year periods.[2]

All figures for the base year 1960 are constructed from available statistical data, although frequently it was necessary to fill statistical gaps with informed guesses. Great care has been taken to make all data internally consistent, and this process leads to discoveries of conflicting data in the basic statistical material. This exercise led, *inter alia,* to a recalculation of the official national income data. It should be pointed out that statistic-economic research in Pakistan has made great strides during the last two-three years. In general, new data do not seriously conflict with the estimates in this study.[3]

Although there is reason to believe that our figures for the base year 1960 are as good as any figures on the economy of Pakistan at the end of the First Five-Year Plan, the same is certainly not true for the figures for 1965, i. e., the last year of the Second Five-Year Plan. These figures were originally based on the targets of the officially approved Second Five-Year Plan, but they were later revised to take into account the revised targets for the Plan and the actual development during the first three years of the Plan period. However, the economy of Pakistan performed far better than anybody could have expected during the Second Plan. The GDP appears to have risen by 29 per cent, instead of 22 per cent as set out in the revision of the Plan. The choice was to retain an unrealistic picture of the situation at the end of the Second Plan and publish the long-term projections based on the hypotehtical figures for 1965 reasonably quickly, or to spend another year on recalculating all figures on the basis of the latest available figures, by which time new figures most certainly would have been forthcoming.[4] The answer was fairly obvious — it is impracticable to keep a study of this kind completely up to date. But it must be clearly kept in mind that the realistic base year figures for the present analysis are those for 1960, not those for 1965.

The second objection which can be raised against the figures is that the targets for the future 20 years are lower than those now put forward by the Planning Commission. This has nothing to do with the method, and will be discussed elsewhere.

B. *The structure of the Gross Domestic Product*

The first basic assumption in this study is that the Gross Domestic Product will grow at a given rate. The assumed absolute figures for the GDP expressed in millions of rupees are shown in Table 10 and the rate of growth in Table 1. The Gross Domestic Product equals the sum of the value added of the various sectors of the economy. If the first basic assumption is to hold, we must show that it is possible for the different sectors of the economy to develop in such a manner that this sum becomes equal to the assumed Gross Domestic Product at the end of each five-year plan period under review.

The value added of one given sector equals its gross output less its purchases of goods and services ('input') from other sectors (including imports). The ratio between output and input may vary with time, particularly if the internal structure of the sector changes or the production methods are under alteration. But given the output of all subsectors within a sector, it is possible to calculate the value added in the sector, even though it must be admitted that the calculation of the input requirements 20 years hence necessarily becomes somewhat uncertain.

The output of the sector is defined as domestic and export deliveries of goods and services produced by the sector, less imports of such goods or services. The domestic deliveries consist of deliveries to households and the government for current purposes ('consumption'), deliveries for fixed domestic investment, increase in inventories of products from the sector, and deliveries to other sectors of goods or services used as input in those sectors.

If we express what has been said in the two previous paragraphs in equations, we find that we have introduced a large number of variables in our system, i. e., value added and output of a selected number of sectors and subsectors, imports of goods or services belonging to all these sectors, and six different types of demand for the output of each individual sector or subsector. Moreover, the 'intermediate' demand for the output of one given sector consists of the sum of the demand from all other sectors or subsectors of the domestic economy. In order to find an answer to our initial question, i. e., how much value is added by each sector which contributes to the GDP, we must introduce as many mutually independent equations as there are unknowns in our system. And not only that, but these equations have to be solved simultaneously. This follows already from the fact that the demand for the output of sector A for intermediate purposes depends on the output of many of the other sectors of the economy, but the output of many of the other sectors may again depend on the demand for inputs by sector A. Also the demand for investment purposes, whether in the form of fixed capital equipment or inventories, depends on the rate of change in the output of all sectors of the economy.

For the purpose of this study no attempt has been made to build up a computable model which includes all the elements which I have wanted to review. It is possible that the elements contained in this study can be fitted together to a model which in principle could be solved. It is more doubtful whether this model could be made computable. Rightly or wrongly, I have concluded that it would not serve the purpose of this study to construct such a model. The Gross Domestic Product has been broken down into more than 200 elements — sectors, subsectors, and producers of individual products in many subsectors. This approach has the advantage of allowing a study of the demand prospects and the potential level of output for many important products. But the introduction of that many boxes in an input-output matrix makes a model very unwieldy. A theoretical difficulty also arises. By breaking down the demand on the output of one integrated industry into demand for individual products (for example, agriculture), it is no longer possible to operate with simplified assumptions as regards the production function in that industry. I have preferred the practical advantages of a study of the demand for, and output of, individual major products to the theoretical advantages of aggregating the output of clearly defined industries in such a manner that the production function and the demand on inputs could be described in computable mathematical formulas.

Having decided against construction of a computable model which can be solved simultaneously, I had to find another approach to solve the model. My solution consists in solving the equations step by step and, in a final reconciliation process, eliminating inconsistencies through an iterative process of adjustments.

The following steps have been taken:

Export demand has partly been estimated as a function of conditions on the world market — this approach is applicable to exports of 'traditional' products from a developing country, i. e., exports the levels of which are dependent on world demand. If the developing country only accounts for a very small proportion of the world trade of a product of this kind, it can, of course, increase its share in the world trade if conditions for the production of such a product seem to be particularly promising. For other products, goods as well as services, the exports by a given industry have been calculated on the basis of the presumed competitive position of the industry. Clearly subjective judgements play an important role in this case. But theoretically as well as practically the export demand can be estimated independently of the other variables of the model.

Consumption demand, by households and the government. This demand is calculated as a function of the total GDP, and is consequently independent of other variables of the model. How consumption demand has been calculated is described in the next section of this chapter.

Demand for fixed investment could be determined as a function of the GDP, or more precisely as a function of the increase in the GDP, by relying on assumed figures for the overall incremental capital-output ratio.[5] The figure for the incremental capital-output ratio depends on the pattern of economic growth. Any figure for the capital-output ratio which is chosen *ex ante* without previous knowledge of the pattern of growth is bound to give a very inexact picture of what will actually happen. This uncertainty would have been of minor importance if the range of possible capital-output ratios was narrow. But it is generally believed that a developing country must count on an incremental capital-output ratio between 3 and 4. Some hopeful voices are raised in favour of 'development strategies' which might result in a capital-output ratio below 3. On the other hand, there are many historical examples of ratios above 4. The choice of a figure for the capital-output ratio has very important implications if the projected rate of growth of the GDP is fast. Thus if the growth rate is set at 7 per cent annually, the necessary rate of fixed investment in relation to the GDP will vary between 20 per cent and 30 per cent depending on whether the capital-output ratio is slightly below 3 or slightly above 4.

In this study the amount of fixed investment which will be required if the projected growth rates are to be achieved is calculated mainly on the basis of the projected growth of the various sectors and subsectors, and in some cases also individual industries, within the economy. In addition, investment in 'infra-structure' of various kinds has been calculated separately, to the extent that such investments cannot be directly related to the increase in the output of certain sectors of the economy.

Total investments in a given year have been calculated as follows:

(1) 'Autonomous' investments in infrastructure, etc., have been estimated on the basis of the need to build up the system of education, the health services, communal services, to serve the growing urban and rural population, and so on (see Chapter 7). Investments in housing have been included under 'autonomous' investments, and have been related to the increased consumer expenditure on housing (see Section C of this chapter). From the point of view of model building, the 'autonomous' investments can be calculated independently, either fairly arbitrarily (on the assumption that such investment decisions can be taken more or less independently of the structural development of the economy as a whole but, of course, on the basis of certain assumptions as regards the rate of growth, the rate of increase of the population in general and the urban population in particular, and the economic and social policy to be followed) or, as regards housing, on the basis of data which can be derived directly from the basic assumptions behind this model.

(2) 'Induced' investments depend on the projected growth of the output of the different sectors of the economy. By breaking down the sectors into subsectors, or even smaller elements, it is justifiable to relate the investments which are required to the projected rate of growth, or in other words, to use the concept of a capital-output ratio in a micro-economic sense. Note that account has to be taken of the time-lag between investments and the increase in output. This time-lag can vary considerably from industry to industry, but the principle is that fixed *net* investments in a given industry in year Y equal the increase in output in year $Y + L$ multiplied by the capital-output ratio for the industry in question. L represents the time-lag between the investment and the increased output. To arrive at the *gross* fixed investments in the industry, it is also necessary to add a figure for the replacement of outworn or outdated productive capital.

The physical output of a given industry can be expressed as a function of demand and of productive capacity, i. e., of investments undertaken in periods prior to or during the reference period. Either demand or capacity will set a limit to the output, provided that voluntary or involuntary stockpiling is counted as demand. The productive capacity is the result of investments which may have been undertaken for a variety of reasons by individual investors; and only occasionally will demand equal the productive capacity at constant prices. The price mechanism will, within limits, ensure that demand is adjusted reasonably well to the productive capacity. It follows from this that it is not admissible to rearrange the functional relationship between investment, output, and demand so that investment in a given sector is a function of the future output which again is a function of demand. Still, this is precisely the procedure which has been described in the previous paragraphs. The assumptions behind this method must therefore be spelled out explicitly.

This method of estimating investments presumes that they depend uniquely on the projected growth of the output of the different sectors of the economy and the economy as a whole (and on political decisions as regards the autonomous investments). It is, consequently, implicitly assumed that there will never be investments in surplus capacity. All investment decisions will be rational and based on perfect foresight and will correspond to the future increase in effective demand.[6] In reality there will certainly be many cases of misdirected investments, and this means that the investment estimates as they are made here should represent the minimum investments needed to achieve a given pattern of growth. The problem of how to make sure that the 'needed' investments will actually take place is outside the scope of this study.

The investment figures must be translated into demand for goods and services from the several sectors of the economy. This means that for each field of activity which requires fixed investments, the investments must be broken down by goods and services delivered by different sectors, so that in the end the figure for total fixed investments can be broken down into deliveries from different sectors.[7]

Induced investments can only be calculated when the growth of the different sectors is known; the growth of many sectors can only be calculated when the demand for investment purposes is known. Consequently, the investment equations form a part of the model which can only be solved simultaneously with other parts of the model. In this study the total demand for investment goods and services and its breakdown have been found through approximations by several steps. While the figures for autonomous investments were taken as firm projections, a first provisional figure for induced investments was introduced in order to find an approximate figure for the demand for investment goods and services. The output targets having been determined in this manner, it was possible to make firmer estimates for the induced investments. These differed, of course, from the provisional ones, and consequently the output figures for certain sectors, subsectors, or industries had to be changed. This process would have been endless, but shortcuts were possible because it was possible to assess in advance the approximate changes in the demand on investment goods and services as a result of a new round of changes in the induced investments. The end result was not perfect, but discrepancies will fall within the margin of error which must be expected in a study of this kind.[8]

Investments in 'inventories' have been estimated as a given percentage of the increase in the Gross Domestic Product. No attempt has been made to refine this particular estimate.

The demand on the different sectors for *intermediate* purposes had to be calculated in much the same manner as the demand for investment purposes. As pointed out earlier, this demand cannot be found until the output of all sectors of the economy is known. The intermediate demand for products from sector A equals the sum of the products of the output of all sectors times their 'coefficients for inputs from sector A' minus the imports of sector A products for intermediate purposes.[9] The final solution of the equations for intermediate demand can only be had through a simultaneous solution of the whole model; but since this method was discarded, an alternative way had to be found, viz. a method of consecutive approximations by the introduction of a provisional solution for each individual sector.

The provisional solution consists in estimating the demand for products of sector A for intermediate purposes as the sum of the demand from two or three main purchasing sectors plus the nonspecified demand which is assumed to rise in line with the output of one sector of the economy which is considered as a good yardstick for the non-specified demand for intermediate purposes on sector A. Another hurdle has to be cleared. One, two, or three main purchasing sectors may in themselves be strongly dependent on intermediate demand for their products. In that case the approach has to be carried one or more steps further, until the output of the main purchasing sectors can be linked with some form of *final* demand.

The justification for this method of making a provisional estimate of the intermediate demand in a given sector is that statistical studies reveal that the bulk of the intermediate demand in many sectors in fact comes from one, two, or seldom more than three sectors. Some of the main purchasing sectors may, in turn, deliver most of their output for intermediate purposes, but these are again concentrated on a few sectors. In many cases, the demand for intermediate purposes can therefore be estimated fairly exactly on the basis of data for final demand for some end-products. In other cases not even an input-output Table provides the answer, because much of the demand in a given sector will be hidden in the category of nonspecified purchases for intermediate purposes by the various sectors of the economy. In such cases there is no other way out than to use the development of one or a group of sectors as an index of demand for intermediate purposes from certain sectors. The item non-specified demand for intermediate purposes represents this method of estimating intermediate demand provisionally. This item has also to be introduced in cases in which the final demand approach is used, but where the demand for specified purposes nevertheless merely represents, say, one-half of total demand. If the estimated demand for specified purposes represents a large part of total demand for intermediate purposes, the provisional figure for total demand for intermediate purposes is calculated also on the basis of the demand from the main purchasing sectors with a constant percentage added for non-specified users.

As soon as provisional estimates became available for all sectors of the economy, it was possible to review the estimates of intermediate demand. Where the discrepancy between the provisional and the derived figures was significant, adjustments had to be made. The final adjustments were made as part of the reconciliation process which was needed at the end of this study, and which is described in section F below.

The *detailed discussions* of the prospects of the *individual sectors,* subsectors, and industries in the economy of Pakistan had to be based on the provisional estimates of demand of investment and intermediate purposes and the firmer estimates of consumption and export demand.[10] However, to the extent that the detailed figures for individual industries etc., had to be altered, this was done; and the figures given in [O], Annex VI, are therefore *not* the original sector estimates, but the adjusted figures. Note that the sector estimates were always changed in conformity with the principles upon which the original estimates were made. Thus if the output of a sector was believed to be determined by domestic demand, the output estimate was changed in line with the demand estimate; but if, on the other hand, the original output estimate was thought to represent the highest possible output, the original output estimates were left unchanged even if the provisional demand estimates were increased significantly.

To *summarize* the procedures which are described above: The output of each sector of the economy has been determined on the basis of the estimated total demand. In cases in which domestic output cannot expand fast enough for some reason or other, such as the scarcity of natural resources, or the probability that domestic production would be too expensive compared to imports, or the impossibility of training enough domestic manpower to run the operations, domestic output equals total demand less imports which are determined as a residuum. Export demand is partly estimated on the basis of the expected world demand and partly on the basis of the competitive position of domestic industries on the world market. Consumption demand — by households or by government — was determined as a function of the postulated Gross Domestic Product (see section C below), whereas investment demand was estimated either independently, on the basis of the growth of the GDP or the development of consumption demand ('autonomous' investments), or as a provisional figure for induced investments in different sectors of the economy. Investment in increases in stocks are neglected for each individual sector of the economy, but taken into account on a global basis. Demand for intermediate purposes is estimated on a provisional basis. These provisional figures for investment demand and for demand for intermediate purposes are reconciled with other data and replaced by final figures at the end of the procedure.

C. *Domestic savings and consumptions*

Savings and consumption are calculated as follows:

Savings at the end of one given five-year plan period equal the savings at the end of the previous five-year plan period plus the increase in the Gross Domestic Product during the given five-year period multiplied by the marginal rate of savings during that period.

It follows from this that the savings at the end of each five-year period under review can be calculated on the basis of the figure for savings in the base period 1960 (and the figure for GDP in 1960) and the two sets of basic assumptions, i. e., the growth of GDP and the marginal rate of savings in each plan period.

Note that 'savings' refers to gross domestic savings, which are taken to mean domestic savings before the deduction of depreciation allowances and before transfer of factor income to abroad.

Consumption, personal and government, equals Gross Domestic Product minus gross domestic savings, and can consequently also be calculated on the basis of the basic assumptions.

One more assumption is then introduced; that government consumption will represent a given percentage of the GDP. Thus government consumption can be calculated, and a last equation gives us personal consumption:

Personal consumption equals total consumption less government consumption.

For the projections of domestic output and imports broken down by sectors of origin it is necessary to know the likely composition of government and personal consumption.

The *breakdown of government consumption* is difficult to estimate, but for most producing sectors a serious error in the estimate of current government demand for their products is less important because such demand represents only a small fraction of total demand. The reason it is difficult to assess the breakdown of government consumption is that virtually no data are available for the base year.

Government demand by types of goods and services falls into two main categories: the government product (i. e., wages, salaries, and other benefits paid to government servants) and purchases from other sectors of the economy.

But government consumption can also be broken down by purpose (general administration, defence, education, etc.). Demand by types of goods and services depends on the purpose of the expenditure. The projections have therefore been carried out as follows:

For the base year, total government consumption was broken down into main purposes, and the pattern of expenditure on types of goods and services under each purpose heading was estimated. The structure of government consumption by purpose was assumed to change considerably with expenditure for general administration and defence growing fairly slowly and with, for example, expenditure for education and health expanding very quickly. Under each heading, the pattern of expenditure on types of goods and services was assumed to remain constant. The global expenditure pattern was thus obtained by adding of the expenditure pattern for the different purposes weighted by the breakdown of expenditure by purpose.

The breakdown of government consumption by types of goods and services which was obtained in this manner was not sufficiently explicit to permit a detailed breakdown by delivering sectors, but it was possible to allocate most government consumption to the more important of these sectors.

Personal consumption is calculated as a remainder. Conceptually this leads to a meaningless result. Actually the personal consumption in the base year equalled the Gross Domestic Product (at *market prices*) less gross domestic saving less government consumption. The concept of personal consumption arrived at as a remainder equals the actual household expenditure on goods and services minus *all* indirect taxes plus *all* subsidies. This is not equal to a concept which might have some real economic sense, namely 'personal consumption at factor cost', i. e., consumer expenditure less indirect taxes plus subsidies paid on products purchased by the consumers, a concept which in itself is difficult to calculate because of the problem of how to distribute indirect taxes less subsidies paid on intermediate goods and services.

There are two reasons why a theoretically meaningless concept of consumer expenditure has been used. First, when this study was commenced, no data were available on the GDP at market prices and the exact amount of indirect taxes less subsidies. Second, as pointed out previously, it is not possible to project the GDP at market prices before the composition of the GDP at factor cost is known.

The main disadvantage in using the concept of personal consumption which is obtained by subtraction from the GDP at factor cost is that it somewhat underestimates the growth of personal consumption. This is caused by the fact that the GDP at market prices happens to show a faster growth than the GDP at factor cost. Since the figures for gross domestic saving and for government consumption are not affected by a change from factor cost to market prices (savings by definition being determined by the growth of the GDP at factor cost, and government consumption already being calculated at actual costs), the figures for personal consumption obtained as a remainder on the basis of GDP at market prices will show a faster rise than those based on factor cost.

Total *personal consumption* must be *broken down* into purchases of products of the different sectors of the economy.

The distribution of personal consumption on purchases of goods and services from the various sectors of the economy is calculated on the basis of the study of potential future changes in the structure of consumption which is presented in [O], Annex III, and summarized in Chapter 5. In the Annex, total personal consumption expenditure is broken down into expenditure by rural households in East Pakistan and West Pakistan respectively and urban households in all of Pakistan. The pattern of expenditure for each of these areas is estimated separately. The demand by households for products from a given sector is, in general, estimated on the basis of the aggregate figure for all of Pakistan. It has not been possible to classify the personal consumption expenditure in a way which corresponds exactly to the breakdown of the economic activities into sectors. In many cases the demand for products from one sector will therefore be expressed as a function of the expenditure under one or several headings. In some cases expenditure broken down by geographical areas is used as a basis for estimates of demand for products of a given sector. (For example, the urban demand for food is assumed to be predominant in determining the output of many modern food manufacturing industries.) It follows from this that it is not possible to express the functional relationship between the demand for products of a given sector and its determining factors in a simple, mathematical manner. (It can, of course, be done but the resulting formula would be very complicated and would not facilitate interpretation of the results. The reader will have to study the details in [O], Annexes III and VI, in order to find out how the demand by households for products from each sector has been estimated.)

D. *Gross Domestic Investment, Gross Domestic Savings, and the Foreign Balance*

The main elements of the national accounts link together as follows:

Exports of goods and services plus personal consumption plus government consumption plus gross fixed investments plus increase in inventories equal the Gross Domestic Product plus imports of goods and services.[11]

The left side of the equation gives the use of available resources, the right side their origin — that is, the GDP and the imports. If exports are moved to the right side of the equality sign, the left side gives the *domestic* use of resources, and the right side gives the availability of resources for domestic use (i. e., the GDP plus the import surplus).

This equation differs from the equation for the individual sectors of the economy which were discussed on page 43. The difference on the left side is that intermediate uses are not included, whereas on the right side the GDP equals the sum of the value added of all sectors, and the sector equations include the gross output as source of supply. This latter presentation is necessary for the individual sectors; but when the sector equations are added together, we can move the total intermediate purchases from the left to the right side of the equality sign, and we obtain gross domestic output less intermediate uses which equals the Gross Domestic Product.

In section C (page 55), we defined personal consumption plus government consumption as the Gross Domestic Product minus gross domestic savings. If we replace total consumption by GDP minus savings in the basic equation for the use and availability of resources, we get GDP on both sides of the equality sign which eliminates that item; and if we rearrange the other items, we obtain the following fundamental equation:

Gross fixed investments plus increase (or, if we prefer, investment) in inventories less gross domestic savings equal imports minus exports of goods and services.

This fundamental equation states that if total domestic gross investments exceed gross domestic savings, imports will have to exceed exports. This holds true regardless of the absolute level of exports. Exports cannot catch up with imports as long as savings do not catch up with investments.

It has previously been shown that for this study the level of gross domestic savings is exclusively determined by the rate of growth of the Gross Domestic Product (at factor cost) and the initial level of savings. No direct relationship has been established between the level of gross investments and the level of savings. This means that it is not possible to know in advance whether the projected investments will exceed or fall short of the projected savings in any given year.[12] The logical result of this is that the projected rate of growth of the Gross Domestic Product is only feasible, under the chosen assumptions for savings, if enough foreign capital is forthcoming to cover the balance of payments deficit which, eventually, is implied in the basic assumptions for growth and savings.

It is easy to object to this crucial assumption, or hypothesis, upon which this study is based. Particularly since the implied flow of foreign aid turns out to be very high, it is quite legitimate to question the realism of the hypothesis. Is there any point in presenting an economic model which makes the implication that the flow of gross foreign aid may have to increase as much as five times between 1965 and 1985?[13]

In order to give a meaningful answer to this question, it is necessary to consider which alternative assumptions could have been made. The evident alternative is to relate the projected domestic savings to the projected level of gross investments in such a manner that the need for foreign aid would decline each five-year period, or at least not increase. Another alternative would be to project increased foreign aid, but at 'a realistic rate'; for example, the amount of foreign aid available would be determined by the projected growth of the national income in the richer countries combined with an assumption of the willingness of these countries to increase the share of their national income devoted to foreign aid. Regardless of the alternative chosen for the future level of foreign aid, the projected figures for domestic savings would have to be related to projected investments and foreign aid in the following manner: domestic gross savings equal gross domestic investments (fixed and inventories) less the import surplus which can be paid by foreign aid, after allowance has been made for debt servicing, etc. This way of determining the level of savings makes the solution of the set of equations in this study more complicated, but the solution can easily be found, even though the iterative process becomes more cumbersome. The item imports less exports would in this case have to be taken as a given parameter.

But even if the new set of equations could be solved in principle, it is by no means sure that a consistent solution could be found. The item imports less exports does not merely depend on the inflow of foreign capital, but also on the size of the two figures for imports and exports. A higher level of domestic savings does not automatically mean that additional resources can be set free for exports and/or that imports will be reduced. On the contrary, the projections of exports in this study are already very much on the optimistic side, so that the lower demand for consumption goods and services which would be implied in a higher figure for savings should at best merely have a very small effect on the projected exports. Lower figures for consumer demand would obviously mean reduced demand for some imported goods and services, but the bulk of the effect would be on domestic production, including transport and trade margins on imported goods. It will be shown in this study that even under the assumption of unlimited foreign aid, it is difficult to get the estimates of the savings deficit and the balance of payments deficit to hang together. The level of domestic savings projected in this study is already so high that it makes rising rates of growth hard to achieve. The alternative of assuming given figures for foreign aid and higher rates of savings is therefore unrealistic, not for policy or other reasons, but because it is not consistent with the inner structure of the model.

The other main alternative is to 'cut the shirt to the body' that is, to calculate the rates of growth of the GDP which would result from two assumptions: (1) foreign aid will be limited, and (2) the gross domestic savings will rise as fast as they can effectively be utilized by the economy. The weakness of this alternative is that it moves away from the original purpose of this study which is to study the structural changes in an economy on the assumption that certain growth targets for the GDP will be achieved.

Both main alternatives imply higher rates of domestic saving than assumed throughout this study. The assumed figures for the marginal rate of savings which have been used here are already very ambitious, but they are, needless to say, not sacrosanct. Nevertheless, when targets for savings are set which are thought to represent the maximum effort which can be expected against the background of poverty and pressing immediate needs of a developing country, it is not very logical to state that these rates are too low and must be increased further to finance the desired investment programme. Of course, it should be possible to raise the rate of savings far above what has been assumed in this study, but this presumes a policy of oppression and a degree of austerity which the present study leaves out of account.

The three main alternatives for the choice of basic assumption imply that one of three major economic magnitudes has to be estimated as a function of all other given and implied factors: (1) the foreign aid, (2) the domestic rate of savings, and (3) the rate of growth of the national income.

Alternative 3 may be considered as the most realistic one, but does not suit the purpose of this study. Alternative 2 is for several reasons the most unrealistic of the three, and may in fact lead more or less to the same results as Alternative 3. Alternative 1 is also hypothetical; but of the three, it is the one which fits the very purpose of the present analysis.

The conclusions which can be drawn from this study, which is based on Alternative 1, have wide implications. They illustrate the magnitude of foreign aid which the richer countries must be willing to provide if they are to enable the developing countries to achieve ambitious growth targets which, although ambitious *per se,* are modest in relation to the enormous needs of those countries. Not only does the study suggest which global amount of aid may be needed, but also the composition of this aid. The projections of the pattern of imports into a country like Pakistan, and the extent to which technical assistance is needed, constitute information which can help in assessing the future structure of foreign aid.

E. *The inter-industry flows of goods and services*

A consolidated system of national accounts is in itself inadequate for the purpose of ensuring internal consistency between the figures contained in this study, which to a large extent is concerned with the gross output (plus imports) of goods and services originating in different sectors, and its uses, end-uses and intermediate uses. The figures contained in this study show that in 1960 33 per cent of total demand was for goods and services for intermediate purposes and that this percentage will rise gradually to reach 38 per cent in 1985. Although it is feasible to arrive at quite good estimates of intermediate uses of a number of important products by relating these intermediate uses to final uses which embody a large proportion of these products, this method can merely give very approximate results.[14] In order to obtain satisfactory results, it is necessary to organize the data on deliveries of goods for intermediate purposes in the form of input-output Tables, one for each year for which projections have been made. In order to control whether the estimated deliveries in fact correspond to intermediate demand, it is furthermore necessary to calculate the input structure of each sector and also organize these figures in the form of input-output Tables. The two sets of figures can then be compared and made mutually consistent.

The use of input-output Tables not only provides a consistency check on the figures for intermediate deliveries, but it also assures a control of the total availability for intermediate and final uses. Adjustments to deliveries for intermediate uses must automatically either lead to adjustments of the deliveries for final uses or of the total availability, i. e., of domestic output and/or of imports.

The construction of a reliable input-output Table for Pakistan for the year 1959/60 is an impossible task, since there are too many gaps in the statistical information. It is nevertheless possible to construct a Table which gives an approximate picture of the inter-industry flows of goods and services.[15] The difficulties are many. Statistical data on the input structure of the different sectors of the economy are only available for modern manufacturing industries.[16] For some other sectors scattered data are available (such as the accounts of the railways), but for most sectors no information can be obtained at all. In order to estimate the input structure it is therefore to a large extent necessary to use 'common sense' supplemented with data from other countries. Extensive use has been made of the detailed input-output studies which have been made of the Italian and Norwegian economies.[17] Italian and Norwegian data have been used in preference to, for example, British or American data which describe the situation in large, thoroughly industrialized societies. The Italian figures refer to the year 1950 when that country still retained many of the characteristics of an underdeveloped country. Norway is relatively highly industrialized; but with its small domestic market, its home industries will in many respects resemble those of a large underdeveloped cuntry with a narrow home market due to poverty.

Two sets of figures were thus available for the base year 1959/60 — the horizontal rows of the input-output Tables showing how the outputs[18] of the different sectors, at producers' prices, were distributed between intermediate and final uses, and the vertical columns showing the structure of the inputs of the several sectors expressed in buyers' prices. To arrive at a consolidated input-output Table, these two sets of figures should be consolidated. For this study such a consolidation had no real purpose. Neither the figures for deliveries nor the figures for purchases are fully reliable, and there is therefore no basis for determining which of two conflicting figures should be used as the basis for a consolidated figure.[19] The input-output Tables, both for the base year and for the future, have therefore been presented in a highly unorthodox manner. Each 'box' is divided in two halves — the upper half makes room for delivery to a sector, or to a final use, at producer prices, the lower half makes room for purchase by the sector at purchaser prices. For the final uses only the upper halves of the boxes have been filled.

In principle, the figures in the upper halves should be the smaller ones, and the difference between the two figures should represent transport costs, trade margins, indirect taxes, and other possible items which account for the difference between producer prices (or import prices c.i.f.) and purchaser prices. As it turned out, the difference between two figures in the same box rarely corresponded to a reasonable difference between the price paid to the producer and the price paid by the user. There are many possible reasons for this: (1) the inputs may be wrong (often underestimated), (2) since the output has been distributed only between the major purchasing sectors, it is quite likely that the calculated delivery to one major sector is overestimated (more should have been allocated to non-specified smaller users), and (3) there may be inconsistencies between the implied prices on the deliveries and the purchases. There are some striking examples of such inconsistencies between the implied prices which can be calculated by dividing the value of deliveries and purchases with the volume of deliveries and purchases respectively.[20] In those cases in which these differences were quite obvious, the figures entered in one or sometimes in both halves of the 'boxes' of the input-output Tables have been changed.

The most striking inconsistencies which were found in the input-output Tables for the base year have been eliminated. Otherwise they would have represented a source of overall imbalance which would have grown bigger, particularly if the inconsistent items grew faster than the average of all purchases or deliveries. But smaller inconsistencies still remain, because much additional research is required in order to eliminate them, and because their influence on the overall picture is less important.

For a number of sectors most of the output which is assumed used for intermediate purposes has been allocated to 'non-specified business uses'. Similarly, a sizeable part of the inputs in many sectors consists of non-specified purchases. It is only possible to reconcile these items globally. The unpublished [O], Annex IX,[21] contains a description of the methods of reconciling inconsistencies in general, and of distributing these non-specified items in particular.

In the construction of these input-output Tables many problems familiar to the input-output statistician were encountered. One of them is the difficulty in reclassifying the industrial statistics in such a manner that the output of a given category of goods is classified under its proper industry, regardless of whether it is produced in that industry or in some other industry. This reclassification was, in fact, undertaken in [O], Annex VI, in which, to the extent that this is possible, the census data on different industries were adjusted for production which does not 'belong to' that industry or inversely for production undertaken in another industry. In principle, therefore, the data are classified in the proper manner, but statistical difficulties have impeded consistent adjustments for all industries.

The treatment of foreign trade, or rather of imports, may surprise many readers. The common approach to the input-output analysis in most countries is to include use of imported goods and services at the bottom of each column so that domestic inputs, indirect taxes less subsidies, imported inputs, and value added, total the gross output of the sector. For final uses the detailed breakdown will only include domestically produced goods and services, whereas the imported goods and services are added in as one item at the bottom of the column in order to obtain the total final use. In this study imports have been broken down according to the sector of origin of the imported goods or services and added to the gross domestic output. The figure which is thus obtained for each sector equals total availability which again equals total demand.

This approach, which is used in France and which was also used by Chenery and Clark in their input-output studies for Italy, has several advantages. (1) It is not necessary to try to distribute imports among different purchasing sectors, (2) it is not necessary to find out how much of the input of one special type of goods in one sector is imported and how much is domestically produced, (3) the presentation allows a direct evaluation of how large a proportion of the total demand for the output of one given sector is covered by imported products, and (4) the columns show the 'true' input structure, that is, the distribution of inputs on sectors of origin, regardless of whether domestically produced or imported.

The disadvantage of the presentation used here is that it does not tell directly how much of the input of each sector is imported.

It is possible to combine the advantages of the two presentations by constructing an import matrix which shows imports by sectors of origin and the distribution of the imports on the several intermediate and final uses. This was, *inter alia,* done in the input-output study of Norwegian industries. But full advantage of this presentation can only be had if the two matrices for domestic production and imports are combined, for example, by making double entries in each box, one for domestic deliveries and one for imports.

The presentation chosen for the present study imposed itself for two reasons: (1) the author had no access to data which would have allowed an approximate distribution of imports on consuming sectors,[22] and (2) the ratio between gross output and imported inputs in most sectors is not constant. The first reason is a purely statistical one; and if it had been necessary, it could have been overcome by an attempt to distribute imports among categories of users. The second reason, however, is fundamental. Whereas almost any sector of the economy depends to some extent on some imported inputs which consequently represent a fairly constant ratio of the gross output of the sector, a substantial part of the imported inputs consists of goods (and to some extent services) which are both produced at home and imported. If in any given year it is assumed that the supply of domestic inputs of a certain type is given, an increase in the output of a sector which obtains at least part of such inputs from domestic sources must result in a more than proportional increase in the demand on imported inputs. Consequently, the imports of one product, or groups of products, originating in one given sector, depend both on the total demand (intermediate demand by all sectors and final demand) and on the domestic output of this product or group of products. The presentation of foreign trade used here corresponds to this manner of calculating imports.

F. *Final adjustments to the findings*

Chapters 5 to 9 summarize the body of this study, which is a detailed analysis of the growth and changes in personal and government consumption, estimates of investment in infrastructure and in the individual productive sectors of the economy, and a review of the growth potential of all sectors, often broken down into major products. The figures which are finally presented in these five chapters are results of several adjustments, based on two subsequent versions of input-output Tables for the economy as a whole. The second version of these Tables is presented as Appendix I. With few exceptions, the figures which are included in the input-output Tables correspond to the figures in Chapter 5 to 9.

The exceptions represent some last-minute adjustments to the input-output Tables which have no bearing on the arguments in Chapters 5 to 9.[23] Apart from unintentional errors, the differences between figures in the body of the report and the input-output Tables are not significant.

The input-output Tables do not, however, represent the final set of internally consistent figures which result from this study. The unpublished [O], Annex IX, describes the global adjustments and the relatively few detailed adjustments which were needed in order to ensure formal consistency between detailed figures and overall assumptions.

These final adjustments concerned several essential problems.

(1) Estimates of indirect taxes and subsidies and calculation of the Gross Domestic Product and its uses at market prices.

(2) The reconciliation of the estimated demand for and the estimated deliveries of goods and services for intermediate purposes.

(3) The calculation of final uses of goods and services at purchasers' prices and the reconciliation of these figures with the figures for deliveries at producers' prices to final uses.

(4) The distribution of the provisional figures for the output of retail and wholesale trade ('the trade margins') between different uses and the calculation of figures for the output of trade which are consistent with other figures.

(5) Final adjustments to the figures for the Gross Domestic Product and imports which follow from other adjustments.

(6) Adjustments to domestic savings resulting from other adjustments.

These final calculations and adjustments led to some fairly important and therefore significant modifications to the assumptions about the growth of the national income and the marginal rate of savings. These initial assumptions are included in Tables 1 and 2, but are discussed further in Chapter 4.

4. Initial Assumptions and Subsequent Adjustments

The basic assumptions of this study are:

(A) The Gross Domestic Product will grow at given rates and the marginal rate of saving will reach given levels.

(B) Government consumption will represent a given (and slightly rising) percentage of the GDP.

(C) Total population will grow at a constant rate, and the urban population will grow much faster than the rural.

(D) The relative difference in output per head in rural and urban areas will remain constant, while the discrepancy in income per head between East and West Pakistan in both rural and urban areas will be closed.

A. *Overall rate of growth and marginal rate of savings*

Tables 1 and 2 of Chapter 2 contain the assumptions regarding the rate of growth and the marginal rate of savings which have been used by the Planning Commission at various stages. They also include the assumptions about rate of growth and marginal rate of savings which were retained for this study. Our assumptions are close to those used by the Planning Commission in the autumn of 1963, when the first guidelines for the Third Five-Year Plan were prepared. We noted that our assumptions for the rate of growth were more modest than those used by the Planning Commission in the final version of the Third Plan, while our assumptions for the marginal rate of savings were far more ambitious.

In Chapter 3, on the methods used in this study, it was shown that the final process of reconciliation of all the figures contained in the study led to the result that the figures for growth and marginal rate of savings had to be altered also. The 'basic assumptions' were therefore used as a working hypothesis; but when they turned out to be in conflict with the detailed figures of the study, they had to be dropped.

Table 4 shows the difference between the figures initially chosen as basic assumptions and those which are consistent with all other figures in this study.

Table 4. *Differences between assumed and obtained figures for the*
rates of growth of the Gross Domestic Product and for the marginal
rate of savings

	Second Plan 1960-65	Third Plan 1965-70	Fourth Plan 1970-75	Fifth Plan 1975-80	Sixth Plan 1980-85
Rate of growth of the GDP per plan period					
Assumption................	22	30	35	40	45
Outcome of this study.......	22.1	33.8	35.3	38.6	41.4
Marginal rate of savings					
Assumption................	18.5	27	28	33	35
Outcome of this study.......	18.1	26.5	26.4	30.6	32.3

Sources: Assumption for the growth of the GDP, Table 1; assumption for the marginal rate of savings, Table 2. Outcome of this study: Table 11.

The final figures for the growth of the GDP show that the growth during the Third Plan can far exceed the target, whereas the growth targets for the Fifth and particularly for the Sixth Plan Period are beyond all practical possibility. The projected strong performance of the economy during the Third Plan Period most certainly corresponds to the real situation. Firstly, as shown in Table 1 (Planning Commission IV) the rate of growth during the Second Five-Year Plan was far faster than 22 per cent, in fact 29 per cent. This means that part of the projected growth during the Third Plan has already occurred. Secondly, the Planning Commission has raised the target for the Third Plan to 38 per cent, on the basis of the present performance of the economy.

The projected 'shortfall' during the Fifth and Sixth Plan periods is in a way disappointing. There are strong reasons to believe that the rate of growth can be accelerated with time. The predominant reason for this is the growing weight of the modern manufacturing sector which means that a *constant* rate of growth of modern manufacturing will lead to an increased rate of growth of the total national income, even if other sectors continue to grow at a constant rate.[1] The reasons for the shortfall during the last two plan periods are analyzed in detail in Chapter 8, but one main cause can be pointed out here — the difficulty of expanding certain industries fast enough, notably the capital goods industries, for which demand will be very high and increase rapidly.

The marginal rate of savings which is obtained as an outcome of this study is lower than the assumed rate of saving in all periods. The 'shortfall' in savings grows with time.

The reader is justified in asking why the outcome of the marginal rate of savings differs from the assumption, since it is clearly fully possible to retain the assumed rate of marginal savings and make adjustments elsewhere. The answer has two sides to it. Firstly, it must be pointed out that the practical difficulties in retaining the assumed marginal rate of savings are formidable. The adjustment to the marginal rate of savings results from the final adjustment to the rate of growth of the Gross Domestic Product. If the marginal rate of savings is retained, the estimates of personal and government consumption have to be changed. Even if these changes in relative terms are fairly small, they would result in changes throughout the economy and in turn to another round of adjustments to the GDP, the rate of savings, consumption, etc. If the analytical gains had been considered to be important, the author would have chosen these time-consuming adjustments, but the analytical gains are not only unimportant, but directly dubious. The alternative of adjusting the marginal rate of savings entails that no further adjustments to consumption, etc., are needed.

Secondly, the adjustments to the marginal rate of saving are in themselves of great analytical interest. They show that on the basis of the structure of the economy at present and during the next couple of decades it is necessary to avoid slowing down the growth of personal consumption too much if the rate of growth of the national income is to reach or approach the desired targets. The reason for the 'shortfall' in savings is closely linked with the reason for the 'shortfall' in the overall rate of growth during the two last five-year periods under review. Rapid growth demands a high rate of investment and a high rate of saving. But the structure of the economy today and during the next couple of decades is such that investments will to a large extent depend on imports. It follows from this that expenditure for investment purposes will not create as much domestic demand as is needed to cause rapid growth in the short run. The 'multiplier effect' of investments is relatively weak because much of it is drained away in the form of imports. Consequently, consumption must contribute the needed stimulus if the desired rate of growth is to be achieved.

For the purpose of this study, the 'shortfall' in the marginal rate of savings has therefore been accepted as something unavoidable. If the postulated rate of savings had been retained, the net effect would have been to reduce the rate of growth of the Gross Domestic Product even further. The assumed figures for the marginal rate of savings are not sacrosanct. They were introduced as a working hypothesis, and to modify them in order to achieve consistent results is fully permissible.

These preliminary remarks on the adjustments to the rate of

growth of the national income and to the marginal rate of savings are made only in order to explain why these adjustments to the presumably basic and immovable assumptions have been made. A more detailed analysis of the problems involved is given later. At this stage it is first of all necessary to underline that the outcome of this study does not yield results which conform fully to the basic assumptions.

Is it possible to build an economic model for Pakistan which conforms to the basic assumptions and which, in particular, maintains the assumption that the GDP can grow 40 and 45 per cent respectively during the Fifth and the Sixth Plan periods and which yields the assumed figures for the marginal rate of savings? Clearly, it is possible to construct such a model which still would be within the range of economic realities. I even have a clear idea as to the basic characteristics of such a model. Since the problem first of all is to raise the level of investments which can be implemented with domestic resources, such a model would call for an even larger programme for building and construction. There is certainly room for such a programme, for example, through a far more rapid expansion of home building and road construction. The secondary effects would be more personal consumption, more investments in factories producing building materials and in transport facilities, and so on; and the end effect would be higher imports, higher foreign aid, and a higher capital-output ratio. My personal opinion is that it is neither likely that such a development strategy would be adopted by Pakistan nor that the aid-giving countries would be willing to 'underwrite' a development plan which would be so costly in terms of foreign aid. I have therefore preferred to deviate from my own assumptions rather than to construct a model which, in spite of certain attractive aspects, nevertheless in my opinion appears to include too many unrealistic assumptions.

B. *The Level of government consumption*

Our figures for 1960 show that government consumption in that year represented 8.5 per cent of the Gross Domestic Product. The working hypothesis in this study was that this percentage will increase by 0.3 percentage points per five-year period, so that government consumption in 1985 will represent 10 per cent of the Gross Domestic Product at factor cost — both government consumption and the GDP expressed in 1959/60 prices. It is important to remember that constant prices are used throughout this study. This is significant in judging the hypothesis for government consumption. Since a large part of government consumption consists of payments to government servants (in Pakistan above 60 per cent), rising salaries are a main reason for the growth of government consumption in relation to national income in most countries. If it is assumed that prices (and consequently also the 'prices' paid for the services of government servants) are constant, the growth in government consumption in relation to national income represents exclusively the growing volume of current government activities. Table 5 below illustrates this point.

There is no logical reason for changing the original assumption that the share of government consumption should grow by 1.5 percentage points from 1960 to 1985. The assumed percentages were therefore applied to the 'latest' estimate of the GDP throughout this study, *except in the very final round of adjustments.* As pointed out in Chapter 3, it was in the end necessary to undertake some global adjustments in order to make all figures internally consistent. These adjustments also affected the size of the GDP. If at this stage the figures for government and personal consumption once more had been changed, another complete round of calculation of the input-output Tables would have become necessary. A more expedient way out was chosen — the figures for government consumption were left unchanged, but the result was that the percentages showing government consumption in relation to GDP were changed. It can rightly be objected that this is an imperfect approach, but the opposite approach would have been unduly perfectionist. The chosen percentages were arbitrary, and what they were supposed to illustrate was merely that there will be a slow growth in the share of government consumption in the GDP. The new percentages show the same thing, and are therefore neither better nor worse than the old ones.

It will be noted that the distribution of the GDP between savings and total consumption differs considerably from the original assumptions. This was caused by an upward revision of investments and GDP in the base year as a result of the final revisions of the input-output Tables for that year.

Table 5 shows that the behaviour of government consumption according to the final figures presented here does not differ significantly from the original assumptions.

The figures for government consumption 'in current prices' take into account the rise in the real wages of government servants which is needed if this category of wage earners shall have its share of the benefits of economic growth. These figures show that the share of government consumption in the GDP will rise by almost one-half in the course of 25 years. In my opinion this is a very reasonable assumption.

Table 5. *Savings and personal and government consumption in*
per cent of Gross Domestic Product at factor cost. Assumptions used
and figures finally obtained

	1960	1965	1970	1975	1980	1985
Assumptions						
Gross savings	6.7	8.8	13.0	16.9	21.5	25.7
Government consumption	8.5	8.8	9.1	9.4	9.7	10.0
Personal consumption	84.8	82.4	77.9	73.7	68.8	64.3
Final outcome						
Gross savings	10.5	11.9	15.6	18.4	21.8	24.9
Government consumption	8.3	8.7	9.0	9.5	9.9	10.3
Personal consumption	81.2	79.4	75.4	72.1	68.3	64.8
NB. Government consumption in						
'current' prices	8.3	8.9	9.5	10.4	11.3	12.3

Sources: [0]: Assumptions, Annex III, Table 1. Final outcome: consumption, Annex IX, Table 2, GDP and savings, Annex IX, Table 20, Alternative A. Government consumption in 'current' prices: Annex X, Table 5.

C. *The size and growth of the population*

The population census of January, 1961, showed a reported population of 93.9 million. Demographers have scrutinized the figures very closely, notably the figures for age and sex distributions, and have concluded that the census gave far too low a figure. Various estimates of the 'real' population have been produced during the last few years. For this study I accepted a figure of 105.5 million for January, 1961, which implied a figure of 102.8 million for the base year 1959/60. These figures were based on the latest available estimate in Pakistan in December, 1963. The Planning Commission now uses a figure of 99 million for 1959/60.[2] This figure is consistent with an estimate published by the Pakistan Institute of Development Economics in the summer of 1963[3] and which concluded that the population in January, 1961, was equal to 102.2 million. I do not know why a higher estimate was used at the end of 1963. The figures used in this study are therefore consistently higher than those used by the Planning Commission. The difference is not very large and does not distort our conclusions.

As shown in Table 1, I have assumed that the population will continue to grow at a rate close to 3 per cent per year throughout the period under review, while the Planning Commission expects the population growth to decline after 1980. This difference is deliberate; the reasons are explained on page 29.

The approach used in the present study requires a breakdown

between urban and rural areas in East and West Pakistan respectively. The Planning Commission has made estimates of the population growth in the two provinces (although they have not been presented explicitly in the Third Five-Year Plan), but no estimate of the expected growth of the urban population has been published.

The assumptions used in this study are crude: (1) the population will grow at the same rate in the two provinces; (2) the total urban population will grow by about 6.5 per cent per year during the Second to Fourth Plan period and by about 8 per cent per year during the Fifth and Sixth Plan period; and (3) the urban population in East Pakistan will grow by 60 per cent per five-year period during the Second to Fourth Plan period and by 65 per cent during each of the two last plan periods. The figures for West Pakistan are obtained from the differences between (2) and (3).

The assumed distribution of the population between rural and urban areas is, as will be shown in the next section of this chapter, very important for the further analysis. These assumptions must necessarily be consistent with the expected employment pattern, because it has also been assumed that there will be no significant urban unemployment. This assumption is not a prediction of events, but an analytical tool. Urban unemployment in coun-

Table 6. *The population estimates and the projected number of jobs in urban areas. (Million persons or man-years)*

	1960	1965	1970	1975	1980	1985
Planning Commission						
Third Five Year Plan						
Total population	99	112	129	148	168	187
Assumptions in this study						
Total population	103	117	133	152	173	199
Rural population	90	99	108	118	123	126
Urban population	13	18	25	34	50	73
Final outcome						
Urban employment	4	5	8	11	16	23
In % of assumed urban population	30	29	30	31	31	31

Sources: Planning Commission estimate [5], 1960 and 1965, p. 1, other years calculated by using the percentage increases in Table 1, p. 19. The figure for 1985 is given on p. 24.

Assumptions: the growth rate for the total population is given in Table 1, the assumptions as regards the growth of the urban population on p. 65. Source of details: [0], Annex II, Table 2. Final outcome Annex VI, Table 6. (Note that the figures given in the Table above are round figures.)

tries in which the number of urban jobs increases very fast is caused by too rapid an influx of job-hunters from the country-side. Against this background it is convenient to treat urban un-employment as 'displaced rural unemployment' rather than as an urban economic and social phenomenon.[4] Our figures of the urban population, and the subsequent analysis of the growth of urban income per head, are therefore based on the assumption that there will be gainful employment for the entire urban labour force.

It follows from this that it is possible to verify the figures for the urban population by comparing them with the growth of the number of urban jobs.

The difference between our figures for the total population and those of the Planning Commission is about 4 per cent for all years except 1985 when the gap grows much wider due to the signifi-cant discrepancy between the assumptions regarding population growth during the Sixth Plan Period.

The figures for the growth of urban employment correspond extremely well to the assumed rate of growth for the urban pop-ulation. This is not entirely accidental since preliminary estimates of the employment pattern were used in order to determine the figures for the growth of the urban population which were finally used.[5]

D. *Differences in output per head between rural and urban areas and between East and West Pakistan*

In almost any country the income per head in rural areas is much lower than in urban areas. This is certainly so in under-developed countries in which most of the rural population de-pends on a traditional low-productive, subsistence agriculture and most of the people whose earnings are from the high produc-tivity modern sector of the economy live and work in urban areas. The income gap between town and countryside would have been much larger were not the urban incomes depressed because of the influx of people from the countryside.[6] It is certainly de-sirable to reduce the gap in income between town and country-side, but this cannot be achieved before agriculture is thoroughly modernized and before the modern sector of the economy offers so many job opportunities that rural under-employment dis-appears. In this study it has been assumed that the relative differ-ence between rural and urban income per head will remain con-stant, or rather that the output per head in rural and urban areas will grow at the same rate.[7]

All available data suggest that income per head is considerably lower in East Pakistan than in West Pakistan. The figures for the base year used as the basis for the assumptions and detailed calculations in this study show that gross regional product per head (in 1959/60 prices) was Rs 242 in East Pakistan and Rs 312 in West Pakistan (see Table 10). The latest official estimate shows that, in 1964/65 prices, income *per caput* in East Pakistan was Rs 297 and in West Pakistan Rs 391.[8]

According to my figures the output per head in West Pakistan was 29 per cent higher than in East Pakistan, whereas the Planning Commission figures show an income gap of 32 per cent. In view of the uncertainties attached to these estimates, the difference between them is not very important.

My estimates illustrate the reasons for the income gap: rural output per head in West Pakistan was 7 per cent higher than in East Pakistan, urban output per head was 17 per cent higher in the West, and the urban population represented 22 per cent of the total population in West Pakistan as against only 5 per cent in East Pakistan. The most important reason for the income discrepancy was the very different distribution of the population between town and countryside.[9]

At the time when this study was started, the existence of a serious income gap between the two provinces was recognized by the government in Pakistan, and it had become a major policy target to eliminate this discrepancy. But this target is difficult to achieve, and it was not until during the preparation of the Third Five-Year Plan that the Planning Commission first suggested that the income disparity between East and West should be eliminated in the course of a given period of time. The period chosen was that of the 'perspective plan', i. e., before 1985.

The present study is, in principle, based on the assumptions made by the Pakistanis themselves. In general, the difference which persist between their and my assumptions are due to two reasons; the Planning Commission altered some assumptions after the main work on this study was terminated, and my basic assumptions were modified as a result of my own analytical work. But in the case of the removal of the income disparity between East and West, I found that the target set by the Planning Commission was too ambitious, and I replaced it by the following assumptions: (1) the differences in output per head in rural and urban areas respectively between East and West will disappear before 1985, i. e., the remuneration for the same kind of work should become the same in the two provinces; and (2) the urban population will grow much faster in East Pakistan than in West Pakistan, i. e., the basic reason for the income disparity will diminish rapidly.[10]

Table 7. *Distribution of gross product* per caput *between regions and between rural and urban areas*

	1960	1965	1970	1975	1980	1985
Gross Domestic (or 'regional') *Product* per caput. (Rs)						
Pakistan......................	274	294	337	397	487	615
All rural areas.................	236	246	272	309	356	419
All urban areas	535	557	616	699	807	950
East Pakistan, total	242	260	299	357	442	572
West Pakistan, total............	312	336	382	446	541	668
GDP per caput, *1960 = 100*						
All Pakistan	100	107	123	145	178	224
All rural areas.................	100	104	115	131	151	178
All urban areas	100	104	115	131	151	178
East Pakistan, total	100	107	124	148	183	236
West Pakistan, total............	100	108	122	143	173	214

Source: Table 10 which gives further details.

The results of the assumptions regarding the growth of output per head in urban and rural areas and in the two provinces are shown in Table 7.

The result of this assumption for the regional distribution of output is that the gap in output per head between the two provinces will become relatively narrower. While the gross product per head in West Pakistan according to the figures used here was 29 per cent higher than in East Pakistan in 1960, the discrepancy in 1985 will be merely 17 per cent. The only reason for the disparity in 1985 will be the projected higher degree of urbanization (which, however, in this case also reflects a further stage of development) in West Pakistan.

It has now become the firm official policy of the Government of Pakistan that the income gap between East and West Pakistan be removed before 1985.[11] It is possible, although by no means certain, that the regional income equalization policy may be helped by the fact that the potential increase in income from agriculture in the long run may be higher in East Pakistan than in West Pakistan. This might lead to higher income per head in rural areas in the East than in the West. But it should be remembered that East Pakistan is far more densely populated, both in relation to the total area and in relation to the cultivable area, than West Pakistan. Furthermore, the rural population in West Pakistan is in this study projected to grow much more slowly than in East Pakistan (by 32 and 45 per cent respectively, see [O], Annex II, Table 2) which will make it difficult for East Pakistan to outrun West Pakistan in rural income per head. It is far more likely that the only way to achieve an economic equilibrium between the two provinces is to accelerate even further the growth of urban areas in East Pakistan than has been assumed here. Admittedly the income gap projected in this study will hardly be politically acceptable, the more so as the absolute gap in output per head is projected to *increase* from Rs 70 to Rs 96. For an outside observer it is very difficult to see how the targets of a high rate of growth for the country as a whole and the closing of the income gap between the two provinces can be achieved simultaneously in the course of the next twenty years. In this context it is worth mentioning that the urban income in East Pakistan is projected to grow by 1,210 per cent between 1965 and 1985 or by 13.7 per cent per year (see Table 10). Such an increase in urban income is only possible if the main urban industries increase at a similar speed. Is it possible for East Pakistan to sustain an increase of, say, 15 per cent per year in industrial production over a period of 20 years? In this study it is implicitly assumed that it is possible, but such an achievement would be most remarkable indeed.

Another major observation which can be made from the figures concerning regional income per head is the wide discrepancy between the rise in income per head for the country as a whole and for rural and urban areas separately. The total national income per head should increase by 59 per cent more than the income per head in rural or urban areas respectively. This is not a surprising result since there is a projected shift of population from low-income rural to high-income urban areas. (The urban population should grow from 12.8 per cent of the total population in 1960 to 37 per cent in 1985, see Table 10). This relative shift in population from rural to urban areas is unavoidable in an economy which is expected to grow on the basis of a modernization of its economic structure. If anything, the projected growth of the urban population is on the low side.

Is it reasonable to assume that the income difference between rural and urban incomes per head will stay constant? This question can be put for two opposite reasons. One is to ask whether it is fair to postulate that income disparities between the predominantly farming population of the rural areas and the rest of the population shall be permitted to remain constant. The other is to ask whether it is realistic to assume that the rural *per caput* income can grow as fast as *per caput* income in the urban areas where the process of modernization is felt much stronger. The first is political and social, the second practical and economic. In fact, the second way of putting the question is probably the most relevant. Historical evidence shows that the rural population tends to lag behind in the development process. Experience from many countries shows that the rural population becomes impoverished while the urban population prospers. One objective of planned economic growth is obviously to bring this tendency to a halt and reverse it. The crucial question is whether this is possible, at least in the short run. Theoretically, the productivity of land could be increased very rapidly if modern techniques were rapidly introduced on all farming land. The introduction of new techniques amongst millions of impoverished and illiterate farmers is bound to take time, and the growth of the yield per hectar will be modest. At the same time the farming population will continue to grow because the modern sectors of the economy are too small to absorb the growing surplus population on the farms. Under such circumstances it would be a great achievement if a country could manage to increase the *per caput* income of its rural population at the same rate as for its urban population, if the urban population does not become abnormally large due to an influx of an army of unemployed, unskilled workers who have fled from the land. As already pointed out, the figures for the urban population used in this study are net of such a displaced, unemployed, rural population. The assumption of a parallel increase in income per head in rural and urban areas implies that the urban unemployment and under-employment remains at a 'normal' level, and that rural income will rise fast enough to be shared with those who are usefully employed on the land only during a part of the year. It would certainly be politically and socially desirable to aim at a faster increase in the income per head in rural areas than in the urban ones, but even the assumption used here seems at the outset to be extremely optimistic.[12]

The only reason why this study includes estimates of the Gross Domestic Product broken down between urban and rural areas and between East and West Pakistan is that the figures for personal consumption have been broken down into three parts: personal consumption in rural areas in East Pakistan, in rural areas in West Pakistan, and in all urban areas. This was necessary because the pattern of consumption in these three 'areas' differs considerably, and because the three population groups in question are projected to grow at widely different rates.[13] Consequently it was necessary to project separately the three parts of personal consumption. In order to do this, independent projections of output, savings, and government consumption in the three 'areas' were needed. We shall return to the distribution of savings later in this chapter.

Since the breakdown of the Gross Domestic Product into three parts (or in fact, four parts, because the urban output was also broken down between the two provinces) was made in order to establish some figures needed as background material for some of the projections, the study of the geographical distribution of the Gross Domestic Product was not pursued further. This field of study is in itself most fascinating and very important, but it would have carried us too far it we had tried a systematic analysis of the geographical location of economic activities in Pakistan. Because East and West Pakistan are more than 1,000 miles apart, the economies of the two wings are to a large extent self-contained. Firm estimates of the distribution of the GDP between the two wings therefore require separate input-output Tables for each of them. It is therefore not possible to tell, on the basis of the material available for this study, how modern manufacturing has to be distributed between East and West in order to achieve the output targets shown in Table 7. The distribution

Table 8. *Growth of the Gross Product in rural and urban areas of East and West Pakistan . assumptions and final outcome*

	Assumptions		Final Outcome	
	1960	1985	1960	1985
Rs per head				
The whole country	274	615	282	631
Rural areas	236	419	243	430
Urban areas	535	950	549	974
East Pakistan	242	572	249	586
West Pakistao	312	668	321	685
1960 = 100				
The whole country	100	224	100	224
Rural areas	100	178	100	177
Urban areas	100	178	1000	177
East Pakistan	100	236	100	235
West Pakistan	100	!14	100	213
Ratio gross product *per caput*				
West Pak.: East Pak.	1.29	1.17	1.29	1.17

Sources : Assumptions, see Table 7, Final outcome. 1960 . all figures were adjusted upward proportionally, by the ratio of the GDP at factor cost according to Table 10, to the final outcome given in Table 11. The assumption that the urban and rural products per head should grow at the same rate, and that they would be, by 1985, the same in the two provinces was maintained, and the 1985 figure for the GDP given in Table 11 was broken down by rural and urban areas in both provinces to conform to this assumption.

of modern manufacturing would have to be used as the item of adjustment in a systematic planning of economic growth between the two wings, since the distribution of the primary activities — agriculture, forestry, fisheries, and mining — is determined by the natural resources, and the distribution of tertiary activities, trade, transport, and other services, is determined by the level and the structure of all economic activities. But the exact level of the tertiary activities can only be estimated on the basis of an input-output analysis.

Figures for the growth of urban and rural output in Table 7 were based on the original assumptions of the growth of the GDP. Table 4 shows that the final outcome differed significantly from the assumptions. How will this discrepancy influence the distribution between urban and rural areas? Table 8 below answers this question.

Table 8 shows that for *the period 1960 to 1985* there is virtually no difference between the assumptions and the final outcome. But Table 4 showed that during the intervening years there were quite significant discrepancies between the assumed figures and those finally arrived at when all detailed implications of the assumptions were figured out. Still, Table 8 serves to reassure us that whatever deviations there are between assumptions and final outcome, they do not significantly disturb the assumed distribution of the gross product between town and countryside, or between East and West Pakistan.

The ultimate reason for breaking down the Gross Domestic Product between rural areas in East and West Pakistan and urban areas was to determine the growth of personal consumption in those three areas, and it follows that figures for savings in the three areas must also be estimated. The assumptions which were used are set out in Table 9, which also shows, as one possible alternative, how the final figures compare with the assumptions.

The figures for 1960 need some explanation. First, the *assumed* percentage for 1960 was much lower than the one which was finally obtained on the basis of a fairly reliable estimate of total investments and firm figures for the balance of payments deficit. Second, the distribution of saving between rural and urban areas is highly arbitrary. But the absolute level of savings (or the *per caput* savings) in the base year has no influence on the calculations of the marginal rate of savings.[14]

It seems reasonable to assume that the marginal rate of savings in the urban areas will be larger than in the rural areas provided that (1) a large proportion of the increased income in the urban areas will consist of profits which will be saved, of higher wage incomes which either can be taxed directly or will result in

Table 9. *The implied savings assumptions – original assumptions and final outcome**

| | Years or Plan periods ending in years | | | | | |
	1960	1965	1970	1975	1980	1985
Savings in per cent of GDP						
Urban areas, assumptions	(3.0)	6.2	12.8	19.6	26.5	30.4
final outcome	(6.8)	9.1	15.2	20.9	26.7	29.8
Rural areas, assumptions	(7.9)	9.9	13.1	15.1	16.9	19.2
final outcome	(11.8)	13.1	15.8	16.8	17.4	18.4
Pakistan, assumptions	6.7	8.8	13.0	16.9	21.5	25.7
final outcome	10.6	11.8	15.7	18.5	21.9	24.8
Marginal rate of savings						
Urban areas, assumptions	n.a.	13.4	25.4	31.7	36.4	36.3
final outcome	n.a.	14.3	26.0	31.7	35.3	35.7
Rural areas, assumptions	n.a.	23.5	28.6	23.4	25.5	30.5
final outcome	n.a.	21.9	27.2	20.8	20.2	24.4
Pakistan, assumptions	n.a.	18.5	27	28	33	35
final outcome	n.a.	18.1	26.5	26.4	30.6	32.3
Marginal rate of savings out of income per caput						
Urban areas, assumptions	n.a.	80.0	75.0	70.2	71.1	53.9
final outcome	n.a.	62.5	59.2	62.2	67.2	51.0
Rural areas, assumptions	n.a.	57.2	43.5	29.8	28.6	33.4
final oucome	n.a.	43.2	35.6	23.9	21.3	25.3
Pakistan, assumptions	n.a.	37.5	42.1	38.6	41.8	41.6
final outcome	n.a.	30.3	36.4	33.9	37.7	38.1

Sources: Assumptions: [0], Annex II, Table 4. (Gross domestic savings in per cent of GDP are calculated on the basis of [0], Table 1, Annex III.)

* Final outcome: for Pakistan as a whole the figures can be calculated on the basis of [0], Annex IX – 20 (Alternative A, which was retained in this study) and Annex II–2 on the data on population. It does not follow from the global figures in Annex IX – 20 how savings and consumptions will be distributed between urban and rural areas. Many alternatives are, in fact, possible. For the purpose of calculating Table 9, one simple alternative has been used: the distribution of personal and government consumption between rural and urban areas has been kept the same as in [0], Annex III – 1. Since the percentage adjustments to the two forms of consumption differ, it follows that savings have been adjusted differently in urban and rural areas.

higher purchases which will lead to larger payments of indirect taxes, and thus a large part of the urban income should be added to private and government savings; and (2) most of the increased farm income will accrue to the peasants who will tend to spend much of their added income on better food (mostly from their own crops) and other consumer goods.[15]

During the Second and Third Five-Year Plan, however, the increase in urban income is too small to provide enough savings, assuming a higher marginal rate of savings in the urban than in the rural areas. The Table shows that even with 'modest' assumptions for the marginal rate of savings in the urban areas during those two plan periods, the *per caput* marginal rate of savings must be extremely high. During the whole period under review the urban population must set aside between 54 per cent and 80 per cent of its added income per head if the original savings assumptions are to be fulfilled.

The result of the revision of the base-year figures for savings and the somewhat lower figures for the country-wide marginal rate of savings implied in the final outcome of this study is that both the marginal rates of saving and particularly the marginal rates of saving out of income *per caput* turn out to be lower than originally assumed in urban as well as rural areas.[16] But the marginal rate of savings out of income *per caput* in urban areas must still exceed 50 per cent throughout the period under review, and in most of the plan periods it must exceed 60 per cent.

The savings assumptions for the rural areas are far more modest. It should also be taken into account that part of the increased rural savings are 'non-monetized' savings, i. e., the value of investment work done by the rural population without compensation which can be consumed.[17]

There is no doubt, however, that the assumed marginal rates in both urban and rural areas are very high. One is bound to conclude that the assumptions concerning savings imply devotion to the development effort on the part of the people and stern determination on the part of the government. An easier way out might appear to be to let the peasantry carry a much larger share of the burden. It is highly questionable whether this would prove to be possible. The development 'strategy' upon which this study is built is one which presupposes a fairly rapid growth of agricultural output. It is unthinkable that any government in a country like Pakistan could avoid basing their planning on such a strategy. First, more food is needed to feed a growing population. Second, the industrial base of the economy is so narrow that during the next couple of decades agriculture must provide employment for a large part of the growing labour force. Improvements in agriculture cannot take place unless the peasants are given incentives to produce more. Incentives to the peasants will undoubtedly lead to higher rural consumption. The savings which can be squeezed out of the rural population are under these circumstances rather limited. The opposite strategy would be a complete regimentation of the peasantry.

A third development strategy can be envisaged — one which concentrates on industrialization, helped by very large and increasing amounts of foreign aid, including rapidly growing imports of food. Such a strategy could give the urban population a real sense of prosperity and progress. Politically it is difficult to envisage such a development policy over a longer period of time: Would the aid-giving countries be willing to augment their aid to a country which lets its agriculture stagnate indefinitely and its rural population become more and more impoverished?

Table 10. *Initial assumptions. Projected growth of Gross Domestic Product at factor cost (in current 1959/60 prices)* Rs million / or Rs *per caput*

	1960	1965	1970	1975	1980	1985
Total Gross Domestic Product at factor costs						
....	28,156	34,350	44,655	60,280	84,385	122,365
GDP *per caput*	274	294	337	397	487	615
GDP *per caput*, 1959/60 = 100	100	107	123	145	178	224
Two main sectors						
GDP *per caput*, 1959/60 = 100	100	104	115	131	151	178
All urban: *per caput*	535	557	616	699	807	950
Rs mill.	7,000	10,090	15,345	23,990	40,520	69,755
All rural: *per caput*,	236	246	272	309	356	419
Rs. mill.	21,155	24,260	29,310	36,290	43,865	52,610
East Pakistan, rural						
per caput	230	241	268	306	354	419
1960 = 100	100	105	117	133	154	182
Rs mill.	12,320	14,390	17,555	22,000	26,975	32,600
West Pakistan, rural						
per caput	247	253	278	313	359	419
1960 = 100	100	102	113	127	145	170
Rs mill.	8,835	9,870	11,755	14,290	16,890	20,010
East Pakistan urban						
per caput	470	505	577	673	794	950
1960 = 100	100	107	123	143	169	202
Rs mill.	1,345	2,275	4,155	7,740	15,085	29,830
West Pakistan, urban						
per caput	550	574	632	713	815	951
1960 = 100	100	104	115	130	148	173
Rs mill.	5,655	7,815	11,190	16,250	25,435	39,925
East Pakistan, total,						
Rs mill.	13,665	16,665	21,710	29,740	42,060	62,430
per caput	242	260	299	357	442	572
1960 = 100	100	107	124	148	183	236
West Pakistan, total,						
Rs mill.	14,490	17,685	22,945	30,540	42,325	59,935
per caput	312	336	382	446	541	668
1960 = 100	100	108	122	143	173	214

Table 11. *Summary Table: Gross Domestic Product, Gross National Product, and use of resources (Final figures* Rs Million)

	1960	1965	1970	1975	1980	1985
GDP at factor cost ...	28,952	35,342	47,301	64,008	88,712	125,455
Indirect taxes less subsidies	1,290	2,200	3,145	4,655	6,890	10,850
GDP at market prices	30,242	37,542	50,446	68,663	95,602	136,305
Personal consumption	24,792	30,259	38,806	50,812	66,490	92,189
Governm. consumption	2,400	3,075	4,260	6,060	8,750	12,880
Gross fixed investm. ...	3,635	6,632	11,711	17,109	26,096	38,422
Stock increase	235	425	605	890	1,335	1,905
Exports*	2,117	2,663	3,688	5,396	8,054	12,173
Total final demand ...	33,179	43,054	59,070	80,267	111,725	157,569
Less imports*	2,937	5,512	8,624	11,604	16,123	21,264
Demand on GDP ..	30,242	37,542	50,446	68,663	95,602	136,305
Gross domestic savings	3,050	4,208	7,380	11,791	19,362	31,236
Net factor income payments abroad ...	30	185	605	1,285	2,335	3,845
Gross National Product at factor cost	28,922	35,157	46,696	62,723	86,377	121,610
Intermediate purchases	16,489	22,667	32,405	45,774	65,956	96,864
Total final and intermediate demand	49,668	65,721	91,475	126,041	177,681	254,433

Percentage distribution

(I) In per cent of GDP at market prices

Personal consumption	82.0	80.6	77.0	74.0	70.6	67.6
Governm. consumption	7.9	8.2	8.4	8.8	9.2	9.5
Gross fixed investment	12.0	17.7	23.2	24.9	27.3	28.2
Stock increase	0.8	1.1	1.2	1.3	1.4	1.4
Exports*	7.0	7.1	7.3	7.9	8.4	8.9
Imports*	−9.7	−14.7	−17.1	−16.9	−16.9	−15.6
Gross domestic savings	10.1	11.2	14.6	17.2	20.3	22.9

(II) In per cent of GDP at factor cost

GNP at factor cost ...	99.9	99.5	98.7	98.0	97.4	96.9

(III) In per cent of total demand

Intermediate purchases	33.2	34.5	35.4	36.3	37.1	38.1

* Exports and imports of goods and services do not include factor income payments from and to abroad.

And would the peasants remain immune to political propaganda and subversive activities if year after year they saw no way out of their misery? Against this background the implied assumptions regarding distribution of savings between urban and rural areas appear to be far less unrealistic. One question remains then; are the global savings assumptions too optimistic? This will be analysed further in the section on the financing of the development effort which shows that considerable sacrifice is required from the richer elements of the population.[18] It is up to the reader to use his own judgement as to whether the sacrifices which are called for can be considered as realistic or not. This judgement must take into account the frame of mind of the educated classes of a country like Pakistan, their hopes and aspirations, their idealism and devotion to the task of building the future of their nation.

5. The Changing Composition of Personal Consumption

A. *Use of elasticities as a tool in projecting consumption*

We may take data which show changes in personal consumption with time for a country as a whole and calculate the implied income (or expenditure) elasticities[1] for the various specified items of consumer expenditure. Such elasticities have only a limited interest for planning purposes. First, changes in relative prices have a double influence on the observed elasticities for individual items. In many important cases relative price increases mean a tendency for expenditure to rise more than would have been the case had prices stayed constant (i.e., on the assumption that the price elasticity numerically is smaller than 1). If we tried to eliminate the effect simply by calculating the ratio between changes in the volume of the various items and changes in real income (i.e., the money income deflated by a price index), income elasticities of items which had become relatively more expensive would be depressed and vice versa. It is therefore necessary to exploit the statistical data further and calculate income and expenditure elasticities under the assumption of constant relative prices. This is technically possible, although one should never pretend to have found 'true and pure' income elasticities, but merely reasonably good approximations. Second, average figures for the consumption pattern of a population hide large variations in consumption pattern per head in different income groups, age groups, occupational groups, rural and urban population, etc. Recorded changes in the consumption pattern over time may in actual fact tell nothing about how the different groups have reacted to changes in prices or income, but merely what has been the combined effect of changes in prices and incomes and in the distribution of the population between groups with different consumption patterns.

In order to make meaningful projections of future changes in the pattern of personal consumption, it is therefore necessary to study the consumption pattern of distinct groups of consumers and estimate reasonably pure income and price elasticities for the various items of consumer expenditure that apply to the different groups of consumers. Forecasts can then be made, under given assumptions, as regards growth of income and changes in relative prices, for the various groups of consumers; and on this basis it is feasible to project changes in the pattern of total consumption.

Even this approach is by no means perfect. It is based on the theory that historically observed 'elasticities' are valid for the future.[2] This may be a realistic position to take for some basic items over a relatively short period of time. Even for major items the element of uncertainty is large, because small changes in elasticities for items which account for a large part of consumer expenditure will have a significant influence on the overall pattern of consumption. For less basic items, for luxuries and for items which can be substituted by other items, historic elasticities are hardly applicable at all. In a high income society, sales promotion and the introduction of new types of consumer goods and services contribute to marked changes in the consumption pattern. In a poor country the growth of the modern sector of the economy will lead to fundamental changes in the consumption pattern. The 'demonstration effect' will prove to be strong, and higher income *per caput* will permit the consumers to satisfy newly created needs.

In spite of the serious criticism which can be directed against using historical elasticities as a basis for projections of the consumption pattern over a quarter of a century, this is nevertheless in principle the only possible method. Accordingly, expenditure elasticities have been used extensively in this study.

The expenditure elasticity for a given item has been calculated as the ratio between the percentage increase in the use *per caput* of the item during a given five-year plan period divided by the percentage increase in total consumption expenditure per head during the same plan period.[3] The personal consumers have been broken down into three groups: consumers in rural areas in East and West Pakistan respectively and urban consumers. Separate elasticities have been used for each of these groups. For a number of items introduction of new products has been taken into account, and consumption per head has, in such cases, been estimated on the bases of the assumed availability of the new products and the receptiveness of the consumers to such products. The corresponding elasticities were then calculated on the basis of the estimated figures for consumption and are therefore *implied* elasticities. The elasticities for individual items are interdependent, since, when they are applied to the consumption pattern in a chosen base year, they must be selected in such a manner that increases in the consumption of the individual items add up to the given increase in total consumption. Consequently, elasticities selected on the basis of historical data had frequently to be modified in order to be consistent with a given pattern of consumption. Elasticities have thus been used as guides in order to project changes in the pattern of consumption, but the figures given in Table 13 are not the elasticities which at the outset seemed the most reasonable on the basis of historical data but those which in the end were found to be both reasonably acceptable and mutually consistent.[4] Therefore the term 'implied' elasticities is used to describe the expenditure elasticities as employed here.

We have already noted that projections of consumer expenditure ideally should be based on relatively small and homogeneous groups of consumers (e. g., farmers, broken down into income groups, etc.). Changes in the age distribution or in the average size of households should also be taken into account. In this study no attempt has been made to break down households into income classes. Data on the income distribution in Pakistan in 1959/60 are available, but they do not appear to be very reliable. What is more important is that projected figures for income distribution in the future would be very tentative.[5] The expenditure pattern is therefore based only on a breakdown of the consumers in rural areas in East and West Pakistan and in urban areas. This breakdown results in three distinctly different consumption patterns. As consumption per head is much lower in rural areas, changes in income distribution which follow from the modernization and urbanization of the economy have partly been taken into account.

The projections have been made on the basis of constant prices. This is a weakness because there are bound to be changes in the relative prices of different types of consumer goods and services. Account has been taken of this in a very cursory manner by somewhat inflating the elasticities for items which will probably become relatively cheaper (such as many consumer durables) and similarly deflating them for items which will become dearer (as, for example, domestic help).

B. *Personal consumption by three groups of consumers*

Personal consumption in rural areas in East Pakistan, rural areas in West Pakistan, and urban areas is calculated on the basis of a breakdown of the Gross Domestic Product and gross savings (discussed in the preceding chapter) and a nominal breakdown of government consumption between the three areas.[6]

Although it is possible to make fairly good estimates of the breakdown of the GDP between the three areas, the breakdown of figures for savings and for government consumption by area is bound to be approximate. The end-result is, however, much more satisfactory than the details because we do obtain a fairly good approximation of the distribution of total personal consumption between the three different groups of consumers. This follows since personal consumption is far larger than either of the other two items or even both together, and therefore fairly large errors in the estimates of savings and government consumption result in relatively smaller errors in personal consumption. Since these errors do not affect total consumption, they will also to some extent offset each other when the breakdown of total consumption is calculated.

Table 12 shows the figures which were used for personal consumption *per caput* in the three areas.

The differences between the original assumptions and the final outcome are fairly small. Since the final figures for the GDP are

Table 12. *Personal consumption* per caput, *for Pakistan and for three major groups of consumers*

	1960	1965	1970	1975	1980	1985
Original assumption Rs per head						
Pakistan..........................	232	242	262	293	335	396
East Pakistan, rural	201	206	219	243	273	310
West Pakistan, rural	211	212	222	241	265	290
All rural areas..................	205	208	220	242	270	303
All urban areas	416	428	443	464	494	548
1960 = 100						
Pakistan..........................	100	104	113	126	144	170
East Pakistan, rural	100	102	109	121	136	154
West Pakistan, rural	100	101	105	114	126	137
All rural areas..................	100	101	107	118	131	147
All urban areas	100	103	106	112	119	132
*Final outcome** (one possible alternative)						
Rs per head						
Pakistan..........................	229	240	269	304	349	409
Rural areas	202	207	226	252	282	313
Urban areas	410	424	454	483	516	573
1960 = 100						
Pakistan..........................	100	105	118	133	153	179
Rural areas	100	102	112	125	139	155
Urban areas	100	104	111	118	126	140

Sources: Original assumptions: [0], Annex II, Table 2.
* See footnote to Table 9.

higher than the assumed figures and the marginal rate of savings lower, the final figures for personal consumption had to be higher. But the difference is not large enough to result in very marked changes in the projected pattern of consumption.

The figures in Table 12 are of considerable interest. Projected personal consumption per head in the three areas grows much more slowly than for the country as a whole. It is striking to observe that the apparent rise in national consumption per head between 1960 and 1985 should be about twice as strong as the rise in consumption per head in the urban areas, which in the original assumptions was only projected to increase by 1.1 per cent per year. This slow increase is partly explained by the assumed high rate of savings in the urban areas. Implication to be drawn from these figures are alarming and are discussed in the section on the financial implications of the model used here. So much can be said at this stage that, as the urban population in 1985 should be much better trained and be employed to a much larger extent in the modern sector of the economy than is the case today, the very slow increase in *per caput* consumption in the urban areas could easily mean that each social category, each group which belongs to the same category of skills, would have a lower consumption per head in 1985 than they have today. One factor weakens this tentative conclusion. Consumption financed from agricultural rent transferred to urban areas represented a large proportion of total urban consumption in 1960 and will become insignificant in 1985.[7] This lessens the growth in urban consumption.

The point has been raised here because it underlines the extreme optimism behind the assumption of a parallel growth of the income level in urban and rural areas. Which is most likely, that the urban population will sacrifice its standard of living in order to share the benefits of progress with the rural population, or that the urban population will continue to harvest the benefits of the modernization process while the standard of living of the peasant will remain stagnant or at the best increase very slowly? The answer to this question is also of crucial importance for the development strategy to be chosen in order to bridge the income gap between East and West Pakistan. If the income per head in rural areas necessarily lags behind, only an ultra-rapid modernization and urbanization in East Pakistan can assure the implementation of the target of equal income per head in the two provinces in 1985. In the present study however, the assumption of parallel growth in rural and urban incomes is maintained throughout.

C. *The changes in the pattern of consumption*

There are no organized data on the pattern of consumption in Pakistan. Some scattered information is, however, available. Sample surveys have been carried out in rural areas both in East and in West Pakistan.[8] They contain, *inter alia,* a breakdown of consumer expenditure in villages in East and West Pakistan. Family expenditure surveys have been carried out in several cities in East and West Pakistan.[9] They contain a breakdown of family expenditure for several social classes. On the basis of data for production, imports, and exports, it is possible to make estimates of consumption of the most important food items, cotton, and certain other clothing, and several other manufactured products.[10]

In this study the breakdown of consumer expenditure has been made on the basis of the sample surveys of family expenditure, but adjustments have been made in cases in which the global data for production, imports, and exports differ significantly from the results arrived at from the sample surveys. For all major items of personal consumption the data presented are thought to be consistent.

The approach has been to estimate *per caput* consumption of 20 main items of food and tobacco and 23 other main items in rural areas in East and West Pakistan and in urban areas. There could be reasons for dealing with urban areas in East and West Pakistan separately, since it is assumed that the proportion of the total urban population living in East Pakistan will increase. But available data are far too weak to make such a breakdown meaningful. The most important part of the problem, the importance of rice in East Pakistan, has been taken care of by assuming that consumption of rice increases as much as consumption of wheat in urban areas, in spite of an underlying assumption that there will be a shift in consumption from rice to wheat.

To determine the likely changes in the pattern of consumption, two approaches are possible; either to assume that the consumers will have a fairly free choice and that the changes depend on income elasticities of demand, or to assume that the government will try to channel the growth of consumption in certain directions. In conformity with the basic assumption of this analysis, that development will take place under a maximum degree of freedom and with substantial participation of private enterprise, it has been assumed that structural changes will be determined mainly by consumers' preferences, which are shown in the form of expenditure elasticities.

To my knowledge no attempt had been made (in 1961) to estimate income or expenditure elasticities in Pakistan.[11] Such studies exist for certain underdeveloped countries, including India. An interesting and promising approach consist of comparing the expenditure structure in countries with different levels of income per head.

Professor Houthakker[12] in a survey article has analysed available information and arrived at some broad conclusions as regards expenditure elasticities to be used for planning purposes in underdeveloped countries. The elasticities which he arrived at after a statistical analysis of available data were:

Food 0.6
Clothing 1.2
Housing 0.8
Other 1.6

His elasticities cannot be used without adjustment in the case of Pakistan. By definition the total expenditure elasticity must be 1.0. If we apply the Houthakker elasticities to the consumption pattern in Pakistan in 1959/60, we get the following results:

Total expenditure elasticity

	Alternative A: housing includes only rent & repair	Alternative B: housing also includes fuel, etc.
East Pakistan rural	0.81	0.75
West Pakistan rural	0.89	0.83
Urban areas	0.97	0.92

The adjustments which have been made to the Houthakker elasticities are shown in Table 13. It was not possible to follow any firm principle for these adjustments, and particularly not for the rural areas in East Pakistan. For West Pakistan rural areas and for the urban areas, I chose to use the Houthakker elasticities for clothing and housing throughout the entire period (housing was defined as including rent, repair, and *local* fuel, the demand for which probably has a low elasticity). For all areas I tried to arrange the figures in such a manner that the Houthakker elasticities for food, clothing, and housing could be used for the period 1979/80 to 1984/85, but for rural areas in East Pakistan I felt compelled to use a higher elasticity for clothing even during that period in order to arrive at smoother changes in elasticities from one five-year period to another. For all three areas I have assumed that, because of existing malnutrition and strong efforts to improve the food standard, the expenditure elasticity for food will be high during the Second Five Year Plan, ranging from 0.9 in rural areas in East Pakistan to 0.8 in urban areas, and that it will decline gradually through subsequent plan periods to reach 0.6 during the Sixth Plan period. The expenditure elasticity for 'other' items is derived as a residuum. It will exceed the Houthakker elasticity, 1.6, for all periods, in all areas, except in rural areas in West Pakistan and in urban areas during the Second Five-Year Plan. It can be questioned whether this result is realistic. In favour of a higher elasticity is a strong world-wide tendency towards higher consumption of modern gadgets and of services. Moreover, it would not be possible to reduce the elasticity for 'other' items without simultaneously increasing other elasticities. We will show later that the elasticities for food can hardly be increased further without leading to very doubtful results as regards *per caput* consumption in terms of calories. Higher elasticity of demand for housing is feasible but not very likely due to the

Table 13. *Changes in the structure of private consumption*
per caput *during five plan periods*
Implied expenditure elasticities

	During				
	Second Plan 1960–65	Third Plan 1965–70	Fourth Plan 1970–75	Fifth Plan 1975–80	Sixth Plan 1980–85
East Pakistan rural					
Food & tobacco	0.9	0.85	0.75	0.70	0.70
Clothing	1.3	1.5	1.5	1.5	1.4
Housing & local fuel	0.8	0.8	0.9	0.9	0.8
Other items..............	1.68	1.87	2.31	2.37	2.24
West Pakistan rural					
Food & tobacco	1.0	0.9	0.8	0.7	0.6
Clothing	1.0	1.1	1.2	1.2	1.2
Housing & local fuel	0.8	0.8	0.8	0.8	0.8
Other items..............	1.1	1.6	1.65	2.06	2.26
Urban areas					
Food & tobacco	0.8	0.75	0.69	0.63	0.57
Clothing	1.2	1.2	1.2	1.2	1.2
Housing & local fuel	0.8	0.8	0.8	0.8	0.8
Other items..............	1.51	1.65	1.74	1.85	1.91
The whole country					
Food & tobacco.	0.81	0.81	0.76	0.71	0.65
Clothing	1.08	1.15	1.23	1.17	1.18
Housing & local fuel	0.81	0.87	0.85	0.88	0.84
Other items..............	1.86	1.79	1.88	1.97	2.62

heavy investment costs involved. Finally, it would be possible to assume higher elasticity for clothing; but as clothing weighs much less in the total expenditure than other items, the elasticity for clothing would have to be increased considerably if it were to have a marked effect on the elasticity for 'other' items.[13]

Table 14 shows how the figures calculated on the basis of the original target figures for GDP have been modified to conform with the final figures on personal consumption.

It is easier to see the implications of these adjustments by looking at the implied expenditure elasticities which are shown in Table 15.

As can be seen from the Table, the adjustment of the figures to the higher rates of growth implies only very small changes in the expenditure elasticities. The only exception concerns the item 'other expenditure' in the period 1960 to 1965. Since the elasticity for the item 'other' was originally obtained as a residuum (pages 93 to 94), this difference is immaterial. The changes for the item

Table 14. *Breakdown of personal consumption of main categories of goods and services. Rs Mill*

	1960	1965	1970	1975	1980	1985
Original data						
Food and tobacco	15,969	18,800	22,758	28,349	35,695	45,775
Clothing	1,892	2,252	2,800	3,655	4,893	6,802
Housing.............	1,215	1,448	1,776	2,324	3,153	4,516
Local fuel	1,036	1,149	1,262	1,385	1,484	1,641
Other goods and						
services	3,731	4,668	6,172	8,690	12,832	19,912
Total 23,843		28,317	34,768	44,403	58,057	78,646
Adjusted data, final						
Food and tobacco	16,633	20,059	25,199	31,985	40,667	52,438
Clothing	1,971	2,407	3,124	4,172	5,655	7,920
Housing.............	1,266	1,548	1,975	2,646	3,638	5,253
Local fuel	1,036	1,149	1,262	1,385	1,484	1,641
Other goods and						
services	3,886	5,096	7,246	10,624	16,046	24,937
Total 24,792		30,259	38,806	50,812	67,490	92,189

Sources: Original data, [0] Annex III, Tables 8 and 9. Bottom line – Table 16 of Annex IX. The other lines under adjusted data have been arrived at in the same manner as the adjusted breakdown of personal consumption in Annex IX – 16, i.e., by inflating the figures so that the global expenditure elasticities are adjusted proportionally. An exception is made for expenditure on local fuel which has not been adjusted because the expenditure on this item has been estimated on the basis of the projected supplies which are assumed to be strictly inflexible.

'local fuel' are relatively large, but this is due to the fact that the absolute figures have not been changed (see notes to Table 14).

Both the original and the adjusted elasticities show in some cases a somewhat irregular behaviour. This is due to the fact that the figures for the country as a whole are obtained by aggregating for the figures for three groups of consumers — rural consumers in East and in West Pakistan and urban consumers. For each of these groups the elasticities behave in a more regular manner (see Table 13), whereas the aggregation leads to more capricious results. These irregularities are in themselves significant and illustrate the inherent weakness in projecting the pattern of personal consumption for a country as a whole.

The most noticeable influence of the relative shift of the population from rural to urban areas can be traced in the item 'housing' in Table 15. The mere fact that expenditure on housing is much higher in urban than in rural areas increases the expenditure elasticity for housing. But the high elasticity for housing is also a result of a specific policy assumption. It has been assumed that efforts will be made to improve the housing situation and there are two reasons for this: (1) the housing standard is very low and improved housing is an essential part of any policy to improve the standard of living; and (2) investments in housing do not require many imports (except for machinery and equipment

Table 15. *Per caput expenditure elasticities implied in the projected figures for personal consumption – on the basis of the original and the adjusted figures*

	1960–65	1965–70	1970–75	1975–80	1980–85
Original data					
Food and tobacco	0.80	0.81	0.79	0.71	0.62
Clothing	1.05	1.17	1.13	1.12	1.12
Housing................	1.08	0.99	1.28	1.30	1.37
Local fuel	−0.53	−0.28	−0.27	−0.21	−0.20
Other items.............	2.45	2.03	2.00	2.02	1.95
Adjusted data, final					
Food and tobacco	0.83	0.82	0.76	0.70	0.65
Clothing	1.01	1.11	1.16	1.15	1.16
Housing................	1.03	0.95	1.18	1.25	1.36
Local fuel	−0.32	−0.17	−0.21	−0.18	−0.19
Other	2.04	1.95	1.95	1.98	1.86

Sources: Calculated on the basis of the figures in Table 14, and the figures for population in Table 6. The expenditure elasticity for a given item over the period of time chosen is defined as the ratio between the percentage change in the expenditure on the given item and the percentage increase in total consumption – all figures expressed *per caput*.

in the building material industries) and do create many jobs. A relatively large housing programme is therefore highly desirable from a social point of view. The high elasticities represent nevertheless a real problem. Empirical studies show that the income elasticity for housing is very frequently below one. In Table 13 this problem was 'solved' by grouping housing, repairs on dwellings, and local fuel together. It may still be doubtful whether the population of their own free will would tend to spend an increasing proportion of their income on rent, even though this would be offset by a sharply declining proportion of expenditure on wood and other local fuel. On the contrary, it is likely that housing would have to be heavily subsidized in order to make the population move away from shacks into better housing. In part it can be done by force, by slum clearance. But experience shows that former slum-dwellers who are moved into better housing will leave their new dwellings if they find the costs too high, and will instead find ways of building new shacks elsewhere. It is likely that the assumptions which refer to expenditure on housing at constant prices imply heavy subsidies, and the financial burden of such subsidies may become very difficult to carry, both for the government and for private industries.[14]

Table 16 shows the changes in the expenditure pattern in terms of percentages. The changes are by no means dramatic, and even in 1985 close to 60 per cent of personal consumption expenditure should still be for food, beverages, and tobacco. This has to be expected in a country in which the income per head remains very low.

Table 16. *Changes in the structure of personal consumption*

	1960	1965	1970	1975	1980	1985
Percentage distribution of expenditure						
Original data						
Food, beverages, tobacco	67.0	66.4	65.5	63.9	61.5	58.2
Clothing, footwear	7.9	7.9	8.1	8.2	8.4	8.7
Housing	5.1	5.1	5.1	5.2	5.4	5.7
Local fuel	4.3	4.1	3.6	3.1	2.6	2.1
Other items	15.7	16.5	17.7	19.6	22.1	25.3
Adjusted data						
Food, beverages, tobacco	67.1	66.3	64.9	63.0	60.2	56.9
Clothing, footwear	7.9	8.0	8.0	8.2	8.4	8.6
Housing	5.1	5.1	5.1	5.2	5.4	5.7
Local fuel	4.3	3.8	3.3	2.7	2.2	1.8
Other items	15.7	16.8	18.7	20.9	23.8	27.0

Source: Table 15.

D. *The growth and structure of personal consumption under an alternative assumption*

In the preceding sections it has several times been pointed out that this study is based on the assumption of a very slow growth of personal consumption per head in the urban areas. The reasons for this assumption have been given. But the assumption will only hold if the urban population shows considerable self-discipline and does not exploit its economic powers in order to obtain more immediate advantages from the rapid modernization of the urban production pattern.

It is of considerable interest to see how the structure of consumption would develop if living standards in the rural areas remained stationary and improved living conditions were limited to the urban areas. Table 17 shows the results of projections of the consumption pattern using this assumption. The calculations are based on the detailed figures upon which this Chapter was based, and no attempt has been made to introduce the final adjustments. Table 16 shows that the effects of those final adjustments on the structure of personal consumption are rather insignificant, and mainly express themselves in a shift from food consumption to other items. The findings in Table 16 can be applied in a crude manner to the figures given in Table 17.

This alternative hypothesis, that only the urban population will enjoy an improvement in their standard of living, results in a significantly different distribution of consumer expenditure between the main categories of expenditure. A comparison of Tables 16 and 18 shows that the change consists almost exclusively of a shift from food consumption to other items. This results from the fact that the implied elasticities for clothing shown in Table 13 were, on the whole, the same for rural and urban areas, that high elasticities for housing were assumed for the rural areas towards the end of the period under review; and that the figure for local fuel has not been changed at all. If all figures are recalculated on the basis of market prices (along the lines of the adjusted data in Table 15), it is certain that one would find an even more pronounced shift from food consumption to other items.

Which 'other items' should such a shift predominantly affect? There should certainly be a strong shift towards items for which there is assumed to be a high expenditure elasticity in urban areas (such as modern accessories, own means of transport, other expenditure on transport, expenditure on health and education, etc.) which should only partly be offset by lower expenditure in the rural areas. The alternative pattern of consumer expenditure would therefore imply that the figures for cars, television sets,

Table 17. *The pattern of personal consumption assuming that
personal consumption per head in rural areas remains constant*

	1960	1965	1970	1975	1980	1985
Absolute figures, Rs Mill.						
Original figures						
Rural areas						
Food, beverages,						
tobacco 12,746	14,247	16,326	19,197	21,754	23,969
Clothing, footwear 1,442	1,608	1,876	2,310	2,773	3,249
Housing............. 914	1,021	1,169	1,439	1,742	2,079
Local fuel 845	941	1,073	1,222	1,326	1,358
Other items.......... 2,447	2,756	3,293	4,318	5,663	7,298
Total 18,394	20,573	23,737	28,486	33,258	37,953
Urban areas						
Food, beverages,						
tobacco 3,223	4,553	6,432	9,152	13,941	21,806
Clothing, footwear 450	644	924	1,345	2,120	3,553
Housing............. 301	427	607	885	1,411	2,437
Local fuel 191	208	189	163	158	283
Other items.......... 1,284	1,912	2,879	4,372	7,169	12,614
Total 5,449	7,744	11,031	15,917	24,799	40,693
Alternative hypothesis:						
Rural consumption per						
head constant						
Rural areas						
Food, beverages,						
tobacco 12,746	14,025	15,318	16,710	17,506	17,833
Clothing, footwear 1,442	1,587	1,733	1,891	1,981	2,017
Housing............. 914	1,006	1,098	1,198	1,255	1,279
Local fuel 845	930	1,016	1,108	1,161	1,182
Other items.......... 2,447	2,692	2,941	3,208	3,361	3,424
Total 18,394	20,240	22,106	24,115	25,264	25,735
Urban areas						
Food, beverages,						
tobacco 3,223	4,711	6,935	10,177	15,512	23,635
Clothing, footwear 450	677	1,088	1,794	2,956	4,859
Housing............. 301	445	700	1,146	1,907	3,186
Local fuel 191	219	246	277	323	459
Other items.......... 1,284	2,025	3,693	6,894	12,095	20,772
Total 5,449	8,077	12,662	20,288	32,793	52,911
All Pakistan						
Food, beverages,						
tobacco 15,969	18,736	22,253	26,887	33,018	41,468
Clothing, footwear 1,892	2,264	2,821	3,685	4,937	6,876
Housing............. 1,215	1,451	1,798	2,344	3,162	4,465
Local fuel 1,036	1,149	1,262	1,385	1,484	1,641
Other items.......... 3,731	4,717	6,634	10,102	15,456	24,196
Total 23,843	28,317	34,768	44,403	58,057	78,646

bicycles, radios, refrigerators, etc., per thousand inhabitants could be raised in relation to the figures which are based on the distribution of consumer expenditure between rural and urban areas as given in the detailed calculations upon which this chapter was based.[15]

Let us imagine that there exists another country in the world in which the situation in 1960 was identical with that in Pakistan. Let us furthermore assume that Pakistan develops along the lines of the pattern assumed in this study and that the 'twin country' raises its national income and personal consumption at the same rate as Pakistan, but that the increased personal consumption per head is concentrated in the urban areas as in the alternative hypothesis shown in Tables 17 and 18. Which conclusions would a student of economic development draw from the two cases? If no reliable statistics were available on the distribution of income, not even between the urban and rural areas, it is quite likely that even the most serious and enlightened student would draw the conclusion that the 'twin country' had been most successful in its development effort. The justification for such a conclusion would be that (1) the population of the 'twin country' uses considerably less of its income on food and (2) that it has far more modern amenities than Pakistan. Both indicators would suggest the conclusion that the 'twin country' was better off than Pakistan. In actual fact Pakistan would provide better living

---

Notes to Table 17

Sources and methods: The original data are taken from [0], Annex III, Tables 8 and 9 (the adjustment for deficit supplies of local fuel). The adjustment to the demand for local fuel has been applied to the urban areas only (which explains the somewhat irregular behaviour of the figure for local fuel in urban areas). The figures for all of Pakistan are given in Table 14.

The alternative hypothesis: For the rural areas the new figures have been obtained by multiplying the population figures for each year (source, Table 6) with the consumption figures per head in 1960. The *total* figures for the urban areas are obtained as the difference between all of Pakistan and rural consumption. The individual items for urban areas are obtained as follows: Food, etc.: It has been assumed that food consumption per head will increase 50 per cent more under this alternative hypothesis than under the original one. This implies that the expenditure elasticities are lower than under the original alternative, but this reduction of the elasticities is entirely logical. Higher elasticities over a period of 25 years would either mean an incredible increase in caloric intake per head (see discussion of this in section D), or such a rapid shift to a better diet that it is hard to envisage how it could take place without very large imports of many foods. Clothing, housing, and local fuel: The same elasticities have been used as in the original calculations. Local fuel is assumed to be in deficit, and the difference between the hypothetical demand for local fuel and supplies (calculated as the total supplies less rural demand) has been added to 'other items'.

Other items: calculated as a remainder.

conditions for its peasants, while 'the twin' let the cities and towns harvest all the benefits of the economic growth.

The reader may object that it is not true that a serious economist would make such a superficial and fallacious comparison between Pakistan and its twin. Unfortunately, there is every reason to believe that such a comparison would be made. There is one way to avoid falling into such a trap — even if no data on the income distribution were available — and that is to compare food consumption per head in the two countries. But international comparisons of consumption levels are very difficult to undertake. Differences in prices represent the main difficulty. Data on calorie consumption per head are often misleading indicators. The economist is therefore frequently compelled to rely on other types

Table 18. *Major differences between the two consumption patterns shown in Table* 17

	1960	1965	1970	1975	1980	1985
Adjustments to the figures for total consumption as given in Chapter III. Rs Mill.						
Food, beverages, tobacco	0	−64	−505	−1,462	−2,677	−4,307
Clothing, footwear	0	+12	+ 21	+30	+44	+74
Housing.............	0	+ 3	+ 22	+20	+ 9	−51
Other items.........	0	+49	+462	+1,412	+2,624	+4,284
Percentage distribution of expenditure under the alternative assumption						
Food, beverages, tobacco	67.0	66.2	64.0	60.6	56.9	52.7
Clothing, footwear	7.9	8.0	8.1	8.3	8.5	8.7
Housing.............	5.1	5.1	5.2	5.3	5.4	5.7
Local fuel	4.3	4.1	3.6	3.1	2.6	2.1
Other items.........	15.7	16.6	19.1	22.7	26.6	30.8
Growth of personal consumption per head, 1960 = 100						
All Pakistan	100	104	113	126	144	170
Urban areas, original assumption	100	103	106	112	119	132
Urban areas, alternative hypothesis	100	107	122	142	157	173

Sources: Adjustments to the figures for personal consumption: figures for Pakistan in Table 17 less figures for Pakistan in Table 14. Percentage distribution: based on Table 17. Growth of personal consumption: two first lines, Table 12; last line, Table 17 and the data for urban population in Table 6.

of information and the percentage of income used on food or the number of cars per thousand inhabitants are constantly used as indicators of the level of development. The two different sets of assumptions presented here serve as a useful reminder of the dangers inherent in measuring the changes in welfare by using some apparently suitable index, such as national income per head, personal consumption per head, or the changes in the structure of personal consumption.

The alternative hypothesis of constant personal consumption per head in the rural areas offers another interesting aspect. Personal consumption per head in the rural areas may well remain constant even when the product per head increases, if additional income *per caput* is drained away through taxes, unfavourable changes in the 'terms of trade' of the rural areas, increased payments of rent, etc., and higher voluntary savings. But a study of the shift in the consumption pattern suggests that constant personal consumption per head in the rural areas also implies that the rural product cannot increase as rapidly as estimated in this study. The main reason for this is that rural food consumption would increase much more slowly. Table 17 shows that under the second alternative, rural food consumption in 1985 would be more than 6,000 million rupees lower than originally estimated (or over 25 per cent). Most of this hypothetical fall would mean less output for use by the farmers themselves. The fact that urban consumption of food is simultaneously revised upwards by Rs 1,800 million does, in any case, offset only part of the fall in rural demand. Moreover, of this increased amount a sizeable part will consist of trade, transport, and processing costs. On the other hand, lower total demand for food should mean that food imports, which are estimated at more than Rs 3,500 million in 1985 (see the input-output Tables), could be eliminated. But even if total projected food imports could be eliminated, the net effect of a fall in food consumption in relation to the figures used in this chapter would probably be some reduction of farm output and consequently of the rural product and income. This fall would be accompanied by a fall in other rural incomes because of lower rural consumer demand, such as lower demand for products from rural food processing industries, for other cottage industries, and for house-building activities.

The fall in rural income should be offset by an increase in urban income, due to higher consumer demand for urban services and consumer goods from the manufacturing industries. But the net effect is difficult to predict. Much of the additional demand would be for products of the metal working industries, and in this study it has been assumed that these industries will expand as fast as is technically possible and economically justifiable. Maybe the output of consumer goods from the metal working industries will expand faster than projected in this study, but on the assumptions used here it will merely mean slower growth of the capital goods industries. Some of the additional urban demand will therefore in one way or other have to lead to higher imports. At the same time demand from the rural sector areas on the urban industries may fall; lower farm output would, for example, mean lower demand for fertilizers. These fragmentary remarks show that if the consumption pattern is drastically altered by introducing the sombre but perhaps realistic assumption that economic progress (per head) will be concentrated in the urban areas, it is not only possible, but also likely, that the growth rate of the Gross Domestic Product will be lower than projected in this study. It would be very interesting to work out an alternative model, but the author believes that it would give less relevant results than the one which has been used throughout this study.

Attention should finally be focused on the bottom part of Table 18 which shows that even if only the urban population is able to increase its personal consumption per head and thereby presumably its standard of living, the growth of the urban standard of living will not be spectacular. As the number of people in the cities grow, their consumption level will grow more slowly than the consumption level of the people as a whole. The figures for the period 1980 to 1985 illustrate this very clearly. Personal consumption per head in the urban areas should rise by 10 per cent; in the rural areas it should remain constant; whereas for the country as a whole the average level of personal consumption per head should rise by 18 per cent. Almost half the increase in the standard of living, as measured by personal consumption per head, should be caused by a move of people from the low consumption rural areas to the much higher consumption urban areas. This is undoubtedly a way in which the standard of living of some people can be increased appreciably, but it does not give any satisfaction to the people who are condemned to remain in the villages, and little satisfaction to those who already live in the urban areas and who enjoy only a modest increase in their consumption level.

E. *Development in food consumption*

We will return to the detailed figures which were used throughout this study as basis for projections of the demand for goods and services from the various sectors of the economy.[16] Amongst these figures, those which describe the growth of food consumption are by far the most important. Domestic demand for food determines *grosso modo,* under our assumptions,[17] the room for expansion in agriculture. The risk of surplus production of food in Pakistan is at present negligible, but unless domestic demand for food increases reasonably, overproduction could occur as a result of a successful programme of improvements in agriculture.

Demand for food must be analysed in detail. In a highly industrialized country expenditure on food is many times higher than the corresponding gross farm income — transport, processing, packing, and distribution of food representing a large proportion of the retail prices. The rapid rate of urbanization in Pakistan also implies that a decreasing proportion of food expenditure will represent income to the farmers. But a sizeable part of the projected increase in food consumption consists of better nutrition standards for the farmers themselves.

Increased consumption of food can take three forms: more calories, more diversified diet, and more processed food. Although the calorie intake *per caput* is very low in Pakistan today, it is fairly obvious that calorie intake per head will increase more slowly than food expenditure per head, even in rural areas where the use of processed food is limited. This follows from the fact that food consumption in Pakistan is not only low in terms of calories, but even more unsatisfactory in terms of consumption of protein or animal fats.

In order to make the projections over food consumptions as realistic as possible, data on calorie consumption per head have been used as control and 'calorie elasticities' have been calculated. This concept was used by L. Jureen in an article on long-term trends in food consumption.[18] He found that the 'calorie elasticity' (i. e., the percentage increase in calorie intake divided by the percentage increase in total consumer expenditure, both figures expressed per head) was between two-thirds and three-quarters of expenditure elasticity for food in money terms. Our figures are shown in Table 19, and they are in general in line with Jureen's findings. A second control was also used — the growth in absolute terms of calorie intake per head per day. The base year figures are conspicuously low — ranging from 1,531 calories per head per day in rural East Pakistan to 2,260 urban areas, or an average figure of 1,656 calories per head per day. These figures are probably too low and reflect an underestimation of the rural subsistence food consumption in the base year. If this is so, output and income in agriculture is also undervalued in the base year. This does not have any significant influence on the present projections of agricultural output which are built on assumptions regarding the scope for relative improvements in yields per acre.

But this possible underestimation in the base year must be kept in mind when judging the postulated figures for calorie intake in 1985.[19]

Data on calorie intake and national income per head on a world-wide basis show that there is no systematic link between income and food consumption per head; but if the data are broken down by regions, there is clearly such a relationship between income and food intake. Pakistan belongs to a climatic region in which calorie intake per head is low even in the more prosperous countries. In the late 1950's calorie intake per head per day in countries in South and East Asia ranged between 1,800 for countries with an income *per caput* of 60 to 70 dollars to 2,200 in Japan with an income *per caput* of 400 dollars. The figures used in this study imply a calorie intake per head of 2,160 in 1985 (or 30 per cent higher than in 1960), a figure which can be raised to 2,330 on modest assumptions as regards the underestimation of food consumption in the base year.[20] On the basis of such a figure, it is fairly safe to state that one cannot expect the calorie intake in Pakistan to rise faster than projected here during the next 20 to 25 years. But there is much room for improvement in the diet. Such improvement can only materialize if domestic agriculture can supply far larger quantities of livestock products, and this is difficult to achieve in the course of a couple of decades. The fig-

Table 19. *Food Consumption – implied expenditure and calorie* elasticities

	Plan periods, or end of plan periods				
	1960–65	1965–70	1970–75	1975–80	1980–85
East Pakistan, rural					
Expenditure elasticity	0.9	0.85	0.75	0.7	0.7
Calorie elasticity	0.65	0.69	0.63	0.47	0.44
Calorie intake per head per day	1,556	1,624	1,736	1,837	1,947
West Pakistan, rural					
Expenditure elasticity	1.0	0.9	0.8	0.7	0.6
Calorie elasticity	0.48	0.64	0.58	0.47	0.41
Calorie intake per head per day	1,625	1,674	1,758	1,840	1,911
Urban areas					
Expenditure elasticity	0.8	0.75	0.69	0.63	0.57
Calorie elasticity	0.53	0.52	0.47	0.39	0.33
Calorie intake per head per day	2,295	2,337	2,389	2,449	2,548

Source: [0], Annex III, Table 4B.

ures on output in agriculture show that large quantities of dairy products must be imported in order to meet the projected demand for such products. Perhaps I have been too pessimistic about the possibilities of raising livestock output quickly, but my conclusion has been that it would be unrealistic to assume a very rapid increase in the consumption of milk, dairy products, and meat during the period under review. This conclusion is furthermore supported by the fact that my studies into the input structure of livestock production suggest that the present prices on livestock products are too low to permit profitable animal husbandry on the basis of added inputs of feedgrain, etc. If prices on livestock products are raised in relation to other prices, the rising demand for such products will be dampened unless, of course, the government keeps down consumer prices through subsidies.

Even so, our figures show that consumption of milk and milk products per head will rise by 69 per cent between 1960 and 1985, and the corresponding figures for meat and for fats and oils are 89 and 119 per cent.

6. Current Use of Goods and Services by General Government

What is called 'government consumption' for short includes purchases by the *general* government for current use. The general government includes the central government as well as regional and local governments. But it does not include government enterprises. The border-line between the general government and government enterprises is sometimes difficult to draw, but the distinction is in principle that a government enterprise receives payment in full for the services which it yields or the goods which it sells, whereas services yielded by units which form parts of the general government are either not paid for directly or, if fees are collected, they do not correspond to the costs of providing the service. The classical tasks of the general government are functions like administration, maintenance of law and order, or defence, but important social and economic services such as roads or general education are also functions of the general government. Difficulties in classification occur when a government branch can be treated either as an enterprise which is subsidized or as part of the general government. In practice railways which run heavy deficits are always treated as subsidized government enterprises whereas public hospitals, which may run small deficits, are treated as part of the general government. In fact, classification will often follow traditional lines even though it is difficult to justify certain classifications on the basis of any definition. In general it may be said that government units which sell economic services will be treated as enterprises, whereas the provision of social services will be treated as part of the general government. In this study the public health and education sector is included under general government, but the actual expenditure is net of reimbursement by the public. Advisory services and other activities to assist agriculture, industry, and other productive sectors are also included under general government. Railways, post and telecommunications, gas and electricity, and port services are included under the enterprise sector. Due to lack of data various municipal services as well as irrigation are implicitly included under the general government.

Current use of goods and services by the government includes most expenditure which is not investment. However, in some few cases certain current expenditure is also included under investment such as research, training abroad, and the cost of foreign technical assistance (foreign teachers) in education.

The use by the general government of goods and services is broken down into two main categories: the government product, and purchases of goods and services from other sectors of the economy (including purchases abroad). The government product is defined as wages, salaries (in cash or in kind), and other payments to government employees. One important adjustment has been made. The earnings of teachers and other personnel in education and of doctors, nurses, and other medical personnel are included under the sectors education and health respectively regardless of whether the personnel is government staff or not. The payment of salaries, etc., to government personnel in the health and education sectors is therefore treated as government purchases of services from those sectors.

No official data were available on the breakdown of government consumption during the financial year 1959/60 by major items of expenditure, neither according to use nor according to types of goods and services bought. The breakdown by type of expenditure which is applied in this study is based on available budget data while the distribution of expenditure under each heading is estimated by the author on the basis of information from other countries.[1] The projections of the future structure of government consumption are necessarily rather speculative, but should nevertheless give a fairly good picture of the magnitudes involved. They certainly give a realistic picture of the contribution to the Gross Domestic Product made by the general government through the remuneration of its personnel; and equally they give a realistic picture of total government purchases from other sectors of the economy. The estimated breakdown of these current government purchases is highly dubious, but this does not introduce any very serious error in projections of total domestic demand since the current government purchases only seldom represent more than a few per cent of the total demand.

The ratio of the pay of government servants to total government consumption is projected at a practically constant figure over the twenty-five years under review (it falls from 62.5 per cent to 60 per cent). The share of the government product will fall from well above half to below one-third. This is explained by the rapidly rising share of pay of educational and medical

Table 20. *Government consumption Rs Mill.*

	1960	1965	1970	1975	1980	1985
1. Total government consumption	2,400	3,075	4,260	6,060	8,750	12,880
2. Pay of government servants	1,500	1,895	2,620	3,700	5,290	7,730
3. In education .	170	285	450	720	1,170	1,900
4. In health	60	120	280	535	950	1,595
5. Government product (line 2 − lines 3 + 4)	1,270	1,490	1,890	2,445	3,170	4,235
6. Domestic purchases	700	980	1,390	2,060	3,110	4,730
7. Transport services	57	66	85	112	156	216
8. Other services	100	164	242	370	578	926
9. Paper, printing etc...........	59	85	116	173	265	411
10. Equipment, engineering goods	23	26	43	67	114	170
11. Fuel (defence only)		10	20	30	30	40
12. Furniture	8	8	9	9	10	16
13. Building materials, construction services .	370	470	619	866	1,266	1,910
14. Miscellaneous .	83	136	196	303	481	781
15. Global adjustment	0	15	60	130	210	260
16. Imports	200	200	250	300	350	420
17. Services, invisible payments	100	125	165	215	260	330
18. Goods, (included under total imports of goods, i.e., treated as domestic purchases)	100	75	85	85	90	90

Sources: Line 1: Table 11. Lines 2, 6, and 16: the original distribution is given in [0], Annex IV − 2. The adjustments (the difference between lines 11 and 7 in [0], Annex IX–2) have been distributed proportionally between the three main expenditure categories. Lines 3 to 5: the original figures which correspond to those in [0], Annex IV–2, are given in [0], Annex VI–116. The upward adjustment of the total pay of government servants is distributed proportionally among health, education, and the government product. Lines 7 to 14: see [0], Annex IV–5. Line 15 represents the total adjustment to the domestic purchases. Line 17: the estimated invisible government expenditure abroad, see Table 51. Line 18 = line 16 minus line 17.

personnel in the total government payroll — this share shows a projected rise from 15 per cent in 1960 to 45 per cent in 1985. At current prices this share will probably rise even more, since the teachers' pay in 1960 was so incredibly low that it has to be increased substantially in order to ensure recruitment to the teaching profession. This sharp rise in the share of health and education personnel in the government payroll is not only explained by the presumed rapid expansion of these sectors, but also by the basic assumption that government expenditure on defence and on general administration will only rise at the same rate as the population. This permits not only the very rapid expansion of expenditure on health and education but also on other social and economic departments.

It may be optimistic to assume that 'classical' government expenditure, on defence and law and order, will remain stable in relation to the number of people in the country. But defence expenditure is very high and the defence system strong, and the administrative apparatus is well developed.

Scope for expansion in new types of government services, such as support to the various productive sectors of the economy, and the creation of a 'welfare state' with adequate social services, appears to be ample.[2]

The breakdown of domestic purchases on different goods and services shown in lines 7 to 14 on Table 20 is illustrative only,

Table 21. *Government consumption.*
Breakdown of major purposes (unadjusted figures) Rs Mill.

	1960	1965	1970	1975	1980	1985
Central and provincial governments						
Defence	975	975	1,105	1,270	1,445	1,660
General administration	525	580	660	755	860	985
Health	85	170	380	710	1,260	2,155
Education	110	245	375	590	960	1,590
Other	440	725	1,020	1,550	2,380	3,730
Local government						
Education	150	185	285	445	725	1,200
Other	115	145	220	345	555	915
Grand total	2,400	3,025	4,065	5,665	8,185	12,235
Global adjustment . .	0	50	195	395	565	645
Adjusted grand total . . .	2,400	3,075	4,260	6,060	8,750	12,880

Sources: Unadjusted figures, [0], Annex IV–2; adjusted grand total, Table 20.

but for lack of other information these figures have to be used in order to assess the impact of government purchases on total domestic demand. The dominant item is building materials and construction services, and *current* government purchases undoubtedly represent a significant part of total demand in these fields,[3] but hardly above 5 per cent. It is the investment programme, private and public, which determines the activities in the construction and building materials industries.

The slow growth of government demand for transport services is explained by the assumed slow growth of the military services which are a large user of transport facilities. The rapid growth of demand for other services reflects the changing structure of government consumption as well as the presumably rapidly growing demand for telecommunication services.

Government imports of *invisibles* include *inter alia* the costs of the Foreign Service, contributions to international organisations, travel by government servants abroad, and other items which are bound to grow even if efforts are made to limit the increase. Line 18 of Table 20 represents goods which have to be imported because they cannot be produced in the country (such as certain types of military equipment, foreign books, or spare parts for imported equipment, etc.). The line is merely included in order to assess the minimum foreign exchange requirements linked with the operation of the general government.

The volume of government consumption and its breakdown depends on policy decisions which cannot be predicted in advance. In this study the projections of government consumption serve the purpose of determining the pattern of part of the demand for goods and services for current purposes. If government consumption were larger or smaller than assumed, personal consumption would have to be correspondingly smaller or larger. If deviations from the assumed distribution between personal and government consumption were small, the influence on the pattern of demand would be marginal. But large deviations would have quite significant influences on the pattern of total demand.

This study assumes a fairly modest growth of the ratio of government consumption to the Gross Domestic Product in constant prices, with expenditure on defence and general administration only rising in line with the growth of population. These assumptions follow, nevertheless, from the basic postulate that maximum efforts will be channelled into development of the economy. Against this background the projected growth and pattern of government consumption is plausible.

7. Investments in Consumption Capital, and Other Investments Classified as 'Autonomous'

A. *The classification of investments into two major groups*

It has been assumed[1] that the level of production in each individual sector will be determined mainly by various types of demand: consumption demand as estimated in Chapters 5 and 6, export demand which will be discussed in connection with each sector in Chapter 8, and investment demand. The level of total investments required will be determined on the basis of the projected development of the volume and pattern of production.[2]

The greater the proportion of industrial activities which are influenced by domestic demand for investment goods and services, the greater will be the degree of uncertainty of the preliminary estimates of production. Most industries which produce investment goods also use intermediate products from other industries. Fortunately during the 25-year period under review this creates only a relatively limited problem for the present method of estimation in the case of Pakistan. Even if the most optimistic expectations are fulfilled in engineering and related industries,[3] Pakistan will *not* be able to satisfy from domestic sources alone the demand for machinery and equipment for investment purposes. Consequently it has been assumed that the growth of engineering industries in Pakistan will not be limited by demand, but rather by the scarcity of skilled manpower, tradition, entrepreneurship, and other factors which will keep the annual growth of these industries down to 'realistic' levels. On the other hand, the activities of the construction industry and the production of most types of building materials can probably be expanded sufficiently to meet the domestic demand. There will certainly be serious problems with regard to supervisory and skilled manpower in the construction industry, but these problems can probably be overcome by the use of foreign engineers and skilled supervisory manpower. The role of the construction industry, and also of industries supplying building materials and transport services to the construction industry, is bound to be important in a developing country. If fairly accurate projections can be made of the output of the industries prior to a complete picture of investments, the process of iteration is simplified.

There is one shortcut which will permit fairly good projections of the output of the construction industry and the building-material industries. This is the estimation of investments which can either be derived directly from the data for private and public consumption or which can be regarded as 'autonomous'. Investments are considered to be 'autonomous' in certain of those sectors in which the capital-output ratio is a particularly unreliable tool of measurement; i.e., they are directly related neither to the projected levels of private of public consumption, nor to production. This shortcut is not altogether defendable from a theoretical point of view. It can, for example, be argued that estimates of investments in education cannot be established before it is known what kind of economy the educational system will cater for. This problem of interdependence is, however, present at all stages of the analysis, i. e., as regards the estimates of private and public consumption in Chapters 5 and 6, or the basic estimates of the distribution of population between urban and rural areas (in Chapter 4), or the projected growth of urban versus rural production in the same chapter. Clearly, the development which will actually take place in consumption, in public expenditure, and in the degree of urbanization, etc., will be strongly influenced by whether growth takes place in large industrial enterprises or in small-scale agriculture.

The choice of investments to be included in this chapter is necessarily somewhat arbitrary. The presentation which is chosen is to include in this chapter the estimates which have been made directly, and which will not be altered subsequently because of changes in the projected pattern of growth.

Investments in the following sectors are included in this chapter:

Education (public and private);
Health services (public and private);
Research (public and private);
Government administration (buildings), general administration as well as specialized services (public only);
Municipal amenities (public only);
Roads (public only);[4]
Housing, including land development (public and private);
Post, telegraph, telephone (public and private);
Broadcasting and television (public and private).[5]

No attempt is made to make separate estimates for public and private investments, nor are associated internal financial transactions considered in this study.

The problem of interdependence makes relevant the question whether it is justifiable to estimate investments in roads and postal, telegraph, and telephone services before the overall pattern of production is known; or inversely, why are investments in railways and ports not also included at this stage. Some of the reasons for the decision taken here are given in the following.

It is not possible to determine with any degree of precision the extent and quality of the road network required for an economy with a certain structure and level of activities. This depends not only on the existence of alternative means of transportation, but also on the priorities attached to road building by the public authorities. There is a substantial difference in the cost of building and maintaining an 'acceptable' network of roads as opposed to an 'excellent' one. Moreover, social and regional considerations are of particular importance. To build roads to remote and sparsely populated areas in which roadbuilding is often excessively expensive leads to much higher expenditure on roads than may be warranted by strict profit considerations. For these reasons it is not possible to assess expenditure on roads on the basis of the projected economic structure of the country. That Pakistan will have an adequate network of roads in 1985 if investments reach the levels projected in this chapter has been the fundamental assumption.

Some comments are needed to show why housing is also included under this heading. There are two reasons, one practical and one theoretical. The practical reason is that on the basis of the projected consumer expenditure on rent, it is possible to estimate investments in housing immediately, whereas other investments which depend on the estimated consumer demand can only be calculated when the output of the supplying industries has been projected. As the output of most sectors of the economy depends not only on consumer demand but also on investment and export demand as well as on the level of imported supplies, it is not practicable to estimate investments on the basis of projected consumer expenditure alone. The only exception is housing which, by definition, is purchase by the personal consumer only and cannot be imported. Since investment in housing constitutes a significant part of total investments, and since it is advantageous to use *final* investment estimates to the largest possible extent in assessing total demand for the purpose of projecting the output of the several sectors of the economy, it is also advantageous to include investments in housing with autonomous investments. There is also a theoretical justification for this approach. Whereas net investments in housing should follow from the net increase in total rent payments, the link between investments and rent in-

cludes a certain interest rate which is generally arbitrary. Consequently, the projected level of investments in housing is 'autonomous' to the extent that the choice of interest rate is an autonomous policy decision, reflecting the extent to which new housing
will be subsidized through lower than normal capital cost.

Investments in ports, railways and internal waterways are much
more directly dependent on the volume of traffic they are expected to handle. This is particularly important in the case of
railways in which a substantial part of investments will be in
rolling stock. Postal and telegraph services may be in the same
category, but for statistical reasons investment estimates have
been combined with investments in the telephone services. The
projections in this chapter make ample allowance for the increased use of telephones for business purposes. The basic assumption is nevertheless that the use of telephones will increase with
urbanization, the rise in national income *per caput*, and the general technological development.

B. *Implications for the strategy of development*

The assumptions made in this chapter determine to a great extent the character of the development strategy which is implied
in the present study for the period under review. In principle, all
assumptions regarding decision-making have been related to
known facts about social and political attitudes, or declared in-
tentions and clearly expressed preferences in Pakistan. It is nevertheless inevitable that in the end many assumptions reflect subjective views on the best strategy of development. Since the
choice of alternatives is particularly wide for 'autonomous' investments, this subjective judgement is liable to be more pronounced in this chapter than elsewhere in the study.

To a great extent the investments projekted in health and education are determined by the projected level of current expenditure, and thus reflect the assumptions made in Chapter 5 on private consumption expenditure elasticities for health and education. Public expenditure on health and education is expected to
increase at a rate similar to that of private expenditure. However,
the projections will show investments in these two fields increasing more rapidly than investments in housing or road-building. Reflecting this expectation, which admittedly is very subjective, far more emphasis will be given to the modernization of
education and health services than to roads and public housing.

In so far as education is concerned, this reflects a decision
taken by the government of Pakistan. The target set in the Second
Five-Year Plan for the development of general education during

the next ten to fifteen years was a very ambitious one. It was found necessary to scale down the Pakistan programme somewhat to make it consistent with teacher-training possibilities.[6] As regards health services, for which there is no official long-term Pakistan programme, the projections reflect the immense need for health services in an Asian country.

The very heavy emphasis on the creation of a modern system of education and medical services bears much resemblance to what has actually taken place in the Soviet Union. The Soviet experience shows that such an ambitious programme is feasible, at least when it is not undertaken simultaneously with other ambitious programmes to increase the stock of consumption capital. The assumptions made here do not imply that the Soviet pattern will be followed in all fields. Although the road and housing programmes may look modest, they will ensure a steady improvement in transport facilities and housing conditions. Nevertheless it could justifiably be argued that the development strategy assumptions are somewhat unbalanced. The reason for this is that the housing programme reflects assumptions about the expenditure elasticities for housing which conform to historical and other empirical data available from a number of countries. The road programme, on the other hand, is based on certain assumptions as regards the development of total government expenditure which may appear relatively slow. However, what is more important is that the end result (that is, the network of roads in 1985) compares favourably with countries whose geographic and/ or economic conditions resemble those projected in Pakistan. Thus, while the projections favour investments in education and health, they are not biased against housing and transport.

C. *The cost of expanding the educational system*

The economic development of a nation depends more on its level of education than on any other definable factor. Nothing demonstrates this more convincingly than the German and Japanese postwar economic 'miracles'. Within a decade these defeated and ruined countries regained their economic strength, and today are second only to the 'super-powers', USA and USSR, in industrial production. Generous economic aid from the United States facilitated their reconstruction, but the pay-off on investments was very high.[7] Relatively moderate investments permitted Germany and Japan to put their trained labour force to work and achieve an annual rate of growth of about 9 per cent per year during the first half of the 1950s. This performance was possible because the available manpower had all the needed skills — skilled workers, supervisors, engineers, and managers were all available.

Theoretical studies which aim at allocating economic growth between the contributing factor labour and capital (including land) show that a very significant proportion has to be ascribed to a 'third factor'. Needless to say any calculation of this type depends on the production function which is chosen, and the distribution of the growth between the factors of production will therefore contain an arbitrary element. Nevertheless, there is no doubt that this 'third factor' exists and that it plays an important role in economic growth.

In a highly industrialized country the third factor is frequently identified with technological progress. But even in the United States, technological progress could not contribute to economic growth unless the labour force were adequately trained.[8] In an economically underdeveloped country, copying techical methods which are in use in the industrialized countries will yield tremendous results. Investments in suitable capital equipment are needed to achieve such progress, but skilled manpower and qualified management must be available to operate the machinery. There is hardly any doubt that shortage of trained personnel represents an almost insurmountable barrier to rapid economic progress in a poor country. Only to some extent can qualified manpower be imported. The mobilization of human resources through the expansion of education and training is therefore essential for economic growth.

It should not be forgotten that education is also a goal in itself. The illiterate or semi-illiterate man and woman cannot fully enjoy the fruits of economic growth. People who starve will temporarily be satisfied if they can fill their stomachs, but when they get used to satisfying their physical appetite, they will inevitable develop the urge for a fuller participation in the life of a nation. The illiterate can never aspire to such full participation in the life of his community.

When this study was started, it was the policy of the Government of Pakistan to make primary-school education universal by 1970 and middle-school education universal five years later.[9] These targets were utterly unrealistic because it would not be possible to train sufficient teachers so quickly. In spite of the fact that this study accepts in general the targets set by the government and the Planning Commission in Pakistan, an exception was made in this case. The Third Five-Year Plan confirms that this deviation from Pakistan's own targets was fully justified.[10] The targets as set out in Table 22 are now probably somewhat more ambitious than the targets at present kept in mind by the Planning Commission and the educational authorities in Pakistan. Calculations made within the framework of this study[11] show that the supply of matriculates, i. e., students who have passed their higher secondary education successfully, will be

Table 22. *The expansion of general education*

	1960	1965	1970	1975	1980	1985
Number of students (thousands)						
Primary schools	4,700	7,200	13,400	21,600	24,550	28,400
'Middle' schools	(830)	(1,170)	3,000	7,000	11,000	14,550
Higher secondary						
schools	(270)	(380)	750	1,150	1,750	2,210
Colleges	110	160	260	450	750	1,000
University under-						
graduates	10	15	23	39	68	103
University post-						
graduates..........	0.7	1	2	3	6	8
School attendance in per						
cent of age-group						
Primary schools	32	42	72	100	100	100
Middle schools	12	14	30	64	87	100
Higher secondary						
schools	6	7	12	17	23	25
Desirable number of						
teachers (thousands)						
Primary schools	127	197	310	470	615	810
Middle schools	(30)	(32)	75	175	300	510
Higher secondary						
schools	(20)	(20)	38	58	88	110
Trained teachers who						
will be available (thousands)						
Primary schools	127	146	215	375	578	770
Middle schools	(30)	31	49	115	265	420
Higher secondary						
schools	(20)	20	25	40	79	113
Enrollment in teacher-						
training institutes (thousands)						
For primary schools ..	7.4	13	40	60	70	75
For middle schools ...	1.1	2	11	28	50	50
For higher secondary						
schools	0.7	1.2	2.8	7.8	12	12

Sources: [0], Annex V, Tables 1, 2, and 3.

Definitions: Primary school, 5 years of schooling between the age of 6 and 11; middle school, 3 years of schooling between the age of 11 and 14; higher secondary school, 2 years of schooling between the age of 14 and 16 (leading up to matriculation); colleges – pre-university training, 2 years: universities, excluding law schools, medical schools, engineering schools, and agricultural colleges.

scarce in relation to the demand for qualified candidates for entry into higher education. The output of matriculates is again dependent on how many students pass their 'middle' school education with enough success to be able to go through the higher stage of secondary education. It has also to be taken into account that a large number of youths with a middle-school diploma will have to undergo various forms of technical training. Unless middle-school education becomes universal, it is doubtful whether it will be possible to achieve the target of 25 per cent of those in the age group 14—16 attending higher secondary schools.[12]

The rapid expansion of general education involves a simultaneous expansion in the number of teachers. The figures for the number of teachers required, which are presented in Table 22, are not excessively high. They are calculated on the assumption that the number of pupils per teacher must go up during the next ten to fifteen years. Thus it is assumed that the student/teacher ratio in the primary schools will rise from 37 in 1960 to 46 in 1975, and in the middle schools from 28 in 1960 to 40 in 1970. Nevertheless it will most probably *not* be possible to meet the demand for trained teachers fully within the next twenty years. This can be seen by comparing the figures for the desired (but by no means ideal!) number of teachers and those for available trained teachers. The situation will be particularly critical in middle schools. Two solutions are possible for the shortage of teachers: (1) the student-teacher ratio can be raised further by two or several shift schools, and (2) untrained teachers can be used. The overall shortage of literate manpower in Pakistan makes the first solution preferable. Multi-shift schools can take several forms — morning and evening classes or school attendance only every second or third day.[13]

The need to increase the number of teachers rapidly makes necessary an extremely fast expansion of the institutes for teacher training. The figures used in this study show that enrolment in the institutes for middle-school teachers must go up from 1,100 in 1960 to 50,000 in 1980 in order to meet 80 to 90 per cent of the need for teachers during the Sixth Five Year Plan. It is probably not possible to plan for an even more rapid expansion, and it would be unwise to do so. Too rapid expansion of training capacity in one specific field will inevitably lead to overcapacity in training facilities. This danger is particularly strong in the field of general education where the demand for teachers will rise rapidly as long as school attendance rises in relation to the number of children in the relevant age groups. But when a desirable level of school attendance has been reached, the need for additional teachers will grow moderately; and as most of the teaching staff will be young, the need for new teachers to replace those who retire will also be comparatively small.

The expansion of specialized education is projected to be even greater than that for general education. Thus, whereas it is expected that the number of college and university students will increase about tenfold, the number of engineering students should increase forty times, the number of medical and dental students twenty times, and the number of students in agricultural colleges eighteen times. At lower levels (except in the case of commercial education) the projected number of students will grow at least fifty times, in some cases far more.

It should be noted that it is assumed that industrial schools will only provide part of the trained workers who will be needed in manufacturing, construction, transport, etc. A large number of workers will have to be trained within the enterprises.

The targets set for education of engineers, technicans, and skilled workers through industrial schools are closely linked to projected employment in the modern sectors of economy, and in particular to employment in the modern manufacturing industries. The formula which has been used is that the number of engineers needed should correspond to 4 per cent of employment in the modern manufacturing industries.[14] However, only half of the engineers should be employed in manufacturing industries — the rest should find employment in construction, transport, public utilities, public administration, and other service industries. The total number of engineers needed in Pakistan was estimated at 120,000 in 1985 on the basis of a preliminary estimate of employment in manufacturing of 3 million people. The final estimate came to 3.4 million so that on the assumptions used in this study the projected expansion of the engineering colleges is on the low side. The need for technicians is estimated to be twice that of engineers.

While the expansion of technical education reflects a well-defined demand for engineers, technicians, and skilled workers linked with the projected growth of the modern sector of the economy, the expansion of agricultural and medical education is based on personal judgement.

On the basis of the assumed expansion of agricultural colleges, 50,000 graduates should be available in 1985. This is a high figure even by international standards. But the modernization of agriculture in Pakistan will require enormous efforts in agricultural extension services, research, general administration, and in other ways. It is also likely that a large number of college-trained agriculturists will be pulled into other occupations (e.g., in the food-manufacturing industries and in trade as salesmen and demonstrators of agricultural machinery, etc). Only a mass injection of first-class skill in agriculture can ensure that the activities which support the development of agriculture will be manned by capable and qualified people. As for persons with diplomas from agricultural schools, there should be 200,000 available in 1985. If half of these worked in the villages, there would still, on the average, only be one per village. The 'rural post-middle schools' referred to in Table 23 include schools which aim at giving further education to gifted rural youth. Fundamental agricultural education should certainly form part of such education which, however, should also aim at making its students better prospective members of their rural communities. It is indispensable that a developing country with a large agricultural population creates forms of education which prevent a mass exodus of men and women to the towns and cities. As long as the craving for further education can only be met in an urban framework, such a mass exodus is inevitable, and employment opportunities in the towns and cities will not be so large that jobs can be found

Table 23. *Expansion of special education*

	1960	1965	1970	1975	1980	1985
Number of students (thousands)						
University level education						
Engineering students	2	4	8.5	22	51	83
Agriculture, animal husbandry, etc.	2	3.5	7	14	27	36
Medical schools, etc.	5	13.5	33	53	85	100
Medium level of education						
Polytechnics, etc.	2.5	8.5	25	40	69	128
Agricultural schools	0.7	1.7	8	18	49	71
Schools for midwives, nurses, health visitors	0.7	2	14	22	37	52
Commercial schools	19	25	45	60	90	115
Other education and vocational training						
Industrial schools.............	3.5	12.5	106	317	605	940
Rural post-middle schools	1.5	3	12	25	62	82
Home economics schools	0.2	2	10	40	150	420

Sources: [0]: Engineering colleges, Annex V–6; agricultural colleges, Annex V–10; medical and dental schools, Annex V–26; polytechnics, Annex V–6; agricultural schools, Annex V–10; schools for midwives, etc., Annex V–26; commercial schools, Annex V–8a; industrial schools, Annex V–7; rural schools (corresponding more or less to the Village AID institutes which were operated in 1960, but with changed curricula), Annex V–10; and home economics schools, Annex V–6a.

for everybody. Home economics schools which, of course, should
be established both in the country and the towns should have the
same aims with regard to female youth engaged in agriculture.

Targets for the *health services* have been set very high in this
study, much higher than by the Pakistan government itself. The
two sets of targets are:

	Pakistan's Perspective Plan[15]	The present study[16]
Inhabitants per unit in 1985		
Doctors	3,000	1,600
Nurses	4,500	1,400
Health visitors	10,000	2,850
Hospital beds	1,000	400

There is no reason to believe that the targets set by the Pakistan
government in 1964 will still guide its actions in 1970 or in 1980.
Of course, the targets which have been used in this study are
extremely ambitious but they are certainly not too generous. The
general health situation in Pakistan is much more difficult than
in countries which have one hospital bed for 100 persons or one
doctor for less than 1,000 persons. Even the ambitious targets
used here are far too modest to safeguard the health of the people
twenty years from now. The crucial question is whether the targets are realistic.

The projected growth in the number of doctors is from 13,000
in 1965 to 125,000 in 1985. In the Soviet Union the number of
doctors was increased from 14,500 in 1917 to 141,000 in 1940.[17]
Consequently such an expansion is feasible. The projected increase in the number of hospital beds is from somewhat above
30,000 in 1965 to 500,000 in 1985, whereas in the USSR the number increased from 150,000 in 1917 to 790,000 in 1940.[18] The absolute increase in the USSR during those 23 years was therefore
considerably higher than the one projected for Pakistan, and it is
important to note that the number of hospital beds per doctor in
the USSR in 1940 was 5.5 against 4 which is projected for Pakistan. One is bound to conclude on the basis of the Russian experience that the ambitious targets set out in this study are not
outside the realms of reality.

One thing is certain — the projected rapid expansion in the
capacity of the medical schools cannot lead to educational standards which can be compared to those in present day USA, USSR,
or Europe. The ground must be prepared for long refresher courses for doctors and other health workers so that their professional

Table 24. *The capital costs of education*

	1960–65	1965–70	1970–75	1975–80	1980–85
Physical facilities (buildings, equipment, etc.) Rs Mill.					
Medical education	66/104	305	305	480	320
Other education	1,067	3,549	6,141	7,831	8,861
Training abroad. Rs Mill.					
Medical students	22	47	93	170	220
Other students	59	122	209	384	608
Foreign teachers					
Medical schools	n.a.	74	108	140	158
Other schools	56	95	175	335	610
Total	1,270/1,308	4,192	7,031	9,340	10,770

Sources: [0], Annex V, Tables 17, 19, and 32.

standard can be raised. Since the science of medicine makes such rapid strides towards greater perfection, such refresher courses are useful even for physicians in countries with the highest medical standards. Education in stages, interrupted by many years practical work, is, therefore, a solution which can give quick results and eventually ensure adequate although not excellent standards.

The expansion of the educational system which is deemed necessary to fulfil the production and income targets used in this study must come at a very early stage so that the impact can be felt soon enough. This is shown clearly by Table 24 which also suggests that from the Fifth Plan onwards *investments* in the educational system will grow much more slowly than total investment costs.[19] Current costs will, however, continue to grow rapidly throughout and after the period under review. (See Table 34 which shows the rate of growth of the various sectors of the economy. The growth of income in the education sector corresponds roughly to the growth of the current costs of education.) Costs of foreign teachers and of training abroad are, in this study, counted as capital costs; and they are projected as representing a sizeable proportion of total investment costs in education.

D. *Improving the health of the people*

The main targets for improved health services have already been summarized in the preceding section on education which included estimates of the costs of training the necessary health personnel.

Table 25. *Investments in health services* (Rs Mill.)

	1960–65	1965–70	1970–75	1975–80	1980–85
Education	88/126	426	506	790	698
Research	15	20	40	70	120
Special health programmes (current expenditure)	120	180	270	370	530
Physical facilities (hospitals, health centres, etc.)	183	577	1,153	2,307	4,613
Total	406/444	1,203	1,969	3,537	5,961

Source: [0], Annex V, Table 32.

Investments in health centres and hospitals, current expenditure on major health programmes (such as programmes against malaria), and research expenditure are much larger than expenditure on education. The total costs of investments in the health services are summarized in Table 25.

In time the cost structure of the health programmes will change character drastically. Investments in buildings and equipment in hospitals and health centres, which during the Second Five Year Plan period represented a mere 45 per cent of total costs, will during the Sixth Plan reach 80 per cent of the total. At the same time the share of education and of the special health programmes will fall drastically, in the case of education from about 25 to barely 12 per cent. This change is to be expected. As long as there is a severe shortage of health personnel, the construction of physical facilities is a mere waste since the men and women who should operate the facilities are simply not there. Investments in education must therefore precede investments in hospitals, and there will be a considerable time-lag between investments in education and the consequences deriving therefrom. The figure for special health programmes is less significant since it has simply been calculated to rise in step with the rise in national income. This is an arbitrary assumption. Alternatively it could have been assumed that the costs of such programmes would rise at the same rate as the total current expenditure on health services, that is, more or less at the same rate as the national income created in the health sector which again is determined by the number of medical personnel. If this assumption was chosen, the total costs of the investments in health would be much higher, and the proportion of the special health programmes in the total costs would fall only moderately.[20] Such health programmes have the character of 'crash' programmes, against malaria, for family planning, etc.;

and when the overall health services become better developed, the need for such programmes will become relatively less important.

The rapid increase in investments in physical facilities will help to contribute to the growth of the construction industry, but will at the same time pull upward the overall requirements for capital to finance the development of the country.

E. *The need for research*

A developing country cannot afford large research programmes because they do not have enough trained manpower to spare for research and because the financial costs are heavy. To some extent a developing country can do without research programmes of its own. The most urgent requirement is that the developing country use research findings from all possible sources, and this requires capital investments and skilled manpower. In the short run it may be better to use skilled manpower and available capital to exploit existing research results rather than to channel resources into the uncertain task of developing new methods. Unfortunately even the most underdeveloped country is faced with problems which have not been satisfactorily resolevd elsewhere and which require new types of research. Furthermore, research activities are in themselves stimulating because of their educational aspect. Therefore some resources must nevertheless be set aside for research, but it is imperative that these scarce resources are not spread so thinly that they are wasted on inadequate efforts which lead nowhere. A very tentative effort has been made to project the cost of future research in Pakistan. The projected expenditure on medical research is given in the preceding section. For other types of *applied* research Table 26 shows the expenditure projected.

The figures for the period 1960 to 1965 were taken from the Second Five-Year Plan, and projections have been based on the

Table 26. *Expenditure on applied research (Rs Mill.)*

	1960–65	1965–70	1970–75	1975–80	1980–85
Research in agriculture	60	120	240	500	1,000
Other applied research	145	435	870	1,740	3,480
Total	205	555	1,110	2,240	4,480
Current expenditure	100	275	555	1,120	2,240
Investments in facilities	105	280	555	1,120	2,240

Source: [0], Annex V, Table 11.

simple assumption that research expenditure will grow in step with the number of available college-educated agriculturists and engineers respectively. In other words, the same proportion of highly skilled manpower will be devoted to research in the future as during the Second Five-Year Plan.

These research programmes can be government financed, government sponsored, or privately financed. They have been included under investments in this study because of their importance for the future growth of the country. The cost of investment in research is not negligible. In 1985 it represents about 30 per cent of total investment in education and research and, as a comparison, it corresponds during the same period to three-quarters of the investment in the health services.

F. *Investment in roads, post, and telecommunications, broadcasting and television, government buildings, and communal amenities*

These items, which constitute important parts of the economic and social infrastructure of a country, have one thing in common; it is not possible to derive exact estimates of these investments from other figures in the present study. They are, like investments in education, research, and medical services, 'autonomous' investments, the level of which is determined by political action rather than by pure economic calculations. It is possible to calculate the rentability of a road, but such calculations are seldom accepted by everybody. Too many subjective judgements enter into the calculations. The choice of interest rate makes a large difference, and the estimates of economic gains caused by a new or improved road include many imponderables. Even if there were undisputed figures for the rentability of roads, social considerations would remain of great importance for road policy. The same holds true for government enterprises such as post and telecommunications. The density of post-offices is not determined by the turnover alone. It is not necessary for the telephone service to expand so that all requests for installation of new telephones are met within a short period, and the fee for installation can be set so high that potential demand is reduced. The broadcasting and television authorities can alternatively use their revenue for better programmes or for investment in more powerful transmitters. The government can also use licence fees from radio and television as a source of income for quite other purposes. The standard of government buildings varies considerably between countries, and a government has a wide range of choice between extreme austerity and excessive luxury in office buildings. Finally, communal, which means here mainly urban, amenities are highly desirable for the wellbeing of the people, but they are also extremely costly and investments in such amenities must be weighed against other needs.

In this study it has in general been assumed that investments in these types of economic and social infrastructure will be adequate — in some cases barely adequate — but that the planners will try to channel as much as possible into investments which give quicker yields. For health and education the assumptions in the present study are that the targets will be bold and ambitious, but these bold targets have the primary goal of facilitating future growth which must be based on a healthy and well-educated population. Good roads, bright street lights, and colour television are assumed to be less indispensable for rapid economic growth.

The results of this road programme can be summarized as follows: East Pakistan which in 1960 had 1,415 miles of superior roads will add 15,915 miles of superior roads, and West Pakistan which had 9,350 miles of superior roads will add another 20,710 miles of such roads. East Pakistan had 19,750 miles of poor secondary roads which will be improved and to which will be added 28,170 miles of new secondary roads. West Pakistan will improve

Table 27. *Improved roads and their costs*

	1960–65	1965–70	1970–75	1975–80	1980–85
New superior roads, miles					
East Pakistan	870	2,000	3,000	4,000	6,045
West Pakistan...............	2,875	3,500	4,500	4,500	5,335
Total	3,745	4,500	6,500	7,500	10,250
Secondary roads, new, miles					
East Pakistan	2,500	4,000	5,500	7,500	8,670
West Pakistan	3,500	6,500	10,000	13,000	15,290
Improved secondary roads, miles					
East Pakistan	4,000	4,000	4,000	4,000	3,750
West Pakistan...............	4,000	6,000	7,000	8,000	9,250
New or improved secondary roads, miles					
Pakistan.....................	14,000	20,500	26,500	32,500	36,960
Costs. Rs million					
Superior roads	570	1,750	2,315	3,335	4,415
Secondary roads.............	125	210	295	370	540
Total	695	1,960	2,610	3,705	4,955

Source: [0], Annex V, Table 54.

its 34,250 miles of secondary roads and add another 48,290 miles. Table 27 shows how this programme is projected to be implemented.

Costs of road-building in East Pakistan are extremely high. Because of recurrent annual floods during the monsoon season, roads which are to be useable all year around must be 'superior' roads, built on embankments and hard surfaced. Main roads of this type will cost about Rs 1 million per mile to build, while even the simpler superior roads will cost about Rs 0.5 million per mile. In West Pakistan superior roads can be built for Rs 125,000 per mile. A large road-building programme is needed in East Pakistan in spite of the enormous costs because the modernization of the economy of the province depends on a cheap and reliable system of transport. Inland water transport is much used in this province but, except for transport of heavy goods on the main rivers, it is slow and expensive. River transport cannot become a cheaper substitute for road transport.

The road programme aims at providing East Pakistan with 0.75 km. of road per sq. km., the densely populated areas of West Pakistan with 0.60 km., and the sparsely populated areas of West Pakistan with 0.10 km. of road per sq. km. These figures are somewhat below the corresponding figures for most European countries at present, but are far above the figures for most poor countries. Investment in roads will in 1985 be smaller than investment in education and research or health — 34 and 83 per cent respectively of such investments — but current and capital expenditure on roads will represent about 1.4 per cent of the GDP against 1 per cent in 1960 if the outlined programme is carried through.

Table 28. *Investments in post and telecommunications and in radio and television*

	1960–65	1965–70	1970–75	1975–80	1980–85
Investments in post and telecommunications, Rs Mill..	316	710	1,220	2,190	3,900
Investments in broadcasting and television, Rs Mill.	40	100	150	200	250

	1960	1965	1970	1975	1980	1985
Physical targets (thousands)
Telephones	75	150	340	720	1,480	3,000
Radio sets	150	300	650	1,600	3,600	7,250
Television sets	–	–	5	110	450	1,200

Sources: [0], Annex V, Tables 67, 68, 69, and 71.

In this study it has been assumed that all work on the second-ary roads will be done by the local population and they have been included in non-monetized investments. There is obviously scope for a further expansion of this part of the programme if it should prove desirable, notably from the point of view of employment.

The bulk of investment in post and telecommunications relates to the expansion of the number of telephones. With 3 million tele-phones in 1985 Pakistan will still only have 15 telephones per 1,000 inhabitants which is a lower figure than in the poorest of the European countries in 1960, and not quite twice the present figure for Egypt. There will certainly be high demand for tele-phones, but investments are heavy and the government will prob-ably be obliged to put a brake on expansion of the telephone system. The figures for the number of radio and television sets are even more modest — 36 radio sets and 6 television sets per 1,000 inhabitants in 1985 are very low figures by international standards. These figures are merely illustrative since the invest-ment figures only include investments in transmitters, studios, and other installations for the programmes and the transmission of programmes.

The projected investments in communal amenities in urban areas are very low. Thus, urban investments per head of urban population will only rise from Rs 29 during the period 1960 to 1965 to Rs 41 during the period 1980 to 1985. If investment is calculated in relation to the increase in the urban population in each five-year period, it will only rise from Rs 106 during the Second Plan to Rs 129 during the Sixth Plan.[21] Such moderate investment will mean very small improvements in municipal

Table 29. *Investments in communal amenities and in buildings for public administration (Rs Mill.)*

	1960–65	1965–70	1970–75	1975–80	1980–85
Investments in communal amenities					
Urban areas	530	745	1,150	2,000	3,000
Rural areas, monetized inv.	145	210	335	475	735
Rural areas, non-monetized investments	145	260	500	830	1,470
Total	820	1,215	1,985	3,305	5,205
Investments in buildings for public administration					
Total	155	190	270	420	790

Sources: [0], Annex V, Tables 48 and 46.

comfort. The picture is somewhat brighter when account is taken of investment in new housing in the urban areas. The cost estimates for housing include land-development costs and installation of water, sewerage, etc., in new housing areas. Still it should be realized that the estimated level of investment in urban amenities is far too low to provide modern living for the residents of towns and cities. Austere public facilities in the urban areas are, however, in line with the assumption of a slow rate of growth of personal consumption also in the cities. Both facts reflect the need to squeeze considerable savings out of the urban population and to divert resources which are available for investments into 'productive' investments which will raise the future productive capacity of the country. It is impossible to assess in advance the *minimum* level of investment which is required in municipal amenities. Heavy investments are needed to ensure good water supplies, adequate sewerage, and other services which are indispensable for the general health of the urban population. The estimates in this study are perhaps too low to ensure such minimum essential amenities, and if this is the case, total investments will have to be increased without a corresponding increase in the growth of the national income. In other words the capital-output ratio would be raised further.

Investments in government buildings have been estimated on the assumption that new offices will have to be built for the increasing number of government servants, but there is no allowance for any significant improvement in quality.

G. *Houses for a growing population*

The estimates of rent for housing which are used in this study are in themselves very dubious. Total rent paid by the consumers in 1960 is estimated at Rs 952 million in Chapter 5. This figure corresponds to a percentage of total consumer expenditure which is in line with what is shown by a number of family expenditure surveys in poorer countries. On the other hand, the most recent estimate of the Gross National Product in Pakistan[22] assesses the value added from ownership of dwellings at Rs 1,772 million. This figure is by definition lower than the rent actually paid by or imputed to the consumer. I have so far seen no data which support this higher figure and have therefore preferred to use the lower figure calculated in Chapter 5.

In the villages most of the people live in huts — bamboo huts in East Pakistan, mud huts in West Pakistan. Other types of houses in the villages are extremely rare. The rent paid in the villages must therefore correspond to the interest on the capital value of the huts plus the annual depreciation and upkeep. Also a large proportion of the urban population lives in huts or in shacks.

Investment in housing therefore falls into two parts — building of huts and shacks and building of more solid houses (or 'pucka' housing to adopt the phrase in general use in the Indian sub-continent).

The assumptions on which these estimates have been made can be read directly from the Table. Throughout the period under re-view there will be some investment in additional huts in the rural areas, which means that part of the growing rural population will live in traditional housing. Nevertheless investment in addi-tional higher quality houses will be very large and the average housing standard in the rural areas should be improved. For the urban areas it has been assumed that additional shacks will be built during the Second and Third Plan periods but that thereafter the shanty towns will not grow further (but existing shanty towns

Table 30. *Investment in housing.* (*Rs Mill.*)

	1960–65	1965–70	1970–75	1975–80	1980–85
Replacement of huts					
Rural areas	2,017	2,240	2,427	2,685	2,830
Urban areas	100	100	175	200	275
Additional huts					
Rural areas	320	325	268	190	80
Urban areas	75	100	0	0	0
Total investment in huts	2,512	2,765	2,870	3,075	3,185
additional huts	395	425	268	190	80
Replacement of 'pucka' houses					
Rural areas*	190	190	190	190	190
Urban areas	170	170	170	170	170
Additional 'pucka' houses					
Rural areas*	350	770	1,920	2,580	3,250
Urban areas	1,975	2,830	4,530	8,430	13,630
Total investment in 'pucka'					
houses	2,685	3,960	6,810	11,370	17,240
additional houses	2,325	3,600	6,450	11,010	16,880
Total investment in housing	5,197	6,725	9,680	14,445	20,325

Sources: [0], Annex V, Tables 37, 38, and 41.

* It has been assumed that 'pucka' houses in rural areas will be built by the local population, and this item is therefore included under non-monetized investment. An allowance is made for purchase of materials (such as corrugated iron for roofing, pipes, some cement, etc.) for non-monetized investment.

will be replaced). This is an optimistic assumption which is reflected in the large figures for investment in new, higher quality housing.

The figure for replacement of existing 'pucka' housing may appear surprising since it suggests that there are more 'pucka' houses in the villages than in the towns and cities. This seems to contradict the statement that the village population lives mostly in huts. Two things should be remembered. First, there were in 1960 seven times as many people in the rural areas as in the urban areas. Second, a large proportion of the urban population moved to the cities and towns during the last 13 years, mostly as refugees from India but also as emigrants from the countryside. Thus perhaps only a minority of the urban population had permanent housing in 1960.

The improvement in urban housing conditions during the course of the period 1960 to 1985 should be very substantial, provided that most of the 'pucka' housing is cheap housing for the low-income groups. On this assumption 85 per cent of the population in cities and towns should live in decent houses in 1985 against an illustrative figure of 50 per cent in 1960. If, however, much of the investment in new housing in the urban areas goes into houses which cost considerably more than Rs 4—5,000 per unit, the number of people in the shanty towns will have to increase very substantially. 'Investments' in additional huts would also become much higher than shown in Table 30.[23]

It is quite obvious that the suggested housing programme for the urban areas does not correspond to the aspirations of the urban population. Comfortable houses in a hot climate must be large and equipped with costly installations such as air conditioners or at least electric fans. The growing urban middle classes will hardly be satisfied with dwellings which cost less than, say, Rs 20,000 per unit and even dwellings having a value of Rs 50,000 would be considered modest by the more prosperous classes. Much more expensive houses are built in large numbers these days in the cities of Pakistan. Attempts to carry through an austere housing programme are bound to run into very determined opposition from the most vocal spokesmen of alleged 'public opinion'. If, however, one of the basic assumptions of this study is fulfilled, viz. the assumption that *per caput* personal consumption in the urban areas will grow only at a rate of 1.1 per cent per year, the austere housing standard will follow as a consequence.[24]

H. *The role of 'autonomous' investments*

The level of autonomous investments will have to grow much faster than the national income, particularly during the Third and Fourth Plan periods. This is clearly shown by the figures for these investments in relation to the Gross Domestic Product. Most of the increased investments will come in the form of monetized investments, i. e., investments which have to be realized through

Table 31. *Breakdown of autonomous investments in major sectors (Rs Mill.)*

	Second Plan 1960–65	Third Plan 1965–70	Fourth Plan 1970–75	Fifth Plan 1975–80	Sixth Plan 1980–85
Monetized investments					
Education, research, etc.	1,273	4,406	7,748	10,946	14,783
Health services	400	1,203	1,969	3,537	5,961
Housing (urban)	2,145	3,000	4,700	8,600	13,800
Administrative buildings.....	155	190	270	420	790
Communal amenities	575	955	1,485	2,475	3,735
Roads....................	570	1,750	2,315	3,335	4,415
Post, telegraph, and telephone	316	710	1,220	2,190	3,900
Broadcasting, TV..........	40	100	150	200	250
Total monetized investments .	5,474	12,314	19,857	31,703	47,634
As % of aggregate GDP.....	3.4	6.1	7.4	8.6	9.0
Imputed investments					
Housing (rural & huts)	3,052	3,725	4,980	5,845	6,625
Communal amenities	145	260	500	830	1,470
Roads....................	125	210	295	370	540
Total imputed investment ...	3,322	4,195	5,775	7,045	8,635
As % of aggregate GDP.....	2.1	2.1	2.2	1.9	1.6
Total investments in the above sectors	8,796	16,509	25,632	38,748	56,269
As % of aggregate GDP.....	5.5	8.2	9.6	10.5	10.6

Monetized investments include those which are accounted for in the Second Five Year Plan.

Imputed investments include both investments in the non-monetized sector, notably investment works in villages, but also building of huts, and investments not accounted for in the second Five Year Plan, i.e., building of 'pucka' houses in the rural areas. Some investments will probably be undertaken in education, health, and administrative buildings the value of which should have been imputed, but the amounts are probably negligible.

Sources: [0], Annex V. Education, Table 19; health, Table 32; housing, Table 43. (Monetized investment: Pucka buildings (urban) – land development, urban areas – land, urban areas. Imputed investments: Pucka buildings (rural)–land development and land, rural East Pakistan – huts.) Administrative buildings, Table 46; communal amenities, Table 48; broadcasting and television, Table 71.

financial resources, and which in most cases will be carried out by government organizations. However, if investments in huts are excluded, the figures imply that the mobilization of local man-power on investment projects which are often carried out with insignificant financial resources will also increase rapidly. Such 'non-monetized' investments will nevertheless only form a small part of total investments.[25]

The percentage distribution of expenditure shows that during the Third Plan period, education should already replace urban housing as the largest single item. Only towards the end of the period under review, when the most urgent tasks of building up the educational system have been fulfilled, will urban housing

Table 32. *Autonomous investments – summary Table*

	1960–65	1965–70	1970–75	1975–80	1980–85
Total autonomous investments, Rs Mill.					
Percentage distribution	8,796	16,509	25,632	38,748	56,269
Monetized					
Education and research	14.5	26.7	30.2	28.2	26.3
Health services (incl. education)	4.6	7.3	7.7	9.1	10.6
Roads....................	6.5	10.6	9.0	8.7	7.9
Post, telegraph, telephone ...	3.4	4.3	4.8	5.7	6.9
Broadcasting, TV...........	0.5	0.6	0.6	0.5	0.5
Communal amenities	6.5	5.8	5.8	6.4	6.6
Government administrative buildings	1.8	1.1	1.1	1.1	1.4
Urban housing	24.4	18.2	18.3	22.2	24.5
Total monetized investments ..	62.2	74.6	77.5	81.8	84.7
Non-monetized					
Huts (rural and urban)	28.6	16.7	11.2	8.0	5.7
Other rural housing	6.1	5.8	8.2	7.1	6.1
Communal amenities	1.7	1.6	1.9	2.1	2.6
Roads....................	1.4	1.3	1.2	1.0	0.9
Total non-monetized investments	37.8	25.4	22.5	18.2	15.3
Autonomous investments in per-cent of aggregate GDP during five-year periods					
All autonomous investments .	5.5	8.2	9.6	10.5	10.6
Monetized investments	3.4	6.1	7.4	8.6	9.0
Non-monetized, other than huts	0.5	0.7	1.1	1.1	1.0
Huts.....................	1.6	1.4	1.1	0.8	0.6

Sources: Tables 30 and 31.

start to catch up with education as the most important form of autonomous investment. Investment in the health sector will grow in relative importance throughout the period, whereas investment in roads is expected to make a jump during the Third Plan but thereafter to rise more slowly than total autonomous investments. A comparison of the figures for 1960 and 1985 shows that investments in education and health, and to some extent also in telecommunications, will become far more important and that this relative gain takes place at the expense of housing. If investment in huts is excluded from the figures, the general picture remains the same.

Table 33 throws some further light on the pattern of growth of different types of autonomous investments. Amongst the monetized investments there are some fast starters — education, roads, health, and broadcasting and TV grow much faster during the Third Plan period than any other monetized investments, and, except for radio and TV, the same pattern prevails during the Fourth Plan. From then on the rate of growth of investments in education and in roads slows down in relation to the average,

Table 33. *Autonomous investments – relative growth during the period 1960–1985 (1960 to 65 = 100)*

	1960–65	1965–70	1970–75	1975–80	1980–85
Monetized investments					
Education and research	100	346	609	860	1,161
Health services (incl. educ.)	100	301	492	884	1,490
Roads (superior)	100	307	406	585	775
Post, telegraph, telephone	100	225	386	693	1,234
Broadcasting, TV.............	100	250	375	500	625
Communal amenities	100	166	258	430	650
Government adm. buildings....	100	122	174	271	510
Urban housing	100	139	219	401	643
All monetized investments	100	225	363	579	870
Non-monetized investments					
Huts (rural and urban)	100	110	114	122	127
Other rural housing	100	178	391	513	637
Communal amenities	100	179	345	572	1,014
Roads (secondary)	100	168	236	296	432
All non-monetized investments	100	126	174	212	260
Grand total, autonomous investments................	100	188	291	441	640

Sources: same as for Tables 30 and 31.

while investment in health grows much faster than the average throughout the period under review. During the later periods this is also the case for investments in telecommunications. In the Sixth Plan Period investments in urban housing, communal amenities, and government buildings pick up speed very considerably. Amongst the non-monetized investments, investments in communal amenities and improved rural housing grow fast throughout the entire period. The slowdown in investments in improved housing in the Sixth Plan partly reflects slower population growth in rural areas.

The data on autonomous investments constitute an important part of the information which is used to project domestic output. For this purpose total investments were broken down into type of expenditure — on buildings and construction, on equipment, etc.[26]

8. The Changing Structure of the Gross Domestic Product

A. *The basis for detailed estimates of structural changes*

Private consumption, government consumption, and autonomous investments in Pakistan corresponded to 86 per cent of total final resources[1] at market prices in 1960, and my final estimates show that they may correspond to 75 per cent of the GDP in 1985. Chapters 5 to 7 include the detailed estimates of these three items of demand which were established at an early stage on my statistical exercise. Consequently, the estimates presented in the previous three chapters cover a very large proportion of total final demand.

In the present chapter export demand will be projected, sector by sector. This will further increase the coverage of final demand which was available as a basis for production estimates when these were initially made. Consumption, autonomous fixed investments, investments in stocks plus exports represented, in 1960, 93 per cent of total available resources for final use, and my projections show that this percentage had fallen to 83 per cent in 1985. Nevertheless, during the whole period under review, these items corresponded to the bulk of final use of resources in Pakistan. Even though it was possible to use only a very sketchy figure for induced investments, the demand estimates were sufficiently broad to allow fairly detailed projections of the final demand for goods and services from the different sectors.

This chapter shows the main results of the estimates of the production pattern. To some extent these were the results of a complex procedure because many sectors produce intermediate products, the demand for which could only be estimated when the final demand for all those products which embody the intermediate products had been calculated.[2] The iteration process which was used to arrive at final results will not be described in detail. The results included in this chapter have been arrived at as follows:

1. The demand for consumption purposes and for investment purposes shown in Chapters 5 to 7 is the major basis for the detailed estimates of production of most goods and services.

2. For individual subsectors the export demand as well as the export supply potential is estimated. This covers another important part of the demand for goods and services.

3. In the case of subsectors which deliver goods and services for investment purposes, preliminary account was taken of the requirements for investments not included under autonomous investment (i. e., 'induced' investments).

4. Within this framework of final demand, the demand for goods and services used as inputs was estimated provisonally.

5. Estimates of induced investments (see Chapter 9) were made on the basis of this first round of projections of the output of the various sectors of the economy. This completed the estimates of final demand. The output of certain sectors had to be adjusted to conform to the firmer estimates of induced investments, simultaneously with consequential adjustments of the figures for induced investments.

6. Figures for outputs, for domestic and foreign deliveries, and for inputs (based on outputs in the different sectors) were brought together in input-output tables which, after elimination of major inconsistencies, gave the results presented in Appendix I. It is these figures for output and value added in the different sectors which have been used in this chapter.[3]

7. At the very end of the statistical exercise global adjustments had to be made to ensure overall consistency. These adjustments also affected the Gross Domestic Product, but they have *not* been carried out in detail, that is, they have not been broken down into sectors and subsectors.

It should be stressed that because it is not possible to establish an entirely consistent and detailed input-output table for the base period, no attempt will be made to arrive at identical figures for supply and demand for each item of goods and services discussed here. The demand estimates were used to assess the *trend* of demand rather than the *absolute level* of demand. It should be noted, however, that in those cases in which there are very significant differences between the demand and the supply figures in the base period, and in which both demand and supply are projected to increase very substantially, it was necessary to reduce the gap between the estimates of supply and demand, in order to avoid obviously meaningless results.

The importance which is attached to each individual sector of the economy in the following depends in part on the effect of the development of each individual sector on the foreign balance and the level of investments. Sectors which cannot operate without significant imports of goods and services or which can earn

foreign exchange (or both) have been studied in considerable detail. Similarly, sectors which can only expand at the expense of
considerable investment expenditure (i. e., those in which the
capital-output ratio is high, or those which are so large that investments will be large even if the capital-output ratio is low)
have also been studied closely. But since it is important to show
how the Gross Domestic Product can, in fact, grow as rapidly as
has been assumed in this study, the remaining sectors could not
be entirely neglected. It was at least necessary to evaluate their
likely growth during the period under review.

Estimates of demand are imperative for the subsequent estimates of output. But demand can be met by domestic production
or by imports or by a combination of both. Certain sectors, notably most of the service sectors, will have to cover the entire
domestic demand, whereas there is no constant ratio between the
demand on one given goods-producing sector and the output of
this sector. Over time such a sector may cover a rising, a declining
or a fluctuating proportion of domestic (and foreign) demand.
The purpose of the detailed studies of the prospects for individual
sectors and subsectors of the economy of Pakistan has been to
evaluate how much of the total demand on one given sector will
be met by domestic output at various points of time during the
period under review and how much will be imported. This has
led to studies of the ability of different sectors to respond to demand.[4] This chapter contains merely the most important figures
and a few of the most important assumptions which have been
used.[5] All figures for output and value added for main sectors and
subsectors are given in Appendix I, the input-output tables.

B. *The changing structure of the Gross Domestic Product*

The Table clearly shows the very uneven growth of the different sectors. Gas and electricity, mining, modern manufacturing,
banking and insurance, and income from business premises are
projected as growing more than three times as fast as the total
GDP between 1960 and 1985; whereas construction, education,
health services, and communications are projected as growing
more than twice as fast. The slow-growing sectors are traditional
manufacturing, forestry, and agriculture.

The sectors which are expected to grow particularly fast, that
is, twice as fast as the national income, are, with two exceptions,
sectors which necessarily will grow relatively fast in an economy
which is being modernized. The two exseptions are mining and
construction. The expansion of the mining industry depends, of
course, on available natural resources. In this study it has been

Table 34. *The growth of the different sectors of the economy*
(Value added, 1960 = 100)

	1950	1955	1960	1965	1970	1975	1980	1985
Agriculture	88	94	100	112	130	157	187	229
Forestry...........	(65)	(86)	100	110	124	139	157	177
Fishing	78	88	100	121	147	190	259	351
Mining (unadjusted)	39	64	100	189	481	1,033	1,937	3,414
Mining (adjusted)...			100	187	408	774	1,355	2,248
Modern manufacturing	22	64	100	161	281	478	806	1,378
Trad. manufacturing (adjusted)........	80	89	100	120	135	153	163	170
Gas, electricity	31	44	100	192	516	971	1,750	3,120
Construction, comm.	37	64	100	171	309	449	723	1,075
Construct., non-monetized	n.a.	n.a.	100	130	162	209	238	288
Banking, insurance .	34	50	100	160	290	480	800	1,367
Government product	80	93	100	117	149	193	250	333
Transport	67	86	100	149	218	310	459	668
Post, telecomm. ...	n.a.	n.a.	100	142	219	342	548	895
Rental, housing	78	88	100	119	145	188	252	355
Rental, business ...	n.a.	n.a.	100	141	281	378	739	1,199
Trade (adjusted) ...	78	89	100	132	178	234	312	434
Education	n.a.	n.a.	100	116	189	360	668	950
Health	n.a.	n.a.	100	126	186	328	574	942
Other services......	70	84	100	120	152	201	267	376
Gross Domestic Product	78	89	100	122	163	221	306	443

Sources: Figures for 1950 to 1960, revised national income estimates, Central Statistical Office, [14], Vol .13, No. 8 (Aug. 1965), Table 29, pp. 2090–2091. Note that the CSO figure for gas and electricity also includes water services; the figure for transport also communications; and the figure for government product also pay to government staff in education and health services. As a result of the final reconciliation process, figures for mining, government product, trade, and traditional manufacturing had to be adjusted (see [0], Annex IX, Tables 14, 19, and 20). For absolute figures for the period 1960 to 1985 see Appendix I (unadjusted figures).

assumed that oil will finally be discovered in Pakistan, and this explains the very rapid growth of the mining industry. However, even if oil is not discovered, the output of natural gas will increase rapidly, and in any case the mining industry will be one of the growing points of Pakistan's economy during the next couple of decades. The output of the modern, 'commercialized' construction industry is expected to grow very fast because the economy is assumed to grow fast, which implies large and rapidly increasing investments.

Among particularly slow-growing sectors are the traditional industries whose markets will expand only slowly as modern products make inroads in the town and villages. The rate of growth projected for traditional industries is, in fact, on the optimistic side. The output from the forests can hardly grow more rapidly because the forests need a long time for improvement.[6]

Rapid growth in agriculture is hard to achieve because it depends on the actions of millions of peasants. The basis for the projection of the output in agriculture will be discussed in section F below.

The other sectors in which the output is projected to grow more slowly than the national income in the period 1960 to 1985 are: Non-monetized construction, government product, fishing, income from housing, and other services. In view of the fact that considerable emphasis must be put on mobilizing local fully unemployed manpower for 'non-monetized' construction work, it may seem surprising that the 'non-monetized construction industry' should grow so slowly. But it should be remembered that in 1960 at least 60 to 65 per cent of the 'output' of the non-monetized construction industry was the building of huts, and that this proportion will probably fall to below 25 per cent by 1985. Other imputed construction activities will therefore increase six or sevenfold between 1960 and 1985. The slow growth of the government product is in part explained by the fact that salaries to personnel in the education and health services are excluded. If they were included, the government product would grow at about the same rate as the GDP. This relatively slow growth is the result of assumed policy decisions to prevent government consumption and current government expenditure in general from growing too rapidly. The slower-than-average growth of the output in fishing, housing, and other services is caused by the dependency of these industries on personal consumption, which is projected to grow considerably more slowly than the national income, in order to permit savings to grow faster.

The pattern of growth of the several sectors of the economy can be seen better from figures which show the average annual growth rates.[7] Table 35, which follows, gives such figures.

One observes that the growth rates of many sectors tend to fluctuate from one five-year period to another. The rate of growth of the commercial construction industry is a case in point. This results from the way in which the projections have been made, on the basis of estimated demand for current and for investment uses. Such fluctuations in the rate of growth are, of course, in reality the normal course of events. In planning economic growth attempts will certainly be made to achieve this smoothly. For the purpose of this study no advantage can be gained by trying to manipulate all kinds of figures in order to achieve smoothly accelerating growth for each sector.[8]

Table 35. *Average, annual growth rate for the different sectors*
of the economy during the period 1950 to 1985

	1950 to 55	1955 to 60	1960 to 65	1965 to 70	1970 to 75	1975 to 80	1980 to 85
Agriculture	0.8	1.2	2.2	2.9	4.1	3.5	4.1
Forestry................	(5.6)	(3.3)	1.9	2.5	2.2	2.5	2.4
Fishing	2.5	2.6	3.9	3.9	5.3	6.4	6.2
Mining	10.8	8.7	13.3	17.0	13.6	11.9	10.6
Modern manufacturing	23.7	9.3	10.0	11.8	11.3	11.0	11.3
Traditional manufacturing .	2.3	2.3	3.8	2.2	2.5	1.3	0.9
Gas, electricity	7.3	17.9	14.0	21.8	13.5	12.5	12.2
Construction, commercial .	11.8	9.4	11.4	12.6	7.8	10.0	8.3
Construction, non-monetized	n.a.	n.a.	5.4	4.5	5.2	2.7	3.9
Banking, insurance	7.6	15.5	9.9	12.7	10.6	10.8	11.3
Government product	3.2	1.4	3.2	4.9	5.3	5.4	6.0
Transport	4.7	3.6	8.4	7.9	7.3	8.2	7.8
Post, telecommunications ..	n.a.	n.a.	7.3	9.2	9.3	9.9	10.3
Rental income, housing....	2.4	2.6	3.5	4.1	5.3	6.0	7.1
Rental income, business prem.................	n.a.	n.a.	7.1	14.8	6.2	14.3	10.2
Trade..................	2.7	2.4	5.7	6.1	5.7	5.9	6.8
Education	n.a.	n.a.	3.1	10.2	13.8	13.2	7.3
Health services	n.a.	n.a.	4.8	8.1	12.0	11.8	10.4
Other services...........	3.7	3.6	3.8	4.9	5.7	5.9	7.1
Gross Domestic Product ..	2.7	2.4	4.1	6.0	6.3	6.7	7.2

Sources: As for Table 34.

The most important conclusion to be drawn from the Table is that it does not include any 'fancy' growth rates which are difficult or perhaps even impossible to achieve. Nine of the sectors which are listed in the Table show growth rates which exceed 10 per cent per year in all or several of the five-year periods under review. For five of these nine sectors, data are available for the period 1950 to 1960, and *all* of these five sectors have in the past exceeded a growth rate of 10 per cent per year in one five-year period.

It is relevant to ask whether many sectors can sustain a growth rate of more than 10 per cent over a longer period. For some of the sectors there is no question that this is the case. Banking and insurance will expand fast if the demand is there, and so will the supply of business premises. In others the essential condition is the investment which needs to be undertaken in human resources or in installations. The supply of gas and electricity will only grow if the power stations, the grid, and the pipelines are built. Education and health services can grow only if teachers and doctors are trained in sufficient numbers. The expansion of telecommunications depends also heavily on investments, and so does the expansion of the mining industry but in this case the natural resources must also be present. Finally, which rate of growth can be sustained in the modern manufacturing sector? The projected rate of growth is slower than the one which prevailed during the period 1950 to 1960, but in 1950 modern manufacturing in Pakistan was almost non-existent. Is it too optimistic to assume that the growth rate (which, in fact, has exceeded 10 per cent per year between 1960 and 1965) can continue above 10 per cent per year during the next twenty years when the industrial base has become much broader? We should remember, however, that *Japan,* after having had an annual growth of industrial production of between 16 and 17 per cent between 1953 and 1961 (and 20 per cent between 1948 and 1961), continued to grow at a rate well above 10 per cent after 1961 also. Such growth rates are possible as long as the markets are present, the labour force trained, and the necessary investments undertaken.

The rate of growth in the construction industry is also very high and this reflects the high and increasing investments which have been projected as a necessary condition for the high growth rate. There is no reason to believe that the construction industry cannot expand rapidly, particularly if foreign assistance is available for tasks for which Pakistan has not sufficient trained manpower.

The real problems connected with the growth rates presented in this study concern sectors with more modest rates of expansion. First, the rate of growth in agriculture appears modest, but in almost any country a growth rate above 3 per cent annually in agriculture is quite an achievement. Second, it can be asked whether expansion in transport and in trade is consistent with that for the economy as a whole. Third, is it right to assume that the traditional manufacturing industries will manage to survive and even expand slowly during a period of rapid modernization? Some of these problems are discussed in Sections F to H below.

If we look for the 'leading sector of the economy', we find that this position is shared by gas and electricity which are on top of the league during the Second, Third, and Sixth Plan periods, and education which shows the highest growth rate during the Fourth and Fifth Plan periods (disregarding the capricious figure for income from business premises). The laggards are traditional manufacturing (except during the Second Plan) and forestry.[9]

C. *The contribution of different sectors to the growth of the economy*

Another way of looking at the pattern of growth is to show how much each sector contributes to the growth of the Gross Domestic Product. This is done in Table 36.

The first and last columns of the Table show that the composition of the Gross Domestic Product will change considerably over a 25-year period. The most striking change is that the contribution of agriculture will fall from 49 to 26 per cent whereas that of the modern manufacturing industries will rise from 6.5

Table 36. *Percentage contribution of the different sectors of the economy to the GDP in 1960 and 1985 and to the growth of the GDP in intervening years*

	1960	1960–65	1965–70	1970–75	1975–80	1980–85	1985
Agriculture	48.6	25.6	22.1	22.8	17.0	16.1	25.7
Forestry	2.3	1.0	0.8	0.6	0.5	0.4	0.9
Fishing	1.4	1.3	0.8	1.0	1.0	1.0	1.1
Mining	0.5	1.9	2.7	3.1	3.4	3.5	2.6
Modern manufacturing	6.6	18.2	19.0	22.5	25.3	29.7	20.9
Trad. manufacturing	4.1	3.8	1.4	1.3	0.5	0.2	1.6
Gas, electricity	0.5	2.1	4.0	4.0	4.6	5.4	3.6
Construction, commercial	2.6	8.4	8.7	6.3	8.3	7.2	6.4
Construction, non-monetized	2.2	3.0	1.7	1.8	0.7	0.9	1.5
Banking, insurance	0.7	1.4	1.6	1.7	1.9	2.3	1.6
Government product	4.4	3.4	3.3	3.3	2.9	2.9	3.4
Transport	5.3	11.9	8.8	8.5	9.3	8.7	8.2
Post, telecommunications	0.4	0.8	0.7	0.8	1.0	1.1	0.8
Rental, housing	3.1	2.7	2.0	2.3	2.4	2.5	2.6
Rental, business	0.3	0.6	1.0	0.5	1.3	1.1	0.8
Trade	8.8	12.7	9.7	8.6	8.0	8.4	8.8
Education	1.4	1.0	2.4	4.1	5.0	3.1	3.0
Health services	1.2	1.5	1.8	3.1	3.6	3.6	2.7
Other services	5.7	5.3	4.5	4.8	4.5	4.9	5.0
All goods-producing sectors	63.5	51.8	46.8	51.3	47.7	50.9	52.8
Goods-producing sectors plus gas, electricity, and construction	68.8	65.3	61.2	63.4	61.3	64.4	64.3
All service sectors	36.4	64.8	50.2	49.8	53.5	52.1	48.4
Service sectors less gas, electr., and construction	31.1	41.3	35.8	37.7	39.9	38.6	36.9
Global adjustment	0.1	–6.6	2.9	–1.0	–1.2	–3.0	–1.3

Sources: as for Table 34. Global adjustments, [0] lines (9) to (11) of Table 14, Annex IX.

to 21 per cent. Thus agriculture will remain the most important single sector of the economy during the period under review, but not for very long beyond 1985.

Another striking change can be found in the contribution of goods-producing sectors to the GDP which will fall from 63.5 per cent to 53 per cent. From an isolated point of view this seems surprising and perhaps outright improbable. But the next line of the Table shows that the goods-producing sectors plus public utilities and construction will almost maintain their share of the GDP, their contribution falling only from 69 to 66 per cent. The shift away from production of goods to production of services is, therefore, far less striking than it seems to be at first sight.

Services proper show a net gain of 6 percentage points, from 31 per cent in 1960 to 37 per cent in 1985.[10] 'Modern' services like banking and insurance, transport, communications, education, and health show a net gain of almost 7.5 percentage points. Consequently, the rising share of services is a logical consequence of the modernization of the economy and the rapid improvement in education and health services. The rise would have been sharper if there were not a simultaneous fall in the contribution of the government product, of housing, and of other consumer services to the GDP.

The figures for the contribution of goods and services respectively to the growth of the GDP in the different five-year periods show that goods (excluding public utilities and construction) consistently contribute far less to the growth of the GDP than they did in the base year 1960, whereas the services consistently contribute substantially more. The most striking change concerns gas, electricity, and construction. These sectors contributed in 1960 only 5.3 per cent to the GDP, whereas in the five following five-year periods their projected contribution is between 12 and 14.5 per cent of the growth. As a result the share of these industries will increase from 5.3 to 11.5 per cent.

A study of the contribution of the individual sectors yields some quite striking results. Unfortunately, the global adjustment disturbs the figures for the Second, Third, and Sixth Plan period considerably, but not enough to invalidate the general picture which can be obtained.

The share of agriculture in the growth of the economy falls fairly smoothly, but during the Fourth Plan it is still agriculture which is projected to contribute most to the increase of the GDP. If we combine the figures for the percentage contribution with those for the rate of growth of the GDP, we find that agriculture contributes 1.05 percentage points to the total growth of 4.1 per cent during the Second Plan, and 1.15 percentage points to the total growth of 7.2 per cent during the Sixth Plan. In terms of contribution to the rate of growth of the economy, agriculture will therefore remain important throughout the period under review. Its falling *share* reflects the increasingly strong performance by other sectors which gradually raise their share of the GDP.

Only agriculture and modern manufacturing contribute sizably to the growth of the economy. No other sector adds more than 0.6 percentage points to the rate of growth. Out of the rate of growth of 7.2 per cent during the Sixth Plan, modern manufacturing alone contributes more than 2 percentage points. It would not be right, however, to measure the importance of any one sector exclusively by its share of the national income or by the amount it adds to the rise in the national income. The smaller sectors together add more to the national income than the two large sectors do. But some of these sectors represent to a large extent, or almost exclusively, cost factors in the economy. This is true of trade and to a large extent of transport or of banking and insurance. From the point of view of what the different sectors mean for the supply of goods and services at the disposal of consumers or investors, the rapid growth of some of these sectors may be a fact to deplore rather than to rejoice over. On the other hand, any one of the sectors creates income and employment, and from this point of view growth in all sectors is a good thing. Account should merely be taken of the fact that the ultimate usefulness of the output of many sectors may be embodied in products and services from other sectors.[11]

The relative contribution of a number of sectors to the growth of the economy increases from one five-year plan period to another: mining, modern manufacturing, gas and electricity, banking and insurance, post and telecommunications (with one minor setback during the Third Plan), education (except during the Sixth Plan), and health services. Except for education and health all these sectors contribute several times more *to the growth* of the GDP during the Second Plan than they did to the GDP in 1960. These seven rapidly growing sectors represented only 11 per cent of the total GDP in 1960 — in 1985 their share will have increased to 35 per cent. Similarly, whereas they are projected to contribute 27 per cent to the growth of the GDP in the period 1960 to 1965, their contribution to growth is projected to increase to 49 per cent in the period 1980 to 1985.

These growth sectors fall in two categories, one consisting of health and education, and another which groups the other five sectors around modern manufacturing. The health and education services in Pakistan are assumed to be built up to the standards of a fairly rich country in the course of these 25 years. As has been pointed out previously, the targets are very ambitious and will require considerable sacrifices in other fields. The accelerated construction of a modern and adequate infrastructure of health and education services in a poor country must give these services a very large role in the economy of the country. Thus, during the Fifth Five-Year Plan they are estimated to contribute more than 8.5 per cent to the growth of the economy. The growth of these two services alone will add almost 0.6 per cent annually to the GDP during the period 1975 to 1980. Their share of the GDP will rise from 2.6 per cent in 1960 to 5.7 per cent in 1985. The growth of these two sectors contributes directly and very substantially to the welfare of the people. In fact, it could probably be demonstrated in one way or another that the contribution of improved education and better health services to raising welfare will far exceed the high percentages of their contribution to the GDP.[12] On the other hand, these sectors will not in the long run continue to make the same relative contribution to the growth of the GDP. In fact, the share of education will fall substantially during the Sixth Plan, and the share of health will not increase. During the following years, when health services and education will grow much more slowly, their share in the growth of the national income will fall very much. Their large contribution to growth is a temporary factor.

The same is not true of the five other sectors. Modern manufacturing is the key sector. It produces goods which are in rapidly rising demand, both for consumption and for investment purposes. The domestic manufacturing industries will not cover more than 81 per cent of domestic demand in 1985 so that the scope for further growth even without any further rapid rise of domestic demand will be large and domestic demand will undoubtedly continue to rise rapidly. Modern manufacturing industries purchase much of the output of mining, a large share of the output of gas and electricity, and are the major clients for services from the communications industry and from banking and insurance. The growth of each of these five sectors is therefore closely linked with the growth of the others. The mining industry could live a life of its own, based on exports, and does so in many poor countries. In the case of Pakistan, however, it is expected that the bulk of the output of the mining industry will be used in or processed by the manufacturing industries. The electricity and gas industries also deliver their services for final uses, but well above half of the output is estimated for use in manufacturing industry in 1985. The role of manufacturing as the leading growth sector, with strong effect on other fast growing sectors, can hardly be over-emphasized.

The contribution of some sectors to the growth of the economy fluctuates considerably, but is still very important. These sectors are commercial construction, transport, and trade.

They will contribute 33 per cent to the growth of the economy during the Second Plan, 27 per cent during the Third Plan, and 24 per cent in the Sixth Plan. Their projected share of the GDP will grow from 16.5 per cent in 1960 to 23.5 per cent in 1985, the whole rise being due to construction and transport. These three sectors are extremely important as sources of income and employment. In many respects there are great differences between these three sectors, and their role in economic growth can be discussed from many points of view.

The productive contribution of *trade* cannot be measured by the national income originating in trade — it represents costs which should be minimized. Trade margins increase the prices which the users must pay and may reduce the prices paid to the producers. Trade is nevertheless part and parcel of the productive machinery of an economy, and a very necessary industry indeed. Without the intervention of the traders, users and producers would often never get in contact with each other. The crucial point is that the better and more efficiently organized the wholesale and retail trade are, the smaller is their contribution to the national income![13] Consequently, it is not necessarily a desirable target that the trade sector should contribute an increasing proportion of the growth of the GDP. It may become an indispensable result of the economic growth, particularly if this entails a rapid move away from a subsistence economy with few trading transactions to a monetized economy in which a large proportion of consumers live in towns and must be served by the trade sector. The figures in this study reflect two conflicting tendencies — the move towards an urban economy which favours the growth of trade, and the relatively slow growth of urban consumption *per caput* which partly offsets the first effect and dampens the growth of the trade sector. Trade must inevitably remain an important sector, but its relative stagnation as shown by Table 36 (i. e. its share of the GDP will be the same in 1985 as in 1960) is not an undesirable aspect of the projected pattern of growth.

To a lesser extent the same arguments apply to transport. The bulk of the income of the transport industry is derived from moving goods from producers to users. The cheaper this move can be organized, the better. As for trade, high output of the transport industry may be a sign of inefficient use of economic resources. Some of the services offered by the transport industry are purchased by personal consumers, but a substantial proportion of these purchases does not contribute to consumer welfare but represents a source of fatigue and a deduction from their disposable earnings. Of course, the commuter prefers to pay and to be squeezed into a crowded bus or train for half an hour rather than to walk for several hours. But the ideal situation is to have one's place of work within easy walking distance. It is inevitable that the role of the transport sector in a modernizing economy will be larger. Factories have to get many of their raw materials from distant places, and must sell much of their output to consumers far away. The modernization of agriculture entails increased transport services, movement of fertilizers and other materials to farms, and the sending of products to urban and foreign markets. The growth of the share of transport in the GDP in Pakistan to a large extent represents inevitable increases in transport costs following the modernization and urbanization of the economy. Part of the growth represents a real gain to the economy, because one-eighth of transport services will be exported in 1985 against 4 per cent only in 1960.[14]

The increased share of construction in the GDP constitutes a dynamic growth factor. The factories, houses, dams, and roads which are set up by this industry add to the productive capacity and the well-being of the country. In the long run the construction industry cannot contribute such a high proportion to annual growth as in the five five-year plan periods included in this study. The growth of the construction industry depends first of all on the growth of fixed investments and secondly on the composition of investments. During the period under review investments have been projected as growing in absolute terms as well as in relation to the GDP. Moreover, the share of the modern construction industry in total fixed investments will be growing — from 47 per cent in 1960 to 50.5 in 1985, notably because projected investments in infrastructure are very important during this period. But during the same period projected purchases of equipment and other products of the modern manufacturing industries will increase from 26 per cent in 1960 to 36 per cent in 1985. The apparent gain of the commercialized construction industry is not real since it has been at the expense of the 'non-monetized' construction industry, the share of which, in fixed investments, will fall from 24 per cent to 8 per cent. It is likely that equipment, machinery, etc., will represent a growing proportion of fixed investments after 1985 and that the share of the modern construction industry must eventually fall. For the period under review the modern construction industry will undoubtedly be a major dynamic growth factor but it cannot be counted upon to play the same role indefinitely.

Some sectors — the government product, income from housing,

other services, and the fishing industry — will contribute somewhat less to the growth of the economy throughout the period
under review than they did in 1960, and consequently their share
of the GDP in 1985 will be lower than in 1960. In all cases the
reason is that the consumption demand for these sectors will grow
more slowly than the national income.

Apart from agriculture, three other sectors will contribute far
less to the GDP in 1985 than in 1960, and their share of the
growth of GDP will fall from one five-year period to another:
forestry, traditional manufacturing industries, and non-monetized
construction.[15] The case of forestry is simple — output from the
forests is bound to grow slowly during the next 20 years because
forest resources cannot be augmented very rapidly, even though
the systematic use of rapidly growing tropical trees may yield
great results over a somewhat longer period. Traditional manufacturing industries are bound to stagnate, partly because many
of them have most of their customers in rural areas where incomes will grow more slowly and partly because some of their
products will inevitably be replaced by cheaper and better products from modern manufacturing. The reason for the relatively
slow growth of non-monetized construction industry has already
been dealt with in some detail on page 140. The projected modest
contribution of this industry to the overall growth of the country
nevertheless raises important political issues. It is generally
agreed that the mobilization of unemployed or underemployed
manpower on works programmes is an excellent way of accelerating economic progress, particularly in rural areas. The figures
suggest that the overall effect of such a policy is modest.

The types of investment which are included under this heading
are manifold. It is possible that the investment effort can be accelerated in relation to what has been assumed in this study, but
such an acceleration also implies that the scope for such investments may be exhausted relatively fast. The non-monetized construction industry is in direct competition with the commercialized construction industry which has the advantage of being able
to complete many projects faster and to tackle far more complex
types of work. The vital assumption upon which this study has
been based, viz. that foreign aid will be forthcoming to an adequate extent, entails the direction of investments in such a way
that they yield relatively quick results in the form of economic
growth. This study therefore projects great possibilities for a
rapid expansion of the more sophisticated, commercial construction industry. The result is that the commercial construction industry will provide many of the jobs which on other assumptions
would have to be created in the non-monetized construction sec-

tor. The slow growth of the non-monetized construction industry is therefore not an unfavourable aspect of the development pattern which can be read out of Table 36, but on the contrary the result of optimistic assumptions as to the possibility of mobilizing surplus manpower within the framework of a modern construction industry which can tackle complex projects of great benefit to the economy.

D. *The changing structure of demand*

Table 37 suggests that there will be some rather fundamental changes in the composition of demand for available supplies (i. e. domestic gross output plus imports) of goods or services from certain sectors. These changes merit some comments. In the case of *agriculture* only a very small proportion of output is exported, which may appear surprising. The reason for this is that major export products like jute, cotton, rice, and tea are part of the deliveries of goods for intermediate use, i. e. for processing in the manufacturing industries. The remainder includes items like hides and skins, raw wool, spices, raw tobacco, etc. In 1960 most of the demand for *forest products* came from consumers in the form of purchases of firewood. Demand for industrial wood (as well as raw rubber which is included here) will rise much faster than the demand for firewood, hence the substantial shift towards intermediate demand. At the beginning of the Second Five Year Plan only a very small proportion of the output of the *fishing* industry went to modern processing plants. This is expected to change substantially during the period under review. Most of the increased export of fish is expected to be in the form of frozen fish and is therefore included under manufacturing. Whereas in 1960 almost 10 per cent of the output of the *mining* industry went directly to final uses (coal to consumers, etc.), those deliveries become increasingly unimportant. A rising proportion of the output of coal will go to industrial uses, and gas and oil will have to go through the gas industry or oil refineries (manufacturing) before they reach final or intermediate users. The most striking change in the case of the *modern manufacturing* industries is the sharp fall in the proportion of the output which goes for export, whereas the distribution of domestic demand between intermediate and final uses does not change at all. The explanation for this is simple: In 1960, 53 per cent of the exports of the manufacturing industries consisted of rice, tea, raw cotton, and raw jute, but this percentage falls to 6 in 1985. If these four products are excluded, the percentage of manufactured products which is exported rises from 9.1 to 9.5 per cent of total available manufac-

Table 37. *Changes in the structure of demand and in imports as % of total supplies.*
Percentage distribution of demand for the gross output per sector

	Inter-mediate		Final				% of total sup-plies im-ported	
			Exports		Domestic			
	1960	1985	1960	1985	1960	1985	1960	1985
Agriculture	66.8	68.7	1.1	0.3	32.1	31.0	3.3	5.8
Forestry.............	13.8	41.6	–	–	86.2	58.4	5.2	23.2
Fishing	–	9.3	8.5	5.4	91.5	85.2	–	–
Mining	89.6	98.9	1.5	0.6	8.9	0.5	24.1	23.8
Modern manufact.* ...	34.7	38.5	19.2	10.1	46.1	51.4	23.8	15.8
Trad. manufactur. ...	3.4	2.8	0.1	0.2	96.5	97.0	–	–
Electricity, gas	63.9	74.7	–	1.0	36.1	24.3	–	–
Commercial constr. ..	7.4	7.7	–	–	92.6	92.3	–	–
Non-monetiz. constr...	–	–	–	–	100	100	–	–
Banking, insurance ...	61.9	71.0	6.2	2.1	31.9	26.9	11.9	11.7
Government prod.. ...	–	–	–	–	100	100	–	–
Transport†	64.0	61.3	7.2	16.1	28.8	22.6	2.6	4.0
Communications** ...	75.4	74.8	–	–	24.6	25.2	–	–
Housing.............	–	–	–	–	100	100	–	–
Business premises	82.0	86.3	–	–	18.0	13.7	–	–
Trade††	18.6	24.6	–3.5	–3.4	84.9	78.8	–	–
Education	–	–	–	–	100	100	2.9	6.6
Health	–	–	–	–	100	100	–	–
(Other services)	–2.9	15.6	5,7	9.8	97.2	74.6	14.0	27.6
Total	33.6	38.6	4.1	5.0	62.3	56.4	6.1	8.7

Sources: Input-output Tables, Appendix I and adjustments, [0] Annex IX.
General: Demand is broken down into three items - intermediate, domestic final, and exports. Supplies correspond to the demand figures, and import ratios are therefore directly comparable with the figures for breakdown of demand.
* See also Table 42, page 212.
† Exports of transport services include transport charges paid to domestically owned enterprises in shipping and air transport on imported goods which are counted cif. under sectors of origin.
** No attempt has been made to calculate seperately exports and imports of communications services.
†† Exports of trade include domestic trade margins on exported goods less earnings on export bonus vouchers (for further explanation, see [0], Annex IX, footnote to Table 7).

tured goods. The demand for the output of *electricity and gas, banking and insurance services,* and *trade services* shows a clear shift from final to intermediate uses which is to be expected in a society which becomes less and less dominated by the subsistence sectors. The same shift also takes place in the transport sector if final domestic demand is compared with the intermediate demand. The share of intermediate demand in total demand for transport services falls because exports increase rapidly as a result of the projected rapid expansion of the international airline and shipping services. The figures for the sector *other services* do not mean very much because all global adjustments have been made to that item. It is fairly obvious, however, that the intermediate demand for the output of this sector rises much more rapidly than final demand which is mainly from personal consumers. The *total* figures show a clear shift from final to intermediate uses and a modest growth in the proportion of total supplies which is exported.

The columns which show imports as a percentage of total supplies should indicate how domestic producers manage to meet the increase in demand. The results do not appear to be very encouraging. The share of imports in *total* supplies is estimated to grow from 6 to almost 9 per cent, and, except in the case of modern manufacturing, the share of imports in supplies will rise or remain stable in the individual sectors.

It is no sign of weakness in the economy of a country that an increasing proportion of the available supplies of goods and services is imported. On the contrary, this is a natural consequence of development from a situation in which a subsistence economy is the predominant feature into one which entails interchange of goods and services inside the country and with foreign countries. The situation is more disquieting when the share of imports in total supplies rises faster than the share of exports. Even this situation can be economically sound if it results from rapid economic growth supported by an inflow of foreign capital, which on our assumptions will be the case for Pakistan in 1985.

Nevertheless it is necessary to examine why the proportion of imports to total supplies is projected as rising or remaining stable in the individual sectors. In the case of *agriculture* the reason is that the projected rise in output is not fast enough to meet the demand of a rapidly growing population which will enjoy a substantial improvement in its nutrition standard. The projected proportion of imports to total supplies is so small that marginal changes in the various assumptions in this study would eliminate imports altogether.[16]

The rapidly growing figure for imports of *forest* products reflects the poverty of forest resources. Imports of raw rubber represent more than 40 per cent of total imports of forest products in 1985. In the case of *mining* the proportion of imports to total supplies is projected as remaining fairly stable. But behind this picture of apparent stability there is a considerable change in the composition of imports of mining products. Solid fuel (i. e. coal) was the main item in 1960 — in 1985 imports will consist of ores and minerals which are not found in Pakistan and which are indispensable raw materials for many industries. The increased imports of forest and mining products are a sign of strength because they reflect a shift away from imports of finished goods to raw materials which are processed in Pakistan.

A fall of one-third is projected in the proportion of imported manufactured goods to the total supply of manufactured goods. The ratio of imports to domestic supplies less exports will fall even more. It may seem pessimistic to project a development in which only one-third of the imports of manufactured goods appears to be substituted by domestic goods in the course of a quarter of a century. But it should be stressed that this result is heavily influenced by the fact that the demand for manufactured goods in 1985 will be quite different from what it was in 1960. This is discussed in the following section.

Detailed figures have been calculated that illustrate in which industries import substitution is projected as going very far and in which it runs into serious difficulties. It should be noted that these details are by no means presented as exact projections of what may happen over twenty-five years. It is evident, for example, that imports of goods from *all* industries will take place because there will always be demand for special products which cannot easily be produced in Pakistan. In fact, no country will make itself entirely independent of imports of all kinds of manufactured goods.

These tentative figures illustrate some important problems connected with import substitution:

1. Imports of goods from the metal-working industries will continue on a large scale, primarily because it is not possible for Pakistan to expand these industries fast enough to meet total domestic demand; but even if this were possible fairly large imports of specialized products would be required.
2. The same is the case for 'miscellaneous' industries which include many highly specialized industries.
3. The wood industries and to some extent also the food-manufacturing industries cannot grow as fast as the total domestic demand due to shortage of raw materials (particularly industrial wood and milk).
4. Industries which have to be based on imported raw materials can nevertheless be expanded to satisfy domestic demand almost entirely, as soon as domestic markets grow large enough (examples include rubber industries based on imported raw rubber, the steel industry based on imported ore and coking

coal, and many chemical industries partly based on imported minerals or other raw materials).

Imports of *services* are, in general, expected to grow faster than domestic demand. This is particularly pronounced in the case of 'other services' but, as previously noted, non-specified imports of invisibles have been included under this heading so that the figures under 'other services' should not be taken at their face value. Imports of education include costs of training students abroad and of foreign teachers. In spite of rapid expansion of the domestic educational services, the need for foreign aid in education is increasing even more rapidly. This reflects the extremely rapid growth in demand for highly skilled manpower in different sectors of the economy.

E. *The import elasticity – income effect and substitution effect*

The figures contained in Table 37, and similar calculations made in more detail for the ratios of total demand for manufactured products covered by imports, permit some estimates of the import elasticity and its components, which are presented in Table 38.

Part A of the Table shows that in 1985 imports of manufactured goods will be 120 per cent higher than projected if no further import substitution takes place between 1960 and 1985, even if this will be partly offset by slower growth in imports of other goods and of services so that total imports only will be 62 per cent higher.

The average annual import elasticity is projected as high as 1.4, i. e. imports are projected as growing 40 per cent faster than the Gross Domestic Product. The rise in projected imports is particularly fast in the services sector.

The second and third columns of part B of the Table show what can be called the effect of import substitution on the import elasticity. If no import substitution were to take place between 1960 and 1985 (whereas, on the other hand, dependence on imports would not grow for any group of goods or services either), the import elasticity would turn out to be as high as 1.7. We may call this the 'income effect'. We will call the difference between this hypothetical import elasticity and the projected elasticity 'the net substitution effect on the import elasticity'. The net substitution effect on the elasticity is therefore minus 0.3, i. e. imports are projected as growing 30 per cent slower in relation to the growth of the GDP than they would have done if no substitution had taken place. In a strict sense this *net* substitution

Table 38. *Effects of import substitution on the structure of imports and on import elasticities*

A. *Imports as percentage of total use of resources in 1960 and 1985*

	1960	1985	
	Actual	Actual	Import ratios as in 1960
Manufactured goods	4.1	5.5	12.1
Other goods	1.2	1.6	1.1
Services	0.8	1.6	0.9
Total	6.1	8.7	14.1

B. *Average annual import elasticities over the period 1960 to 1985*

No further import substitution between 1960 and 1985

	Actual figures Elasticities	1960 import ratios Elasticities	'Substitution effect'
Manufactured goods	1.3	1.9	−0.6
Other goods	1.3	1.0	+0.3
Services	1.6	1.2	+0.4
Total	1.4	1.7	−0.3

Sources: Input-output Tables, Appendix I, and adjustments, [0], Annex IX.
Note that the hypothetical calculation of imports of manufactured goods in 1985 is based on the breakdown of demand for and imports of manufactured products by subsectors. The elasticities are calculated as the ratios between the average annual ('compound') growth rate of imports and the average annual rate of growth of the GDP (6.04 per cent per year).

effect is only a meaningful concept if it is assumed that it is possible to conduct an economic policy which maintains the import ratios at the same level as in 1960. This is obviously *not* possible for a number of goods and services which have to be imported such as forest products, ores and minerals, and also different types of services. On the other hand, if no further efforts were made to substitute domestically manufactured products for imported ores, the import demand for raw materials for the manufacturing industries would be lower. Consequently, the net substitution effect is still valid as an approximate measure of the effect of import substitution on the propensity to import.[17]

The economic meaning of the 'substitution effect' is highly questionable, for two widely different reasons, First, as has been pointed out in the footnote on page 155, total demand depends on the structure of domestic output mainly because almost 40 per cent of the demand for available resources in 1985 will be for intermediate goods and services, but also because a different economic structure will have some influence on the demand for goods and services for investments. Therefore any crude calculation which shows how much higher or lower imports would be if domestic demand were the same while the domestic output was different is highly speculative. Such a calculation would only be valid if all the implications of a different structure of output were calculated. Second, the import elasticity is dependent not only on the structure of domestic output but equally on the relationships between the growth of investments, savings, exports, and the Gross Domestic Product.[18] If the projected figures for import substitution were raised and all other relevant figures remained the same (investments, savings, exports), imports and the import elasticity would not be changed. In our terms, the 'substitution effect' would be higher, but so would the 'income effect', and the two changes would cancel. Other examples which imply that one or several of the other relevant figures would change can equally well be given. Thus, import substitution could lead to lower exports; and as the balance of payments deficit should remain the same (investments and savings having not been changed), lower imports would be offset by lower exports. Import substitution could lead to higher investments; and if savings (and exports) remained the same, the import surplus and imports would be higher in spite of the higher degree of import substitution. Finally, import substitution could lead to higher profits and savings; and if investments remained the same, the balance payments of deficit and imports could, in fact, be lower.

The figures which show the 'substitution effect' have therefore only the limited meaning of illustrating the changes in the rate of growth of imports which, *ceteris paribus,* are caused by the fact that a rising or falling proportion of domestic demand is met by domestic production. The figures, as presented in Table 38, therefore give some insight into the changing dependency of the economy on foreign supplies only on this *ceteris paribus* assumption.

F. *Limits to the expansion of agriculture*

Agriculture will remain the key sector in Pakistan's economy. It will provide a livelihood for a very large part of the population[19] and as late as in 1985 agriculture will contribute more than one-fourth of the total Gross Domestic Product. Slow growth in agriculture will necessarily slow down the growth of the whole economy.

Three factors limit the rate of expansion of agriculture: natural resources, human resources, and demand. In East Pakistan there is very little land available which is not already cultivated. In West Pakistan shortage of water prevents the cultivation of enormous tracts of unused land, and the scope for further improvements in irrigation is limited. All over Pakistan the peasants are on the whole illiterate and poor, and it is a Herculian task to encourage and persuade millions of peasants to adopt modern production methods which can multiply the output of the land. Ultimately the demand for agricultural output will set a limit to the extent to which production can be expanded.

In this study projected output from agriculture does not rise so fast that dangers of overproduction could result. On the contrary, as is shown in Table 37, the country will be more dependent — even in relative terms — on imports of agricultural products in 1985 than it was in 1960. The target for output from agriculture could have been set at least 10 per cent, probably 15 per cent, higher for 1985 without any danger of overproduction.[20]

If the output target for 1985 had been set 12 per cent higher than in the present study, the annual rate of growth of agriculture would have been raised from 3.4 per cent to 3.8 per cent per year for the period 1960 to 1985. The difference seems to be marginal — if the lower figure is possible, why not the higher one? But 'marginal' improvements in the productivity of agriculture are not that easy to achieve. The present projections are based on assumptions which I personally consider to be optimistic, and I will summarize these assumptions so that the reader may pass his own judgement on the projections.

These figures show:

1. that in East Pakistan methods must be found to increase the double (or triple) cropped areas from 40 per cent of the sown area to 87 per cent, while at the same time the sown area must be increased by 20 per cent from 21 million acres to 25.4 million acres;
2. that in West Pakistan water must be found to irrigate another 19 million acres annually;[21]
3. that in both provinces a substantial proportion of very poor pastures will be improved;
4. that the output per acre in the period 1965 to 1985 will increase by 15 per cent per five-year period (or more than 70 per cent over the 20-year period);
5. that in order to achieve this the use of fertilizers will increase

almost 100 times in East Pakistan and almost 50 times in West Pakistan; and

6. that the output of milk and meat will increase many times as a result of great improvements in animal husbandry.

Assumption 2 is unrealistic, and it has therefore been assumed that yield per acre in West Pakistan will increase more than 15 per cent per five-year period, in order to offset the shortage of water which limits the expansion of the cropped area.[22] Significant increases in output per acre in West Pakistan can be expected as a result of large schemes to curtail water logging and salinity.

Table 39. *Basic assumptions behind estimates of output in agriculture*

	East Pakistan 1960	East Pakistan 1985	West Pakistan 1960	West Pakistan 1985
A. *Land use in East and West Pakistan* (1,000 acres)				
Area under major crops	24,180	35,795	28,533	36,905
of which				
Rice	21,151	23,250	2,937	2,600
Wheat	138	1,240	12,092	16,800
Maize................................	7	6,700	1,110	2,580
Area under minor crops	5,220	6,600	4,025	7,600
Area under new fodder plants	0	2,500	0	7,000
Total area under crops	29,400	44,900	32,560	51,500
Double cropping needed East Pakistan *	8,400	19,450		
Improved pastures	0	1,020	0	3,730
B. *Changes in yields*	(yields in tons per acre.)			
Rice	0.40	0.72	0.33	0.68
Wheat	0.21	0.36	0.31	0.60
C. *Use of fertilizers* (Rs mill.)				
On major and minor crops	16	1,420	32	1,135
On pastures	0	120	0	355
D. *Output of milk and meat – absolute figures, and per animal.* 1,000 tons				
Milk	1,000	5,650	5,300	14,050
Meat	115	390	225	775
Number of animals, weighted (1960 = 100) ...	100	140	100	150
Output per animal (1960 = 100)				
Milk	100	400	100	175
Meat	100	240	100	230

Sources: [0], Annex VI, Tables 16, 17, 23, 24, 25, and 30.
* In fact, part of the area may be under triple cropping.

Between 1960 and 1985 the projected *gross* output of crops will rise by 143 per cent in East Pakistan and by 179 per cent in West Pakistan, and the gross output of livestock products by 350 per cent in East and 180 per cent in West Pakistan. Inputs will have to grow faster than gross output, so that the projected *value added* from crop production will increase by 120 per cent in East and 145 per cent in West Pakistan whereas the value added from livestock will increase by 225 per cent in East and 85 per cent in West Pakistan. It is important to note these rather striking differences between the rate of increase in the gross output and in the value added. The modernization of agriculture implies much more use of purchased inputs. This development cannot take place unless the peasant is given incentives to make such purchases. Share cropping is a serious disincentive because purchases of current inputs (fertilizers and others) may represent as much as 25 per cent of the added output, to which must be added depreciation costs of modern machinery and equipment. In the case of livestock production, present prices are probably too low to encourage better feeding. The price data which are available are not very satisfactory, but they do suggest that the profit derived from purchasing feed grain for more intensive production of milk and meat is very small, if not outright non-existent. The assumed modernization of animal husbandry in Pakistan therefore seems to entail higher prices to the farmers, and, unless these higher prices are offset by government subsidies, also higher prices to be paid by the consumers. This should be kept in mind when judging the implied expenditure elasticities for livestock products.[23] At *current* prices these may become higher than at constant prices.

The projected expansion of agricultural income in Pakistan is almost exclusively based on the expansion of domestic demand for food. Of the total projected increase of gross agricultural output between 1960 and 1985, just above 50 per cent represents major crops except textile fibres, 28 per cent livestock products, 15 per cent minor crops (of which fruit and vegetables are very important), and only 6 per cent textile fibres. The growth of agriculture depends, on these assumptions, on a fairly rapid growth of domestic consumption. It has been shown (Table 17) that if rural consumption per head stagnates and economic progress takes place mainly in urban areas, food consumption will grow much less than projected in this study. In one way this means that agriculture can pull itself up by its own bootstraps — higher income in agriculture would lead to higher rural consumption and higher food consumption and thereby higher demand for agricultural products. But this assumes that the higher physical output in agriculture will in fact result in higher income, and that the rural population is not forced to save an unreasonably large proportion of its additional income.

The second condition for the projected growth of agricultural income is that the output of livestock products will rise rapidly. If most or all of the increase in agricultural output takes the form of foodgrains and other plant products, the domestic markets will probably not be able to absorb the increased output. Only if there is a shift towards a more varied diet is it reasonable to assume that total food consumption will increase as much as is shown in Chapter 5.

The final question which should be put is whether it would be possible to base an expansion of agriculture on a large-scale export programme, so that farm output could expand regardless of what happened on the domestic market. If it were reasonable to assume that Pakistan was one of the few now less-developed countries which could manage to expand its output of food rapidly and that more slowly developing countries had foreign exchange available for large-scale food imports, then Pakistan could happily plan to expand its output of food-grains and other food products destined for exports. However, this study is made in the context of the general assumption that most less developed countries will manage to get their economies off the ground which implies that most of the other poor countries will be able to solve their food problem as rapidly as Pakistan. For this reason the food and textile projections for Pakistan must be mainly based on domestic demand. (Jute is, of course, excepted, and for cotton it has been assumed that exports of cotton goods and hence production of raw cotton can be expanded substantially. Other exceptions could be mentioned, such as the promising export of fine rice.)

G. *The changing face of modern manufacturing*

The central role of modern manufacturing in the economic growth process of Pakistan has already been discussed in considerable detail. Manufacturing is the only sector where projected output covers a substantially higher proportion of the country's needs in 1985 than in 1960.

Modern manufacturing consists of so many completely different industries that it is useful to look into the pattern of industrial growth.

The upper part of Table 40 shows that over the twenty-five year period, growth will be very unevenly distributed. Thus the petrochemical industry will grow 20 times as fast and the basic metals industry 10 times as fast as the textile industries. These

Table 40. *Rates of growth of modern manufacturing industries*

	1960	1965	1970	1975	1980	1985
A. Growth of value added (1960 = 100)						
Food manufacturing ..	100	166	277	449	727	1,195
Beverages	100	171	305	527	1,045	2,291
Tobacco	100	127	201	325	560	950
Textiles	100	141	194	272	380	512
Footwear	100	142	224	373	650	1,178
Clothing	100	353	811	1,468	2,426	3,690
Printing, publishing ..	100	138	224	385	690	1,332
Wood products	100	183	562	1,014	1,711	2,669
Pulp, paper, paper prod.	100	215	381	668	1,114	2,047
Leather, leather goods.	100	153	210	300	425	625
Rubber goods	100	282	624	1,409	2,674	5,705
Chemicals	100	209	434	783	1,263	2,000
Petrochemicals	100	623	1,477	3,531	5,990	10,727
Non-met. minerals prod.	100	237	514	901	1,644	2,830
Basic metals	100	278	928	1,629	2,922	5,418
Metal working	100	158	304	619	1,208	2,336
Cotton ginning, jute bal.	100	114	128	137	141	148
Misc. industries	100	142	216	416	821	1,642
Total	100	161	281	478	806	1,378

B. *Growth of value added, annual (compound) rate per five-year period and per whole period*

	1960–65	1965–70	1970–75	1975–80	1980–85	1960–85
Food manufacturing	10.6	10.8	10.2	10.1	10.4	10.4
Beverages	11.4	12.2	11.6	14.7	17.0	13.3
Tobacco	5.0	9.5	10.1	11.5	11.1	9.4
Textiles	7.2	6.5	7.0	6.9	6.1	6.7
Footwear, clothing	8.7	10.8	11.0	11.5	12.1	10.8
Wood products...........	12.8	25.5	12.5	11.1	9.3	14.0
Pulp, paper, paper prod. ..	16.5	12.2	11.9	10.8	12.9	12.8
Printing, publishing	6.7	10.1	11.5	13.4	14.0	10.9
Leather and leather goods .	8.8	6.6	7.4	7.2	8.1	7.6
Rubber goods	23.0	17.2	17.7	13.7	16.4	17.5
Chemicals	15.9	15.8	12.6	10.0	9.6	12.7
Petrochemicals	44.1	18.9	19.0	11.2	12.4	20.0
Non-met. minerals prod. ..	18.8	16.8	11.9	12.8	11.5	14.3
Basic metals	22.7	27.3	12.0	12.4	13.1	17.4
Metal working	9.5	14.1	15.3	14.3	14.1	13.4
Cotton ginning, jute bal....	2.7	2.3	1.4	0.5	1.0	1.6
Miscellaneous industries ...	7.3	18.2	14.0	14.6	14.9	11.5
All modern manufacturing .	10.0	11.8	11.3	11.0	11.3	11.1

Sources: Input-output Tables, Appendix I.

cases may be regarded as exceptional since initial production was very small. But industries like the pulp and paper industries and the non-metallic mineral goods industries which contained large, modern units in 1960 are also expected to expand four to five times as fast as the textile industries.

The lower part of the Table helps to interpret the picture given in the upper half. It shows that the average annual growth rate ranges between 6.7 per cent for the textile industries to 17.4 and 17.5 per cent for the basic metal and rubber goods industries. The cotton-ginning and jute-baling industries are a special case at the lower end of the scale, whereas the rate of growth of the petro-chemical industry is above 20 per cent because the industry consisted of only a very small petroleum refinery in 1960.

Most of the sectors are projected as growing more than 10 per cent per year on an average. The exceptions merit some special comments. The cotton-ginning industry will grow in line with the increase in the output of raw cotton whereas the jute-baling industry will decline as exports of raw jute decline. This sub-sector would in any case grow relatively slowly, but the growth rate is exceptionally low due to the fall in exports of raw jute. The rate of growth of the textile industries is in fact high, taking into account that growth is based on consumer demand and on export demand. As personal consumption expenditure is projected as rising more slowly than national income, and as new export markets are hard to find, the rate of growth can hardly be expected to exceed 7 per cent annually. The growth of the leather and leather goods industry over the period as a whole is dependent on domestic supplies of hides and skins, although some additional growth can be permitted because in 1960 a significant part of domestic supplies was exported as raw hides and skins. The tobacco industry was already well developed in 1960 (Pakistan was virtually self-sufficient in cigarettes), and the scope for growth is therefore limited.

In the case of industries where the projected growth rate is faster than 10 per cent annually, it can be noted that in most five-year periods the rate of growth is between 10 and 15 per cent. The exceptions have the following background: The wood industries will grow fast as soon as the building of modern saw mills is under way, replacing traditional hand sawing. The rubber goods industry is expected to grow particularly fast during the Second Five-Year Plan period when production of tyres and tubes for motor vehicles will be started. The growth of the petrochemical industry is particularly rapid during the first five-year periods, partly because a refinery to cover a large part of domestic consumption was set up early during the Second Five-Year Plan period and partly because of the assumption that oil will be found in Pakistan and will be refined there. The basic metals industry will grow very fast during the Second and Third Plan periods when an integrated steel industry is scheduled to be set up. The non-metallic minerals goods industry will also grow particularly rapidly during the first ten years under review, partly because of the fast expansion of investments which require large additional supplies of cement and partly because a large-scale modern brick industry is expected to be started.

The exceptionally high growth rates for certain industries have therefore a reasonable explanation, and so have the 'low' rates of growth in certain other industries. With the exception of the cotton-ginning and jute-baling industries, the normal situation in most five-year periods is that the most rapidly growing industries do not grow much more than twice as fast *per year* as the slowest growing ones. As the upper half of the Table shows, however, these differences in growth *rates* add up to very considerable differences in total growth over a twenty-five-year period.

The importance of a given industry for the overall rate of industrial growth of the country depends both on its own rate of growth and on its initial share of total industrial output.

A few very striking changes are projected in the structure of modern manufacturing. The combined share of seven industries in total output will fall by 32 per cent of total output. Most of this fall is accounted for by the textile industries, and most of the remainder by the cotton-ginning and jute-baling industries. In both cases the trend suggests that their share will continue to decline also beyond 1985. The relative decline of the other five industries is modest (except in the case of leather industries which, however, count for little in absolute terms) and at least two of them, clothing and footwear, and printing and publishing, may increase their share again after 1985.

The steady decline of the importance of the textile industry is a direct consequence of its very large share in the base year 1960. Such a large share cannot be maintained in the long run unless total industrial growth is fairly slow. The cotton textile industry is the first example of a very significant success in the modern industrial field in Pakistan. Its development started as late as 1952—53, but already in 1955 it assured reasonably adequate supplies of cotton yarn and cloth for the domestic consumers and in 1959 it earned large amounts of foreign exchange on exports. The falling share of the textile industries is not a tale of the failure of the textile industries but one of the success of other industries.[24] The growth of the jute industry was equally impressive.

The metal-working industries[25] will gradually gain the position of the most important of the modern manufacturing industries. In the period 1980 to 1985 these industries are projected as contributing 9 per cent to the total growth of the GDP, that is,

Table 41. *Modern manufacturing industries:*
Percentage contribution of various subsectors to total output in 1960
and 1985 and to the growth of output in intervening years

	1960	1960–65	1965–70	1970–75	1975–80	1980–85	1985
Food manufacturing	9.0	9.7	8.4	7.9	7.7	7.4	7.8
Beverages	0.3	0.3	0.3	0.3	0.5	0.6	0.5
Tobacco	4.6	2.1	2.9	2.9	3.3	3.1	3.2
Textile	36.2	24.5	16.0	14.4	11.9	8.4	13.5
Footwear, clothing	2.0	1.6	1.7	1.7	1.9	2.0	1.9
Wood products...........	0.8	1.1	2.5	1.8	1.7	1.3	1.5
Pulp, paper etc.	2.2	4.0	3.0	3.1	2.9	3.5	3.2
Printing, publishing	2.9	1.8	2.1	2.4	2.7	3.3	2.8
Leather, leather goods.....	0.8	0.7	0.4	0.4	0.3	0.3	0.4
Rubber goods	0.6	1.8	1.8	2.4	2.3	3.2	2.5
Chemicals	8.3	14.8	15.7	14.8	12.2	10.7	12.1
Petrochemicals	0.4	3.2	2.7	3.9	2.8	3.1	2.9
Non-met. minerals prods...	4.4	9.8	10.2	8.6	10.0	9.1	9.0
Basic metals	1.9	5.5	10.3	6.7	7.5	8.3	7.5
Metal working	15.8	15.4	19.5	25.4	28.5	31.3	26.9
Cotton ginning, jute bal....	6.8	1.6	0.7	0.4	0.1	0.1	0.7
Misc. industries	3.0	2.1	1.8	3.0	3.7	4.3	3.6
Four largest contributors* .	69.3|	64.5	61.5	63.2	62.6	59.5|	61.5
Industries classified by products† ...							
Consumer goods	55.8	40.7	31.8	30.0	28.3	25.1	30.1
Investment goods.........	21.0	26.3	32.2	35.8	40.2	41.7	37.4
Intermediate goods	20.2	30.9	34.2	31.2	27.8	28.9	28.9
Mixed goods	3.0	2.1	1.8	3.0	3.7	4.3	3.6
N.B. Share of the modern manufacturing industries in GDP or in the growth of GDP	6.6	18.2	19.0	22.5	25.3	29.7	20.9

Sources: Input-output Tables, Appendix I.
* Four largest contributors: 1960, Textiles, metal working, chemicals, and food manufacturing. In 1985 and in all intervening periods (except 1965 to 1970, the non-metallic mineral goods industries take the place of food manufacturing. In 1965 to 1970, basic metals replace temporarily the non-metallic minerals goods industries.

† Classification by products: *Consumer goods:* Food, beverages, tobacco, textiles, footwear, clothing, printing and publishing, leather and leather goods. *Investment goods:* Wood products, non-metallic minerals goods products, and metal working industries. *Intermediate goods:* Pulp, paper, paper products, rubber goods, chemicals, petrochemicals, basic metals, cotton ginning, jute baling. *Mixed goods:* Miscellaneous industries.

they will contribute more than any other sector of the economy except agriculture (see Table 36). Demand is unlikely to set a limit to the expansion of the metal-working industries in Pakistan before the end of this century, provided that the economy grows rapidly. The limit is set by the ability to mobilize enough human resources to run these industries economically and to produce high quality goods. They require very skilled management which is able to plan the production process, to design or choose the right products, and to supervise and train an army of skilled workers. In this study it has been assumed that the shortage of management and skilled workers will limit the expansion of these industries to doubling of the output per five-year period (or an annual rate of growth close to 15 per cent).

Other industries which will increase their share of total industrial output by 4 per cent or more are the basic metal industries (i. e. mainly the steel industry), the non-metallic mineral goods industries (which mainly produce building materials), and the chemical industries (the products of which are needed in most sectors of the economy). These industries may reach their peak shares of total industrial output during the period under review — the chemical industries already by 1975. The reason for this is that they are expected to meet fully domestic demand fairly early during the period under review, and the demand for their products will probably not rise noticeably faster than total demand for manufactured goods after 1985.[26]

The classification of industries according to the use of their products is tentative and differs from other classifications which are used. The criteria employed here are based on the input-output Table for 1958. The industries are classified according to the destination of the largest part of their output in that year. An exception is made for leather, the intermediate use of which is almost exclusively in a consumer goods industry, and for wood products which are used to a very large extent in the construction industry. Steel is usually classified under capital goods. Here it has been included under intermediate goods. This is a useful deviation from the traditional classification since it helps to offset the significant error which results from classifying all metalworking industries under investment goods industries.[27]

The overall picture which is obtained from the figures in Table 41 is certainly plausible — there will be a substantial change in industrial output away from consumer goods to investment goods, and the output of intermediate products will become far more important than in 1960. The industrial base will gradually be broader in the sense that more subsectors will contribute substantially to industrial growth and total industrial output. This statement seems to be contradicted by the line in Table 41 which shows the contribution of the four largest industry groups to value added. This figure is, however, heavily influenced by the rapid growth of the metal-working industry. If this group is excluded from the four largest contributors, their share can be shown to fall from 60 per cent in 1960 to 42 per cent in 1985.

Table 42 shows the changes in the structure of demand for manufactured goods (excluding those produced by the traditional industries) and the proportion of manufactured goods which will be imported.

The most striking changes in the structure of demand (apart from the very sharp relative fall in the demand for ginned cotton and baled jute) are the sharp fall in the share of the textile industries and the increase in the share of the metal-working industries. These changes have to a large extent their explanation in

Table 42. *Percentage distribution of the demand on the gross output of the different modern manufacturing industries. The share of demand which is covered by imports*

	Share of each industry in total demand		Share of imports in demand	
	1960	1985	1960	1985
Food manufacturing	14.7	18.3	6.6	8.5
Beverages	0.1	0.3	0	0
Tobacco	2.0	1.9	0	0
Textiles	20.6	10.6	0	0
Footwear, clothing	1.2	1.5	8.8	0.8
Wood products....................	0.5	1.9	29.5	44.2
Pulp, paper, paper products.........	1.7	2.4	26.1	4.9
Printing, publishing	1.3	1.6	0	0
Leather, leather goods..............	1.2	0.6	0	0
Rubber goods	0.7	1.9	55.0	0
Chemicals	7.0	9.0	43.7	13.5
Petrochemicals	3.6	3.4	89.4	0
Non-metallic minerals products.......	2.4	4.9	20.9	0.5
Basic metals	4.0	6.1	70.8	6.5
Metal working	18.2	28.5	55.2	34.2
Cotton ginning, jute baling	17.7	3.5	0.5	3.8
Misc. industries	2.0	2.6	43.8	28.3
Non-specified (imports only)	1.1	1.0	100.0	100.0
Total	100.0	100.0	23.8	15.8

Sources: Input-output Tables, (Appendix I) and, for final modifications of the figures, [0], Annex IX (these modifications include a slight increase of non-specified imports of manufactured goods, and a significant reduction of the imports (and demand) of goods from the metal-working industries.)

the relative shift of demand from consumption goods to capital goods. Simultaneously there will be a shift in the structure of demand to consumer goods produced by the metal-working industries (cars, bicycles, radios and TV sets, and various appliances). The share of some consumer-goods industries in total demand (e. g. food manufacturing) will rise because of the increasing degree of urbanization which entails a shift in demand from agriculture and the traditional food-manufacturing industries to modern food industries.

The changes in import ratios show the effects of import substitution. The wood products and the food industries are expected to suffer from shortage of domestic raw materials (lumber, milk, and raw materials for vegetable oils) so that they will cover a smaller proportion of total domestic demand in 1985 than in 1960. The figures for the metal-working industries illustrate the difficulty these industries will have in catching up with domestic demand, and support the inference that the growth of these industries will not be impeded by inadequate demand, at any rate until the end of this century.

The relatively rapid rise in the demand on the wood product industries and the non-metallic minerals goods industries is partly explained by a shift in demand from traditional to modern industries, but part of the rise is caused by the sharp increase in construction activities during the period under review.

H. *The pattern and the dynamics of growth*

It would be a mistake to point at the most rapidly growing sectors of the economy and state that these are the main causes of the rapid economic growth which is projected for Pakistan up to 1985. Economic growth stands on two legs — demand and production. Without expanding demand, present or expected in the near future, output will not expand either. On the other hand, increase in demand is useless if the producers do not respond by raising their output.

It is futile to ask which comes first, demand or production. The two factors are closely interlinked. In the present analysis demand has been put first because interest is centred around the question how an economy will develop if it responds adequately to a given rise in demand. But demand will not materialize (with some qualifications) if output does not rise in such a way that it generates the income and the demand which is the underlying assumption of the study.

To some extent it is true that increased output creates demand for itself. This is noticeably the case for subsistence agriculture.

Within the limits set by the starvation level and the 'full' satisfaction for food, fluctuations in the output of substistence agriculture will be followed by similar fluctuations in the consumption of food. If the harvest fails, the curious situation develops that the fall in output will result in increased demand for the products of the monetized sector of the economy. This is only possible in a modern society in which the government has the means to offer famine relief, by purchasing food outside the famine area and delivering it practically free of charge to the starving peasants. On the other hand, if the output of subsistence agriculture exceeds what traditionally can be consumed by the farmers themselves, the increased output will not lead to increased demand for farm products but for other products which the peasants will buy in exchange for their surpluses. In the case of all other sectors of the economy, increased output, if sold, will result in demand for the output of other sectors, with only a small fraction of the increased income initially or indirectly being spent on the output of its sector of origin. The scale of the increased output of any given sector is therefore dependent on whether other sectors will also increase their output and income and spend enough of their income on the increased output of the given sector. The input-output analysis helps to trace these inter-relationships between the different producing and using sectors of the economy, but it cannot tell which sectors are the prime movers of economic growth.

Input-output Tables give a static picture of the economy. They represent a photograph of the economy at a given point of time — the fact that the shutter of the camera is kept open for a whole year does not alter this essential truth. To arrive at a dynamic picture of the economy, it is necessary to study not only the rates of growth but also the rates of changes in the rates of growth. Mathematically this can be done in a neat manner by using calculus which allows a study of changes in indefinitely small intervals. Such mathematical analyses can throw considerable light on many growth phenomena. In practical terms, however, it is not possible to break down the growth process in periods shorter than a year. The year represents a fundamental reality in the important sector of agriculture. It does not matter very much whether the 'year' is counted from 1 January or, say, 22 May although in different parts of the world the logical beginning of an agricultural year may differ considerably. The seasonal changes in the course of the year are also important for most other sectors. In a northern country the use of electricity will vary considerably with the seasons. The output of education depends on the school year. Manufacturing, transport, and trade are influenced by seasonal movements. It becomes imperative therefore to measure annual changes in order to study economic growth.

The dynamic analysis contained in this study is apparently very simple and unsophisticated. No attempt has been made to express the dynamism in the form of mathematical formulas containing multi-degree derivatives. Nevertheless this is a dynamic analysis and it is based on the rates of change of demand and of domestic output. The changes in demand are calculated on the basis of the presumed *global* changes in domestic output and income. The *detailed* changes in domestic output and income represent the response of producers to the changes in demand. As has been seen, this approach as used in the present study means that the ultimate global changes in output and income differ from the initially presumed changes, since domestic producers may be found to respond more or less readily to the challenge of demand than initially implied.

If it is kept in mind that the pattern of growth of output is not only determined by the capacities of the different sectors to grow, but also by the demand for goods or services from each individual sector, it is possible to go back to the figures in Tables 34 to 36 and give them a broader interpretation. It can then be said that the development of demand favours an extremely rapid expansion of the gas and electricity industry, and that this industry will prove capable of meeting the rapid increase in demand, and that it therefore will contribute significantly to the growth of the economy. In contrast it can be said that the demand for the output of the traditional industries is only going to increase slowly, and that these industries therefore will be unable to contribute very much to the overall growth. These two statements could not be based on Table 34 alone — we have to know something about why the growth of one sector is projected much slower than the growth of another sector. Thus, the fact that agriculture is expected to expand by only 130 per cent and forestry only by 75 per cent over the 25-year period does not by itself in any way prove that demand for the products of these two sectors will not allow a steeper increase. In these two cases the relatively slow growth is due to scarce natural resources and the slow adaptability of the labour force. On the other hand, the value added in mining and in modern manufacturing industries projected shows a very fast growth. This does not mean that these two industries will manage to meet the total demand for their products. Also in these two cases it is the scarcity of natural and human resources which sets the limit to the rate of growth. The sectors or the subsectors which contribute most to the growth of the economy are those in which the two conditions converge — large and rapidly rising demand, and a large capacity for production which can be expanded to meet the increasing demand.

The extent to which each sector contributes to economic growth is strongly dependent on technical factors. In a primitive primary sector the value added is approximately equal to the gross output. If such a sector is modernized its output may rise sharply, but only a part of the additional output may be shown as increased value added in the primary sector itself. The rest will represent inputs purchased from other sectors, and will be shown as additional value added in a number of sectors and, in part, as additional imports. Which sector or which sectors have initiated the growth? Is it the primary sector which has modernized itself and has increased its output or the 'supporting' sectors which have made possible the increased output of the primary sector? The answer is clearly that all the sectors have contributed to the additional output, in proportion to their increased value added. It must be kept in mind that hardly any sector can be expanded at will; its expansion will to a large extent depend on the pattern of growth of the economy as a whole. Growth in the sectors which mainly deliver goods or services for final uses depends on the proportion between investments and consumption in total final demand, and on the changes in the structure of consumer demand as well as in investment demand. Growth in the sectors which mainly deliver their output for intermediate uses depends almost entirely on changes which take place in the industrial structure of the economy.

The *stimulus* to growth must come from increased demand. In practically all countries with a modern economic sector demand increases, partly because of population growth and partly because income per head rises. In the short run there will be cyclical or other fluctuations around the trend. The less-developed countries are characterized by having a comparatively small modern sector which does not grow fast enough to ensure any appreciable growth — in some cases the growth has been too slow to allow the average *per caput* income to rise. The problem which these countries face is the need to *raise* the rate of growth, which in turn entails the need to *accelerate* the increase in demand.

Any one economic unit is subject to restraints which limit its ability to increase its level of demand by independent action. These restraints are determined by the degree of dependency on imports and on the flexibility of the economy. The smallest economic unit is the family unit. A family which is fully integrated in a monetized economy is almost fully dependent on 'imports'. Such a family cannot in the long run raise its demand without increasing its 'exports' or, in plain terms, without earning more money so that it can buy more goods and services.[28]

An independent country, with a banking system of its own, can raise demand initially by pumping out more money. The effects of such a step on the domestic rate of growth are clearly dependent on the initial dependency on imports and on the flexibility of the economy. If the country in the initial position already imports a large proportion of its supplies of goods and services — which is the case for most small countries regardless of whether they are highly developed or underdeveloped — increased domestic demand will only partly result in higher domestic output. The rest of demand will be directed towards imports, which means that the country, like the monetized family unit, will use its 'savings' of foreign exchange. The economy of an underdeveloped country which is dominated by a large and inflexible subsistence sector may import relatively little in the initial position but additional demand will result in a large increase in imports because the subsistence sector cannot respond to the increased demand and the 'modern' sector is too small and not diversified enough to absorb the demand.[29]

Within certain limits a country can increase its domestic demand without a significant increase in its imports if the increased demand is not created indiscriminately through higher money incomes but through a strategic channelling of demand in directions which will stimulate domestic output. An underdeveloped country can, for example, start large-scale public works, which in part are financed by taxes on imported goods so that the effect on imports is reduced as much as possible. But the limits are very narrow. If the country is short of food in the initial position, the additional demand for food which is created through the payment of wages to construction workers will have to be met by additional imports. The inflexibility of subsistence agriculture sets a limit to almost any form for increase in domestic demand, unless strict rationing of food is imposed and the additional demand is ruthlessly channelled in the direction of domestic goods and services the output of which can be increased.

Let it be assumed that a country can surmount the difficulties and increase domestic demand in such a manner that domestic output will increase correspondingly. It will not be very long before it will become necessary to carry through a diversified investment programme in order to sustain the higher rate of growth over a protracted period of time. A country which may be able to carry through a simple, but large, investment programme in public works and thereby stimulate economic growth, will not necessarily have enough productive capacity to follow up the initial effort with a much broader investment programme. Even though imports of consumer goods may be held in check, the need for imports of capital goods will become pressing. In some form or other the inflexibility of the economy will set a limit to autonomous action of the country to stimulate growth through a well-designed policy of stimulating demand.

It is at this point that the need to expand foreign exchange earnings enters the picture. If *exports* can be expanded rapidly, and if appropriate steps are taken to increase domestic savings, it is theoretically possible for a poor country to carry through its own development policy without foreign aid or capital imports. But increased exports are not easily realized by a country with an inflexible economy. Firstly, if the economy is inflexible, increased exports may mean reduced domestic supplies. In the aggregate, however, it is possible to achieve increased exports on this basis if domestic demand is reduced through higher savings. Secondly, it is very difficult for a country in this situation to find markets for increased exports because its industrial structure will probably lack growth industries for which world demand is increasing rapidly.

In most developing countries capital imports and foreign aid are therefore the only practical alternative. Capital imports and foreign aid give far more freedom of action. The government of a developing country does not, in this case, have to limit its imports so strictly that there will be a scarcity of consumer goods as well as of essential capital equipment. Inflow of foreign capital, through investment or aid, will allow a country to modernize its economy, make this more flexible, build up competitive export industries, and strengthen its own capital goods industries. The present growth model for Pakistan is built on the assumption of ample foreign aid. Foreign aid will allow investment programmes to be continued which will only yield benefits in a relatively distant future. The immediate impact on demand can be offset through higher imports.

At the same time a large part of the demand created by the investment programmes will directly or indirectly stimulate demand for many of the goods and services produced by Pakistan's own economic sectors. More investments not only mean more imports of machinery and equipment but more work for the construction workers in the country, more output from cement factories and brick works, more transport of building materials, and, indirectly, as incomes are earned in these expanded activities, further increases in effective demand both for domestic and imported products. And more activity will be created in trade and transport regardless of whether the goods bought are domestic or imported.

The essential dynamic element in the economic growth of Pakistan as projected in this study is precisely investments in dams, factories, irrigation canals, power stations, roads and harbours, and not least in human resources in the form of better educated children and youth. These investments will be made to meet demand in the future — not always a distant future, but often several years ahead. The resulting pattern of growth, as outlined in Tables 34 to 36, is one which corresponds to this process of modernizing the economy in anticipation of future economic growth. It should be pointed out once more that this pattern of growth is based on the assumption that foreign aid will take care of the deficit on the balance of payments. On this assumption the projected pattern is one of efficient response to the challenge of demand — demand for consumer goods and services as well as for investment purposes.

9. Total Investments and Capital-Output Ratios

A. 'Autonomous' and 'induced' investments

The concept of 'autonomous' investments as used in this study is defined and discussed in Chapter 7. For reasons of convenience 'autonomous' investments were defined within very wide limits and included some investments which equally well could have been classified as 'induced' investments. Induced investments undertaken in a given sector in the course of a given period of time consist of:

1. Investments in new or expanded capacity in order to achieve the postulated growth of output linked with the investments in the chosen period;[1] and
2. Replacement investments which are needed to maintain the existing productive capacity.

The sum of new investments and investments for replacement purposes represents the minimum amount of investments which are needed to achieve a given increase in output on the assumption that the productive capacity will be reasonably fully and efficiently utilized. If, initially, existing productive capacity is under-utilized, it follows that some increase in output can be obtained without investments. The existence of unused capacity does not create any serious problems for our estimates, since whatever unused capacity existed in 1960 will be very small in relation to new investments over the next 25 years. Efficient utilization, however, constitutes a far more complex problem. In so-called operation-controlled industries capacity will normally be efficiently utilized, although an inexperienced labour force may cause frequent breakdowns of the machinery and thus reduce the output below normal levels. In industries in which skilled management and skilled labour are both important there is in a developing country a wide margin between the performance of new factories and other new productive units and full and efficient utilization of capacity. It is not possible to estimate with any degree of precision the efficency rating of capacity utilization and how this changes over time. In this study I have estimated capital-output ratios for subsectors based on less than fully efficient utilization of new capacity during the earlier five-year plan periods under review, but assumed that there will be a gradually improved capacity utilization during the later five-year periods. This is one of the reasons why in this study it has been found that the capital-output ratios for individual subsectors will fall with time.[2]

The general assumption behind the figures for induced investments which are shown in this chapter is therefore that the new capacity will in most cases be utilized as fully as is technically possible, i. e. that there will be few cases of investments in capacity which remains partly unused due to marketing difficulties. The figures for induced investments therefore represent minimum investment needed to achieve the projected pattern of growth.[3]

B. *Different ways of calculating investments for different sectors*

It should be kept in mind that the purpose of this study is not to make precise predictions of what will happen in the different sectors of the economy. The purpose is to get a global picutre which takes into account the diversity of economic development. It follows from this that more effort had to be put into estimates of output and investments for sectors which account for a large proportion of investments than for sectors which merely represent a small share of the total demand for investment goods. Thus, far more detailed estimates were needed for agriculture, manufacturing, electricity production and transmission, gas transmission, and transport than for forestry, fishing, trade, or construction.

With few exceptions, the estimates of induced investments are based on sector capital-output ratios. In some cases these ratios are derived directly, as the ratio between the investments in expansion of capacity and the increase in value added (with appropriate adjustments for time lags and for investments to replace existing capacity). In other cases the investment costs are calculated on the basis of the expansion of the physical capacity (investments per additional ton of cement, per ton of additional refined mineral oils products, or per additional KWh generated, etc.) with the same type of adjustments for time lags and replacements. Finally, in yet other cases investments in certain key types of capital equipment have been calculated directly (storage capacity for grain, new railway engines or coaches, tonnage of new ships, etc.). In all cases, however, there is a clearly defined link between the increase in output and the investment in expansion.

But some investments have been calculated independently of the increased output — such as investments in irrigation and flood control in agriculture, investments in reforestation, in improved ports and airports, etc. The link between increased output and investment is still present, but it is often vaguely defined.[4] These investments are therefore of a nature approaching the autonomous investments dealt with in Chapter 7.

Special assumptions regarding time lags and replacements have been used only for some sectors for which these two factors are very important. For manufacturing industries, for example, capital-output ratios for all subsectors, and even for some individual

Table 43. *Methods of estimating induced investments by sectors*

Method	Sector or subsector
1. Ratio gross investment to increase in value added five-year periods. No adjustment for time lag, no specific figure for replacements	*Fisheries* (broken down into subsectors); *Mining* (other than coal, petroleum, and natural gas); *Modern construction; Banking and insurance; Air transport; 'Other' transport services* (except ports); *Trade; 'Other' services; Business premises for rent*
2. As for 1, but with separate figures for replacements	*Traditional manufacturing industries* (broken down into subsectors)
3. Ratio gross investment *per year* to increase in value added, adjusted for time lag, plus replacement investments	*Modern manufacturing* (broken down into subsectors, and often also into individual industries. Increase in physical output in some cases used as basis instead of increase in value added)
4. Ratio gross investment to increase in physical output (no replacements, time-lag not specified)	*Mining* – coal and petroleum. *Transport* – oil pipelines
5. As for 4, but adjustment for time lag.	*Mining* – natural gas. *Electricity* (production and distribution) and *natural gas* (distribution).
6. Investments in specified types of physical capital related to increase in output (in money or physical terms)	*Agriculture* (farm buildings, grain storage, livestock); *Transport* (railway rolling stock, road transport vehicles, inland water and ocean shipping, boats, barges and ships)
7. Increase in physical capital, not directly linked with increase in physical output or value added.	*Agriculture* (irrigation, flood control, land improvements, tractors and machinery); *Forestry; Transport* (railways, other than rolling stock, ports)

Sources: [0], Annex VII.

industries, have been used, and in each case time lags and replacement costs have been taken into account. Gross investments in a given subsector in year A thus equals the increase in value added (or in physical output) in year A + L (L representing the time lag) multiplied by the subsector capital-output ratio, *plus* investments in replacements which in general are calculated as a percentage of the value added in year A.[5] In cases where this detailed approach has been used, investments in a five-year period represent the sum of investments in the five years of the period, all calculated on the same basis.[6]

In other sectors the investments during a five-year period have simply been calculated as the increase in value added during the same period multiplied by the capital-output ratio for the sector. Investments during the end year of a given plan period were arrived at on the basis of crude estimates based on the five-year totals. Table 46 which shows assumed capital-output ratios adjusted for time lags gives very poor figures for sectors in which the investments are calculated on the basis of increased output during a five-year period. These sectors count little in the global picture, however.

Table 43 summarizes the methods which have been used to calculate induced investments for the different sectors of the economy.

C. *Summary of main results*

Table 44 summarizes the investment picture, and, furthermore, gives details for the breakdown of induced investment by sector.

The breakdown of investment between the different sectors shows at first sight a remarkable stability, particularly as regards agriculture and modern manufacturing which together account for about half of total investments throughout the period under review. The share of agriculture is projected as rising during the Third and Fourth Plan periods whereas the share of manufacturing is somewhat lower in the Third to Fifth Plan periods than during the Second. Investments in agriculture finish at a somewhat higher percentage of total investments in the Sixth Plan than in the Second, whereas the share of modern manufacturing is slightly lower.

The changes shown for some of the other sectors are far more significant. Thus the investments in such economic infrastructure as power supplies and transport will represent 8.5 per cent less of total investments during the Sixth Plan than during the Second, with the fall equally distributed between the two sectors. This is an encouraging result since it suggests that investments in this kind of infrastructure will tend to be less burdensome in the future than they are at present. It is possible, however, that the assumptions used for investment requirements in power supplies are somewhat on the optimistic side. Nevertheless it is probably true, within limits, that when basic networks of transport and

Table 44. *Summary of all gross investments with details for induced investments by plan period*

	2nd Plan 1960–65	3rd Plan 1965–70	4th Plan 1970–75	5th Plan 1975–80	6th Plan 1980–85
Absolute figures, Rs Mill.					
Total gross fixed induced investments	17,420	33,465	48,975	74,280	107,165
Autonomous investments	8,795	16,510	25,630	38,750	56,270
Stocks	1,350	2,300	3,450	5,150	7,900
Grand total gross investments	27,565	52,275	78,055	118,180	171,335
Gross fixed induced investments:					
Percentage distribution					
Agriculture	17.2	23.3	24.0	21.7	18.4
Forestry..................	0.5	0.4	0.5	0.5	0.5
Fishing	1.5	0.9	1.0	1.2	1.1
Mining	2.8	3.2	3.5	3.8	4.3
Modern manufacturing	31.1	28.7	29.3	28.3	30.8
Traditional manufacturing ..	2.4	1.2	0.9	0.6	0.5
Electricity, gas transmission .	15.1	13.0	13.2	11,8	10.9
Construction (equipment) ...	1.3	1.5	1.8	2.2	2.7
Banking, insurance	0.8	0.8	0.9	0.9	1.3
Transport	22.7	19.7	19.4	19.2	18.3
Business premises	3.2	5.5	2.7	6.4	5.7
Trade.....................	0.7	0.8	1.2	1.9	2.9
Other services..............	0.7	1.1	1.6	1.5	2.6
Total gross fixed induced investments	100	100	100	100	100
of which:					
Land	1.4	1.3	1.2	1.1	1.0
Non-monetized investments in:					
Agriculture	3.8	8.1	6.8	5.8	4.5
Fishing	0.6	0.4	0.3	0.2	0.2
Traditional manufacturing	1.1	0.6	0.4	0.3	0.2
Transport (country boats) .	0.9	0.5	0.4	0.2	0.2
Investments in stocks in percentage of fixed investm.	7.7	6.9	7.0	6.9	7.4

Source: [0], Annex VII, p. 45.

power supplies have been established, it will cost relatively less to expand them to meet increasing demand. Note that the figure for transport does not include road-building which will become very expensive once roads and streets start to become crowded by cars. This will probably only happen before the end of this century in a few large cities of Pakistan.

Whereas investments in economic infrastructure may tend to become less burdensome, investments in modern services will become more important. The share of investments in banking, trade, other services, and business premises (mainly for retail trade and for offices) will rise by 7 per cent between the Second and the Sixth Plan periods. Investments in trade include modern warehouses, etc., for the expanding modern type of wholesale trade, and larger retail shops as well as delivery vans and other equipment for transport and handling of materials. Other services include the hotel industry which will require substantial investments.

Two other sectors will increase their proportion of total investments — mining, because it is projected as a very rapidly expanding industry dominated by oil and gas which require considerable investment, and the construction industry, both because it will expand rapidly and because it will use relatively more modern construction equipment.

The share of the traditional manufacturing industries will obviously fall sharply since their share of the GDP also falls. Fishing is not expected to grow as fast as total national income, and it is therefore not surprising to find that its share of total investments will fall.

Non-monetized investment in relatively declining industries such as traditional fishing, manufacturing, and transport will inevitably fall. (No figure has been calculated for investments in the traditional road transport industry, i. e. bullock carts, etc. and draught animals.) In agriculture, however, non-monetized investments are projected as rising rapidly between the Second and the Third Plan due to the stimulation of the efforts by the farmers themselves to improve existing irrigation systems, reclaim land, etc. The fact that these investments will represent a falling share of the total investments from the Third Plan period onwards reflects the relatively limited scope for works of this kind. The increase in livestock holdings is included under non-monetized investments.

Investments in stocks in relation to fixed investments will fluctuate somewhat from one plan period to another. This simply reflects changes in the capital-output ratio. Since the ratio of stock increase to the increase in the GDP is assumed to be constant, a higher overall capital-output ratio will mean a lower proportion of investments in stocks, and *vice versa*.

The ratio between autonomous investments and induced investments will remain approximately constant during the period under review. The implied capital-output ratios throw more light on this point.

D. *What will happen to the capital-output ratio?*

The very crude capital-output ratios shown in Table 45 can only be used to obtain a summary picture of what happens to the capital-output ratio. There are two main sources of error:

(1) The time lag. Obviously not all investments undertaken in one plan period will effect the GDP during the last year of the plan period. Since investments are rising during the period under review, this means that the capital-output ratios are systematically overvalued.

(2) The fact that fixed investments are counted gross of depreciation. This means that in some sectors which grow slowly only a small proportion of the total investments will contribute to further growth while most of the investments are necessary to maintain output at the old level. This factor is particularly significant for traditional manufacturing and for housing. During the Second Plan period, half of the investment in housing was in huts (most of this for replacement purposes), whereas during the Sixth Plan less than one-sixth of the investments will be in huts. This explains the remarkably high capital-output ratio for housing in 1960—65 and the substantial fall between then and 1980—85.

A further analysis of the capital-output ratios will be undertaken on the basis of Table 46 which contains estimates of capital-output ratios per year under the assumption that there is a two-year time lag between the investment and the corresponding increase in the value added of the sector, or the total GDP. This estimate reduces the importance of the error caused by the time lag, although it produces very odd figures for some smaller sectors in which the investment estimates have been made by calculating the investments needed to produce a given increase in the value added during a plan period.[7] No attempt has been made to calculate capital-output ratios based on figures for net investment. Net figures would have given completely different figures for traditional manufacturing, but will not differ very much from the gross figures for the other sectors. (Under autonomous investments, for which details are not given in Table 46, net figures would have given quite different results for housing, but would hardly have influenced the other sectors.)

Table 45. *Implied incremental capital-output ratios per plan period*

	2nd Plan 1960–65	3rd Plan 1965–70	4th Plan 1970–75	5th Plan 1975–80	6th Plan 1980–85
A. *Induced investments*					
Agriculture	1.8	2.9	3.1	3.8	3.3
Forestry	1.5	1.4	2.7	3.3	4.0
Fishing	3.0	2.9	2.9	3.1	3.2
Mining	3.0	2.9	2.9	3.1	3.2
Modern manufacturing	4.4	4.0	3.7	3.2	2.9
Trad. manufacturing	1.7	2.4	2.1	3.7	5.7
Electricity, gas	19.6	9.2	9.7	7.7	5.9
Construction	0.4	0.5	0.8	0.8	1.1
Banking, insurance	1.6	1.3	1.5	1.5	1.6
Transport	5.2	6.3	6.7	6.2	6.1
Business premises	15.3	15.0	15.1	15.0	15.1
Trade	0.1	0.2	0.4	0.7	1.0
Other services	0.5	0.9	1.1	1.2	2.2
B. *Autonomous investments illustrative figures*					
Government	7.1	8.4	8.8	10.2	10.3
Communications	6.6	8.1	8.7	9.3	9.9
Housing	29.1	26.5	23.5	23.1	20.2
Education	17.4	11.9	8.7	6.3	8.1
Health	3.9	5.2	3.8	3,7	4.1
Capital-output ratios for the whole economy					
All fixed investments	4.0	4.1	4.3	4.5	4.3
of which:					
Induced	2.7	2.8	2.9	3.0	2.9
Autonomous	1.3	1.3	1.5	1.5	1.4
Stocks	0.2	0.2	0.2	0.2	0.2
Total capital-output ratio	4.2	4.3	4.6	4.7	4.6

Sources: [0], Annexes V–72 and VII–45 for investments, Annex IX–20 for GDP, and the input-output Tables as adjusted in Chapter IX for the value added of the sectors.

Method: The 'implied' incremental c/o-ratio has been calculated as the investments during a plan period divided by the increased value added *in the same plan period*. Note that investments which are assumed to correspond to the government product include roads, communal amenities, and government administrative buildings. The investment figures under education exclude investments in research.

All figures exclude investments in land.

A comparison between Tables 45 and 46 shows that the way the capital-output ratios have been calculated makes a considerable difference. Note that for many of the smaller sectors — notably traditional manufacturing, fishing, banking, construction, business premises, and trade — the estimates of investments have

Table 46. *Implied incremental gross capital-output ratios assuming*
a two-year time lag

	1960	1965	1970	1975	1980	1985
Capital output-ratios *for individual sectors*						
Agriculture	1.6	1.8	2.6	3.3	3.1	(3.1)
Forestry......................	1.3	1.1	1.8	2.8	3.6	(4.0)
Fishing	3.9	2.9	2.0	2.3	3.1	(3.0)
Mining	2.7	3.3	2.9	2.9	3.0	(2.9)
Modern manufacturing	3.0	3.3	3.3	3.1	2.6	(2.4)
Traditional manufacturing	1.2	2.3	2.0	4.0	5.9	(11.0)
Electricity, gas	13.3	9.6	8.7	7.7	6.1	(4.8)
Commercial construction	0.3	0.4	0.7	0.6	0.9	(1.0)
Banking, insurance	1.1	1.0	1.3	1.3	1.3	(1.4)
Transport	4.0	5.0	6.0	5.4	5.5	(4.9)
Business premises	(7.2)	(8.3)	(21.8)	(7.4)	(16.4)	(12.5)
Trade........................	0.1	0.1	0.3	0.5	0.8	(1.0)
Other services.................	0.2	0.4	0.7	0.9	0.9	(1.5)
Capital-output ratios *for the economy as a whole* All gross investments						
(land excluded)...............	3.15	3.13	3.93	3.92	4.02	(3.77)
Fixed investments less land ...... of which:	3.0	3.0	3.7	3.7	3.8	(3.6)
Autonomous investments	1.1	0.9	1.2	1.2	1.3	(1.2)
Other investments	1.9	2.0	2.5	2.5	2.6	(2.4)
Gross investment less land as percentage of GDP	13.4	19.9	26.0	28.1	30.9	31.4

Sources: Investments, Table 47; increase in value added two years later than the investments, calculated on the basis of the input-output tables as modified in [0], Annex IX, and the growth rates in the various plan periods. Growth figures for the Seventh Plan, and therefore the figures for the increase of the value added in 1987, are crude estimates on the basis of trends.

been made on a crude basis, and it is the capital-output ratios in Table 45 which illustrate the underlying assumptions about investments needed to increase the output by one unit. Thus in the case of business premises it has been assumed that if value added per year is to increase by one million rupees during a five-year period, Rs 15 million must be invested. The capital-output ratios for business premises in Table 46 are completely meaningless. For the other sectors for which the need for investments by five-year periods is the base of the estimates, the results in Table 46 become less meaningless, but they will on the whole show a downward bias. Investments in 'other services' are a good example. In this case capital-output ratios based on the annual investment figures, assuming a two-year time lag, are far lower

Table 47. *Summary Table – Annual investments. (Rs Million)*

	1960	1965	1970	1975	1980	1985
Fixed investments in sectors producing goods & services						
Agriculture (incl. water)	520	910	1,900	2,645	3,515	4,250
Forestry.............	17	20	35	65	90	115
Fisheries	43	56	68	122	217	272
Mining, oil, natural gas	60	175	260	420	680	1,065
Modern manufacturing	670	1,380	2,270	3,530	5,260	8,150
Traditional manu- facturing	80	80	85	95	100	100
Electricity, gas transmission	305	720	1,000	1,530	2,150	2,930
Construction (equipment)........	25	70	130	235	420	700
Banking, insurance ...	18	35	65	110	200	375
Transport	557	967	1,571	2,269	3,239	4,545
Trade (excl. stocks) ...	17	31	77	178	460	960
Other services........	13	37	100	185	295	770
Business premises (for rent)	50	175	350	400	1,100	1,400
Total of above	2,375	4,655	7,910	11,785	17,725	25,630
'Autonomous' investments	1,340	2,145	4,105	5,800	9,085	12,765
Total fixed gross investments	3,715	6,800	12,015	17,585	26,810	38,395
Increase in stocks.....	245	405	605	900	1,345	1,940
GRAND TOTAL ...	3,960	7,205	12,620	18,485	28,155	40,335
Less investments in land						
Investment I.......	45	90	200	300	485	680
Investment II	30	70	90	140	185	245
Non-monetized investments	5	9	15	35	45	50
GRAND TOTAL, adjusted (excl. land)	3,880	7,035	12,315	18,010	27,440	39,360
Non-monetized investment incl. in the sector estimates						
Agriculture	100	225	595	705	900	1,030
Fisheries	19	23	27	30	33	35
Trad. manufacturing..	40	39	40	43	44	43
'Autonomous' in- vestments	595	740	940	1,295	1,500	1,890
Total, non-monetized .	755	1,025	1,600	2,070	2,475	3,000
GRAND TOTAL, less non-monetized	3,205	6,180	11,020	16,410	25,680	37,340
Total fixed investments less non-monetized and land	2,880	5,605	10,110	15,035	23,620	34,425
Total fixed investments, less land	3,635	6,630	11,710	17,110	26,095	37,420

than the figures based on five-year periods which reflect the assumptions which have been used.

Figures for mining, modern manufacturing, gas and electricity, and transport have been calculated on the basis of certain assumptions about time lags, and the implied capital-output ratios in Table 46 therefore illustrate well the underlying assumptions. In the case of agriculture and forestry there is a much weaker link between investments and increased output. A large proportion of investments in these sectors consists of costly programmes, the benefits of which are not fully felt until after several decades. This is particularly true of forest regeneration programmes, but also partly of large irrigation projects.

Both Tables show the important fact that the implied capital-output ratio in modern manufacturing will be falling. The reason for the expected fall in the capital-output ratio for modern manufacturing is partly that relatively more capital is required to set up entirely new industries than to expand them, but partly also because within the modern manufacturing sector there will be a relative shift away from investments in very capital-intensive industries (fertilizers, cement, steel) to less capital-intensive ones (notably the metal-working industries).[8] In 1960 only 17 per cent of investments went into industries with a capital-output ratio of 2 or lower; in 1985 almost 35 per cent of investments will go into these industries.

The high capital-output ratio in agriculture will surprise most observers. Investments in irrigation and 'other', which *inter alia* includes settlement on reclaimed land, will fluctuate between 65 and 75 per cent of total investments in agriculture in the period 1960 to 1980, and fall to 61 per cent in 1985.[9] With this very rapid increase in investments in irrigation and improvements of the land the total level of agricultural investments will grow faster than the increase in agricultural output. It would not be correct to infer from our derived figures that any increase in agricultural value added necessitates direct investments in agriculture which are three times as high. But in order to achieve the *rate of increase* which is assumed in this study (on the technical assumptions made here), the capital-output ratio will exceed three during most of the period under review. Increased output in agriculture is ascribed to three main factors: more and better land, more water on existing land, and better methods applied to the existing land. To improve land through drainage, de-salinization, flood protection, etc., and to bring more water to the land, implies very costly investments, whereas better methods do not require high direct investments in agriculture. If one satisfies oneself with the increase in output which can be had through better methods, the capital-output ratio in agriculture will become much lower. It should be pointed out, however, that better methods lead to substantial investments in other sectors, first of all in the fertilizer and chemical industries. In a country which is poor in farm land in relation to its total and to its farm population, the capital-output ratio in agriculture will tend to become very high.

The high implied capital-output ratio in agriculture makes it appropriate to ask whether it is rational to aim at a rapid growth of farm output. In other words, does it make sense to stimulate food production at almost any cost? This question is the more relevant when it is known that many rich countries have great difficulties in keeping food output down and in avoiding mounting agricultural surpluses.

There are three factors which must be taken into consideration in trying to answer this crucial question. First, the agricultural surpluses in the rich countries, although large, may prove quite inadequate to feed the rising population in all less-developed countries. Certainly in the long run the American prairies cannot produce enough food to satisfy hundreds of millions of Asians if these do not cover most of their food requirements through their own efforts. Second, the development of agriculture is a goal in itself in developing countries. Most of their peoples make their living in agriculture, and during the next two or three decades other sectors of their economies cannot grow fast enough to create jobs for the large agricultural surplus populations. For an equitable distribution of the gains of economic growth it is indispensable that a substantial part of economic growth take place in agriculture itself. Third, the burden of investments in agriculture, through land improvement, irrigation, etc. may be very high, but at the same time these investments create jobs and income for many people. Heavy investments in agriculture accentuate the problem of financing investments and impose policies to restrain consumption and increase savings. But in a country in which the engineering industries are poorly developed, which will be the case in less-developed countries for most of this century, investments in large-scale construction works in agriculture give much more stimulus to internal economic growth in general than the same amount of investments in machinery and equipment in other sectors. Investments in land improvement of different types therefore help to solve the employment problem.

E. *Can the capital-output ratio be lowered?*

Is it possible to design a development strategy which leads to a lower, global capital-output ratio? In the short run the answer is probably yes, but it is doubtful whether such a strategy would be acceptable from a political point of view or desirable from a social point of view. The key to such a development strategy can be found in Table 17, which shows the effects on total personal consumption of major categories of goods and services on the hypothesis of an alternative pattern of growth of urban and rural consumption. This alternative is based on the assumption that rural consumption per head stays constant, whereas urban consumption per head rises more rapidly. The main effect would be a change in consumption from food to other items, mainly manufactured products.

The assumption of constant rural consumption *per caput* would obviously have to be linked with an assumption of almost or fully stagnant rural income per head. This would mean less growth in agriculture and less rural construction work. As has just been pointed out, a lower growth rate in agriculture could very well lead to a lower capital-input ratio in agriculture, and this again would lead to less rural construction work. On the other hand, higher urban demand for manufactured goods and services would lead to more rapid expansion of sectors or subsectors with low capital-output ratios: many consumer goods manufacturing industries, trade, services. Lower construction activities would reduce the demand on manufacturing industries with high capital-output ratios — the steel industry, the cement industry. Also, less transport of heavy construction materials (and also of domestically produced food products) would reduce the need for the expansion of the transport services, probably so much that it would easily offset the increased urban demand on transport services. Finally, the overall demand for gas and electricity might also be lower.

Thus, investments in sectors or subsectors with high capital-output ratios (transport, gas and electricity, building materials industries, agriculture) could be reduced, and investments in sectors with low capital-output ratios (manufacturing of consumer goods, consumer services) be increased. Table 17 also shows that the demand for housing, which is a sector with a very high capital-output ratio, would be reduced.

A development strategy of this type is not out of the question. On the contrary, there are many examples of countries which have developed along this pattern — i. e. the modern urban sector has expanded while the rural sector has stagnated. On paper, such a development pattern can lead to impressive results: Industrial production increases rapidly, national income *per caput* grows at a reasonably high speed, the use of modern gadgets becomes widely spread, etc. But the drawbacks are also familiar — hopeless conditions in the rural areas, and an exodus of surplus man-power from the countryside to the shanty-towns at the outskirts of the rich modern cities.

A low capital-output ratio should not be a goal in itself. It can appear to be a fundamental target, if the rate of growth of the national income is stated to be the primary objective, not a means of enhancing the welfare of the people. If the growth rate of the national income is the ultimate measure of success, and if the resources available for investments are limited, the search for a low capital-output ratio becomes a logical consequence. But when we measure the impact of different growth patterns on the welfare of the people, we may well find that a nominally slower growth rate, or a more costly growth pattern in terms of investments, will create more additional welfare than a development pattern which merely stresses the overall growth rate. In particular the government will generally opt for a strategy which stimulates economic growth in all geographic regions of the country, not only in one or a few growth centres, even at some cost to the rate of growth. The Government of Pakistan has clearly stated that increased welfare shall be reasonably equally distributed between different regions and different groups of the people. I feel confident, therefore, that the planners in Pakistan will adopt a development strategy broadly in line with the one used in this study, even though a fast rate of growth in these circumstances will be more difficult to achieve.

10. The Balance of Foreign Payments

A. *The basis for the balance of payments estimates*

The balance of payments can be defined in many ways. In this study we are mainly concerned with the *current* balance which shows the total income from exports of goods and services, the total expenditure abroad on imports of goods and services, and the balancing item which is the current surplus or deficit. In imports and exports are included 'factor income payments' to and from abroad, items which in many countries are dominated by capital income payments. For our purpose it is convenient to exclude capital income payments from exports and imports, and treat net capital income payments to (or from) abroad as a separate item.

The input-output Tables (see Appendix I) include detailed projections of imports and exports of goods and services other than capital services (and other factor income payments). These figures for imports had to be somewhat adjusted in order to be internally consistent with other figures in this study and notably with the figures for gross domestic investments and savings.[1] These adjustments were not carried out in all details, and Table 50 includes, therefore, an item 'global adjustments' to imports.

By definition imports less exports of goods and services (both items excluding capital income payments) equal gross domestic investments less gross domestic savings (i. e. savings before deduction of net factor income payments to abroad).

Data on the complete current balance of payments are necessary in order to estimate the need for net capital inflow from abroad. As will be shown in Section D, figures for the total current balance of payments depend entirely on the assumptions chosen for the terms under which Pakistan will receive 'foreign aid'.

Finally, in order to estimate the gross inflow of foreign capital it is also necessary to make assumptions as regards the payment of foreign debt. Examples of the need for gross inflow of foreign capital under different alternatives are also given in Section D.

B. *How can exports grow fast enough?*

The overall foreign balance depends ultimately on the difference between domestic investments and domestic savings and *vice versa*. If savings persistently fall short of investments, no efforts to increase exports can close the balance of payments deficit. This problem has, however, another equally important aspect. Let it be assumed that Pakistan manages to increase her savings to such an extent that the *prospective* balance of payments deficit falls within what can vaguely be termed as 'reasonable limits', i. e. it will not exceed what can be hoped for in terms of inflow of foreign capital to cover the deficit. The *actual* balance of payments deficit, however, is the difference between imports and exports. As the development effort must lead to a rapid increase in imports in spite of all efforts to substitute imports by domestic production, rapid increase of exports will become an indispensable condition for keeping the balance of payments deficit down to the level determined by *ex ante* investments and savings.[2] The export projections which are shown in this section are consistent with the projections of imports and of the savings deficit.

These figures show that the export drive has to be very hard indeed, and that its success depends on an extremely rapid growth

Table 48. *The pattern of the projected growth of exports*

	1960	1965	1970	1975	1980	1985
Total exports of goods and services (except factor income from abroad), Rs Mill. (1959/60 prices)	2,117	2,663	3,688	5,396	8,054	12,173
(1960 = 100)						
All exports	100	126	174	255	380	575
of which:						
Food and tobacco	100	135	230	335	400	480
Raw materials	100	108	105	97	70	40
Fuel	100	55	135	470	1,520	3,570
Finished and semi-						
finished products ..	100	150	270	445	730	1,120
Invisibles............	100	150	250	470	850	1,460
Some examples:						
Textiles	100	135	220	330	485	615
Other products of						
modern manufact. ..	100	220	510	1,065	2,250	4,450
Transport services .	100	200	400	800	1,480	2,580
Tourist income.....	100	500	1,250	5,000	12,500	25,000

Sources: Tables 52 and 53 which give absolute figures.

of exports of certain types of goods and services. Total exports must on the average grow by 7.2 per cent per year between 1960 and 1985, and by 7.9 per cent between 1965 and 1985. Since export of raw materials (which represented more than half of total exports in 1960) are assumed to fall, most other exports must rise far more rapidly than total exports. Even exports of textiles, which are bound to meet substantial resistance in the world markets, will on the average have to rise faster than total exports.[3] Even with the help of the projected rapid expansion of exports of textiles, exports from other manufacturing industries will have to expand 45 times between 1960 and 1985. The rapid rise in exports of fuel, which *inter alia,* also include some exports from modern manufacturing (oil refineries), is based on the assumption that petroleum will be found in large enough quantities to leave an exportable surplus of refined petroleum products. By comparison, projected exports of liquified gas are small. Invisible earnings are expected to grow very fast, partly because income from international airlines and shipping is assumed to grow fast and partly because of a projected rise in income from foreign tourism from Rs 4 million in 1960 to Rs 1,000 million in 1985. These projections for transport and tourism are probably *not* unduly optimistic. The targets which will be most difficult to fulfil are those for the manufacturing industries, including the textile industry. Whether exports of fuel will rise as projected or not depends entirely on how much oil will be found during the next couple of decades.

The structure of exports will change radically during the period under review, but these changes are closely related to changes which already took place in the decade preceeding 1960.

The projected changes in the trade structure are dramatic. If the 'manufacturing industries' which undertake crude processing of agricultural goods[4] are treated as part of agriculture, the share of agriculture in exports will fall from 55 per cent to less than 5.5 per cent. This fall is absorbed by modern manufacturing (30 per cent) and invisibles (20 per cent). Almost the entire increase in the case of manufacturing falls on industries other than textiles, whereas the share of transport and tourism has a projected rise of 22 per cent, i. e. more than the total rise for invisibles. Other changes are marginal. It can be noted that exports of natural gas through pipelines will account for merely 0.5 per cent of total exports in 1985.

Exports directly from agriculture in 1960 consisted mainly of loose jute, hides and skins, and wool. Exports of loose jute and of hides and skins are expected to cease during the period under review on the assumption that these raw materials will be processed entirely in Pakistan. Exports of raw wool are also expected to fall towards the end of the period because of rising domestic demand and higher exports of woollen textiles. Exports of agricultural raw materials and food from manufacturing industries in 1960 took the form mainly of baled jute and ginned cotton. At the end of the period projected milled rice will account for 45 per cent of these exports, whereas exports of baled jute are assumed to disappear almost completely.

Exports from manufacturing industries other than the textile industries were very small in 1960 and consisted mainly of re-exported petroleum products, leather, and products of miscellaneous industries (such as sporting goods and scientific instruments). In 1985, a projected 35 per cent of such exports will come from the metal-working industries, 19 per cent from petroleum refining, 10 per cent from the fertilizer industry, 6 per cent from miscellaneous industries, 4 per cent from the footwear and clothing

Table 49. *Changes in the structure of exports*

A. *Percentage distribution of exports*	1960	1965	1970	1975	1980	1985
By types of export						
Food and tobacco	6.1	6.6	8.1	8.1	6.5	5.1
Raw materials	52.0	44.6	31.3	19.7	9.7	3.6
Fuel	1.2	0.6	0.9	2.2	4.7	7.3
Finished, semi-finished goods	23.9	28.8	37.1	42.0	46.1	46.7
Non-spec. goods	3.0	3.0	2.8	2.6	2.4	2.3
Invisibles	13.7	16.5	19.8	25.4	30.7	34.9
Total	100	100	100	100	100	100
By sectors of origin						
Agriculture	9.5	6.5	5.4	4.4	2.6	1.2
Manufacturing: crudely processed agricultural goods*	45.3	40.6	29.6	19.0	9.4	4.1
Fishing	2.2	2.1	1.8	1.5	1.2	1.0
Mining	0.2	0.3	0.2	0.3	0.4	0.3
Modern manufacturing (except items above)	26.3	31.2	40.1	46.7	53.7	57.0
of which:						
Textiles	21.9	23.6	27.4	28.5	28.0	23.4
Other	4.4	7.6	12.7	18.8	25.7	33.6
Trad. manufacturing	0.2	0.4	0.4	0.4	0.3	0.2
Natural gas	–	–	0.5	0.7	0.6	0.6
Non spec. goods	3.0	3.0	2.8	2.6	2.4	2.3
Invisibles (except repair services, included under manufacturing)	13.3	15.9	19.1	24.4	29.4	33.3
of which:						
Transport services	4.0	6.3	9.1	12.5	15.5	17.8
Tourism	0.2	0.8	1.4	3.7	6.2	8.2

* Rice, tea, ginned cotton, baled jute.

(Table 49, continued)

B. *Percentage contribution to the growth of total exports per five-year period*

	1960 −65	1965 −70	1970 −75	1975 −80	1980 −85
By types of export					
Food and tobacco	8.4	11.8	8.2	3.2	2.5
Raw materials	15.9	−3.2	−5.2	−10.7	−8.2
Fuel	−2.0	2.0	4.9	9.9	12.5
Finished, semi-finished goods	47.6	58.5	52.8	54.3	48.0
Non-specified goods	2.9	2.4	2.0	1.9	2.1
Invisibles.............................	27.1	28.5	37.3	41.5	43.2
Total	100	100	100	100	100
By sectors of origin					
Agriculture	−5.1	2.5	2.3	−1.2	−1.6
Manufacturing (crudely processed agricultural goods)	22.3	0.9	−3.8	−10.2	−6.0
Fishing	1.6	1.0	0.9	0.8	0.6
Mining	0.9	0	0.3	0.7	0.1
Modern manufacturing (except items above)	50.1	63.2	60.9	68.2	63.5
of which:					
Textiles	30.0	37.3	31.0	26.9	14.4
Other.............................	20.1	26.9	29.9	41.3	49.0
Trad. manufacturing..................	0.9	0.5	0.3	0.2	0.1
Natural gas	0	2.0	1.2	0.4	0.6
Non-specified goods	2.9	2.4	2.0	1.9	2.1
Invisibles (except repair services included under manuf.)..............	26.2	27.5	35.8	39.6	40.8
of which:					
Transport services	15.4	16.3	19.8	21.5	22.5
Tourism	2.9	2.9	8.8	11.3	12.1

Sources: [0], Annex VIII, Tables 1 and 3.

industries, and 6 per cent from industries which process agricultural raw materials into finished or semi-finished products. The expansion of these types of exports depends therefore to a large extent on the ability of the metal-working industries to achieve competitive advantages for certain of their products, and on the discovery of mineral oils.

Part B of Table 49 illustrates how during most of the period under review the export targets depend on four items: textiles, other modern manufacturing, transport services, and tourism. It should be noted that the gross figures for each item sometimes hide changes in the sub-items. Thus increased exports of rice will help to offset the fall in exports of raw jute, and the small contribution of the fishing industry does not take into account increased exports of frozen fish. In the total picture these exceptions are, however, insignificant. The figures shown in the Table certainly point to the crucial sectors in the export drive as projected in this study. It can be noted that the textile industries will play an important role during the Second to the Fifth Plan period. Beyond 1980, however, they can hardly play the same relative role in the growth of exports, even with very optimistic assumptions about world markets for textiles. Only if the cotton textile industries in the highly developed countries were to decline into insignificance, while cotton still remained the most important textile fibre of all, would it be reasonable to expect that exports of textiles from Pakistan could grow at a very high rate also after 1985.

The role of transport services is very important during the whole period, but it is likely that its share of the growth in exports will stagnate or even decline towards the end of the century, by which time a substantial part of traffic to and from Pakistan, by air and by sea, will be by domestic craft. Even tourism may tend to reach a plateau as an earner of foreign exchange, although the expansion of world tourism could well surpass the most optimistic dreams. The responsibility for a steady and rapid growth of Pakistan's exports during the period under review is to be borne by industries other than textiles. Their share in the growth in exports is projected as rising from 20 per cent during the Second Five-Year Plan to almost 50 per cent in the Sixth Plan, and this share will almost certainly have to rise even further — see the remarks above on textiles, transport services, and tourism.

A cursory review of these export projections may suggest that the role of the manufacturing industries can have been exaggerated. Perhaps so, but it is very difficult indeed to justify any error. Domestic demand on the output of agriculture is projected so high that imports of food will be needed. Under these circumstances it is not very realistic to project a large rise in agricultural exports, or even a much slower decline than projected here. Of course, it is possible to assume that fewer raw materials will be processed in Pakistan — which would mean more exports of raw materials and less of manufactured goods. In that case, total exports would be lower since the value added created by processing raw materials would not be included in exports. The export targets for the manufacturing industries will certainly be difficult to achieve. If, however, exports of manufactured goods cannot be raised as rapidly as suggested here, there are only two other alternatives. The one is to reduce imports by further import substitution. This may be possible but only under very optimistic assumptions for the growth potential of certain important sectors,

Table 50. *The projected pattern of the growth of imports*

	1960	1965	1970	1975	1980	1985
Total imports of goods and services (except factor income payments to abroad). Rs Mill. (1959/60 prices)	2,937	5,512	8,624	11,604	16,123	21,264
1960=100						
All imports	100	188	294	395	549	724
By types						
Food, tobacco	100	270	420	515	675	710
Raw materials	100	260	320	520	835	1,420
Fuel	100	92	82	28	0	0
Finished, semi-finished products	100	180	300	415	560	700
All goods	100	190	300	395	535	680
Invisibles.....................	100	160	265	400	645	1,035
By sectors of origin						
Agriculture	100	260	400	470	560	495
Forestry.....................	100	115	190	315	445	980
Mining	100	335	685	955	1,330	2,270
Manufacturing .... of which:	100	170	265	365	510	675
Metal working	100	220	370	530	745	985
Other manufacturing	100	120	140	180	255	335
Non-specified goods	100	150	230	340	510	765
Percentage distribution of imports *By types*						
Food and tobacco	16.3	21.5	17.4	14.3	16.7	15.3
Raw materials	7.5	10.4	8.2	9.9	11.4	14.8
Fuel	10.8	5.3	3.0	0.8	0	0
Finished, semi-finished	52.5	49.0	47.3	49.2	49.9	50.0
Global adjustment	–	2.8	12.4	12.9	7.1	1.6
Invisibles.....................	12.8	11.0	11.6	12.9	15.0	18.3
Total	100	100	100	100	100	100
By sectors of origin						
Agriculture	16.9	23.6	23.1	20.1	17.3	11.6
Forestry.....................	1.2	0.8	0.8	1.0	1.0	1.7
Mining	1.7	3.0	3.9	4.0	4.0	5.2
Manufacturing .... of which:	65.4	60.0	59.1	60.2	60.8	61.1
metal-working	28.6	33.5	35.9	38.2	38.8	38.9
Other.....................	36.8	26.5	23.2	22.0	22.0	22.2
Non-spec. goods (raw mat.)	2.0	1.6	1.6	1.7	1.9	2.1
Invisibles.....................	12.8	11.0	11.6	12.9	15.0	18.3
Total	100	100	100	100	100	100

Sources: [0], Annex VIII, Tables 1 and 3. Note that the global adjustment done in [0], Annex IX, Table 19, has been divided between goods from agriculture and from manufacturing, but not between types of goods. However, in the figures showing imports as a percentage of 1960 imports, agricultural goods are included under food and tobacco, and manufactured goods under finished and semi-finished goods.

notably the engineering industries. The other is to let the balance of payments deficit be higher than projected. However, this might also mean, *inter alia,* a slower rate of growth of the Gross Domestic Product (because total effective demand on the domestic output would become lower).

Finally, note should be taken of the fact that in the projections of exports in this study the role of exports of invisibles may have been exaggerated more than the role of the manufacturing industries. Their contribution to the growth of exports is assumed to be very high. Whether or not it is a good thing for Pakistan to build a large merchant fleet is difficult to judge. The one great advantage of such a policy is that it will lead to saving of foreign exchange on transport costs to and from Pakistan. As regards the growth of income from international airlines, one is on much safer ground. Pakistan International Airlines have grown very fast, and there is every reason to believe that it will capture more than its share of the growing air trafic in Asia. The projected tourist incomes may appear high, but the onslaught of tourists from Europe and America is spreading further and further afield. It is not impossible that the projections of a level of tourist income of 200 million dollars in 1985 will in fact turn out to be surpassed even by wide margins.

C. *The rise of imports*

At first sight the Table shows a remarkable stability in the pattern of imports with three notable exceptions: The share of invisibles in total imports, after a temporary fall, is shown to increase substantially; the share of raw materials in total imports will double; and fuel imports, which represented 11 per cent of total imports in 1960, will disappear. There are also other important changes. Thus, products from the metal-working industries will represent an increasing proportion of total imports, while imports of other manufactured goods will become less important. The reason why imports of such goods will not fall further in relative importance after 1975 can be ascribed to the rapid increase in imports of dairy products which in 1985 is projected as 5 per cent of total imports (against a mere 0.2 per cent in 1960).

Food imports remain important throughout the period under review, but in 1985 one-third of such imports will consist of manufactured agricultural products, imports of which were negligible in 1960. This change leads to the apparent fall in imports of agricultural products. It is true that imports of this group are projected to fall, but imports of manufactured products with a very high content of agricultural raw materials will rise. The rise in imports of raw materials, as well as in imports of forestry and mining products, reflects the poor supplies of domestic raw materials of different types (wood, raw rubber, minerals, ores). Amongst the imported manufactured raw materials, forest products (sawn lumber, pulp) are predominant, followed by raw materials of agricultural origin like vegetable oils.

The rise of the share of invisibles in total imports can almost fully be ascribed to a single item, viz. expenditure abroad on account of shipping and airlines. Such payments represented only 1 per cent of total imports in 1960, but this percentage will rise to 5 in 1985.

During the period under review, imports are expected to rise by 8.3 per cent per year (or considerably faster than exports at 7.2 per cent per year). For the period 1965 to 1985 the position is different, however. Imports are projected as growing 7 per cent per year against a growth of 7.9 per cent for exports.

The annual increase of imports per five-year period shows a projected change as follows. (The annual import elasticity is calculated on the basis of these figures and the figures for the annual rate of growth of the GDP.)

Table 51. *Import elasticity*

	1960–65	1965–70	1970–75	1975–80	1980–85
Annual increase in imports during each five year period, %	13.4	9.4	6.1	6.8	5.7
Rate of growth of GDP, %	4.1	6.0	6.3	6.7	7.2
'Import elasticity'	3.3	1.6	1.0	1.0	0.8

Source: Tables 50 and 35.

The import elasticity during the Second Five Year Plan was exceptionally high and reflects a sharp increase in development expenditure which could be matched neither by increased domestic output of many investment goods, nor by an equally steep increase in domestic savings. During the Third Plan import elasticity is also projected high, but thereafter it will fall considerably and reach a level below one during the Sixth Plan. The combined effects of a higher domestic rate of savings and import substitution will then begin to be felt fully.

From the point of view of foreign supplies the most interesting aspect of the projected development of Pakistan's imports is the gradual concentration of imports of goods in two fields: engineering and related products; and food, raw materials, and manufactured products based on raw materials which are scarce in Paki-

Table 52. *Imports and exports of goods – projections for the period 1959/60 to 1984/85* (Rs Million)*

	1960	1965	1970	1975	1980	1985
A. *Imports*						
(at cif. prices)						
Food and tobacco	479	1,185	1,504	1,658	2,685	3,264
Raw materials	221	572	710	1,144	1,843	3,141
Fuel	318	293	260	90	0	0
Semi-finished, finished						
goods	1,544	2,700	4,081	5,715	8,038	10,630
Final, global adjustment ..	–	156	1,073	1,497	1,141	339
Total	2,562	4,906	7,628	10,104	13,707	17,374
B. *Exports*						
Food and tobacco	130	176	297	437	522	625
Raw materials	1,100	1,187	1,154	1,065	781	442
Fuel	25	14	34	117	380	893
Finished and semi-finished						
goods	507	767	1,367	2,269	3,711	5,688
Non-specified goods	64	80	105	140	190	275
Total	1,826	2,224	2,957	4,028	5,584	7,923
C. *Trade balance*	–735	–2,680	–4,670	–6,075	–8,125	–9,450

Source: [0], Annex VIII, Table 1.

* The global, final adjustment of the figure for imports was necessary in order to arrive at internal consistency in the model – see [0], Annex IX, notably Tables 12 and 19.

stan. The choice between imports of raw materials or products made of raw materials in short supply in Pakistan depends on the type of raw material required. If it is perishable or bulky, it will mostly be imported as a semi-finished or finished product, unless there are very special economic reasons in favour of localizing production close to the markets. Iron ore and coking coal may be imported rather than steel, whereas there is hardly any choice but to import dairy products if the shortage of milk products is to be covered.

D. *The foreign deficit and how it can be financed*

By definition, the realized surplus of imports of goods and services over exports of goods and services (excluding factor income payments in either direction) equals the amount by which gross domestic investments exceeds gross domestic savings.[5] Table 54

Table 53. *Imports and exports of services ('invisibles') –*
projections for the period 1959/60 to 1984/85 (Rs Million)

	1960	1965	1970	1975	1980	1985
A. *Imports*						
1. Foreign travel	29	50	80	130	235	470
2. Transport, insurance...	(85.0)	140	220	345	585	1,035
of which						
3. Freight and insurance on international shipments	..........included in imports of goods......					
4. Other transport	(60.0)	100	150	225	385	695
5. Other insurance	(25.0)	40	70	120	200	340
6. Government	(99.7)	125	165	215	260	330
7. Miscellaneous.........	(161.0)	291	531	810	1,336	2,055
of which						
8. Expenditure on international shipping and airline operations	(28)	66	141	295	581	1,095
9. Other..............	(133)	225	390	515	755	960
10. Total	(375)	606	996	1,500	2,461	3,890
B. *Exports*						
11. Foreign travel	4.3	20	50	200	500	1,000
12. Transport, insurance...	84	168	335	673	1,245	2,170
of which						
13. Airline income	(35)	70	140	280	560	1,120
14. International shipping	..	30	100	250	480	750
15. Other transport (ports etc)	(49)	68	95	143	205	300
16. Insurance	(13)	16	21	30	45	60
17. Government exp.......	67.6	80	100	120	135	150
18. Miscellaneous.........	124.0	155	225	345	545	870
19. Total	291.0	439	731	1,368	2,470	4,250
20. *Invisible balance* (Imports surplus –, exports surplus +)	–84	–167	–265	–132	+9	+360

shows that the figures used in this study in a formal sense are
internally consistent. It also shows the size of the foreign deficit
for six different years.

The present study is based on the assumption that the foreign
deficit will be covered by an inflow of foreign capital. The present section will deal with the form in which this inflow of foreign capital will take place, and the effect this will have on the
total current balance of payments (i. e. including factor income
payments).

Table 54 shows that the balance of payments deficit will grow

Table 54. *External and savings deficit*

	1960	1965	1970	1975	1980	1985
Imports of goods and services (except factor income payments to abroad)	2,937	5,512	8,624	11,604	16,123	21,264
Exports of goods and services (except factor income payments from abroad)	2,117	2,663	3,688	5,396	8,054	12,173
Gross fixed domestic investments (less land) plus increase in stocks ..	3,870	7,057	12,316	17,999	27,431	40,327
Gross domestic savings	3,050	4,208	7,380	11,791	19,362	31,236
Import surplus = savings deficit................	820	2,849	4,936	6,208	8,069	9,091

Sources: Tables 48, 50, and [0], Annexes VII – 45 and IX – 21.

considerably during the period under review. Table 55 shows how the balance of payments deficit develops in relative terms and throws some light on the reasons for its growth.

In isolation, the first and second lines of Table 55 give a very dismal picture of the economic development of Pakistan. In 1985, Pakistan will have to rely on foreign aid to pay for 43 per cent of its imports against 28 per cent in 1960, and the foreign deficit in relation to the GDP will have grown more than two and a half times. We should note, however, that considerable progress is projected as taking place between 1965 and 1985; i. e. if we make comparisons with the situation after instead of before the epoch

Table 55. *Imports and exports, investments and savings, and the balance of payments deficit; in relation to each other or to the GDP*

	1960	1965	1970	1975	1980	1985
Imports paid by exports, per cent...................	72.1	48.3	42.8	46.5	50.0	57.2
Balance of payment deficit, per cent of GDP	2.8	8.1	10.4	9.7	9.1	7.2
Gross investments financed by dom. savings, per cent	78.8	59.6	59.9	65.5	70.6	77.5
Gross savings and investments, per cent of GDP						
Savings	10.5	11.9	15.6	18.4	21.8	24.9
Investments	13.4	19.9	26.0	28.1	30.9	32.1

during which the development efforts had started to influence the foreign balance, the prospects are far less gloomy.

The third line, however, throws some light on this seemingly very unsatisfactory performance. Whereas domestic savings in relation to domestic investment will fall abruptly between 1960 and 1965, savings rise faster than investments from then onwards and by 1985 domestic savings will cover almost the same percentage of investments as in 1960. There are two reasons why exports will cover a much lower proportion of imports than in the base year (see Table 54). Firstly, throughout the period the absolute figure for imports is much smaller than investments so that the same absolute deficit represents a larger proportion of imports than of investments; secondly, investments grow much faster than imports.

Lines four and five show the tremendous relative increase both of investments and of savings. In spite of a most spectacular increase in savings, particularly during the later part of the period, the gap between investments and savings, as a percentage of the GDP, remains much wider than in 1960 when investments were relatively modest.

Even lines one and two have their promising aspects. Whereas 57 per cent of imports will have to be covered by foreign aid in 1970 and only 43 per cent from Pakistan's own resources, the situation is reversed in 1985. And there are signs that the gap will be closed at an accelerating speed. Similarly, the net addition to domestic resources through foreign aid will be cut by almost one-third between 1970 and 1985.

The main arguments and assumptions on the inflow of foreign aid and the form it may take are summarized here.[6] The capital inflow can take two forms, 'grants' or 'loans'. Grants include all capital inflow on which no interest charges are paid and which will never be repaid. Loans include all foreign capital which will have to be repaid, whether interest-bearing or not. Thus 'loans' include also direct foreign investments in profit-making enterprises. The average return on 'loans' is assumed to be 6 per cent per year (taking into account that many short term and private loans may carry higher interest than 6 per cent and that the return on private capital often may be considerably higher). It is furthermore assumed that 5 per cent of all outstanding debt at the end of one year is due to be repaid the following year.[7]

The future of Pakistan's balance of payments has been calculated under two alternatives: A: 75 per cent of the foreign capital inflow comes in the form of loans and 25 per cent in the form of grants; and B: 25 per cent comes as loans and 75 per cent as grants.

Table 56 gives a shocking picture of the future foreign balance of a country like Pakistan which aims at a high rate of growth, assisted by a liberal inflow of foreign capital. Under Alternative A, which on present indications is a fairly realistic alternative, Pakistan will need 27,000 million dollars in fresh capital inflow during its Sixth Plan period. Of this large amount more than one-third will be needed to pay interest on old debt (or dividends on foreign investments), a little less than a third will be needed to convert old loans or permit withdrawal of foreign private investments, and only one-third will be available for financing the country's import surplus of goods and services during that plan

Table 56. *The total balance of payments deficit, under two assumptions regarding the terms under which capital inflow takes place*

| | Rs Mill per five-year plan period | | | | |
	1960 to 65	1965 to 70	1970 to 75	1975 to 80	1980 to 85
Accumulated deficit, net of factor income payments	8,865	22,265	28,340	37,310	43,015
Alternative A					
Interest payments, etc., on foreign debt (net).	1,320	5,735	14,205	27,300	46,825
Total current deficit	10,185	28,000	42,545	64,610	89,840
Repayment of foreign debt, etc. ...	880	4,225	11,130	21,815	37,945
Total fresh capital inflow needed ..	11,065	32,225	53,675	86,425	127,785
Total net foreign debt at the end of plan periods	9,140	31,570	67,035	109,270	201,400
Alternative B					
Interest payments, etc., on foreign debt (net)	560	2,070	4,950	9,385	15,995
Total current deficit	9,425	24,335	33,290	46,695	59,010
Repayment of foreign debt, etc. ...	395	1,540	3,890	7,510	12,970
Total fresh capital inflow needed ..	9,820	25,875	37,180	54,205	71,980
Total net debt at the end of plan periods......................	3,520	11,160	23,195	41,905	68,655

Source: [0], Annex VIII, Table 4.

Alternative A: 25 per cent of the current deficit net of factor income payments covered by grants from abroad. The rest of the deficit, payments of interest to abroad, and repayment of foreign loans, and foreign private investments to be covered by new loans or private investments.

Alternative B: 75 per cent of the current deficit net of factor income payments to be covered by foreign grants.

period, excluding payments of factor income to abroad. Alternative B, which assumes that the present tendency in donor countries to give foreign 'aid' in the form of loans rather than grants, will be reversed, gives a less disturbing picture. But even under this alternative more than one-fifth of the gross inflow of foreign capital during the Sixth Plan period will be needed for interest and dividend payments, a little less than a fifth for repayment of old debt, so that 60 per cent will be available for current purchases of goods and services.

It is obvious that the interest rate chosen has a fundamental influence on these calculations which do not represent forecasts of what may happen but merely illustrate what a steady and large inflow of foreign capital will mean if a fairly big proportion of it takes the form of relatively high-interest-bearing foreign investments.

The figures used in Table 56 have also been calculated on an

Table 57. *Balance of payments – current and capital account (Rs Mill.)*

	1960	1965	1970	1975	1980	1985
Deficit on balance of goods and services	820	2,849	4,936	6,208	8,069	9,091
Alternative A						
Net factor income payments to abroad	30	480	1,710	3,705	6,805	11,270
Total current deficit	850	3,330	6,645	9,915	14,875	20,360
Repayments of debt.......	(25)	330	1,290	2,930	5,465	9,165
Total need for fresh capital inflow	875	3,660	7,935	12,845	20,340	29,525
Alternative B						
Net factor income payments to abroad	30	185	605	1,285	2,335	3,845
Total current deficit	850	3,035	5,540	7,495	10,400	12,935
Repayment of debt	(25)	135	460	1,015	1,875	3,125
Total need for capital inflow	875	3,170	6,000	8,510	12,275	16,060
Total current deficit as % of GDP						
Alternative A	2.9	9.4	14.0	15.5	16.8	16.2
Alternative B	2.9	8.6	11.7	11.7	11.7	10.3
Total need for fresh capital inflow as % of GDP						
Alternative A	3.0	10.4	16.8	20.1	22.9	23.5
Alternative B	3.0	9.0	12.7	13.3	13.8	12.8

annual basis, so that it is possible to calculate a complete balance of payments for Pakistan at five-year intervals.

The percentages in Table 57 illustrate the effects of debts and debt repayments on the balance of payments of Pakistan. The total need for fresh inflow of capital will, under Alternative A, continue to rise in relation to the GDP throughout the period under review, and even under Alternative B it will only fall somewhat after 1980. The total need for 'fresh' capital supplies under Alternative A, where grants amount to 25 per cent of capital inflows, will approach one-quarter of the GDP in 1985. Under Alternative B, however, where three-quarters of the capital thus supplied is provided in the form of grants, the annual inflow of fresh capital will be little over one-eighth of the GDP and will tend to decline in later plan periods.

These figures have wide political implications. The willingness of donor countries to provide fresh aid to such an extent as is here suggested for Pakistan can be doubted, at least against the background of present attitudes to foreign aid in most industrialized countries. These attitudes may gradually change, and the growing affluence of the rich countries may make them far more willing to give aid than at present. The real problem arises first of all from the point of view of the receiving country. It appears highly unlikely that a country like Pakistan would be willing to accept a situation in twenty years' time in which foreign capital inflows as high as one-quarter of Gross Domestic Product would be required. If such a situation developed, Pakistan would probably not maintain development targets at the levels suggested in this study.

Even the implications of the more generous Alternative B might be objectionable from the point of view of the receiving country, except perhaps for a limited period.

The illustrations given in this section therefore raise the whole problem of how and on what terms a developing country can achieve rapid economic growth through foreign aid. Imagine a developing country meeting with a 'consortium' which is considering the granting of a guarantee that assures the developing country that external finance will be made available for a 20 year 'perspective plan'. The donor countries might make the following declaration: 'We realize that a part of your expenditure abroad will be for purposes which will not yield significant economic benefits in the relatively near future. We will therefore give you some help in the form of grants, through technical assistance, gifts of food surpluses, and other grants. We estimate that these grants will correspond roughly to one-quarter of your current balance of payments deficit, net of factor income payments abroad. For the rest we will guarantee you an inflow of loans and private foreign investments which will permit you to build up your economy and pay your interest charges and dividends on previous investments. But this flow of foreign capital will considerably strengthen your economy, and there is therefore no reason why you should receive it free of charge. We will also generously guarantee that the foreign debt which each year has to be repaid will be converted into new debt, so that debt repayments will not create undue difficulties for you.'

Such a declaration of intent corresponds to Alternative A developed above. If Pakistan were given this offer, and if it were basing its perspective planning on the assumptions in this study,[8] the planners would have to draw the following conclusions: 'At the end of the Sixth Five-Year Plan our net foreign debt will have grown to more than Rs 200 *billion,* which corresponds to 160 per cent of our projected Gross Domestic Product (or 175 per cent of our projected Gross National Product). The net interest burden will have mounted to 9 per cent of the Gross Domestic Product (or 10 per cent of the Gross National Product or 93 per cent of our total export earnings); the repayments which are to be made during the last year of the Sixth Plan will correspond to more than 7 per cent of our GDP. Our plans tell us that in 1985 our total export earnings, i. e. before payment of interest on existing debt, will still not be able to pay for more than 57 per cent of the imports of goods and services which we need to continue our investments and our high rate of growth and to supply our new industries with the raw materials and external services which are needed for their operations. We will, in other words, at the end of our Perspective Plan have to ask the donor countries for an inflow of foreign capital which in total will exceed one-quarter of our total Gross *National* Income. Frankly, we cannot play poker with the future in this manner and leave our economy entirely at the mercy of the political opinions in the donor countries 20 years from now.'

If, however, Pakistan were offered foreign capital on terms corresponding to Alternative B — which under present circumstances would appear very generous on the part of the donors — the situation would be much improved but still not satisfactory: The accumulated foreign debt in 1985 would correspond to 55 per cent of the Gross Domestic Product, annual interest payments to 3 per cent of the GDP or more than 30 per cent of export earnings, repayment of debt to 2.5 per cent of the GDP and above 25 per cent of export earnings. These figures are very high. A country like Norway, which for very long periods has been running persistent deficits on its balance of payments (or in other words has financed a considerable part of its domestic investments through foreign finance), pays less than 1 per cent of its GDP in net interest to foreign countries, and its foreign indebtedness is only about 10 per cent of its GDP.

The problem must also be looked at from the point of view of the capital-exporting (or 'donor') countries.

In the above table, 1965 has been chosen as the base year, because the level of foreign capital inflow during the year 1964/65 was very close to what has been shown in Table 57. The inflow of foreign capital to Pakistan at the end of the First Five Year Plan was fairly modest.

The 'real burden' on the donor countries — i. e. the transfer of goods and services to Pakistan (however financed) — will on the average grow by 6 per cent annually between 1965 and 1985. If the national income of the rich countries grows by 5 per cent per year over the same period, the proportion of their resources transferred to Pakistan will increase by only 20 per cent between 1965 and 1985. But at no time would the donor countries be compelled to increase their *real* sacrifices by more than slightly above one-third in relation to what they are today. There is therefore no reason to fear that Pakistan's need for additional resources from abroad during the next twenty years will be too large in relation to the richer countries' ability to sacrifice part of their resources for the development of the poor countries.

At this stage it is appropriate to raise the point that Pakistan is not the only underdeveloped country in need of help. Pakistan expects to receive about 550 million dollars in official loans and

Table 58. *Growth of transfer of capital from the capital exporting ('donor') countries to Pakistan*   1965 = 100

	1960	1965	1970	1975	1980	1985
Transfer of goods and services (except capital services) to Pakistan	29	100	173	218	283	319
Inflow needed to cover Pakistan's total current balance of payments deficit						
Alternative A	26	100	200	298	447	611
Alternative B	28	100	183	247	343	426
Inflow needed to cover Pakistan's *gross* need for capital from abroad						
Alternative A	24	100	217	351	556	807
Alternative B	28	100	189	268	387	507

Source: Table 57.

grants, technical assistance and private investments in 1965.[9] The total net flow of long-term financial resources from the DAC countries to the developing countries in 1963 is estimated at around 8 billion dollars.[10] On the basis of these figures, therefore, Pakistan received less than 7 per cent of the total 'foreign aid', or a figure which corresponds almost exactly to Pakistan's share of the population of the underdeveloped countries in Asia, Africa, and Latin America (excluding the people's democracies in Asia.)[11] If the case of Pakistan should be typical of the need of all developing countries, the need for foreign aid *in the form of transfers of goods and services* should only rise moderately in relation to the national income of the rich countries during the next couple of decades.[12] In any case, the needs of Pakistan are certainly not projected to rise so rapidly that they would seem to place undue burdens on the shoulders of the rich countries.

While the need for *net* transfer of goods and services shows a reasonable rate of increase, the transfers from the rich countries to the poorer ones which have the sole purpose of enabling the poor countries to pay interest and dividends to the rich countries represent merely a flow of financial resources to the developing countries and then back to the rich countries. Fundamentally, this also applies to transfers to the poor countries in order to enable them to pay off old debts. This is also a circular flow of financial resources. There is one crucial difference, though. In the first case, new capital must be raised to pay current interest and dividend payments to citizens and organizations in the rich countries, whereas the other case merely implies a decision on the part of the rich countries to maintain in the developing countries the capital which is already invested there.

Transfer of resources to the developing countries to enable them to meet their obligations to the richer countries does represent financial sacrifices which can have very substantial implications. These transfers must be financed out of the savings of the rich countries which thereby will be faced with the problem either of saving more, which involves a sacrifice in terms of lower consumption, or of investing less at home (or in other rich countries).

The problem merits a deeper analysis than can be attempted here. This analysis would particularly have to take into account the relative profitability of investments at home and in the developing countries. It would illustrate many of the financial problems which are created in donor countries by large foreign aid programmes. Even without such analysis it should be clear, however, that levels of consumption and investment in the rich countries depend fundamentally on their real resources and on production, not on their financial resources. The financial system can be manipulated to fit into the framework of real resources.

In conclusion it can be said that from the point of view of the donor countries a policy of transfer of resources to developing countries in the form of loans and private investment instead of as grants creates as many problems as it solves. In the short run, while the financial problems are still manageable, it may be easier to finance foreign aid through loans and private investment than through grants; but as the toll of interest charges and repayments mounts up in a growing number of receiving countries, the problems behind this kind of aid policy will become more and more evident.

The crucial fact is that rapid growth in developing countries demands such a high level of investment that it is not feasible for these countries to finance such investments fully themselves, nor is it realistic to assume that they will be able to pay normal capital charges on the foreign capital which is required.

E. *What kind of foreign aid?*

If Alternative B in Table 57 is used as the only reasonably realistic alternative for the breakdown of foreign capital inflow between grants and loans, the total aid picture can be illustrated as shown in Table 59.

The Table shows what already could be seen from Table 57 — whereas 94 per cent of the inflow of aid in 1960 was used to pay for imports of goods and services, this percentage will have fallen to 57 in 1985.

The main purpose of Table 59 is to throw some light on the question whether aid will be directed to projects, to special programmes, and to technical assistance, or whether it will have a more general character.

The import items which have been specified in the Table include most imports which would be financed under project aid, food aid, or technical assistance. Aid for specific projects will, under present procedures, mainly cover foreign-exchange expenditure which mostly consists of machinery and equipment (included under imports from the metal-working industries) and engineering and consultant services (included under services). Technical assistance would, on the whole, fall under import of services, including education, The five items which are listed in the Table are therefore typical of imports financed under project aid. The totals shown in the Table will also include, however, a substantial proportion of imports from the metal-working industries of spare parts, components, consumer goods, and other items which are not imported for investment purposes, and fall outside the type of commodities financed under project aid programmes. The percentages which show these selected imports in relation to total inflow of foreign aid will, therefore, overstate the extent to which foreign aid could be allocated to specific projects or programmes. The trend in these percentages, which is clearly downwards, is of importance as it suggests that the percentage of total aid which can be allocated to special projects and programmes must fall, at least up to 1975. This implies a shift from project help and technical assistance to general programme support.

Table 59. *The use of the inflow of foreign resources*

	1960	1965	1970	1975	1980	1985
Total inflow, Rs Mill.	(875)	3,170	6,000	8,510	12,275	16,060
of which to cover (per cent distribution)						
Deficit on balance of goods and services ...	(94)	90	82	73	66	57
Interest charges and dividends............	(3)	6	10	15	19	24
Repayments of loans and foreign investments ..	(3)	4	8	12	15	19
Total imports of specified goods and services	1,391	3,177	4,897	6,503	9,541	12,302
Of which:						
Food grains............	413	1,098	1,354	1,365	2,013	2,022
Dairy products	6	10	55	180	525	1,040
Goods from metal-working industries ...	839	1,844	3,098	4,433	6,248	8,280
Education (training abroad, foreign teachers)	(12)	15	80	100	200	270
Services (includes research, consultants, engineering, etc.)	(121)	210	310	415	555	690
Imports of certain specified goods and services expressed as % of total capital inflow..	159	100	82	76	78	77
In % of total deficit on balance of goods and services	170	112	99	105	118	135

Sources: Table 57 (Alternative B). Data for imports, [0], Annex VIII, Tables 1 and 3.

11. The Gross National Product and Disposable National Savings

The Gross National Product equals the Gross Domestic Product less net factor income payments to abroad.[1] The figures given in Table 57 permit a calculation of the Gross National Product. Total gross national savings equal gross domestic savings less factor income payments abroad. Another concept can also be introduced — *disposable* gross national savings which equal gross national savings less repayments of foreign debt. The meaning of disposable gross national savings is the amount of national savings which is available to cover new investments and depreciation allowances over and above those accounted for by repayments of foreign debt. The figure for the disposable gross national savings shows the ability of the country to participate in the financing of its investment programme, or the flow of gross savings which are retained in the country.

The figures for the Gross National Product shown in Table 60 depend on which of the two alternatives for the form of foreign aid is considered. The Table shows the influence on the level and growth of the GNP and, particularly, on the level and growth of savings.

Under Alternative A the Gross National Product in 1985 will be 9 per cent lower than the Gross Domestic Product; under Alternative B the difference will be far less important — 3 per cent. Over the period 1960 to 1985 the GNP will grow by 295 per cent under Alternative A, and 321 per cent under Alternative B against the projected growth of 333 per cent for the Gross Domestic Product. The annual rate of growth of the Gross National Product will under Alternative A be about 0.5 per cent lower than the rate of growth of the Gross Domestic Product.

This drain is, however, small compared with the gains achieved through foreign investment. In the period 1965 to 1970, 40 per cent of the gross investments will be financed by foreign capital, that is, under Alternative A, 30 per cent by foreign loans. Assuming that investment financed by foreign loans will be responsible for 30 per cent of growth, the growth rate of the GDP will only

Table 60. *Gross National Product and national savings*

	1960	1965	1970	1975	1980	1985
Gross Domestic Product						
(at factor cost) Rs Mill...	28,950	35,340	47,300	64,010	88,710	125,450
Gross National Product						
Alternative A, Rs Mill...	28,900	34,860	45,590	60,300	81,900	114,180
Alternative B, Rs Mill...	28,915	35,155	46,700	62,725	86,380	121,610
Growth per five-year period ending in year						
Per cent						
Gross Domestic Product ..		22.1	33.8	35.3	38.6	41.4
Gross National Product						
Alternative A		20.6	30.8	32.3	35.8	39.4
Alternative B		21.6	32.8	34.3	37.7	40.8
Annual rate of growth (%) *during each five-year period, ending in year*						
Gross Domestic Product ..		4.1	6.0	6.3	6.7	7.2
Gross National Product						
Alternative A		3.75	5.5	5.75	6.3	6.9
Alternative B		4.0	5.85	6.1	6.6	7.1
Percentage of GDP in net factor payments to abroad						
Alternative A	0.2	1.4	3.6	5.9	7.7	9.0
Alternative B	0.1	0.5	1.3	2.0	2.6	3.1
Gross national saving in % *of GNP*						
Alternative A	10.5	10.7	12.4	13.4	15.3	17.5
Alternative B	10.4	11.4	14.5	16.8	19.7	22.5
Gross disposable national saving in % *of GNP*						
Alternative A	10.3	9.7	9.6	8.5	8.7	9.5
Alternative B	10.3	11.1	13.5	15.1	17.5	20.0
Grosss domestic savings in % *of GDP*	10.5	11.9	15.6	18.4	21.8	24.9
Percentage of gross domestic savings used for						
Interest payments abroad						
Alternative A	1.8	11.4	23.2	31.4	35.1	36.1
Alternative B	1.2	4.4	8.2	10.9	12.0	12.3
Repayment of foreign debt						
Alternative A	0.8	7.9	17.5	24.9	28.2	29.3
Alternative B	0.8	3.2	6.2	8.6	9.7	10.0

Sources: GDP [0], Annex IX – 20, net factor income payments abroad, Table 57 (GNP = GDP less net factor income payment abroad). Gross domestic savings, Table 54 (Gross national savings = gross domestic savings less net factor income payments abroad). Repayment of foreign debt, Table 57. (Gross disposable national savings = gross national savings less repayments of foreign debt).

be 4.2 per cent without foreign loans against the actually projected rate of 6 per cent.

It should be stressed that the assumption that three-quarters less foreign aid would only reduce investments by 30 per cent is unrealistic and, moreover, it is equally unrealistic to assume that if investments were curtailed by 30 per cent because of less foreign aid, the growth rate would fall by only 30 per cent. The drastic reduction of imports which would follow from a sharp reduction in foreign aid would impede domestic production to such an extent that investments nominally financed and carried out by domestic resources would certainly be curtailed as well. As regards the second assumption about the proportional fall in investments and the rate of growth, a fall in investments financed by foreign aid would most certainly affect investments in sectors with relatively low capital-output ratios and would therefore cut back the rate of growth proportionally more than the reduction of the investments.

If this is accepted, it follows that the gains will offset the payments abroad many times.

It is the impact on domestic savings which shows the inherent problems in a development effort financed to a large extent by interest-bearing foreign capital. The figures for gross domestic savings as a percentage of the Gross Domestic Product illustrate the efforts which must be made in order to divert domestic resources from consumption to investments and so ensure a more rapid economic growth. Table 55 (p. 199) shows how *domestic* savings, from 1970 onwards, slowly but steadily start to catch up with investments. It would, of course, be preferable if savings could approach investment more rapidly, but as is shown in Table 9 (p. 74) even the assumptions used in this study imply very determined efforts on the part of the population.

Table 60 shows how the savings efforts are drained away for servicing of foreign debt, particularly, of course, under Alternative A. Alternative B only slows down the development, so that the difference between gross domestic investments and the gross disposable national savings will widen to its maximum in 1980 and thereafter narrow slightly. Under Alternative A, however, the gap between gross disposable national savings and gross investments, both expressed as a percentage of the GNP, will persistently widen durin gthe period under review. In other words, as far as savings are concerned, therefore, Pakistan would seem to be further away from the take-off into self-sustained economic growth in 1985 than in 1960 under Assumption A.

It is reasonable to object that the use of gross *disposable* national savings exaggerates the picture, since, after all, the savings which are used for repayments of foreign debts nevertheless form part of the national income of Pakistan. The picture remains much the same, however. Under Alternative A the gap between gross national savings and investments will attain its maximum in 1980 when it reaches 18.2 per cent of the Gross National Product, and will decline very little by 1985, to 17.8 per cent. Under Alternative B the maximum gap will also be reached in 1980, with 12.1 per cent of the GNP, but the fall between 1980 and 1985 will be more substantial as it then will have dropped to 10.7 per cent. As the ultimate target must be that it should be possible for Pakistan to finance an adequate investment programme out of its own resources, it is obvious that even under Alternative B the country will be very far from reaching this goal by 1985.[2]

The figures which have been produced here show that even if three-quarters of the annual deficit of goods and services were covered by interest-bearing foreign loans or private investments, the rise in the national income which results will be easily large enough to offset the added payments of factor income abroad. It can be shown that this would be the case even if the entire import surplus was financed on 'commercial terms'.[3]

On the other hand, the figures show that the breakdown of foreign aid between 'grants' and 'loans' has a tremendous influence on the country's future ability to finance its own investments and pay for its imports. These two facts hang together since the gap between national savings and investments is identical to the export-import gap. The higher the proportion of foreign 'aid' a country receives in the form of interest-bearing loans and private loans and private foreign investments, the further removed is the day when it can finance its own growth.

12. The Thorny Road
towards Full Employment

A. *The difficulties in measuring employment*

In any circumstance it is difficult to assess the employment situation in an economy dominated by agriculture. Even when statistical data are available, the actual employment, under-employment, seasonal unemployment, and permanent unemployment in agriculture cannot be shown with precision. Most farmers are partially unemployed during some seasons and overemployed during others. It is obvious that farmers with under-sized holdings are under-employed during the better part of the year. In economically advanced countries such farmers often find work outside the farm and will take time off for sowing and harvesting, while their wives manage to look after most of the daily work (like feeding the animals when the husband is away). Also in a less-developed country small farmers may have a second form of employment in cottage industry, transport, trade, or construction. In both cases it is extremely difficult to assess how much time must be spent on the land and with the livestock.

An estimate of total employment in Pakistan, where almost three-quarters of the labour force are classified as in agriculture, is virtually impossible. The attempt which is made in this study corresponds reasonably well to other estimates, but this does not mean that any of the estimates can be regarded as fairly exact.

Unfortunately, the employment data for other sectors of the economy are also highly uncertain. Whilst employment in government service, in modern manufacturing industries, and in certain parts of the transport sector (like the railways) is known, the data on trade, traditional manufacturing, construction, and services are highly questionable. Different sources give conflicting results. Census figures cannot be taken as the ultimate answer because the classification problem is so difficult. For example, most of the employment in the traditional food manufacturing industries is seasonal so that the majority of the workers in these industries will probably be counted in the census as farmers, traders, or as having some other occupation. Nevertheless, these industries represent an important source of income and employment.

The employment estimates in this study are mainly based on calculations of the number of *man-years* worked in the various sectors of the economy. In some cases such figures may be fairly close to the actual employment during the whole year, in other cases they may reflect peak employment periods with many times more workers in jobs than the number of man-years would suggest, whereas employment throughout the year will represent a small fraction of the number of man-years. An attempt has also been made to estimate employment in the non-monetized sectors of the economy. One good example is collection of firewood. It certainly represents a good million man-years, but it will never appear in the employment statistics, nor in the population census. Moreover, a good deal of the work may be done by people who statistically are not included in the labour force, like young children or women. This is one explanation why the figures for apparent unemployment in this study are lower than figures which have been presented elsewhere. This lower figure for unemployment and under-employment is fictional, and should not be taken literally. Other ways of presenting the figures show to what extent the employment situation is expected to improve during the next twenty to twenty-five years.

Unemployment in a poor country in which there are innumerable productive tasks to perform may be looked upon as an anachronism. Unfortunately, it requires a certain amount of organizational talent and willingness to make sacrifices if the labour force of any country is to be mobilized fully. In the present study it has been assumed that organizational talent will be forthcoming and that enough ·sacrifices will be made so that unemployed labour can be put to work. The present situation is so difficult, however, that unless some forced mobilization of labour takes place, the achievement of full employment within the next twenty years is an almost impossible goal. On the other hand, it should be possible to create enough jobs for the rising population and even gradually reduce the number of unemployed, not only as a proportion of the total labour force, but in absolute terms as well.

B. *The total employment situation*

The figures used in Table 61 can be questioned for two reasons: First, they show that the agricultural labour force represents a lower proportion of the total labour force than official statistics show (61 per cent according to Table 61 against 74 per cent according to the Population Census).[1] Most of the difference is explained by the fact that official statistics do not include any figures for employment in forestry and fishing (1.6 million man-years according to the figures used in this study) and the official

Table 61. *Summary of employment projections (1,000 man-years)*

	1960	1965	1970	1975	1980	1985
Non-agricultural activities						
'Modern' sectors						
Forestry.................	10	13	18	22	30	36
Fishing	7	15	23	38	65	95
Mining	31	57	97	146	219	326
Manufacturing	574	758	1,096	1,590	2,301	3,414
Electricity, gas	3	9	21	34	53	82
Construction	720	1,250	1,965	2,685	3,925	5,320
Government	550	700	900	1,200	1,660	2,400
Banking, insurance	75	110	175	270	410	640
Transport	440	645	1,165	1,520	2,100	2,650
Communications	70	95	125	165	215	265
Trade...................	2,000	2,380	2,900	3,500	4,250	5,400
Education	310	355	545	1,020	1,790	2,500
Health services...........	140	180	297	549	937	1,582
Other services...........	2,137	2,537	3,123	3,936	4,998	6,453
Total 'modern' sectors	7,100	9,100	12,500	16,700	22,950	31,150
'Traditional' sectors						
Forestry (fuel wood mainly)	1,215	1,350	1,350	1,350	1,330	1,250
Fishing	415	470	485	515	540	560
Quarrying	120	200	300	375	450	470
Traditional manufacturing	2,080	2,415	2,460	2,510	2,505	2,435
Construction ('self-help') ..	1,270	1,650	1,850	2,150	2,250	2,500
Traditional transport	1,030	1,320	1,185	1,130	980	895
Total 'traditional'........	6,100	7,400	7,600	8,000	8,025	8,100
Total non-agricultural	13,200	16,500	20,100	24,700	30,975	39,250
Total labour force	33,700	38,300	43,500	49,800	56,850	65,200
Difference: Per definition agricultural labour force	20,500	21,800	23,400	25,100	25,900	26,000
'Minimum' employment agriculture.............	17,600	18,100	17,900	17,700	15,700	14,300
'Maximum' employment agriculture.............	17,600	18,300	20,400	23,800	25,100	28,600
'Economic' employment agriculture.............	17,600	18,700	19,600	20,900	21,500	22,200

Sources: [0], Annex VIB, Tables 145 to 148. Employment in agriculture: 'minimum'='reasonable' assumption about increase in labour productivity per acre and animal; 'maximum' = no change in such labour productivity; 'economic'=based on calculation of the ability of agriculture to pay its labour (see footnote Table 62).

figures for traditional transport, construction, trade, and services are considerably lower than the figures used here. In absolute figures the difference represents about 4.5 million people. The discrepancy is therefore more apparent than real. Second, I have made no allowance for the unemployed in the non-agricultural labour force (estimated at 700,000 persons in an unpublished document). This unemployment is, however, hidden behind the figures for very low earnings per man-year in a number of traditional occupations. These low earnings imply that many workers will be unemployed part of the year.

The figures for employment in agriculture in the future are shown as an illustration. If these figures are taken to represent the employment opportunities in agriculture, and if urban unemployment is set at zero *per definition* (i. e. urban unemployment is considered as displaced agricultural unemployment, on the grounds that urban unemployment in fact results from a too rapid exodus of people from the rural areas and not from lack of employment opportunities in the towns), and if no account is taken of the potential labour force absorbed as students in schools at various levels, then the number of unemployed in agriculture will be higher throughout the period up to 1985 than in 1960. Under this assumption the agricultural labour force will be above its 'permissible' level — i. e. the level at which the value added per head in agriculture will grow at the same rate as total

Table 62. *The total labour force and its distribution by occupation*
(Millions of man-years)

	1960	1965	1970	1975	1980	1985
Total labour force employed	33.7	38.3	43.5	49.8	56.8	65.2
Modern sectors, etc.	7.1	9.1	12.45	16.7	22.95	31.2
Trad. industries, etc.	6.1	7.4	7.7	8.0	8.0	8.1
Agriculture (illustrative) ...	17.6	18.7	19.6	20.9	21.5	22.2
Agr. unemployed	2.9	3.1	3.8	4.2	4.4	3.75
Total agr. labour force	20.5	21.8	23.4	25.1	25.9	26.0
Total agr. labour force, 'permissible' level	20.5	21.75	22.8	24.35	25.1	25.9

Sources: Labour force 1960, unpublished estimate. The labour force is assumed to grow at the same rate as the total population. Employment – Table 61, 'economic' employment for agriculture. Total agricultural labour force equals total labour force less non-agricultural employment. The 'permissible' level of the agricultural labour force is the one which allows value added per head of the agricultural labour force to grow at the same rate as the rural product per head (see comments [0], Annex VI – 148). Note that the proportion between the illustrative example of employment in agriculture and permissible labour force remains constant.

rural income. The difference between the estimated and the 'permissible' agricultural labour force is shown as fairly large in the period 1970 to 1980. In other words, the structural development of the economy as projected in this study will not lead to an improvement of the employment situation, but rather the opposite, If this conclusion is right, it is evident that the authorities will have to conduct a more active employment policy and create additional jobs for millions of people. This can be done through 'works programmes' which thus would lead to higher output and employment in the construction industries ('commercial' as well as non-monetized). This would in turn lead to a higher national income than the one projected in this study. Such employment policies could only be implemented if domestic savings and/or the inflow of foreign capital ('foreign aid') could be raised sufficiently to finance additional investments. These additional investments would have very little impact on the growth of national income and would raise the capital-output ratio further.

The level of agricultural unemployment may turn out to be considerably higher or considerably lower than shown in Table 62. Useful employment in agriculture may in fact be considerably lower in 1985 than in 1960, and unemployment in agriculture 6 to 8 million man-years higher than shown in Table 62. Such lower employment estimates in agriculture represent situations which will occur if all efforts are concentrated on efficiency in all employment of rural labour, or conversely if the modernization of agriculture is permitted to run its course without counterbalancing efforts to try to maintain the level of employment in agriculture as high as possible.

C. *The effects of expanded education on employment*

The estimates of the level of unemployment in agriculture would be considerably lower if account were taken of the fact that the number of juveniles aged 12 and above who attend schools will increase much faster than the number of people in these age groups. Consequently, a lower proportion of people in the age groups 12 to 22 years will belong to the labour force. Table 63 gives alternative estimates of the unemployment in agriculture, taking into account (1) higher productivity in agriculture, or (2) higher school participation, or (3) a combination of both. Note that in deducting the higher school attendance from the total labour force, it is implicitly assumed that there will be no tendency to higher participation in the labour force of people above school age. This assumption may be wrong. It is quite possible that the modernization of the economy will raise the proportion of the labour force to total population in the adult age groups, partly because more women will seek employment. Three factors may contribute to increased participation of women in the labour force: the general tendency towards the emancipation of women; the higher level of education amongst women; and the desire for

Table 63. *Adjusted employment figures – account taken of school attendance and of possible higher productivity in agriculture* (1,000 man-years)

	1960	1965	1970	1975	1980	1985
Un-employment, first estimate	2,900	3,100	3,800	4,200	4,375	3,750
Reduction of unemployment because of higher school attendance	0	135	780	2,065	3,585	4,970
Increase of unemployment because of higher productivity in agriculture						
Lower estimate...........	0	400	1,100	2,400	4,500	6,000
Higher estimate	0	600	1,700	3,200	5,800	7,900
Adjusted unemployment estimates						
Lowest level	2,900	2,965	3,020	2,135	790	–1,220
Highest level............	2,900	3,700	5,500	7,400	10,175	11,650
Combined effect of education and higher productivity in agriculture (lower estimate)	2,900	3,365	4,120	4,535	5,290	4,780

Sources and methods of estimation. Unemployment, first estimate, Table 62. Effect on the labour force of higher school attendance: Data for school attendance are given in [0], Annex V. For all schools above primary school level the following calculation has been made: the projected number of students is compared with a hypothetical number of students calculated on the assumption that the number of students will have grown at the same rate as total population. The difference represents an expression of the higher rate of school attendance in absolute numbers. It has been assumed that the following percentage of this higher level of school attendance will be drawn from the labour force: 2 first years middle school 20 per cent, third year middle school 30 per cent, all other schools except vocational training institutes 40 per cent and vocational training institutes 50 per cent. Note that the Census of Population 1961 shows following percentage for participation in the labour force for the relevant age groups: 10–11 years 24 per cent, 12–14 years 36 per cent, 15–19 years 46 per cent, and 20–24 years 52 per cent (source, [15], p. 40–41). Effects of higher productivity in agriculture: Source [0], Annex VI–148. The difference between cases (iv) and (iii) respectively and case (v). The lowest figures for unemployment are obtained by deducting the number of school children and juveniles who otherwise would have been in the labour force from the estimated unemployment figures. The highest figure for unemployment is obtained by disregarding the effect of education on the labour force and adding the effect of higher productivity in agriculture to the first estimate of unemployment.

a higher standard of living which will encourage more women to seek work.

Table 63 gives four alternatives for total unemployment. The first estimate shows that unemployment will increase from about 3 million man-years in 1960 to about 4.5 million in 1980 and fall below 4 million in 1985. If labour productivity in agriculture does not increase more than assumed in Table 62, and a larger number of young people are withdrawn from the labour force because they go to school, unemployment will remain at 3 million during the first ten years but then drop sharply and become negative in 1985. This does not mean, however, that there will be a shortage of labour in 1985 since there is considerable scope for increased participation in the labour force. But it means that if there still is unemployment in 1985 (based on the assumptions about productivity in agriculture used in the first estimate of unemployment), this will have been caused by a rising participation rate in the labour force, not by a failure of emlpoyment to grow in step with the rising population.

If there is a considerable increase in labour productivity in agriculture, and the higher school attendance has no effect on the labour force (because this effect is offset by a higher participation in the labour force by other groups), unemployment will rise sharply during the period under review and will reach almost 12 million man-years in 1985.

Finally, if the labour force is reduced because of higher school attendance, and productivity in agriculture rises considerably, unemployment will grow considerably up to 1985. This last alternative is perhaps the most realistic one. Children between 10 and 14 years old represent about 10 per cent of the total labour force in agriculture, and if all these children go to school there will presumably be an automatic effect on productivity in agriculture, more so because the children who nominally will be outside the labour force nevertheless certainly will take part in urgent seasonal work on the farms.[2] Therefore it looks as if the unemployment situation may develop even more unfavourably than shown in Table 62. Moreover, it should be remembered that none of these estimates takes into account the very real possibility of a much higher participation of *women* in the labour force.

The unemployment which is projected in Tables 61 and 62 will mainly take two forms: under-employment on the farms, and urban unemployment caused by an inflow of migrants from the rural areas. There may also be unemployment amongst hired agricultural labour.

The unemployment may turn out to be less serious than suggested here, mainly because of deliberate or unintentional waste of labour in many trades. If the unemployed are to be employed in a rational manner, it would, as discussed above, be necessary to carry through more ambitious investment programmes than assumed in this study. It seems in any event obvious that the unemployment problem will not be solved automatically through the process of development during the next couple of decades.

D. *The growth of non-agricultural employment*

Table 61 shows that 82 per cent of the growth of the labour force between 1960 and 1985 will be absorbed in non-agricultural employment. Where will 26 million additional jobs be found in the course of these 25 years? This is suggested by the picture drawn in Table 64.

One is immediately struck by the fact that the role of the goods-producing sectors in creating jobs in modern and/or predominantly urban sectors is so small. Their share of the employment in these sectors is expected to rise only from 9 to 12.5 per cent, and over the period 1960 to 1985 will contribute less to increased employment in modern or predominantly urban sectors than any of the other five groups of sectors under this heading.

Three groups of sectors will increase their share of the total modern or predominantly urban employment very considerably: construction, health and education, and modern services (e. g. transport, banking and insurance, gas and electricity, government services, and 'other' services). These three groups will between them create 58 per cent of the new non-agricultural jobs in modern or predominantly urban sectors (excluding most traditional occupations). It should be noted, however, that the contribution of the construction industry is projected as being very large during the first couple of five-year periods under review, and will tend to fall when the share of investments in the use of national resources ceases to rise very rapidly. Neither will health and education continue to contribute such a notable share of new jobs as in the 1970s; when these services have been built out satisfactorily, their share in creation of new jobs will fall considerably. The share of other modern services in providing employment opportunities seems, however, to be rising. The share of trade and of traditional services in the total number of jobs is falling, and this fall will certainly continue in the case of traditional services. The higher percentage shown for trade between 1980 and 1985 is significant, however. At the end of the period under review personal consumption is expected to start rising more rapidly, and with this, the turnover of consumer goods. Trade, therefore, may con-

Table 64. *Percentage break-down of non-agricultural employment by major groups and the contribution of these groups to the increase in employment*

	1960	1965	1970	1975	1980	1985
Modern sectors (including also traditional services except traditional transport services)						
A. *Absolute figures* (mill. man-years)	7.05	9.1	12.45	16.70	22.95	31.15
B. *Percentage distribution*						
Goods-producing sectors ..	8.8	9.3	9.9	10.8	11.4	12.4
Construction	10.2	13.7	15.8	16.1	17.1	17.1
Health and education	6.4	5.9	6.8	9.4	11.9	13.1
Trade..................	28.3	26.1	23.3	21.0	18.5	17.3
Other services, modern	17.1	18.2	20.6	21.0	21.5	22.1
Trad. services (exc. transp).	29.3	26.8	23.7	21.8	19.6	18.0
Total of above	100	100	100	100	100	100
All non-agricultural employment						
A. *Absolute figures* (mill. man-years)	13.2	16.5	20.1	24.7	31.0	39.3
B. *Percentage distribution*						
Modern sectors, incl. trade.	37.9	40.4	47.3	52.8	59.6	65.1
Traditional sectors, including transp., excluding other services	46.4	44.9	38.0	32.5	25.9	20.7
Other trad. services	15.6	14.8	14.7	14.7	14.5	14.3
Total	100	100	100	100	100	100

Contribution to the growth of non-agricultural employment per five-year periods	1960 to 85 (%)	1960 to 65 (%)	1965 to 70 (%)	1970 to 75 (%)	1975 to 80 (%)	1980 to 85 (%)
Modern sectors and trad. services other than transport.						
Goods producing sectors ..	13.5	10.8	11.7	13.3	13.0	15.3
Construction	19.1	26.0	21.4	17.0	19.8	17.0
Health and education	15.1	4.2	9.2	17.2	18.4	16.5
Trade..................	14.1	18.7	15.5	14.2	11.9	14.0
Other services, modern ...	23.6	22.1	27.0	22.2	23.0	23.8
Trad. services (exc. transp.)	14.6	18.2	15.2	16.1	13.9	13.4
Total of above	100	100	100	100	100	100
All non-agricultural employment						
Modern sectors, incl. trade.	78.9	50.3	79.4	76.6	86.2	85.7
Trad. sectors, incl. transp. excluding other services .	7.6	38.5	6.3	8.6	−0.1	1.0
Other trad. services	13.5	11.2	14.2	14.7	13.9	13.3
Total non-agr. employment	100	100	100	100	100	100

Source: Table 61.

tribute relatively more jobs after 1985 than during the period under review.

The figures in Table 64 suggest that there will be a relative shift away from employment in traditional industries, to the modern sectors and trade. It may appear surprising that the traditional services will almost maintain their share of non-agricultural employment. This is due to the increasing urbanization of the economy which will lead to a rapid increase in demand for all kind of services. Apart from the period 1960 to 1965 the traditional goods-producing industries and transport will contribute little, if anything, to the increase in non-agricultural employment.

The following figures which show the distribution of non-agricultural employment among goods-producing sectors, construction trade, and 'pure' services, suggest that employment in services will increase far more than employment in the goods-producing sectors.

It should be noted that the share of health and education in total non-agricultural employment is projected to increase from 3.5 to 10.5 per cent and this increase represents almost half of the increased share of the modern services.

It seems surprising to see figures which suggest that the total share of goods-producing sectors in non-agricultural employment will fall from more than one-third to less than 22 per cent. Clearly part of this fall is due to a relative shift of manpower from

Table 65. *Non-agricultural employment, broken down by goods-producing sectors, construction, trade and other services* (Per cent)

	1960	1985
All goods-producing sectors	*33.9*	*21.9*
of which		
modern	4.7	9.9
traditional	29.0	12.0
Construction	*15.1*	*19.9*
of which		
modern	5.5	13.5
non-monetized	9.6	6.4
Trade	*15.2*	*13.7*
Other services	*36.0*	*44.4*
of which		
modern	12.5	27.9
traditional	23.5	16.5

Source: Table 61.

low productivity traditional industries to high productivity modern industries. Another reason for the relative expansion of employment in services at the expense of the goods-producing sectors (including construction) is the increase in productivity of goods-producing sectors.

Nevertheless, the projected shift in employment towards the 'service industries is so strong that it seems to contradict most historical studies of economic development. This contradiction is merely apparent. There are three major causes for the employment paradox shown above. Firstly, as has already been pointed out, the strong increase in productivity in the goods-producing sector (e. g. the value added per man-year in modern plus traditional manufacturing will increase 4.3 times between 1960 and 1985). Secondly, in contrast to most services, goods can be imported. Since in the present study a large import surplus is projected throughout the period under review, output from and employment in service industries will be relatively higher than in a country without an import surplus. Thirdly, since manpower will remain cheap, services will also be relatively cheap, thus stimulating demand for services. A fourth point could also be added. The tremendous expansion of the health and education services is a major element in the growth of employment in the service sectors as a whole.

The most important practical conclusion which can be drawn from these estimates of the future employment pattern is that it is completely misleading to consider employment opportunities only in the modern manufacturing industries and in some other modern sectors when assessing future employment opportunities in a developing country. It is all too obvious that modern sectors like large-scale manufacturing, modern transport, and gas and electricity production and distribution will only provide employment for a fraction of the growing labour force in a developing country and cannot help in the least to reduce under-employment in agriculture.

It would be dangerous if people, on the basis of this depressing conclusion, were to argue that the modernization of the economy must be held back because it will not help to solve the employment problem. Indirectly, the modernization and industrialization of the economy will substantially help to solve the employment problem. It will induce a rapid expansion of the construction industry which is very labour-intensive; it will create employment in transport and trade and numerous service sectors; and it will pump purchasing power into the economy, resulting in increased job opportunities in a number of fields. The attempt to create many jobs in agriculture in a country such as Pakistan, where scarce land and water set definite limits to the expansion of output, is doomed to fail because the modernization of agriculture will sooner or later lead to the more efficient use of manpower on land and hence reduce the number of jobs.

E. *Employment in rural and urban areas*

For several reasons it was necessary in this study to estimate the future distribution of the population between rural and urban areas (see Chapter 4). It is, of course, of great interest to see whether the projected employment data are consistent with the assumed distribution of the population.

Table 66 is frankly hypothetical, since reliable data on the occupational distribution of the labour force between rural and urban areas are not even available for the base year 1960. The future trends are also very difficult to assess. In the case of commercial construction the data on the future investments in building and other construction work suggest that the proportion of the work undertaken in rural areas will fall considerably. It is also quite obvious that rural share of employment in trade will fall substantially. As regards modern manufacturing, however, the suggested figure is a pure guess, based on the assumption that there will be distinct tendencies for manufacturing industries to grow in towns and that industrial towns will grow up around many factories in the rural areas. Similarly (but of very little importance as regards total employment), it has been assumed that much of the mining activities will result in the springing up of mining towns. All percentages are, of course, approximate and should not be taken too literally. It should be remembered that some people working in banking, insurance, or in modern services will live in rural areas, and there will be farmers, farm workers, and forest workers living in the urban regions.

Taking all these reservations into account, it may nevertheless be justly concluded from the Table that the projected growth of the urban population in relation to the total population largely seems to reflect the projected changes in the employment pattern. In Table 66 no account has been taken of urban unemployment, nor of the effect of the far higher degree of school attendance. Both these factors would tend to increase the urban population in relation to the rural one. On the other hand, the Table may underestimate the effect of commuting between rural and urban areas and of temporary employment of rural workers in the towns.

The percentage distribution of the labour force in the rural areas seems to change relatively little. The figures show a shift from agriculture to modern sectors, whereas rural unemployment

Table 66. *Employment, labour force, and population in urban
and rural areas*

	1960	1965	1970	1975	1980	1985
Rural areas						
Population, mill.	89.7	98.7	107.8	117.6	123.2	125.5
Labour force, mill.	29.7	33.1	36.0	39.1	41.4	42.5
Labour force in per cent. of population	33.2	33.5	33.4	33.4	33.4	33.9
Percentage distribution of labour force:						
Agriculture, actively employed............	59.2	56.5	54.5	53.5	52.3	52.2
Agriculture, unemployed	9.8	9.4	10.6	10.8	10.6	8.8
Traditional sectors	23.7	26.4	24.8	24.6	24.1	24.2
Modern sectors	3.3	4.3	5.9	6.9	8.8	10.6
Trade.................	4.0	4.3	4.3	4.2	4.1	4.2
Urban areas						
Population, mill.	13.1	18.1	24.9	34.3	50.2	73.4
Labour force, mill.	4.0	5.3	7.5	10.7	15.7	22.7
Labour force in per cent. of population	30.2	29.0	30.2	31.1	31.2	30.9
Percentage distribution of the labour force ...						
Traditional sectors	28.9	27.6	22.1	19.0	16.6	15.1
Modern sectors	50.9	54.3	59.7	63.7	67.1	69.0
Trade.................	20.2	18.1	18.2	17.3	16.3	15.9

Sources and methods of estimation. Population, [0], Annex II, Table 2, Employment, Table 61. Distribution of employment between rural and urban areas: Exclusively rural employment: agriculture, forestry, mining (imputed income), non-monetary construction. Exclusively urban employment: modern fishing, electricity and gas, banking and insurance, modern services. Rural proportion of employment in other sectors: traditional fishing, three-quarters of total; modern mining, falling from 100 per cent to 50 per cent of total; modern manufacturing, falling from 10 per cent to 5 per cent of total; commercial construction, falling from 50 per cent to 30 per cent of total; government servants, distributed between rural and urban areas in the same proportion as government consumption is distributed (see [0], Annex III, Table 1). Trade, falling from 60 per cent to 33 per cent of total; education, falling from 30 per cent to 25 per cent of total; health, rising from 3 per cent to 10 per cent of total. Traditional services, distributed between rural and urban areas in the same proportion as consumer demand for servants, etc, and personal care (see [0], Annex III, Table 8). Modern transport, falling from 30 per cent to 20 per cent of total (and as regards unskilled workers occupied on cartage for the construction industry, from 50 per cent to 30 per cent of the total).

Traditional sectors comprise forestry (except exploitation of national forests), traditional fishing, 'mining' of sand, stones, etc., traditional manufacturing, transport, traditional services, and non-monetized construction.

and employment in the traditional sectors and in trade represent practically the same proportion of the total labour force at the end of the period as at the beginning. Within the traditional sectors, however, there should be a relative shift away from traditional manufacturing and transport to non-monetized mining and construction and traditional services. It is the migration to urban areas which has to provide an outlet for the population growth in the rural areas. It follows from the urbanization of the economy that a declining proportion of employment in the modern sectors will be in rural areas — the proportion of total rural employment in modern sectors is assumed to fall from 33 per cent in 1960 to 22 per cent in 1985.

In the urban areas there will be a marked shift from employment in traditional sectors to employment in the modern sectors. Employment in other traditional sectors than services is projected as falling from 16 per cent of the total urban labour force in 1960 to 3 per cent in 1985. The employment in traditional services will probably grow almost as fast as the urban population. A fall in the share of trade in total employment must also be expected, as other types of urban employment will grow very rapidly.

13. Income Flows, Savings and Consumption

A. *The financial flows*

The pattern of growth and its influence on the flow of goods and services shown in the earlier chapters is not independent of outside factors. We have already to some extent studied population growth and movements and the growth and pattern of employment, and we have concluded that there is no inconsistency between the flows of goods and services and the development of the population and employment pattern. In the financial field, however, only transactions with foreign countries have had to be analysed as an integrated part of the present analysis. The reason for this is obvious: financial transations with foreign countries have their counterparts in the form of a flow of goods and services to and from foreign countries.

Flows of goods and services will result in, and will simultaneously be determined by, domestic financial flows. It has been assumed here that it will always be possible to manipulate the domestic financial flows in such a manner that changes in the flows of goods and services ('real resources') can take place as projected. The government can manage this through its financial and monetary policies — but only within limits. It is possible to construct a model for the flow of real resources which implies such drastic changes that it would be difficult to envisage how the government could implement the changes merely through financial and monetary policies.

In this study it has been explicitly assumed that the growth will take place in a society which will not undergo revolutionary social and organizational changes. Two of these assumptions have been stressed several times: consumers will have freedom of choice, and private enterprises will play an important role. These two assumptions do not exclude rationing of certain consumer goods and services, control of investments in enterprises or licensing of imports, and they certainly do not exclude the use of indirect taxes, subsidies, and tariff protection as means to guide the economic development. But it is implicitly assumed that such means will be used with moderation and not lead to a situation in which consumer choice and freedom of private enterprise have become illusory.

The question then arises: Is the projected pattern of development, as expressed in the flows of goods and services, possible within this framework of relative economic freedom? Or in other words, will the financial flows *resulting* from the production of, and trade in, goods and services be distributed in such a manner that the *pattern of demand* will be as assumed in this study?

Domestic financial flows consist of flows of income and its current use and flows of capital (borrowing and lending). Income flows, and particularly the distribution of income between current consumption and savings, are more fundamental in determining the growth pattern than are capital flows. In actual fact, however, an imperfect capital market, which prevents available capital from moving into the most profitable or the most desireable investments, can prove to be more of a deterrent to economic growth than inadequate savings out of current income. The organization of the capital market is to a large extent a question of institutional arrangements, and one is probably justified in stating that satisfactory institutional arrangements can be made and that savings out of current income are the crucial problem.

B. *A basis for estimates of income flows*[1]

As it has been concluded that the income flows are fundamental whereas the domestic capital movements are merely of secondary importance,[2] the question must be posed whether it is possible to obtain a reasonably realistic picture of the income flows.

This study has provided us with one important element in the examination of income flows, i. e. *value added* broken down into sectors. Value added (at factor cost) consists of labour income and capital income. The latter includes depreciation of the fixed capital invested in the sector.[3] If depreciation *and* interest payment on debt are deducted, we arrive at net profits before taxes.

We have no basis for making such a detailed breakdown of the value added of the different sectors of the economy. What has been done is to split value added between labour income and capital income. Labour income includes all renumeration of labour, i. e. also the 'labour income' of self-employed persons or of owners of non-corporate enterprises. This had been done by multiplying the employment in each sector with the estimated average labour income per man-year. This approach has the great advantage of eliminating the effects of changes in the ownership structure with time. But it must be underlined that the distinction between 'labour income' and 'capital income' of, for example, self-employed farmers is nominal.

For all sectors and subsectors of the economy, figures for employment in terms of man-years have been calculated.[4] In a number of cases it has been specifically assumed that value added per man-year will increase. Real earnings per man-year will have to rise. In order to calculate this rise it has been assumed that earnings in predominantly urban occupations will rise at the same rate as private consumption per head in urban areas, and similarly for predominantly rural occupations. For mixed occupations a combination of the two series has been used. For some sectors it has furthermore been assumed that earnings will rise more, taking into account the effect of 'up-grading' of the personnel (i. e. more skilled and less unskilled manpower) on average earnings.

In four sectors — government product, health services, education, and 'other' services — no assumption was made in Chapter 8 about increases in productivity. That is, value added in those sectors, in constant prices, was calculated on the basis of the employment multiplied by the average earnings in the base year. Consequently, the calculated labour income in those sectors exceeds the value added which has been used as a basis for the calculations of the growth of the Gross Domestic Product. This dilemma has been resolved by recalculating the distribution of the GDP, government consumption, and private consumption in 'current' prices. The assumption that the GDP is expressed in 1960 prices is maintained, but allowance is made for changes in relative prices. This adjustment has been made in a very crude manner — the relative prices of manufactured products (produced by the modern manufacturing sector) are assumed to fall whereas the relative prices on the above-mentioned services are assumed to rise. The value added in the four service sectors is adjusted upward and the value added in modern manufacturing adjusted downward by the same amount. Government consumption in so-called current prices has been obtained by adjusting it upward by the higher incomes of government servants, including personnel in the health and education sectors. Private consumption has been adjusted downward by the same amount, on the crude assumption that the consumers, directly or indirectly, will benefit from the relative fall in the prices of manufactured products.

The *capital income* is obtained by deducting labour income from value added and it includes therefore depreciation, direct taxes, interest on debt paid domestically or abroad, dividends and payments to partners within the sector or outside the sector (in the country or abroad), and retained profits.

C. *The use of labour and capital income*

Labour and capital income has been broken down into three components: consumption, savings and direct taxes. (In the case of capital income in agriculture a fourth component is added, viz. rent.) Consumption and taxes (and agricultural rent) are, in general, treated as functions of the capital or the labour income in the individual sectors.[5] Savings are consequently calculated as a remainder. This rather mechanical approach is used in order to arrive at a distribution of income between consumption and savings which, as far as possible, is not too strongly influenced by the author's attempts to manipulate the figures in line with his own judgements. Of course, the base-year figures are heavily influenced by guesses since very few relevant statistical data were available. The base-year figures had to be manipulated in order to become consistent with calculated consumption and savings in the base year (and with its distribution between urban and rural areas). But the pattern thus arrived at did to a very large extent determine the projected distribution of income between consumption and savings in later years.

The figures obtained for *savings* must be interpreted with care. They are gross figures (since they include depreciation of capital equipment). But they also include income which will be transferred abroad as interest or dividend payments. For each sector the savings out of capital income have been compared with the estimated gross investments in the sector. The difference has been labelled 'monetized savings', a figure which can be negative or positive. It would be wrong to conclude, however, that a sector which shows positive monetized savings will automatically be able to finance its own investments, because some of the savings of the sector will be drawn out of the sector in the form of contractual payments to shareholders, partners, and creditors.[6]

D. *The growth and the use of capital income*

Table 67 shows the growth of the capital income in relation to value added.

It should be noted that the share of the capital income in value added in sectors dominated by corporate enterprises in 1985 is reduced from 68 to 59 per cent as a result of the downward adjustment of relative prices, value added, and capital income in modern manufacturing. In most sectors, the share of capital income tends to rise because it has been assumed that labour productivity in general will rise faster than real wages. Traditional

Table 67. *Capital income as a percentage of value added*

	1960	1985
Agriculture	25	38
Other traditional sectors	11	7
Sectors with a mixture of corporate and non-corporate enterprises	31	32
Sectors dominated by corporations	59	59
Sectors, mostly govt. owned	61	79
Ownership of buildings	100	100
All sectors	28	37

Source: [0], Annex X, Table 2.

sectors are an exception. The share of capital income in the GDP will rise, both because of changes in individual sectors and because sectors with high capital income in relation to value added will tend to grow the fastest. As depreciation charges increase with the modernization of the economy, it is necessary for capital income to grow faster than value added.

To capital income from the productivity sectors of the economy has been added a nominal figure for government interest payments (based on estimates of the public debt).

Table 68 shows the development of and the use of private capital income (i. e. including government interest, but excluding capital income from predominantly government-owned sectors).

Table 68. *The use of private capital income* (Rs Mill.)

	1960	1985
Private capital income from productive sectors	7,460	40,470
Government interest payments	310	8,800
Used for		
Land revenue	220	1,600
Other direct taxes	425	5,485
Consumption	4,195	14,500
Gross investments	2,460	25,065
Monetary savings:		
Out of government interest	210	7,000
Positive, out of other capital income	1,075	3,545
Negative	−810	−7,925
Global adjustment	+ 18	−1,635
Total private savings out of capital income	2,950	26,055

Source: [0], Annex X, Table 3.

The percentage distribution of private capital income shows therefore the following projected development:

	1960	1985
Direct taxes (incl. land revenue)	8	16
Personal consumption	55	35
Gross investments	33	65
Monetary savings	4	—16
Gross savings	37	49

Two important conclusions can be drawn from this illustration:

(1) Personal consumption will rise much more slowly than private capital income, and
(2) in spite of this, the private sector (or more correctly, the enterprise sector) will need a large inflow of capital in 1985, whereas it was able to finance its own investment in 1960.

E. *Reconciliation of two sets of consumption estimates*

Total labour income is estimated to grow from Rs 20,920 million in 1960 to Rs 78,670 million in 1985, and personal consumption out of labour income is estimated to rise from Rs. 20,600 million to Rs 75,640 million during the same period.[7]

Table 69 shows estimates that have been made of consumption and its distribution between rural and urban areas.

We are confronted with the surprising result that during the early period, when the country is poorest, savings will tend to grow too fast in Pakistan and will tend to grow more slowly than assumed from 1970 onwards.[8]

We furthermore find that rural consumption is persistently shown to be above the target figures. This could be for the obvious reason that the rural product as calculated on the basis of the detailed breakdown of the domestic product was considerably higher than the rural product used as the basic assumption for this study. But this is not the case.[9]

The reason for the discrepancies between the target figures for consumption and the figures based on the calculated income distribution must therefore be found elsewhere. The answer is the following.[10] Rural consumption rises faster than assumed because consumed capital income in rural areas rises much faster than the target for total rural consumption. This is again caused by the growing prosperity of the farmers. In urban areas, on the other hand, consumption out of capital income is projected as rising only half as fast as total consumption, and the somewhat faster rise of consumption out of labour income (caused by the upgrad-

Table 69. *Reconciliation of two different consumption estimates* (Rs mill.)

	1960	1965	1970	1975	1980	1985
Target personal consumption, adjusted						
Total	24,790	30,185	38,575	50,195	66,220	89,610
Of which						
Rural	18,780	21,085	25,130	30,455	35,620	40,280
Urban	6,010	9,100	13,455	19,740	30,600	49,330
Personal consumption out of labour and capital income						
Out of labour income	20,595	24,485	31,205	41,220	55,205	75,640
Out of capital income	4,195	5,210	6,390	8,120	10,630	14,500
Total	24,790	29,695	37,590	49,335	65,835	90,140
of which						
Rural	18,780	21,565	25,265	30,510	36,245	44,055
Urban	6,010	8,130	12,325	18,830	29,595	46,085
Discrepancies						
Calculated less target consumption						
Total	0	−490	−980	−860	−385	+530
Rural	0	+480	135	+55	+625	+3,775
Urban	0	−970	−1,120	−910	−1,005	−3,245

Sources: [0], Annex X, Tables 6 and 8.

ing of labour in many sectors) is not strong enough to offset this. Consumption out of capital income in the towns is estimated to have accounted for 26 per cent of total urban consumption in 1960; in 1985 the percentage is projected as having fallen below 15. The main reason for this is the shrinking importance of rent from agriculture as a source of income to be spent on consumption in urban areas.

The model depends on a fairly rapid increase in personal consumption. If consumption falls short of targets, this will lead to a fall in the Gross Domestic Product and not to an increase in savings. It can be shown how the consumption targets can be reached.[11] This implies, *inter alia,* a lowering of the relative prices of agricultural products during the Fourth to the Sixth Plan periods. In other words, the previous assumption that rising relative prices for services are offset by lower relative prices for manufactured goods is modified so that agriculture will account for a share of the falling relative prices.

F. *Government finances and total savings*

Goverment finances, under the assumption of no changes in the tax structure, show the development projected in Table 70.

The picture of the development of government finances looks quite plausible. Current government income also includes income from government-owned enterprises. This income will rise fast enough to cover most of the interest on government debt, and the tax income will increase faster than government consumption.

But there is considerable scope for significant changes in the picture of government finances as presented in Table 70. Firstly, taxes may be raised. This would raise the government surplus and, consequently, also the ratio between public and private savings. Secondly, the government may be able to cover a large part of its need for borrowing through grants from foreign countries. This would reduce interest payments, thereby increase government current surplus, and again lower the need for further borrowing. Thus, although the figures are quite plausible, they can very well be far off the mark.

Finally, attention should be called to the bottom lines of Table 70. Private savings out of capital income include debt servicing abroad. According to Table 55 these may, in 1985, amount to Rs 20.5 billion under the 'worst' alternative and Rs 7 billion under

Table 70. *Government finances and total domestic savings* (Rs Mill.)

	1960	1985
Government current income	2,600	27,465
Government current expenditure	2,710	24,260
Of which		
Government consumption	2,400	15,460
Interest on debt	310	8,800
Government current surplus	–110	3,205
Government investments	1,490	15,235
Of which		
In enterprises	765	6,300
Other	725	8,935
Government need for borrowing	1,600	12,030
Total domestic savings:..............................	3,050	30,710
Of which		
Private out of capital income	2,950	26,055
Private out of labour income	210	1,450
Government current surplus	–110	3,205

Sources: [0], Annex X, Tables 5 and 6.

the more favourable one. If the more favourable form for capital aid to Pakistan is realized, we shall find that private capital accumulation in Pakistan will account for very large sums. This is quite natural in a free enterprise economy, but it may lead to political complications. Such capital accumulation in a poor country may be resented by those who do not directly benefit from it. This observation leads also to the conclusion that taxes may be raised above their 1960 level, so as to enable the government to account for a larger proportion of the national savings. Such a policy would also have the practical purpose of financing a larger proportion of government investments out of government revenue. For the many reasons listed above, the figures in Table 70 must not be considered as forecasts.

14. Perspective Planning in Pakistan

A. *Projections versus planning*

The projections contained in this study are in many respects different from, and in some cases even very different from, the figures published by the Government of Pakistan on long-term perspectives in its Third Five Year Plan.[1] A systematic comparison of the two sets of projections is relevant and of considerable interest for two main reasons — the methodologies and some of the basic assumptions differ. It could not, therefore, be expected that the results of the projections should turn out to be similar.

It should also be borne in mind that a comparison between Pakistan's Perspective Plan and this study covers two exercises which have been carried out for different purposes. The Perspective Plan is an attempt at long-term planning on the basis of policy targets to which the Government of Pakistan is committed. The present study is an academic analysis of a likely development pattern under assumptions chosen by its author, on the basis of what is know about the attitudes and aspirations of the Government of Pakistan, and which, it is hoped, will therefore be acceptable to the Pakistanis. In some doubtful cases I found it necessary to scale down certain ambitious policy targets contained in the Perspective Plan, not because I rejected them but because I found that it would be impossible to reach them within the time span of the present study and of the Perspective Plan. Such cases are discussed in detail in section C of the present chapter.

The present study does not pretend to be anything more than an academic exercise, whereas the Perspective Plan is a policy document; but the methodology used for the present study could equally well have been used for the Perspective Plan. All evidence suggests that the Perspective Plan is based on a relatively simple macro-economic model, whereas the present study is built upon a series of detailed investigations into various sectors of the economy. This method entails a large number of calculations, and has the distinct disadvantage that it is not possible to test the different sets of assumptions as with a computable model. It is therefore rigid, and any significant change in the initial assumptions leads to time-consuming re-calculations of the many details of the model. Within limits, however, it is possible to build a simple macro-economic model on the basis of the information contained in this study, because it is justifiable to assume that the macro-economic coefficients which can be derived from the present study will not change significantly through minor alterations in the basic assumptions about growth, the rate of savings, etc.

The crucial difference between the Perspective Plan and the present study is that while the former appears to be based on assumed figures for the capital-output ratio, the import elasticity, and the rate of saving, in the latter both the capital-output ratio and the import elasticity have been calculated on the basis of details within the model, while the rate of saving initially assumed was modified to make it consistent with the results of the detailed calculations.

To a great extent differences between the two sets of projections can be traced back to another reason, *viz.* the implicit disregard of the pattern of consumption and investment demand respectively in a macro-model. Planners must avoid the pitfall of planning for a development pattern which may be very satisfactory from the point of view of low cost-benefit ratios and a high employment potential, but which disregards to a dangerous extent the breakdown of demand, and only takes into account broad aggregates of demand. Formal consistency is not enough if projections of demand are not broken down sufficiently to provide some guidance as to the pattern of growth by sectors.

There is every reason to suggest that a relatively simple perspective planning process will contain certain inherent weaknesses. A macro-economic model will include certain global coefficients which cannot be determined in a very exact manner. Three such coefficients merit special mention: the capital-output ratio, the import elasticity, and the rate of saving. Slight deviations from the figures used for these three coefficients are bound to cause fundamental changes in the conclusions drawn from the planning model. The capital-output ratio is strongly influenced by the pattern of growth, not only in a macro-sense (i. e. the distribution of growth among agriculture, industry, and services), but also in a micro-sense. Not all capital-goods industries are capital-intensive; not all consumer-goods industries are labour-intensive. Within the service sector some activities are very capital-intensive (e. g. power supply and transport and communications), whereas others involve very little investment. It might be possible to increase output in agriculture up to a certain rate without very heavy investments, whereas efforts to push up the

rate of growth even further may entail very substantial investments (e. g. in irrigation and flood control). A global figure for
the capital-output ratio will remain a very crude guess as long as
it is not based on thorough studies of capital requirements under
a given pattern of growth. Similar problems occur with regard to
import elasticity. The ratio between the growth of imports and
the growth of the national income depends fundamentally on the
pattern of industrial growth behind the growth of the national
income. Finally, the rate of saving is highly dependent on the industrial structure of the national income as well as on the distribution of personal incomes.

These remarks are merely meant to draw attention to the considerable uncertainty implicit in long-term projections, uncertainty which becomes more pronounced the less detailed the perspective planning model. They should not be taken as an absolute condemnation of the use of a simple macro-economic model
for perspective planning purposes. A crude perspective plan is
much better than none at all. It will under all circumstances
contribute to a better understanding of the problems ahead. It
will also compel a government which embarks on perspective
planning to state its objectives and policies in clear, quantitative
terms. Here one must utter a word of warning, however. There
is an inherent danger that optimistic assumptions will be used
too lavishly. This will automatially mean that the danger of
significant shortfalls and disappointments will become very
pronounced. An over-optimistic perspective plan can easily become a political burden for the government. Of course, the opposite argument can be advanced: that under more pessimistic assumptions the future prospects may look so bleak that both
government and people are discouraged, and lose the impetus to
undertake a determined development effort. It should be remembered, however, that the development problem can also be presented in terms of the need for foreign 'aid' or capital inflow. In
essence, pessimistic or 'realistic' assumptions lead to the conclusion
that foreign aid cannot taper off, but must rather increase if certain essential economic and social targets are to be reached. This
is in itself a very healthy conclusion, because it reminds the
'donor' countries of their long-term obligations. The political
burden which results from using too optimistic assumptions can
thus be seen to have two sides: the people would be disappointed
if targets proved beyond reach, and the donor countries, who had
been led to believe that foreign aid could be reduced shortly,
might wrongly conclude that assistance to developing countries
is useless because they never learn to stand on their own feet.

It is true, of course, that I implicitly argue in favour of very detailed studies of the development prospects in a given country before it embarks upon a formal perspective plan. But the benefits to be derived from a more detailed, and perhaps a more sophisticated, mathematical analysis than the one I have used must be weighed against the costs in terms of money and particularly in terms of the use of scarce, skilled manpower. I would personally advocate that priority be given to careful project analysis and stringency in short-term planning rather than to sophisticated perspective planning. Pakistan's economic success in recent years is, indeed, largely based on its determined efforts to carry through and modify its five-year plan, and it has without a doubt been right to concentrate on short-term planning and plan implementation rather than on long-term model building. However, it would clearly be worth while for the Planning Commission in Pakistan to keep its Perspective Plan under review, and to take into account questions raised in this and other studies of Pakistan's development potential.

B. *Perspective Planning in Pakistan*

Pakistan is one of the few countries which up till now have begun to utilize perspective planning as part of their planning procedure. Reference to the work done in Pakistan has been made in many places in this study. Since this chapter is devoted to a comparison between the results of the present study and the forecasts contained in Pakistan's own Perspective Plan, it is necessary to review in a more systematic manner the Perspective Plan and the way in which it has been established.

Although the Perspective Plan is built around a very simple macro-economic model, it is nevertheless a real effort in perspective planning because it contains not only macro-economic forecasts, but also some well-defined policy targets. These are quoted below *in extenso*.

The explicit aims of the Perspective Plan are:

(a) a quadrupling of the Gross National Product from about Rs 43,365 million in 1964—65 to about Rs 174,300 million in 1984—85; more than doubling *per caput* income from Rs 386 in 1965 to Rs 932 in 1985;

(b) provision of full employment to the entire labour force by about the middle of the Perspective Plan period;

(c) parity in *per caput* incomes between East and West Pakistan;

(d) universal literacy; and

(e) elimination of dependence on foreign assistance.[2]

These five main policy objectives represent, in terms of concrete achievements, extremely ambitious expectations. This does not mean that the objectives are unrealistic and unattainable. On the contrary, I believe that in the course of the next decade we shall witness an acceleration of the rate of growth in the developing countries which few people would have believed possible only a few years ago. But since the objectives are ambitious, they can only be achieved through a combination of strict and sensible planning, a series of necessary policy measures, and a willingness on the part of both the leading citizens and the masses of the people to work hard and sacrifice short-term advantages. The fact that some of the objectives are inherently conflicting makes them even more ambitious. A short review of the implications of the objectives will illustrate these points.

Objective (a) implies first that the average annual compound rate of growth of the GNP at market prices must reach 7.2 per cent during the Perspective Plan period 1965—85, as against a rate of 2.5 per cent from 1950 to 1960, and 5.2 per cent during the sucessful Second Five-Year period 1960—65; and secondly, that in order to achieve the planned increase in income per head, the annual rate of population growth must be reduced, through family planning measures, from an estimated 2.7 per cent during the Third Plan period 1965—1970 to 2.1 per cent during the Sixth Plan period 1980—1985.

Objective (b) implies that between 1965 and 1975, 14.6 million jobs will be created, or employment increased by almost half. Half of the jobs will have to be created in non-agricultural activities. This may prove hard to do, for the simple reason that the objective of raising national income fast, as stated in the Perspective Plan, 'implies a rapid increase in the application of modern technology, which tends to be very capital-intensive'. By shifting resources to labour-intensive industries, the rate of growth may be reduced.[3]

Objective (c) implies that during the Perspective Plan period the GNP of East Pakistan will grow at an annual compound rate of 8.0 per cent, as against 6.4 per cent in West Pakistan. During the decade 1950—1960, the rate of growth in East Pakistan was 1.9 per cent, and jumped abruptly to 5.4 per cent during the Second Plan period, whereas in West Pakistan the growth rate reached during the pre-Second Plan decade was 3.1 per cent, and during the Second Plan 5.0 per cent. It would be wrong to put too much emphasis on the fact that East Pakistan increased its share of the GNP during the Second Plan period; this was due, to a great extent, to a sharp increase in the output of rice from a depressed level at the end of the First Five-Year Plan. On the whole, in the immediate future, growth prospects are best in West Pakistan, which still possesses the bulk of modern economic activities in Pakistan. Objective (c) implies that one accepts, as stated in the Perspective Plan, that 'it may be necessary to slow down the rate of growth in one region in order to accelerate the growth of another'. This means a shift of resources to East Pakistan where they may yield smaller results, at least for some years, than they could have done in West Pakistan.

Objective (d) is not quite as ambitious as it looks. The intention is to enrol all children in the relevant age groups in primary schools for 5 years by 1980, and in lower secondary schools for 3 years by 1985. The Perspective Plan makes no mention of any system of adult education aimed at those persons who have not been to primary schools before 1980. In terms of numbers the programme is very ambitious: in the course of twenty years enrolment in primary schools should rise from 7 million to 26.7 million, or by almost 20 million, and in the lower secondary stage from 1.1 million to 15.2 million, or by 14 million. In East Pakistan, the number of children in lower secondary schools should increase twenty-fold.

Objective (e) does not mean that there will be no inflow of foreign capital in 1985. This is a very wise decision. The phrase 'elimination of dependence on foreign assistance' can be interpreted in many ways which all, however, imply a continued sizeable inflow of foreign capital (or, inversely, a sizeable deficit on the current balance of payments). The inflow of foreign capital should not be so great that its sudden cessation would lead to a drastic curtailment of investments or a sharp cut in imports, both with disruptive influences on the domestic economy, nor should it be greater than can be met by normal lending operations and/or an inflow of private, direct investments. The target figure of a foreign capital inflow of Rs 2,000 million in 1985 meets these criteria. It represents less than 5 per cent of gross investment, and only 12.5 per cent of imports, and it is likely that Pakistan could find this amount without relying on foreign aid agencies. Nevertheless, strenuous efforts will be required if this objective is to be reached. Exports must grow by 7.9 per cent per year, and the annual average increase in imports must be kept down to 4.2 per cent, or less than 60 per cent of the annual growth of the GNP, and domestic savings must rise by 11.5 per cent annually and amount to almost 22 per cent of the GNP in 1985, as against slightly over 10 per cent 20 years earlier. Whereas the inflow of external resources will in absolute terms only fall from Rs 3,940 million in 1965 to Rs 2,000 million in 1985, in relative terms it will fall from 8.1 per cent to 1.1 per cent of the

GNP. The fall of imports in relation to GNP is equally striking — from 15.3 per cent in 1965 to 8.6 per cent in 1985.[4]

This short survey of the implications of the five main policy objectives does not *a priori* suggest that any of them is unattainable. Admittedly, on the basis of past experience it looks doubtful whether, for example, an annual rate of growth of national income of 8 per cent can be sustained for two decades in East Pakistan. However, it would be unduly restrictive to presume that past experience is the sole valid measure for planned, future growth. The very purpose of planning is to surpass past achievements. But past experience is highly relevant in detailed planning. It tells us, for example, what yields we may expect from soil of different qualities for different crops, and under which conditions the desired yields can be obtained. Planning consists of pulling all available data together and showing which steps have to be taken in order to reach set targets. In the end, what matters is whether the individual targets for the different sectors of the economy are realistic or not. This again depends on technical factors, as well as on the speed at which human attitudes and qualifications can be modified, and on the policy measures which will be taken to implement the targets. If all details in a plan are realistic — and, needless to say, mutually consistent — the global target in terms of national income will also be realistic, regardless of whether it looks high on the basis of past experience or not.

Pakistan's Perspective Plan does not contain much information to permit us to evaluate whether it is realistic or not, because it does not set detailed targets and show the measures to be taken to reach them. But the Third Five Year Plan represents the first phase of the implementation of the Perspective Plan, and that Plan is generally looked upon as realistic, even if it is ambitious. Thus, prior to a closer examination of some of the basic assumptions behind the Perspective Plan, there is, in my opinion, no reason to reject it as too ambitious or unduly optimistic.

Before embarking upon a comparison of the results of the present study and the Perspective Plan, it would have been useful to know something about the *methodology* behind the Perspective Plan. Unfortunately, I have been unable to get hold of any detailed description of the method used. On the other hand, I have studied working papers prepared in the Planning Commission in 1963 and 1964, and these show that much intellectual effort and ingenuity are behind the figures which in the end were published. The 1963 working paper presented a ten sector econometric model, containing 114 different equations, but no actual figures, neither for the base year nor for 1985. The second working paper, dated April, 1964, was built on a quite different model, which contained 9 sectors, but a much reduced number of equations.[5]

In the Perspective Plan the number of sectors was reduced to five (three main sectors — agriculture, manufacturing and other sectors, with manufacturing broken down into three sub-sectors). Five sectors which were specified in the April, 1964, working paper were thus grouped together under 'other' sectors in the published Perspective Plan. It may be, of course, that the Planning Commission did use the same model for unpublished estimates, but chose to use simplified Tables when publishing the results.

Some of the figures in the Perspective Plan are the same as in the April, 1964, working paper, whereas others have been substantially altered. The target growth rate for agriculture was raised, certainly because of the very encouraging progress in agriculture towards the end of the Second Five Year Plan, i. e. between the preparation of the April 1964 working paper and the presentation of the Third Five-Year Plan in the first half of 1965. However, the growth rates for the three subsectors of manufacturing were also substantially altered, which suggests that some changes in methodology took place during the last year before the publication of the Perspective Plan. But there is no evidence which suggests that the Plan was based on significantly more detailed calculations than those shown in the April 1964 working paper.

From a formal point of view the figures in the Perspective Plan are undoubtedly internally consistent (although sometimes it is not possible to reconcile different published figures without access to more detailed data). However, it is not enough to show, for example, that *total* demand for consumer goods and services can be satisfied by x per cent from domestic resources and by y per cent from imports, or that out of *total* domestic production of consumer goods and services z per cent will be consumed inside the country and w per cent will be exported. It is also necessary to show that such relationships hold true for important categories of goods and services as well, such as agricultural products, lumber, textiles, and so on. None of the information available on the Perspective Plan suggests that such consistency tests were carried out. Although the method described in the April, 1964, working paper is very ingenious, it does not, in my opinion, ensure consistency between supply and demand in sufficient detail.

Indeed, the authors of the Perspective Plan admit implicitly that it is open to criticism. Thus in the chapter on long-term perspective in the Third Plan, it is stated that 'most of the thinking of this model is tentative'. It is likely that lack of stringent and fairly detailed supply/demand consistency tests represents the most serious weakness of the Perspective Plan.

C. *A comparison between the present study and the Perspective Plan*

The simplest and most straightforward way of comparing the two attempts to project Pakistan's development prospects up to the fiscal year 1984/85 is to compare the figures in the Perspective Plan with those of the present study, Table by Table. It is not necessary to compare figures for each five-year period, except in those cases where such comparisons are particularly important.

1. *The policy objectives*

These differ considerably, as can be seen from the synoptic table below:

Table 71. *Comparison of policy objectives*

The Perspective Plan	*The present Study*	
A. Growth of the GNP:		
1. absolute figures	Four times	3.5 times
2. per head	140 per cent	103 per cent
B. Provision of full employment	By the middle of the Perspective Plan period	5.5 to 7.5 per cent unemployed at the end of the Plan
C. Relation between *per caput* incomes in East & West Pakistan	Parity between total *per caput* income in 1985	Parity in rural and urban incomes per head between provinces in 1985
D. 'Universal literacy' (i.e. universal primary and lower secondary education)	Yes	Yes
E. Elimination of dependence on foreign assistance	Yes (current deficit in 1985 Rs 2,000 mill)	No (current deficit in 1985 Rs 13,000 mill.)

Sources: The Perspective Plan, [5], p. 17; the present study: (A' 1). Table 60 (Alternative B), (A, 2). Table 60 plus population figure Table 7; (B) – Tables 61, *62*, and 63; (C) Chapter 4, Section D – see Tables 8 and 9; (D) Chapter 7, Section C – see Table 22; (E) Table 57, Alternative B.

It is evident that the projections in the present study are far from satisfying the avowed policy objectives of the Government of Pakistan. To some extent the differences are accidental, but in the main they are due to differences in the methods of projecting the economic development. Whereas the Perspective Plan is based on the assumption that the five major policy objectives can be made mutually consistent, the conclusion of the present study is that they cannot. These questions have been discussed in earlier chapters, but the main arguments will be repeated below in connection with the discussion of the various Tables in the Perspective Plan.

2. *The basic framework of Pakistan's long-term growth*

There are two fundamental differences which make it impossible to compare the *absolute* figures. Firstly, the figures in the Perspective Plan are expressed in 1964—65 prices, and in the present study in 1959—60 prices. A comparison of two sets of figures from the Third Five-Year Plan reveals that for the GNP at factor costs, prices were 7 per cent higher in 1964—65 than in 1959—60.[6] Secondly, the figures for 1964—65 are actual (although provisional) figures, whereas in the present study they are calculated on the basis of the actual 1959—60 figures and revised plan figures for the Second Plan period 1960—1965. As the GNP in fact increased by 29 per cent between 1960 and 1965, in-

Table 72. *Key Magnitudes*

	Perspective plan			Present study		
	Rs Mill.		Annual growth 1965–85 %	Rs Mill.		Annual growth 1965–85 %
	1965	1985		1965	1985	
Gross National Product (market prices) .	45,540	187,300	7.2	37,355	132,460	6.5
Gross investment .	8,400	42,800	8.5	7,057	40,327	9.1
Gross national savings*	4,460	40,800	11.7*	4,022	27,392	10.1
External resources*	3,940	2,000	–3.5	3,035	12,935	7.5
Exports	3,050	14,000	7.9	2,663	12,173	7.9
Imports A†	n.a.	n.a.	n.a.	5,512	21,264	7.0
Imports B†	6,990	16,000	4.2	5,697	25,109	7.7

*Figures in the Perspective Plan for 1965 have been modified by me, i.e. the use of foreign-exchange reserves has been deducted from savings and added to external resources.

†Imports A: imports of goods and services, excluding factor income payments abroad.

Imports B: total imports of goods and services.

Sources: The Perspective Plan, [5], Table 1, p. 19; and the present study, Tables 11 and 57.

stead of by 22 per cent as planned, the 1965 figures in the present
study are about 6 per cent too low. In addition, the revised figure
for the Gross National Product in 1959—60 used in the Third
Five-Year Plan is about 9 per cent higher than the one used in the
present study.

These differences in absolute figures make it impossible to
undertake meaningful comparisons between the projected absolute figures without undertaking several adjustments, but they
do not preclude comparisons between rates of growth, percentage
distribution of product and expenditure, etc., although, of course,
such comparisons will not be entirely exact.

The picture which emerges from a comparison of the growth
rates given in Table 72 is broadly the following:

The Perspective Plan expects the GNP to grow 0.7 per cent
faster than the present study, i. e. at a rate which is about 10 per
cent greater than the one used here. This difference has two independent reasons: (1) the present study was based on the long-term
target rate of growth suggested by the Planning Commission at
the end of 1963, since then the Planning Commission has raised
its sights; and (2) the model used in the present study yielded as
one main result that it would be extremely difficult to achieve a
rate of growth higher than the one finally used in the present
study. Thus the difference between the two growth rates has one
accidental and one fundamental reason.

The Perspective Plan expects investment to grow somewhat
more slowly and savings considerably faster than the present
study. We shall return to the reasons for these differences shortly.
The combined result of these, in themselves fairly small, differences is striking, however. The Planning Commission expects
that reliance on external resources can be cut by half, whereas
the present study concludes that the need for external resources
will be four times as great in 1985 as in 1965. At this point it is
worth noting that in the Perspective Plan a reduction of the dependence on 'foreign assistance' is an explicit policy goal, whereas the present study treats the inflow of foreign capital as a residuum, and does not worry about the size of this inflow. This difference in approach could have been a reason for the difference in
the projections, *viz.* the Perspective Plan could have been built
on more strongly planned efforts to raise the rate of savings and
exports and to reduce investment and imports than the present
study. In actual fact, however, the present study is also built on
the assumption that the growth of imports will be limited as far
as possible, and that investment will be no higher than is abso-

lutely necessary to reach the output targets. Furthermore, as will be shown below, the present study assumes relatively more rapid increases in savings and exports than the Perspective Plan. This is not apparent from Table 72, because the rate of growth of the GNP is lower in the present study.

Finally, Table 72 shows that the Perspective Plan expects imports to grow much more slowly than the present study, whereas the rate of growth of exports is the same in both sets of projections. The difference in the development of imports is, of course, linked with the differences in the figures for savings, investment, and dependence on external resources. It should be noted, however, that there is no reason why these differences should only express themselves in different *import* ratios. The Perspective Plan could well have sought part of the solution in a much higher export ratio than the present study.

Table 73 helps to illustrate the more basic differences between the two sets of projections. The figures for 1965 are reassuringly similar. The slight differences are easy to explain. The present study includes a higher figure for imputed investment than the Perspective Plan, and this raises the percentages for investment and savings. The lower percentage for exports (and consequently the higher percentage for external resources) in the Perspective Plan is due to the fact that the rate of growth of exports did not exceed the Second Plan target as much as the rate of growth of the GNP. The figures for 1985, however, are fundamentally different. Only the figures for savings are reasonably similar. The present study projects investment to absorb one-third more of the GNP than the Perspective Plan, and imports to be more than twice as high in relation to the GNP.[7] Finally, in relation to the GNP the export target in the present study is substantially

Table 73. *Key magnitudes as percentages of GNP*

	Perspective plan		Present study	
	1965	1985	1965	1985
Gross investment	18.4	22.9	18.9	30.4
Gross national savings..............	9.8	21.8	10.8	20.7
External resources	8.6	1.1	8.1	9.8
Exports	6.7	7.5	7.1	9.2
Imports	15.3	8.6	15.3	19.0

Source: Table 72. Note that the percentages for savings and external resources in 1965 differ from the figures in the Perspective Plan, because in the Perspective Plan the use of foreign-exchange reserves was counted as savings. In Table 73 all four columns are calculated on the same basis.

(23 per cent) more ambitious than the target in the Perspective Plan.

The heading of Table 74 is the one used in the Perspective Plan. However, in the present study only two of the lines in the Table represent *assumptions, viz.* the population growth rate and the marginal rate of savings B. Two other lines are derived directly from assumptions (about the rate of growth of the Gross *Domestic* Product and the gross *domestic* savings), *viz.* the growth rate of the GNP and the marginal rate of savings A, both of which are obtained through the intermediary of the figures for net factor income payments abroad. The capital-output ratio and the two lines for marginal propensity to import are results of the detailed calculations in the model. It is not clear from the Third Five-Year Plan whether the figures for the capital-output ratio and the marginal propensity to import in the Perspective Plan represent pure assumptions (i. e. in reality, informed guesses), or are based on an analysis of detailed figures behind the Perspective Plan.

A straight comparison between the figures in the two sets of projections reveal some minor discrepancies and some very fundamental differences. The former concern figures which have been assumed in both sets of projections and the latter figures which, in the present study, are results of detailed calculations and not assumptions.

The assumed growth rate in the present study is lower than in

Table 74. *Key assumptions*

	Perspective plan			Present study		
	1965 to 70	1980 to 85	1965 to 85	1965 to 70	1980 to 85	1965 to 85
GNP growth rate*	6.5	7.5	7.2	5.9	7.3	6.5
Population growth rate ...	2.7	2.1	2.6	2.6	2.8	2.7
Marginal rate of savings A .	22.0	25.0	25.0	22.0	26.5	24.5
Marginal rate of savings B .	n.a.	n.a.	n.a.	26.5	32.3	30.0
Capital-output ratio	2.9	3.0	2.9	4.2	4.4	4.4
Marginal propensity to import A	n.a.	n.a.	n.a.	25.0	13.0	16.5
Marginal propensity to import B	12.0	4.0	6.0	28.3	17.0	20.4

Sources: The Perspective Plan, [5], p. 19; the present study, Tables 6 and 11. Marginal rate of savings A – ratio between the increase in gross *national* savings and GNP at market prices; B – ratio between increase in gross *domestic* savings and GDP at factor cost. Import A excludes and import B includes net factor income payments abroad.

*Compound annual growth rates in per cent.

the Perspective Plan, but it is worth nothing that the gap is far smaller towards the end of the Perspective Plan period. A major reason for this discrepancy is the fact that the present study was based on an expected performance during the Second Plan period which was much poorer than the actual outcome. The Perspective Plan therefore sets a much higher target for the Third Plan period than the present study. In addition it should be noted that for the present study it was assumed that the growth rate during the Sixth Plan could significantly exceed 7.5 per cent, but that this target had to be lowered as it was not consistent with the pattern of demand for the domestic output. The difference between growth rates is in itself not very large, but in the course of a period of 20 years the Perspective Plan projects a figure for the Gross National Product that is 17 per cent higher than the one projected in the present study (if the figure for the base year 1965 had been the same in both projections).

The present study assumes a somewhat faster population growth than the Perspective Plan for the period as a whole, but the difference is particularly large for the Sixth Plan period. The reason for this lies in my subjective judgement that during the next twenty years the effect of better health services will offset an eventual fall in the birthrate due to strong family planning measures. The effect on the projected population figure of this discrepancy in the assumptions is very small, however.

The savings assumptions appear to be practically identical. In fact, if anything, the basic figure for the marginal rate of savings is higher in this study than in the Perspective Plan. The marginal rate of savings B was used as a basic assumption in the present study (i. e. the ratio between the growth of gross domestic savings and the growth of the Gross Domestic Product at factor cost). As the present study results in a far larger deficit in the current balance of payments, and consequently in a far more rapid growth in factor income payments to abroad, the gap between the marginal rates of savings A and B is undoubtedly larger in the present study than it would have been in the Perspective Plan had both figures been available.[8]

It is worth noting that the assumptions in the two sets of projections do not differ very much. The most important difference concerns the GNP growth rate, and part of this difference is due, not to different assumptions, but to the fact that the model on which the present study is built produced the answer that the assumed growth rate was somewhat too ambitious.

The remaining two key figures in Table 74 are the capital-output ratio and the marginal propensity to import. The differences here are fundamental, and represent the very reason why many of the key figures in the two sets of projections differ so drastically. The present study leads to the conclusion that the capital-output ratio will be about half as high again as that assumed in the Perspective Plan, whereas the marginal propensity to import will be more than three times as strong for the period as a whole, and more than four times as strong during the Sixth Plan period. These differences are so great that one of the two projections, or both, must be fundamentally wrong. It is too easy to maintain that because the present study is based on a detailed review of necessary investments and imports, while the Perspective Plan is, or appears to be, based on assumed figures for the capital-output ratio and the marginal propensity to import, it is the Perspective Plan which is fundamentally wrong. One must, however, review again the basis for the figures included in the present study if one is to resolve the problem as to which figures for investment and imports are the more realistic projections of what may happen in the future. The next section deals with the capital-output ratio, and the import projections will be dealt with in the section on the balance of payments projections.

3. *The capital-output ratio*

The 'capital-output ratio' is a much used and much criticized tool of development planning. It must be admitted that it is an indispensable part of any kind of growth model. But it must also be recognized that it is a very crude concept, which cannot be expected to be reliable. Internationally, the 'incremental capital-output ratio' differs very considerably, and within one country it changes a great deal from one period to another. It is hardly exaggerated to maintain that in almost any developing country reasons can be advanced for expecting a gross capital-output ratio of anything between 2 and 5 for a long planning period. It is not possible to estimate a valid capital-output ratio on the basis of data from other countries, because it is impossible to find any country in which conditions, during a period for which an historical capital-output ratio is available, are sufficiently like the conditions in a developing country planning for rapid growth. Similarly, in a developing country in which the economic structure is changing rapidly, and which is accelerating its economic growth, observed data on the capital-output ratio in the past are not indicative of the future capital-output ratio. Finally, it must be remembered that observed capital-output ratios for shorter time periods are frequently influenced by conjectural factors, such as unused capacity which is gradually absorbed, or an investment boom which results in a substantial increase in unused capacity.

The large margin of error that is necessarily implicit in any long-term estimate of the capital-output ratio makes projections based on such an estimate highly uncertain. Thus, if in the Perspective Plan the capital-output ratio for 1984—85 should turn out to be 25 per cent higher than expected (i. e. 3.5, which is quite a 'normal' figure for the incremental gross capital-output ratio), *ceteris paribus* the need for external resources would become Rs 12,500 million, or three times the need in 1965, instead of Rs 2,000, or half the need in 1965.[9] To express it in another manner, the simultaneous achievement of the policy objectives in the Perspective Plan is more than anything else dependent on the assumption that it will be possible to keep the capital-output ratio below 3 during the Perspective Plan period.

The results obtained from the present study suggest that this fundamental assumption is impossible. Before accepting this statement as a firm conclusion, we must examine whether the estimates of the capital-output ratio in the present study suffer from any bias which would tend to pull them upwards. There are two facts which suggest that such a bias might exist; the capital-output ratio during the Second Plan turned out to be much lower than projected in the present study, and the growth potential in agriculture appears to be far more promising than assumed here.

The gross capital-output ratio during the Second Plan period (1959—60 to 1964—65) turned out to be 2.8.[10] In the present study this ratio was projected to be 3.9. Most of this difference can be ascribed to the fact that between 1960 and 1965 the GDP at factor cost increased by 29 per cent, instead of 22 per cent as planned and as assumed in the present study. This higher rate of growth was achieved without any significant increase in investment. If the investment figure used in the present study for the

Annual rate of growth during the Second Plan period

	Actual figures %	Projections present study %
Agriculture	3.5	2.2
Large-scale manufacturing	13.0	10.0
Small-scale manufacturing	2.6	3.8
Other sectors	6.7	5.1
GDP at factor cost	5.2	4.1

Sources: Actual figures, [5], p. 20. Projections, Table 35.

Second Plan period is combined with the actual rate of growth, the capital-output ratio would only be between 2.9 and 3.0, or only slightly above the Perspective Plan figure. The remaining difference can, in fact, be traced back to a higher figure for imputed (non-monetized) investment in the present study. This explanation only confirms that the projected investment figure for the Second Five Year Plan period was reasonable, but it still suggests that the implied capital-output ratio was too high. To refute this suggestion it is necessary to determine whether the growth of the GNP during the Second Plan period was conditioned by the level of investment during that period. A partial answer to this can be found in the following figures.

The evidence available indicates that:

1. Progress in agriculture was faster than projected, partly because better methods were introduced more rapidly than was foreseen, partly because of a greater use of tubewells, and partly as a result of favourable climatic conditions. The experience of the Second Plan period does suggest, however, that agriculture can progress more rapidly during the Perspective Plan period than was previously expected, without any significant amount of additional investment.

2. Progress in manufacturing was very rapid due to better supplies of raw materials, etc., which led to better capacity utilization. This lowered the capital-output ratio, but for one plan period only.

3. Progress in other sectors was faster than planned due to the faster growth of agriculture and manufacturing. In many service sectors output grew faster with insignificantly larger investment (e. g. trade), whereas in others the existing capacity had to be utilized more intensively (public utilities, transport). In the longer run, however, investment in gas, electricity, transport, and communications will have to be raised in order to respond to higher demand. Thus it is reasonably obvious that in other sectors also the capital-output ratio during the Second Plan was lower than should normally have been expected.

I would not hesitate to conclude that the relatively low capital-output ratio for the Second Plan period cannot be used to prove that the implied capital-output ratios in the present study are far too high, nor that the capital-output ratio during the Second Plan period can be taken as a basis for the projected capital-output ratio during the Perspective Plan period. (In the Perspective Plan the capital-output ratio for the Plan period is 2.9, or only slightly above the 'depressed' capital-output ratio of 2.8 for the Second Pland period.) It is evident, however, that if the growth potential in agriculture is as promising as is suggested by experience during the Second Plan and as projected in the Perspective Plan, the implied global capital-output ratio in the present study is systematically too high.

The effects of better growth prospects in agriculture on the projected capital-output ratio in the present study can be estimated in the following crude manner. Let us assume, for the purpose of estimating an alternative global capital-output ratio on the basis of the data in the present study, that between 1965 and 1985 agriculture can grow at the rate shown in the Perspective Plan, without any investment above that included in the present study and that all other figures remain unchanged.[11] This increases the value added in agriculture in 1985 from Rs 32,260 million to Rs 46,630 million, and the GDP at factor cost from Rs 125,455 million to Rs 139,835 million. Consequently, between 1965 and 1985 the rate of growth is raised from 6.5 to 7.1 per cent, and the capital-output ratio lowered from 4.4 to 4.0. Thus, the possible underestimate of the growth potential in agriculture (discussed further below) is responsible for a possible 10 per cent overestimate of the capital-output ratio. But the capital-output ratio as shown in this study still remains more than one-third higher than the assumed capital-output ratio in the Perspective Plan.

This gap can have two explanations: (1) the growth pattern in the present study may imply a relatively more rapid growth of sectors or subsectors with high capital-output ratios than in the Perspective Plan, and (2) the capital-output ratios applied to the individual sectors or subsectors in the present study may be higher than those assumed in the Perspective Plan. Unfortunately, no details are available on the pattern of growth or assumed capital-output ratios for subsectors in the Perspective Plan. This does not preclude that part of the difference between the two sets of global capital-output ratios could eventually be explained on the basis of specific differences between the projected patterns of growth or capital-output ratios for individual industries, subsectors, or sectors. What is unlikely, however, is that the entire difference could be explained on the basis of differences in the growth pattern alone. On the contrary, the little information available on the growth pattern (see the next section) in the Perspective Plan suggest that the projected growth patterns are rather similar. If this is the case, the difference between the global capital-output ratios must on the whole result from differences in capital-output ratios for individual sectors and subsectors. As no details are available for the Perspective Plan, it is only possible to refer the reader to Tables 45 and 46 of the present study, which show the capital-output ratios by sectors used in the present study. If these seem on the whole to be on the high side, the global capital-output ratio will also be on the high side. But if they seem reasonable, the implied incremental gross capital-output ratio for the economy as a whole is, of course, also reasonable. When looking at the two Tables on capital-output ratios, the reader should also take note of the remarks in the text which explain some of the figures which might appear strange at first sight. In addition, it should be remembered that I recognize that the capital-output ratio in agriculture may be far too high. By adopting the much higher growth rate for agriculture which is used in the Perspective Plan, the capital-output ratio for agriculture as shown in Tables 45 and 46 is cut almost by half.

Due to lack of information on the details behind the Perspective Plan, this discussion of the global capital-output ratio is very rudimentary. But I cannot accept as realistic the assumption by the Planning Commission that the global capital-output ratio will be as low as 2.9 for the period 1965 to 1985. I have several times re-examined my own figures, and although there are some individual ratios which may be on the high side, there are at least as many which may be on the low side. A gross incremental capital-output ratio of 4 per five-year period (or a significantly lower ratio if time lags are expressed explicitly — compare the figures in Tables 45 and 46) appears to be quite a reasonable figure, and I would consider it as a rather optimistic assumption to locate the probable capital-output ratio between 3.5 and 4. I feel bound to conclude that the capital-output ratio assumed for the Perspective Plan is very much on the low side.

4. *The growth pattern*

Table 75 in itself needs little comment. The only fundamental difference concerns the projected growth rates in agriculture. This is sufficiently important to merit a section of its own. It should be noted, however, that the ratio between the growth rate for other sectors and for the economy as a whole differs in the two projections. In the Perspective Plan this ratio is only 1.07, whereas it is 1.17 in the present study. This difference is so great that at first sight it looks as if one or the other of the two studies must have misjudged the growth potential of the service-producing sectors. In fact, the difference is easy to explain. Because the present study assumes that the foreign-exchange deficit will increase, not only in absolute, but also in relative terms, it also implies that domestic demand will grow faster than the GNP. The opposite is the case in the Perspective Plan. As the growth of the output of the service-producing sectors is closely linked with the

Table 75. *The Projected Growth Pattern 1965 to 1985*
(Annual compound rate of growth 1965–85)

	Perspective plan per cent	Present study per cent
1. Agriculture ....?..............	5.6	3.7
2. Manufacturing	10.2	9.6
a. consumer goods	(7.2)	(6.2)
b. intermediate products	(13.7)	(12.6)
c. investment goods	(10.0)	(14.4)
3. Other sectors	7.7	7.6
GDP at factor cost	7.2	6.5

Sources: The Perspective Plan, [5], p. 20; the present study, the input-output Tables. The classification of manufacturing by subgroups differs somewhat between the two sets of projections

growth of domestic demand, it follows that these sectors should be projected to grow relatively faster in the present study than in the Perspective Plan. This presumption is reinforced by the fact that the present study projects a much faster growth of investment demand than the Perspective Plan, and this leads directly to a much faster growth of sectors like construction and transportation, which represent a large part of the output of 'other sectors'.

5. Growth in agriculture

The rate of growth in agriculture projected in the present study is not slow. It should be noted that whereas value added is projected to grow by 3.7 per cent per year, the corresponding annual increase in gross output is 4.3 per cent. This gap is due to the rapid increase in the use of purchased inputs in agriculture. As land is scarce in East Pakistan and water in West Pakistan, these projections were based on an assumed increase in average yields per acre of the order of magnitude of 15 to 17 per cent per five-year period in the two provinces. Over a twenty-year period it represents an increase in average yields of 75 to 90 per cent. Of course, the technological possibilities of increasing yields are far larger, but this revolution in agriculture must be carried out in 100,000 villages by millions of small farmers.

However, progress in agriculture during the last years of the Second Five Year Plan was most encouraging, and a large number of farmers have introduced new and efficient methods far more quickly than was expected only a few years ago. It is therefore most appropriate for the two provincial governments in

Pakistan and the Planning Commission to postulate new and ambitious targets in agriculture.

During the Second Five-Year Plan, crop production in West Pakistan increased by about 25 to 30 per cent, or by approximately 5 per cent per year. Of this increase 12 per cent can be explained by more groundwater, 6 per cent by more use of fertilizer, and 8 to 10 per cent by other factors, such as more surface water (irrigation canals), better seed, plant protection, and other inputs. The real sensation behind this splendid achievement was the rapid installation of privately owned tubewells, which are estimated to have increased available irrigation water by 9 per cent during that five-year period. Including public tubewells, the groundwater supply increased by 14 per cent. About 32,000 private tubewells had been installed by the end of the Second Plan, and most of them had been installed in the course of the Plan period. It is expected that the rate of installation of tubewells by private farmers and by the government will be increased substantially during the Third Plan, so that the water supply will be increased by almost another 30 per cent from tubewells only. Increased use of fertilizers is closely connected with better water supplies, and the use of fertilizers is for this and other reasons projected to increase sharply. Thus from 1960 to 1965 fertilizer consumption rose from 32,000 to 88,000 nutrient tons, or by 56,000 tons, and during the Third Plan it is expected to increase by 175,000 nutrient tons. It is estimated that increased water supplies (mostly groundwater) will lead to an annual increase of crop production of 4.2 per cent, and that increased use of fertilizers will lead to an increase of 2.3 per cent. The total increase in crop output in West Pakistan during the Third Plan has been projected at 49 per cent (8.4 per cent per year), which should lead to an increase in value added of 7.9 per cent per year, and in total value added in agriculture of 6.2 per cent per year.[12]

The above projections for the Third Plan period were based on the assumption of a modest rate of growth (3 per cent per year) in livestock, forestry, and fisheries (which were included under agriculture in the above estimate) and on the assumption that water and fertilizers would account for almost four-fifths of the growth in crop production. Recent experience, however, suggests that use of better seed can contribute to an even more explosive growth in yield per acre in West Pakistan. Wheat experts from Mexico believe that by using Mexican dwarf wheat (and new Pakistan varieties developed on the basis of Mexican wheat), West Pakistan should be able to double its output of wheat in the course of five years.[13] This optimistic assessment is based on extensive use of Mexican seed in various regions of West Pakistan. During the harvest season 1965—66, 12,000 acres of wheat were planted with these new varieties, and the average output was about 1.6 metric tons per acre as against a normal yield of just above 0.4 metric tons per acre on irrigated land. To achieve such yields substantial quantities of fertilizers have to be used, but the higher yields result from a combination of these two factors. The experience has been so successful that Pakistan may expect to become self-sufficient in wheat in two or three years, and will have to plan for alternative uses for between one-third and one-half of its wheat land in the course of some few years.

The most important aspect of the recent experience of agricultural development in West Pakistan is that tens of thousands of farmers have been making heavy investments in relation to their resources, or have been willing to try new seed varieties or the use of chemical fertilizers. The conditions are certainly very favourable for a sustained and rapid increase of the crop output. At the end of the Third Plan as much as 85 per cent of the potentially available groundwater in West Pakistan may be exploited, which means that the tube-well revolution will peter out in about five years' time. Only 77 per cent of the total water available for irrigation will be exploited in 1970, but the development of the use of surface water is a much more expensive and slow proposition.[14] On the other hand, progress resulting from more use of fertilizers and better practices, including the use of improved seed, means of plant protection, etc., can continue at a fast rate over several decades. As far as West Pakistan is concerned, it seems justified to hope that the rate of growth in crop production can significantly exceed the projections in the present study.

Recent experience in East Pakistan also suggests that rapid progress is possible. During the Second Plan period the output of rice increased considerably, after a decade of stagnation (or rather 'one of large fluctuations about a rather steady level'). Output in agriculture is estimated to have risen by about 3.5 per cent per year during that Plan period, of which 1 per cent was accounted for by more area under cultivation; and of the remaining 2.5 per cent, it is estimated that 0.6 per cent came from greater use of fertilizer, 0.2 per cent from plant protection, 0.5 per cent from improved seeds, 0.1 per cent from irrigation facilities, and slightly more than 1 per cent from increased and improved labour inputs. During the Third Plan it is estimated that the crop output can increase by 6.2 per cent per year, and the total output by 5.6 per cent. Of the increased annual output, 1.9 per cent should be due to fertilizers, 2.1 per cent to water (of which three-quarters due to larger cropped area), 0.5 per cent each from improved seeds and plant protection, and 1.2 per cent from labour (of which one-third due to a larger cultivated area). Thus yields should increase by about 4.2 per cent per year, and a larger cropped area will contribute 2 per cent.[15]

The background for the optimistic projections of agricultural growth in East Pakistan during the Third Plan period is the change from stagnation to growth that took place during the Second Plan period. This change was not due to one major factor as in West Pakistan. But as in West Pakistan there was a marked change in the attitude of the farmers during the plan period. Fertilizer consumption rose even faster than in West Pakistan, and the use of better seed played a significant role in raising rice output. As noted above, about one-third of the increase in yield was caused by more and better labour inputs, which also contributed to the higher acreage under cultivation. This does not necessarily mean that attitudes and technology have been changed. Indeed, increased population pressure has undoubtedly led to more intensive cultivation of land by traditional methods, and to cropping of marginal land. But two other factors have been important in East Pakistan. Better cultivation methods have been adopted, e. g. the so-called Japanese method of rice cultivation, and the Rural Works Programme has led to higher yields (and more useful acreage) directly through the renovation of drains and indirectly through the reconstruction of secondary roads and additional purchasing power in the villages. The Works Programme has had important psychological effects on the rural population through its effective demonstration of improvements which could be undertaken at low cost by the use of surplus labour.[16]

It is impossible to judge whether the projections for growth in agricultural output in East Pakistan are too optimistic or not. On balance, it seems fairly obvious that the basis for the projected acceleration of the growth rate in agriculture in East Pakistan is weaker than it is for West Pakistan, where technical factors such as the rapid installation of tube-wells and better seed come in addition to changes in attitudes and improved practices in general. However, it is by no means impossible that the targets for 1970 in East Pakistan can be reached and even surpassed. If the targets for both provinces are reached, value added in agriculture during the Third Plan will apparently increase by 5 per cent per year.[17] This is somewhat below the projected average rate of growth for the Perspective Plan period as a whole (5.6 per cent). It is probably reasonable to assume that as soon as an agrarian revolution is really under way, it will lead to a further increase in the rate of growth.

I am willing to accept — albeit hesitantly — that technical, organizational, and sociological factors favour an average, annual

Table 76. *Estimated use of gross output in agriculture –*
1965 and 1985. Rs Mill.

	1965	1985
Value added, agriculture, etc.	21,055	62,500
Gross output, agriculture, estimate....................	21,600	70,000
Imports of food, estimate	1,000	nil
Output of non-food products, estimate	−2,000	−6,000
Exports of food, estimate	− 200	−5,000
Food (of agricultural origin, including fishing, at farm prices) available for domestic consumption	20,400	59,000
	Rs	Rs
Food (of agricultural origin, including fishing, at farm prices) available for *per caput* consumption	182	315
Total personal consumption, *per caput*	344	715
Implied expenditure elasticity for food from agriculture at farm prices	0.76	

Notes. Value added agriculture, source [5], p. 20. The other figures have been estimated for the purpose of the present Table on the following basis; gross output – purchased inputs in agriculture excluding crops used for feeding live-stock will increase from 2.5 per cent to 12 per cent of gross output; imports of food will be eliminated; exports (at farm prices) will correspond to 35 per cent of total projected exports of goods and services, at f.o.b. prices; output of non-food products will increase three times.

compound rate of growth of value added in agriculture of the order of 5.6 per cent per year during the two decades between 1965 and 1985. But I am somewhat perplexed by the *economic* implications of such a rate of growth, which implies that value added in agriculture will triple in the course of twenty years. A very crude numerical example will illustrate why I have some doubts about the economic feasibility of the projected growth in agriculture.

Table 76 has deliberately been prepared in such a manner that the implied figure for available supplies of food for domestic use in 1985 is on the low side, rather than the opposite. Thus, it is very optimistic to assume that the output of non-food products can be tripled, since jute and cotton account for about two-thirds of these products at present, and the demand for jute will grow only very slowly. Also, the projected exports of food have no-thing in common with the only projection of the composition of Pakistan's exports in 1985 which I have seen hitherto.[18] Indeed, the actual supply of food at farm prices might easily exceed the figure shown in Table 76 by 10 per cent, in which case the im-plied expenditure elasticity would be about 0.90.

Table 77. *Income (value added) per employed person or per head of labour force under different price alternatives*

	1965	1985	1985 in % of 1965
Constant 1965 prices			
Total economy			
Value added, Rs million	43,365	174,300	
Employment, million....................	29.700	59.700	
V.a. per employed person, Rs	1,460	2,920	200
Labour force, million	37.250	62.300	
V.a. per head of lab. force, Rs............	1,164	2,797	240
Agriculture			
Value added, Rs million	21,055	62,500	
Employment, million....................	19.300	29.500	
V.a. per employed, Rs...................	1,091	2,119	192
Labour force, million*	26.850	32.100	
V.a. per head of lab. force, Rs............	784	1,947	248
Non-agriculture			
Value added, Rs million	22,310	111,800	
Employment, million*...................	10.400	30.200	
V.a. per employed, Rs...................	2,145	3,720	173
Changes in relative pricees, Alternative A			
Agriculture			
Value added, Rs million	21,055	57,850	
V.a. per employed person, Rs	1,091	1,962	180
Non-agriculture			
Value added, Rs million	22,310	116,450	
V.a. per employed person, Rs	2,145	3,856	180
Changes in relative prices, Alternative B			
Agriculture			
Value added, Rs million	21,055	48,800	
V.a. per head of lab. force, Rs............	784	1,520	194
Non-agriculture			
Value added, Rs million	22,310	125,500	
V.a. per head of lab. force, Rs............	2,145	4,157	194

*All unemployed have been counted as members of the agricultural labour force.

Sources: Value added [5], Table 2, p. 20; labour force and employment, [5], Table 7, p. 25.

When judging the implied expenditure elasticity, it must be taken into account that a growing proportion of the farm output will be delivered to towns and cities, and that the average margin between farm prices and consumer prices will therefore increase, due to higher trade, transport, and processing margins. If the sum of these margins were to increase by 10 per cent, the implied expenditure elasticity of 0.76 shown in Table 76 would be raised to 0.9. Similarly, the implied elasticity of 0.9 referred to in the previous paragraph would be raised to above 1. It seems highly unlikely that the expenditure elasticity for food could be as high as anything between 0.9 and 1.0.

The above elasticities are calculated on the basis of constant prices. If prices of food fall in relation to other prices, the expenditure elasticity for food at current prices will be lower than at constant prices. This is a real possibility, if we stick to the figures given in the Perspective Plan.

By comparing the figures for value added, employment, and labour force, it is possible to get a picture of how income per employed person or per head of the labour force will change between 1965 and 1985 under different price alternatives.

The first part of Table 77 shows that if relative prices do not change, value added per employed person in agriculture will rise considerably faster than value added per employed person outside agriculture. If the total number of unemployed is included in the agricultural labour force (which is a fair approximation of the real situation since most of the unemployed labour force represents under-employment in agriculture), the growth of value added per head of labour force is much faster in agriculture than outside. Such a development would, of course, be very favourable, since it would help to close the very large gap in income between agriculture and other activities. However, nothing specific is said in the Perspective Plan about a policy of closing the gap in income between urban and rural areas.[19]

Alternative A in Table 77 is based on the assumption that income per employed person will grow at the same rate in agriculture and in all other activities taken together; whereas alternative B builds on the same assumption, but takes income per head of labour force as its basis. In both cases it has been assumed that the average price level will remain constant, but that the current value added in agriculture will be lower than it would have become at constant prices (and vice versa in other activities). Under Alternative A, the average value added in agriculture is 92.6 per cent of constant prices, and in non-agriculture 104.2 per cent; whereas under Alternative B the corresponding figures are 78.0 per cent and 112.3 per cent. These figures exaggerate somewhat the necessary changes in the relative prices of agricultural and non-agricultural products, since they refer to value added and not to gross output. If it is assumed that gross output in agriculture is 113.7 per cent of value added (the assumption used in Table 76), and in non-agricultural activities 200 per cent of value added, and that the prices of purchased inputs do not change on the average, it is found that under Alternative A, prices of agricultural goods must fall by 6.5 per cent, and prices of all other goods and services must increase by 2.1 per cent; whereas under Alternative B agricultural prices must fall by 19.3 per cent and other prices rise by 6.2 per cent. Under Alternative A the 'terms of trade' of agriculture will in 1985 be 91.6 per cent of what they were in 1965, under Alternative B they will fall to 76.

The purpose of this exercise is to find the expenditure elasticities for food at current prices. There are two ways of calculating these: on the basis of the change in agricultural prices in relation to the average price level, or in relation to the prices of other goods and services. The latter alternative is used here, since it has the greatest effect on the figures, but the two methods yield approximately the same results. In any case, it must be assumed that prices of food and non-food products of agricultural origin change at the same rate. The results are shown below.

The critical figure in Table 78 is an expenditure elasticity of 0.65. It should be noted that expenditure elasticities may be

Table 78. *Implied expenditure elasticities for food, under two assumptions of changes in relative prices*

Based on farm prices, and total food supplies as shown in Table 76.

Alternative A	0.65
Alternative B	0.38

Based on the figures used above plus 10 per cent (which either represents 10 per cent higher food supplies at farm prices, i.e. more realistic assumptions about food exports, or the figures in Table 76 plus 10 per cent increase in the trade margin)

Alternative A	0.78
Alternative B	0.51

Based on consumer prices (i.e. 10 per cent increase in the average trade margin between 1965 and 1985) and 10 per cent higher food supplies than in Table 76

Alternative A	0.92
Alternative B	0.65

slightly higher than income elasticities during the Perspective Plan period, because savings should grow faster than disposable personal income. But the discrepancy will be small, so that an expenditure elasticity for food of 0.65 corresponds to an income elasticity which exceeds 0.6. It is likely that an income elasticity for food that exceeds 0.6 is higher than most students of consumer demand will accept (see [46], also referred to in Chapter 5 of the present study). However, in the present study a much higher expenditure elasticity has been assumed (see Table 14). It should be noted that this is based on constant prices, and that in the present study consumption per head is only assumed to grow by 70 per cent between 1965 and 1985, as against 105 per cent in the Perspective Plan. If an expenditure elasticity of 0.65 is ruled out as far too high, Alternative A is unrealistic, regardless of whatever other assumptions are used. Even Alternative B is then unrealistic, on the assumptions in the last section of Table 78, which represent the most realistic set of assumptions as regards other uses of agricultural goods. Under other assumptions Alternative B appears realistic.

The conclusions to be drawn from the preceding discussion are that the projected increase in agricultural output cannot be sold unless:

(1) the 'terms of trade' of agriculture in relation to other activities fall by about one-fourth between 1965 and 1985; and

(2) a substantial proportion of the increase in food production can be exported (and indeed a much higher proportion than that which seems to be under discussion at present).

Although the problems of organizing rice exports from East Pakistan or diverting wheat land to other uses in West Pakistan have been mentioned in reports on agricultural prospects in the two provinces, the Perspective Plan itself does not stress the marketing problems and the need for structural changes which the projected rapid expansion of value added in agriculture involves.

6. *Structural changes*

As regards the figures for the base year 1965, the output figures are fairly close to each other. The lower figure for agriculture in the present study is, as already noted, due to the fact that the 1965 figure is a projected figure based on the Second Plan forecasts, which did not take into account the unexpectedly rapid growth in agriculture during the years 1960 to 1965. The employment figures for 1965 differ considerably, however. The statistical base for employment estimates in 1965 is very weak, and both sets of figures are based on 'informed guesses'. I find the figure for employment in manufacturing used in the Perspective Plan on the high side, however, and I also believe that employment in traditional services is somewhat underestimated. The last line shows imputed employment, which in the present study absorbs a large proportion of the unemployment shown in the Perspective Plan. This problem is discussed further under the section on the employment forecasts.

The structural changes projected in the present study are far deeper than those in the Perspective Plan. The reason is, of course, the very different projected growth rates for agriculture. It is worth noting, however, that both as regards output and employment, the present study projects a much more important role for other sectors than the Perspective Plan. This feature has already been discussed under Section D above. This difference persists if the figures in brackets in Table 79 are used instead of those derived from the present study. The figures in brackets are calculated by adjusting the growth rate for agriculture so that it becomes the same as in the Perspective Plan, leaving the figures for manufacturing and other sectors unchanged. Under these assumptions the projected employment in the present study would

Table 79. *Structural changes in the Perspective Plan:*
Percentage distribution of output and employment

	Perspective plan		Present study	
	1965	1985	1965	1985
1. *Output*				
a. agriculture	49	36	47	27 (34)
b. manufacturing	12	21	13	22 (20)
c. other sectors	39	43	40	51 (46)
Total	100	100	100	100
2. *Employment*				
a. agriculture	65	49	62	40 (47)
b. manufacturing	11	14	10	10 (9)
c. other sectors	24	37	28	50 (44)
Total	100	100	100	100(100)
+ imputed employment not included above	n.a.	n.a.	17	10 (4)

Sources: Perspective Plan, [5], p. 21, Table 3; the present study, output – the input-output Tables, employment – Table 61. Imputed employment includes 'forestry' (mainly collection of firewood), non-monetized construction (to a large extent building of huts, particularly in 1965), traditional transport (country boats and other), traditional fishing, and non-monetized mining (i.e. notably quarrying, for use in non-monetized construction, etc.). Figures in parentheses: estimated on the basis of the same growth rate for agriculture as in the Perspective Plan (see also text below).

have exceeded the labour force by about 2.5 million persons, even if the imputed employment were eliminated altogether. Such a situation of projected 'over-full' employment is explained (1) by the fact that employment in relation to value added in agriculture is projected to be higher in the present study than in the Perspective Plan, and (2) by the much higher projected employment in other sectors. The employment aspects of Table 79 are discussed further under the section on the labour force and employment.

7. *Domestic savings*

The assumed development of domestic savings is one of the key assumptions in perspective planning. As has been shown in subsection (2) above, the assumptions used in the Perspective Plan and in the present study are very close to each other. The present subsection deals with some of the detailed assumptions.

Table 80 shows that the projected distribution of the increase in GNP per head between consumption and savings is exactly the same in both sets of projections. Because of the difference in the projected rate of growth, the similarity stops here. Thus, the Perspective Plan projects that consumption per head will increase by 113 per cent and savings by 450 per cent, whereas the corresponding increases, according to the present study, are 85 and 300 per cent.

During the Perspective Plan period the time phasing of the marginal rate of savings differs somewhat between the two sets of projections, although the figures for the total period are prac-

Table 80. *Increase in* per caput *incomes, consumption, and savings*

	Perspective plan		Present study		
	(Increase 1965–85)		(Increase 1965–85)		
	Rs	%	Rs	Rs	%
Per caput income					
(GNP per head)	598	100	346	(441)	100
Per caput consumption	421	70	243	(309)	70
Per caput savings	177	30	103	(132)	30

Sources: The Perspective Plan, [5], Table 4, p. 22; the present study, based on Tables 6 and 11. The figures in parentheses have been obtained by 'inflating' the figure for income per head in 1965 so that it becomes the same as in the Perspective Plan. It is thereby possible to compare the changes in the absolute figures.

tically identical. The slight difference in time phasing is never-theless significant. The Perspective Plan is built on the assumption that the savings effort as measured in terms of marginal rates of savings can be reduced somewhat after 1980, whereas the present study is based on the assumption that, in principle, the savings effort must be increased continuously. This discrepancy also has its roots in the widely different figures for capital-output ratios.

The figures for the Second Plan period are widely different, but most of this is due to statistical discrepancies for the year 1960 (1959—60). The Third Five Year Plan shows that the amount of foreign assistance received in 1959—60 was Rs 1,580 million, but a figure of Rs 850 million has been used in the present study. All the other Pakistan sources which have been available as background material for the present study support the lower estimate used here. The present study also includes higher figures for imputed investment. The result is that whereas for the present study savings in 1960 were estimated at Rs 3,020 million, they were only Rs 1,850 million according to the Third Plan. In my opinion, savings in 1960 are underestimated by about Rs 730 million in the Third Plan (only because of an overestimate of the current foreign-exchange deficit); and if an adjusted figure for savings in 1960 were used as the basis for calculation of the marginal rate of saving during the period 1960—65, the result would be that Table 81 would show a marginal rate of saving of 14 (instead of 22) under the heading of the Perspective Plan. Thus, the discrepancy between the two sets of figures for 1960 to 1965 has a statistical explanation.[20]

Table 81. *Marginal rates of savings* %

	Perspective plan		Present study	
	From total income	From *per caput* income	From total income	From *per caput* income
Second Plan (1960–65)	22	31	14	18.5
Third Plan (1965–70)	22	28	22	28.5
Fourth Plan (1970–75)	25	31	21	27.5
Fifth Plan (1975–80)	28	32	25.5	30.5
Sixth Plan (1980–85)	25	28	26.5	31.0
Perspective Plan (1965–85)	25	30	24.5	30.0

Sources: The Perspective Plan, [5], Table 5, p. 22, and Table 1, p. 19 ; the present study, based on Tables 6 and 11.

Tables 80 and 81 show that as regards savings both attempts to project the economic development up to 1985 are fundamentally based on the same assumptions. This is very important, because the evaluation of the likely magnitude for the marginal rate of savings is the most important single policy assumption in perspective planning. It shows implicitly the willingness of the government to rely on a combination of two methods of raising savings: steps to restrain consumption through austerity in government consumption, taxation of consumer goods and services, and other taxes on private income; and policies which permit substantial enterprise profits (public or private enterprise) which will frequently be saved, either in the form of re-investment in the enterprise or as investment in other enterprises or other sectors of the economy. The fact that the savings assumptions in the Perspective Plan and the present study are practically identical makes comparisons between the two sets of projections meaningful.

8. *Balance of payments*

It is difficult to compare the Table in the Perspective Plan with the data in the present study, because of the difficulty in classifying imports under the three categories — consumer, intermediate, and capital goods. The Table in the Third Five Year Plan on which Table 82 is based only refers to 'goods' and 'products', but it is clear from another Table in the same document that imports of invisibles as well as debt servicing are in fact included under imports of goods and products.[21]

Table 82 illustrates well the very different conclusions arrived at in the two sets of projections. Of course, the size of the current balance of payments deficit is determined by the assumptions about savings and the capital-output ratio. Thus the far larger deficit in the present study results from its higher implied capital-output ratio. It is nevertheless of considerable interest to compare the projected import patterns. The crucial difference concerns *intermediate goods and services,* for which the present study projects a rate of growth that is twice as fast, on an annual basis, as the one in the Perspective Plan. Part of this difference may be due to differences in classification and part to the high imports of such products in 1965 according to the Perspective Plan. Nevertheless, there is undoubtedly a very substantial difference in the underlying assumptions as regards the need for imports of raw materials and semi-manufactured products as well as intermediate services. It should be noted that the projected imports of intermediate goods and services in the present study depend only

Table 82. *Balance of payments in the Perspective Plan*

	Rs mill. 1965	Rs mill. 1985	Annual compound growth rates 1965–85 (%)
I. *The Perspective Plan*			
1. Exports	3,050	14,000	7.9
2. Imports	6,990	16,000	4.2
a. consumer goods	1,830	3,000	2.5
b. capital goods	2,015	4,500	6.0
c. intermediate products	3,145	6,500	3.7
3. Balance of payments deficit	3,940	2,000	−3.5
4. Percentage of imports financed from exports.................	44	88	
II. *The present study*			
1. Exports	2,663	12,173	7.9
2a. Imports (excluding factor income payments abroad)	5,512	21,264	7.0
a. consumer goods & services ..	1,966	6,366	6.1
b. investment goods & services .	1,474	6,135	7.4
c. intermediate goods & services	2,072	8,763	7.5
2b. Imports (including factor income payments abroad)	5,697	25,109	7.7
a. investment goods & services plus factor payments	1,659	9,980	9.4
3a. Balance of payments deficit (imports 2a)	2,849	9,091	6.0
3b. Balance of payments deficit (imports 2b)	3,034	12,936	7.5
4. Percentage of imports financed from exports.................			
a. excluding factor inc. paym...	48	57	
b. including factor inc. paym...	47	48	
III. *Teh present study – adjusted figures* (no imports of food in 1985)			
2a. Imports (excluding factor income payments abroad)	5,512	17,469	5.6
a. consumer goods & services ..	1,966	2,571	1.4
2b. Imports (including factor income payments abroad)	5,697	(21,314)	(6.8)
3a. Balance of payments deficit (imports 2a)	2,849	6,520	4.2
3b. Balance of payments deficit (imports 2b)	3,034	(10,365)	(6.3)
4. Percentage of imports financed by exports...................			
a. excluding factor inc. paym...	48	70	
b. including factor inc. paym...	47	(57)	

Sources: The Perspective Plan, [5], Table 6, p. 24; the present study, data prepared on the basis of the input-output tables and detailed adjustments. For the sake of simplicity all imports of agricultural products plus products from the food manufacturing industries have been counted as food imports.

to a small extent on assumptions as regards the ratio between investment and savings. I would consider the rapid growth of raw materials, etc., as an unavoidable consequence of the modernization of the economy. In my view, this is a factor which makes rapid growth of imports in a developing country unavoidable, and which suggests that *a more rapid growth of exports* is an indispensable companion of higher savings as a practical means of reducing the balance of payments deficit.

The different projections of imports of consumer goods and capital goods depend on specific aspects of the two projections. Thus, as Part III of the Table shows, if the present study were based on the assumption that no food imports would be required in 1985, the annual growth in consumer goods imports would only be 1.4 per cent as against 2.5 per cent in the Perspective Plan. This suggests that, apart from agriculture, the present study is based on more hopeful assumptions about the possibility of import substitution for consumer goods than the Perspective Plan.[22]

Finally, if investments were much lower than shown in the present study, imports of investments goods and services would also be lower. It should be repeated once more that the fundamental difference in the import projections relates to the very different rates of growth of imports of intermediate goods and services. The Perspective Plan apparently bases its projections on a global estimate of the demand for and the domestic output of intermediate goods. In a formal sense this is an entirely valid approach, but it neglects the restraints on the domestic production of various types of intermediate goods, notably raw materials, but also many semi-manufactured goods which cannot be produced economically in Pakistan, or the production of which cannot rise rapidly enough due to technical difficulties. The use of input-output tables makes it possible to analyse the demand for intermediate goods and services and to assess how much of this demand must be met by imports. Table 83 shows the development of demand for imported goods and services.

With few exceptions, domestic industries have been projected to cover a much larger proportion of the demand for intermediate goods and services in 1985 than in 1965. Nevertheless, imports are projected to cover exactly the same proportion of total demand for intermediates in both years. This results from a rapid growth of economic activities which depend to a considerable extent on imported intermediate goods and services (such as the metal-working industries; the basic metal industries, which are assumed to depend on imported ores; the chemical industries, which in part depend on imported minerals such as sulphur and

Table 83. *Demand for and imports of intermediate goods and services. Projections in the present study*

	Imports as a percentage of domestic demand for intermediates		Percentile distri- bution of imports of intermediate goods and services	
	1965	1985	1965	1985
Forestry products	37	56	2	4
Mining products	50	27	8	12.5
Manufactured products..........	31	15	76.5	53.5
Wood products...............	83	62	3	8
Pulp. paper	5	6	0.5	1
Chemicals	56	19	16.5	11.5
Petro-chemicals	52	0	7.5	0
Non-met. minerals...........	6	0	1	0
Basic metals	55	7	12.5	4
Metal-working	63	30	23.5	27.5
Cotton, jute-processing	(20)	4	(10.5)	1.5
Misc. industries	(52)	1	(0)	0
Banking, insurance	19	17	2	4
Transport	4	6	5	8
Invisibles*....................	100	100	3	12.5
Other........................	n.a.	n.a.	3.5	5.5
Total	9.55	9.56	100	100

*Expenditure of shipping and air transport companies abroad.
Sources: Input-output Tables, after adjustments (see also Table 53 and [0], Annex VIII, Table 1).

phosphates; and shipping and airlines). Goods and services from five sectors or subsectors (*viz.* mining, wood products, chemicals, metal-working industries, and invisible imports by shipping and airlines) are projected to represent 72.5 per cent of the total imports of intermediates in 1985. In my opinion the projected imports under these five headings are well justified.[23] Without pretending to have found the ultimate answer to the question of the necessary imports of intermediate goods and services, I do maintain that the projections in the present study are well enough substantiated to permit the conclusion that the projected growth of such imports in the Perspective Plan is very much on the low side.

In Table 74 the tendency to import was expressed through the 'marginal propensity to import', i. e. the ratio between the absolute figures for growth in imports and growth of the GNP in a given period. Another statistical concept can also be used: the import elasticity, i. e. the ratio between the percentage growth of imports and of the GNP. For the period as a whole the Perspective Plan shows an import elasticity of 0.58, whereas the present study shows a figure of 1.18, or 1.08 if factor income payments are excluded from imports. If the figures for growth in the GNP and imports in the present study are modified so as to take into account the better growth prospects for agriculture, the import elasticity is reduced to 0.96, or lower than 0.83, excluding factor income payments.

As import elasticities below 1 are exceptions both in developing and highly developed countries, the unadjusted figures for import elasticities derived from the present study seem to be most in line with empirical evidence. However, as stressed many times in the present study, perspective planning or projections for developing countries which undergo deep structural changes cannot be based on empirical evidence. *A priori,* the low figure for import elasticity implied in the Perspective Plan should therefore *not* be taken as an indication of over-optimistic assumptions as regards the future course of imports. Nevertheless, an import elasticity below 0.6 suggests a degree of import substitution which may prove extremely difficult to achieve.

The Perspective Plan does not contain any breakdown of projected *exports*. The only fairly authoritative study of the export prospects during the Perspective Plan period which I have come across is a working paper prepared in 1964.[24] This was built on the assumption that exports would have to reach Rs 11,300 million in 1985, whereas the figure for exports in the Perspective Plan as published one year later was Rs 14,000 million. It is likely that due to the greatly improved prospects for agriculture, the Planning Commission expected far larger exports of food than those shown in the working paper prepared in 1964. That working paper was, of course, based on forecasts of exports in 1964—65, and not on actual achievements. A comparison between the export projections in that paper and the projections used in the present study has nevertheless a certain interest, and such a comparison is made in Table 84 below.

At the outset it should be noted that the Planning Commission study based its figures on more recent information about the likely 1965 exports than the present study. Thus exports of raw cotton and rice, as well as of some 'new' manufactures, proved to be higher than projected in the present study, whereas exports of cotton manufactures and some other products fell short of the targets.

The Planning Commission study projects goods exports in 1985 to be about Rs 1,400 million higher than this study. The source of this difference can be ascribed primarily to five items: raw jute, + Rs 470 million; jute manufactures, + Rs 150 million,

Table 84. *Comparison between two export projections. Rs mill.*

	Planning Commission		Present Study	
	1965	1985	1965	1985
I. *Traditional products*				
Raw jute	800	550	743	80
Jute manufactures	360	1,650	350	1,500
Raw cotton	400	700	273	178
Cotton manufactures...	150	950	270	1,300
Other (hides, skins, wool)	160	200	143	89
Subtotal I	1,870	4,050	1,789	3,147
II. *Natural resources products*				
Rice	150	750	75	225
Other................	165	580	141	568
Subtotal II	315	1,330	216	793
III. *Manufactures based on natural raw materials*	15	1,250	48	1,489
IV. *Manufactures based on traditional skills .....*	47	275	42	270
V. *New manufactures based initially on domestic market*	31	785	16	960
VI. *Other goods (not specified in the Planning Commission study)*				
Tea	n.a.	n.a.	23	22
Manufactured goods specified in the present study	n.a.	n.a.	15	967
Non-specified goods ...	70	1,610	80	275
Subtotal VI	70	1,610	118	1,264
VII. GOODS, TOTAL	2,400	9,300	2,224	7,923
VIII. *Services*				
Tourism	n.a.	n.a.	20	1,000
International shipping, airlines	n.a.	n.a.	100	1,870
Other (or non-specified)	550	2,000	319	1,380
SERVICES, TOTAL .	550	2,000	439	4,250
GOODS AND SERVICES, TOTAL	2,950	11,300	2,663	12,173
PERSPECTIVE PLAN	3,050	14,000		

Sources: Planning Commission, [36], Annex, Table 1; the Perspective Plan, [5], Tables 1 and 6, pp. 19 and 24; the present study, based on Table 53 and [0], Annex VIII, Table 1.

raw cotton, + Rs 520 million; rice, + Rs 525 million; and non-specified, + Rs 345 million; or, in total, about Rs 2,000 million. Amongst the major items for which the present study sets higher targets (which partly offset the five items above) can be mentioned cotton manufactures, + Rs 350 million; manufactures based on natural raw materials, + Rs 240 million; and new manufactures, based initially on domestic markets, + Rs 175 million.

The projections of exports of jute and jute goods in the Planning Commission study are based on a considerably more optimistic appreciation of the future world market for jute goods than the present study (although the Planning Commission assumes a fall in prices, which means that in constant prices the gap between the two forecasts is even wider). I believe that the Planning Commission estimates on that point are too optimistic. The higher estimates of exports of rice and raw cotton in the Planning Commission study are soundly based on recent agricultural achievements. I believe that as regards cotton, it will prove easier to expand exports of cotton goods than of cotton. The very rapid expansion which is projected for non-specified goods in the Planning Commission study is not well substantiated, but may nevertheless be credible, because of the capricious behaviour of international trade. Success in exports depends very much on individual entrepreneurs, and the planners in Pakistan are right in hoping for pleasant surprises in the field of exports.

The projected increase in exports of services in the Planning Commission study is very modest. There is every reason to believe that in the course of the next twenty years airlines, shipping lines, and tourism will contribute very much to Pakistan's foreign-exchange earnings.

In the Perspective Plan the export target for 1985 has been raised Rs 2,700 million above the target in the 1964 study by the Planning Commission. It is likely that a considerable part of the increase in the export target is accounted for by goods from agriculture. It is, of course, also possible that the Planning Commission has raised its expectations as regards exports of services.

The export targets in both the Perspective Plan and in the present study are ambitious, but an annual increase in exports of the order of 8 per cent is undoubtedly necessary, and should even be surpassed, if Pakistan is to be able to sustain a high rate of growth of its national income without becoming unduly dependent on capital imports and foreign aid.

9. *Employment prospects*

The difficulties inherent in estimating employment in a developing country are discussed at the beginning of Chapter 12. Both in the Perspective Plan and in the present study, employment in agriculture in the base year is estimated on the basis of the number of cropped acres and domestic animals. In the present study, the projected employment figure in agriculture represents the number of man-years which can be remunerated at an acceptable level (see Chapter 12). It is feasible, and probable, that the ef-

Table 85. *Labour force and employment, 1965–85 (mill. man years)*

	Perspective plan		Present study	
	1965	1985	1965	1985
Labour force......................	37.25	62.30	38.30	65.20
Employment......................	29.70	59.70	30.20	55.80
Employment, including imputed empl.	n.a.	n.a.	35.20	61.45
a. agricultural...................	19.30	29.50	18.70	22.20
b. non-agricultural...............	10.40	30.20	11.50	33.55
of which				
modern manufacturing	n.a.	n.a.	0.75	3.40
traditional manufacturing	n.a.	n.a.	2.40	2.45
total manufacturing	(3.25)	(8.20)	3.15	5.85
Other.......................	(7.15)	(22.00)	8.35	27.70
c. imputed employment	n.a.	n.a.	5.00	5.70
Unemployment as percentage of the				
labour force	20	4	21	14
Imputed employment deducted from				
unemployment	n.a.	n.a.	8	6

Sources: The Perspective Plan, [5], Table 7, p. 25; the present study, Table 61. The figures for employment in manufacturing in the Perspective Plan have been calculated on the basis of [5], Table 3, p. 21.

fective demand for labour in agriculture may grow more slowly than projected, or even fall. Judging from the discussion of the employment prospects in agriculture in the April, 1964, working paper on the Perspective Plan prepared in the Planning Commission, the employment projections in the Perspective Plan are based on planned increases in cropped area and the number of livestock.

In other sectors the employment projections in both studies are based on ratios between growth in output and growth in employment, i. e. assumed rates of growth of productivity of labour. The implied productivity assumptions in the two sets of projections are:

	Perspective plan	*Present study*
Agriculture	3.4	2.8
Manufacturing	5.2	6.3
Other sectors	1.9	1.3

(Increase in output per man-year, compound annual rate during the period 1965—85. Estimates based on Tables 75 and 85.)

There is no purpose in comparing the two implied rates of growth of productivity in agriculture since the employment estimates have been established on the basis of completely different methods.[25]

What is certain, however, is that both projections of employment in agriculture are based on a substantial amount of 'wishful thinking'. Even if output per acre rises substantially, and even if in some cases this increase is due to more labour intensive methods (such as the Japanese rice-growing technique), it is not at all certain that employment per acre will remain unchanged on the average during the next twenty years. On the contrary, it is overwhelmingly likely that the technical revolution in agriculture will lead to mechanization and to a more general use of labour-saving methods. The estimates of the level of unemployment in 1985 stand and fall with the estimates of employment in agriculture. If these are much too optimistic, unemployment will remain a serious problem throughout the Perspective Plan period.

In the other sectors, the Perspective Plan shows a slower increase in productivity in manufacturing and a faster increase in productivity in other activities than the present study. The difference in the case of manufacturing is clearly caused by the fact that the Perspective Plan is based on a substantial increase in employment in small-scale industries. I believe that the Perspective Plan overestimates substantially the employment potential of the manufacturing industries. After all, about 75 per cent of the total employment in manufacturing in 1965 was accounted for by traditional industries (which should not be confused with *small-scale industries* in general) which are bound to stagnate.[26]

Whereas the Perspective Plan appears to over-estimate the increased employment opportunities in manufacturing, it may under-estimate the potential growth of employment in other sectors. It should be remembered that per definition productivity in many service activities cannot increase (for example, government administration, education, health).

For non-agricultural activities as a whole, both sets of projections show practically the same rate of growth in employment between 1965 and 1985. The present study shows higher absolute figures; and until the present employment situation in Pakistan has been surveyed more thoroughly, it is not possible to determine the absolute level of employment, either present or future.

The present study includes an estimate of 'imputed employment' in mostly non-monetized activities.[27] In my view some of this employment must be taken into account in assessing the present level of unemployment and under-employment, e. g. employment on country boats and in traditional fishing in East Pakistan, and at least some of the employment in traditional land transport all over Pakistan. Other jobs, such as the collection of firewood or the construction of huts, are usually done by women and children who are not included in the labour force estimates. It is likely, however, that by 1985 more of the 'imputed employment' will cover work done by people included in the labour force, particularly since by then all children should be in school up to the age of 14, which will substantially reduce the amount of child labour.

In the present study no effort has been made to devise a development strategy that will reduce or eliminate under-employment and unemployment. Thus, the figures for employment shown in Table 85 are an automatic consequence of the projected pattern of output. Nevertheless, they show a significant reduction in the percentage of unemployed. But in the final analysis it is primarily what happens in agriculture that will determine the employment situation. If the agrarian revolution leads to less labour intensive farming methods, Pakistan will have to face a very serious unemployment problem during the next couple of decades.

10. *The targets for education*

The educational targets for 1985 are the same in the present study and the Perspective Plan. But Table 86 below shows that the time phasing is more ambitious in the present study. The reason for this is that at the time the present study was started, the official policy in Pakistan was based on the targets set by the National Education Commission, which were universal primary education by 1970, and eight years of universal elementary education by 1975.[28] The present author considered that these targets were beyond reach and modified them accordingly. The government of Pakistan has evidently found that these targets had to be modified even further, which is understandable, since the cost of building schools and training teachers and the current running costs must rise very steeply if the targets given in the present study are to be attained.

It should be noted that in the present study the targets for enrolment of students in teacher-training institutes in 1970 was set at 40,000, or the same figure as in the Third Plan.[29] The same

Table 86. *Targets for education*

| | Percentage of age groups enrolled in | | | |
| | Primary stage | | Lower secondary stage | |
	Perspective plan	Present study	Perspective plan	Present study
1960	34	32	11	12
1965	44	42	12	14
1970	70	72	19	30
1975	90	100	45	64
1980	100	100	70	87
1985	100	100	100	100

Sources: The Perspective Plan, [5], Table 8, p. 28; the present study, Table 72.

considerations seem to have prevailed in both cases, since the planned figures for enrolment of pupils in the primary schools by 1970 are practically identical in both projections. In my opinion, the educational targets in the Perspective Plan are feasible, but will require very determined efforts.

11. *The regional income distribution*

It is a major policy objective of the Perspective Plan to close the gap in income *per caput* between East and West Pakistan by 1985. Though fully aware of the political necessity of such a target, I was unable to accept it as feasible. This question is discussed in some detail on pages 69 and 70 of this study.

The Perspective Plan does not explain how to achieve income equality between the two provinces, but in the April, 1964, working paper on the Perspective Plan it was assumed that in 1985 East Pakistan would still be less urbanized than West Pakistan, and that in order to reach the target of income equality, rural incomes *per caput* in East Pakistan would have to be higher than in West Pakistan.[30] The Perspective Plan may have been built on the assumption that the ratio of urban to rural population would be the same in both provinces in 1985, in which case the gap in *per caput* income could be closed if rural and urban *per caput* incomes were the same in both provinces.[31]

A priori there is no reason why the average urban income per head in East Pakistan should not catch up with that of West Pakistan in the course of the next twenty years. Even though West Pakistan will probably remain the centre of government and the armed forces, there is no obvious reason why wage and income

Table 87. *Pattern of regional growth in the Perspective Plan*

	Perspective plan		Present study	
	East Pak.	West Pak.	East Pak.	West Pak.
Income *per caput* 1965 (Rs) ..	340	442	260	336
Income *per caput* 1985 (Rs) ..	932	932	572	668
Growth rate in regional product 1965–85 (%)......	8.0	6.3	6.8	6.3
(Data from working paper on the Perspective Plan)				
Income *per caput* 1965 (Rs) ..	325	430	260	336
Income *per caput* 1985 (Rs) ..	790	790	572	668
Rural income *per caput:*				
1965 (Rs)........	310	345	241	253
1985 (Rs)........	620	550	419	419
Urban income *per caput:*				
1965 (Rs)........	580	695	505	574
1985 (Rs)........	1,220	1,220	950	950
Growth rates 1965 to 1985				
Income *per caput*	4.5	3.1	4.0	3.5
Rural income *per caput*	3.5	2.3	2.8	2.6
Urban income *per caput*	3.8	2.9	3.2	2.6
Rural product	4.8	4.0	4.2	3.6
Urban product	15.1	7.6	13.7	8.5

Sources: The Perspective Plan, 3 first lines, [5], Table 9, p. 29; other lines, [37], Table 12, p. 58; the present study, Table 7.

levels in general should not be about equal in the urban areas in both provinces. But given the fact that the urban population in West Pakistan is more than three times as large as that of East Pakistan, and that the total population of East Pakistan will probably remain larger than that of West Pakistan, it is not very likely that the degree of urbanization in East Pakistan can catch up with West Pakistan in the course of only twenty years.

At present it looks as if the prospects for a rapid growth of the total rural income, as well as of rural income *per caput,* are considerably brighter in West than in East Pakistan (see subsection 5 on agriculture in the present section). In 1959—60 there were 0.9 acres of cropped area per head of rural population in West Pakistan as against 0.55 acres in East Pakistan. Because of the 'tubewell revolution' it is likely that available irrigation water will increase by two-thirds during the ten-year period 1960 to 1970, and some further increase is possible. Double and triple cropping are to a large extent possible in East Pakistan, but cropping seasons overlap, and it will require much ingenuity to increase the acreage considerably through extended irrigation and multicropping. It is therefore likely that during the next twenty years irrigation alone will increase the potential agricultural output in West Pakistan more than in East Pakistan. Table 87 shows that the working paper on the long-term perspectives of the Pakistan economy assumed that not only rural incomes *per caput* but also the rural product in itself would grow faster in East than in West Pakistan. At present it is overwhelmingly likely that at least the rural product, and possibly also the rural product *per caput,* will grow fastest in West Pakistan.

In view of the fact that East Pakistan is already very densely populated, one cannot avoid concluding that the *per caput* income in East Pakistan cannot catch up with that of West Pakistan until, in relative terms, East Pakistan is at least as urbanized as West Pakistan. And until the urban sector of East Pakistan has grown so large that the population pressure on agricultural land ceases, it seems unlikely that rural incomes per head in East Pakistan can catch up with those in West Pakistan. Even the assumption in the present study, i. e. that rural incomes per head will be the same in both provinces in 1985, is fairly unrealistic.

It is, of course, not good politics to maintain that East Pakistan will remain poorer than West Pakistan at the end of the present Perspective Plan. It would be possible to retard growth in West Pakistan so much that East Pakistan could reach parity in *per capita* income by 1985 (by means such as preventing the agrarian revoultion in West Pakistan by diverting all available fertilizers to East Pakistan, etc.), but such policies would be meaningless and would not hasten growth in East Pakistan. Two years ago I would have defended the thesis of aiming at parity in rural and urban *per caput* incomes respectively between the two provinces. This would have made sense in many respects. But the very promising agricultural prospects in West Pakistan make it unlikely that even this goal can be reached by 1985. In relation to West Pakistan rural incomes in the East will be depressed due to the shortage of land, and urban incomes may also be depressed, because of a relatively greater inflow of landless peasants to the towns and cities.

The only feasible policy is to accelerate the industrialization of East Pakistan as fast as is humanly possible. This will in turn accelerate urbanization, which is the one most important precondition for *per caput* income parity between the two provinces. Such a policy will inevitably mean some brake on development in West Pakistan. Thus, available foreign aid should be diverted to East Pakistan without, however, harming the all-important agrarian revolution in West Pakistan, and, similarily, foreign investments should be channelled into East Pakistan through all available means. But even so it will certainly prove very difficult to raise the annual growth of the urban product in East Pakistan above the 14 per cent assumed in the present study, or the even higher percentage implicitly assumed in the Perspective Plan. Regional *per caput* income parity is certainly the most pressing domestic policy objective in Pakistan, but as economists we must be prepared to admit that this cannot be achieved within the life-time of the present Perspective Plan.

12. *Concluding remarks*

The foregoing analysis of the Perspective Plan on the basis of the material contained in the present study leads to several important conclusions. It should be kept in mind that these conclusions depend on a large number of underlying assumptions in the present study, but no information available to this author tends to undermine or cast serious doubts upon these many detailed assumptions. It is the very detailed approach used in the present study that is responsible for an analytical outcome that in many respects differs significantly from the corresponding results in the Perspective Plan.

A. It will certainly not be possible for Pakistan to reach its target growth of national income and at the same time reduce and almost eliminate its dependence on foreign assistance and any other inflow of foreign capital. There are two main and internally consistent reasons for this conclusion.

Firstly, the global incremental capital-output ratio will certainly prove to be significantly higher than assumed in the Perspective Plan. Therefore, gross investment as a percentage of Gross National Product will, under the given growth assumptions, become so high that it would be unrealistic to assume that gross national savings could be raised enough to close, or almost close, the gap between investment and savings. This gap must be filled by foreign assistance and other capital inflow from abroad.

Secondly, it is likely taht, in spite of determined efforts to create import substitution industries, imports will have to grow about as fast as the Gross National Product. As Pakistan initially had a large current balance of payments deficit, exports would have to grow much faster than national income if the balance of payments gap were to be closed, or almost closed, in the course of two decades. Whereas Pakistan must plan to increase its exports very fast, it is almost inconceivable that it could manage to increase them fast enough to reduce its current balance of payments deficit substantially by 1985.

Thus, independent examinations of each of the two 'gaps' lead to the same conclusion, namely an increased rather than decreased need for inflow of foreign capital.

It is probable that similar studies of other developing countries would in most cases lead to the same result, i. e. that if the rate of growth of national income is to be high enough to be politically acceptable, both within the countries themselves and internationally, the need for foreign aid must grow rather than decline during the next two to three decades.

B. The heavy reliance on rapid growth in agriculture as a means of achieving fast economic development has not yet been adequately analysed. An examination of the Perspective Plan suggests that the planners have implicitly assumed that the domestic demand for food will grow at a rate that may prove to be unrealistically high. Theoretically, the problem could be resolved by a drastic reduction of food prices in relation to other domestic prices, i. e. by planning for an unfavourable change in the terms of trade of agriculture in relation to other economic activities. But such a policy might well prove self-defeating, since it would reduce incentives to increased agricultural production, stimulate the use of labour-saving devices in farming, and thus aggravate the unemployment situation, and prevent the gradual closing of the income gap between urban and rural areas (and thereby also slow down the process of closing the gap in income *per caput* between East and West Pakistan). In addition, it is by no means certain that relative price reductions on food would raise domestic food consumption sufficiently to ensure demand for the projected rapid increase in food supplies. In general, the price elasticity for food is low.

The projected rapid expansion of agricultural production should therefore logically lead to a strong increase in exports of food and other agricultural raw materials. There is no clear indication in the Perspective Plan of a projected increase in exports of agricultural products large enough to absorb domestic surpluses. Neither does the Perspective Plan discuss the modification of the structure of land use and agricultural production, which is a pre-condition for the successful implementation of the global plan targets for agriculture.

These observations are universally valid for most developing countries. Against the background of stagnating or at best slowly increasing food production in most developing countries, we are becoming more and more obsessed by the danger of world-wide famine and a dangerous degree of pauperization of the less-developed countries. But those developing countries which do succeed in bringing about an agrarian revoultion and a steep growth in output of food and other agricultural raw materials will quickly be faced with problems of demand. On a world-wide basis, a short spurt in food output is needed, followed by a 'normal' rate of growth to ensure adequate food supplies in the future. This strategy makes sense from the point of view of ensuring adequate food supplies, but it is not satisfactory as a basis for sustained growth in the developing countries, for rapid rural development and for a policy of full employment, which for decades to come must be based on the highest possible level of employment in agriculture. Moreover, it is probable that the agrarian revolution will take the form, *not* of a short spurt in output, but of a movement which will gain momentum.

I do not dispute the wisdom of policies designed to increase productivity in agriculture, but I feel that a word of warning is appropriate, otherwise we risk our planned agrarian revolution becoming a monster rather than a servant of mankind.

C. It is unlikely that parity in income between East and West Pakistan can be achieved by 1985. This conclusion is based on the observation that such parity probably cannot be achieved until the distribution of employment between urban and rural areas has become roughly the same in both provinces. Within the Perspective Plan period, and under the overall growth assumptions in the Plan, this would entail an inconceivably rapid rate of growth of non-agricultural activities in East Pakistan. The alternative solution, that rural output per head of labour force should become higher in East Pakistan than in West Pakistan, is equally unconvincing, taking into account that East Pakistan would have a far larger proportion of its labour force in agriculture, and far less arable land per head of agricultural labour force, than West Pakistan. However, the relative income gap should be reduced, and parity of income *per caput* should be feasible in the course of this century. The idea of keeping West Pakistan's growth rate down for the benefit of East Pakistan is not relevant, because it would involve reducing the overall growth rate below the planned target.

D. Employment projections are very weak, both in the present study and in the Perspective Plan. Although the composition of *non-agricultural employment* differs somewhat between the two sets of projections, the global figures are of the same order of magnitude. However, this does not mean that the results are realistic. On the contrary, it is quite likely that both projections are on the optimistic side. The two sets of figures for projected *agricultural employment* are also roughly the same. Both projections are based on similar assumptions, *viz.* limited use of labour-saving machinery and widespread use of very labour intensive cultivation methods. This suggests that the projected employment potential in agriculture is also on the optimistic side. Both projections lead to the conclusion that unemployment and under-employment will be practically eliminated, although the present study concludes that there will be some unemployment. A critical examination of the figures in both projections suggests that unless extraordinary and spectacular steps are taken against un-employment, there is every likelihood that Pakistan will continue to suffer from both unemployment and under-employment during the Perspective Plan period.

E. Finally, there is a grave, inherent danger in relying on the use of assumed macro-figures for capital-output ratio, import elasticity, and demand for broad categories of goods and services in perspective planning. Assumed figures will, of course, be based on empirical experience, and may be the outcome of very refined statistical studies. They may nevertheless be irrelevant, because no future situation can be a reproduction of one, or a combination of several, past situations. No one will deny that the use of global figures implies a very wide margin of error. Nevertheless, it is likely — and the Perspective Plan is a case in point — that in choosing macro-economic coefficients for planning purposes, the planners may tend to choose figures which are close to the border of the range of possible figures. Thus the likely errors will be one-sided. The analysis in this chapter shows that such systematic errors are present in the Perspective Plan, and that these errors are responsible for the analytical weaknesses stressed in Conclusions A and B above.

Planners in a developing country are compelled to present a reasonably bright picture of the long-term economic prospects, and this author will not criticize the Planning Commission in Pakistan for having used very optimistic assumptions on a number of points. *They* cannot plan for increased foreign aid which is unrealistic on the basis of the donor countries' present attitude and unacceptable from a domestic political point of view; *they* cannot advise against the over-production of agricultural goods, partly because it would look unrealistic against the background of the present world food shortage, and partly because it would reduce the incentives to transform agriculture which is the most urgent need of most developing countries; neither can *they* proclaim that it will take the rest of the century to acheive *per caput* income parity between East and West Pakistan. In contrast, the present study is an academic study in which it is not merely permissible, but mandatory, to spell out a series of 'dismal' conclusions and to raise new issues which must be discussed, analysed further, and faced by the policy makers in the highly industrialized as well as in the developing countries.

To resume, these policy issues are:

(1) The need for foreign aid, defined as the transfer of goods and services from 'rich' to 'poor' countries, is likely to become greater during the next two or three decades if the developing countries are to maintain a sufficiently high rate of growth;

(2) The need for foreign aid, defined as the need for capital inflow to cover the current balance of payments deficit, including capital income payments abroad, plus contractual repayments of loans, etc., will grow very rapidly if foreign aid continues to take the form of interest-bearing and repayable loans and direct private investments;

(3) Although an agrarian revolution is the most important step in the transformation of the economies of the developing countries, it is necessary to foresee the effects of such a revolution on the supplies of food and agricultural raw materials, and to design alternative strategies for development which can be implemented when the threat of over-production in agriculture becomes a reality;

(4) The elimination of regional inequalities in the course of a relatively short time will not be possible unless the overall rate of growth reaches levels which are almost inconceivable today; and

(5) It will not be possible to create full employment until the economy of a typical developing country is thoroughly modernized, unless either the wage level in non-agricultural activities is kept so low that under-employment in agriculture becomes an economically irrelevant concept, or large-scale programmes of mobilizing labour for investment purposes are carried through in one way or another.

None of these five problems makes rapid economic growth in developing countries impossible. But they all suggest radical re-thinking of many policies, in both the rich and the poor countries.

Appendix I: Input-output Tables for Pakistan for the Years 1960, 1965, 1970, 1975, 1980, and 1985

The 'input-output Tables' which have been prepared as a part of the study of possible structural developments inside the economy of Pakistan during a 25-year period are not input-output Tables in the strict sense of the word. They have not been properly consolidated since neither the products of certain sectors (notably trade and transport) nor indirect taxes less subsidies have been distributed between receiving sectors.

The Tables as presented here consist of two sets of Tables, superimposed upon each other. Each 'box' has room for two figures — the upper figure which is expressed in producers' prices and the lower figure which is expressed in purchasers' prices. The *upper* figures have been estimated on the basis of the gross domestic output of the various sectors plus the imports of goods and services which per definition are produced by the different sectors (i. e. whether actually produced in Pakistan or not). The total availabilities have then been distributed between the different intermediate and final uses. Thus the upper figures give a complete picture of the rows in an input-output table, with one major exception: the output of the trade sector has not been distributed between various uses. Moreover, as the domestic output (and imports) are expressed in factor costs, total availabilities are also expressed in factor costs.

The *lower* figures cover merely intermediate uses, and are based on the estimated input structures of the different sectors. These figures therefore may be said to represent the columns of the input-output Table, and are expressed in market prices. The reason why there are no lower figures for final uses is that the break-down of the estimates of the final uses (private and public consumption, fixed investments, investments in stocks and exports) in Chapters 5, 6, 7, 9 and 10 of this study is not made according to sectors of origin, but according to types of goods and services.

Ideally, the upper and lower figures should be consolidated into one set of figures, and this is, of course, what is done when an input-output table is being constructed. For the purpose of this study, however, such a consolidation is not necessary. The purpose of the Tables as set out here is to spot and eliminate obvious inconsistencies. This can be done by comparing the upper and lower figures for the intermediate uses and deliveries, and by reviewing the estimates of the final uses together with the figures for deliveries for final purposes.[1]

Note that imports are shown as a column, not as a row as in many input-output Tables. This presentation is by no means unique. It is used by the French and also, for example, by Chenery and Clark in their input-output study of Italy in 1950.[2] Both ways of including imports are in some respects unsatisfactory. If imports are included as a row, it is easy to see how much of the inputs in various sectors is imports, and similarly how much of private consumption, investments, etc., consists of imported goods and services. But the Table does not give any information as regards the sectors of origin of imported goods and services. This limits severely the direct usefulness of the Table since it is not possible to tell from the Table what *direct* influence on imports increases in certain types of demand will have. Even for intermediate uses there exists no 'law' which says that the use of imported inputs will rise at the same rate as the use of domestic inputs (or as output). The use of imported inputs may rise faster than output and the use of domestic inputs if imports are caused by an inflexible domestic supply of certain inputs. On the other hand, the use of imported inputs will rise more slowly than the use of domestic inputs if import substitution is taking place. Only when imported inputs consist exclusively of items which are not domestically produced, and the input-coefficients remain constant, will imports of inputs have to rise at the same rate as the output of the sector which uses the inputs. As regards final uses, it is even more obvious that the ratio of imports to a certain category of demand will not stay constant.

The alternative presentation has the advantage that it makes it possible to see the link between imports and domestic output, i. e. imports equal total demand less domestic output. In most cases it is possible to draw rather far-reaching conclusions from this equation, but in some cases the equation gives false results. This is due to the aggregation which is implied in an input-output table with a reasonable number of sectors. One example will illustrate this: an increase in the output of cement or of sulphuric acid will in both cases lead to a higher demand for minerals (limestone and gypsum in the first case, sulphur in the other).

Pakistan has abundant supplies of limestone and gypsum, but virtually none of sulphur. Increased output of cement will therefore lead to increased output in the Pakistan mining industry, while increased output of sulphuric acid must lead to increased imports of mining products. This cannot be read directly out of the input-output matrix.

A double set of input-output tables which includes domestically produced and imported items separately in each 'box' would be of great help, but would provide no answer to the problem discussed above. If, for example, in the base year the sector pulp and paper industry only purchases domestic forest products, it would not be justified to conclude that a tripling of the output of pulp and paper products would lead to a tripling of domestic purchases of forest products. Limited forest resources may well compel the industry to cover most of its additional needs from abroad. On the contrary an industry which has depended exclusively on imported supplies of products from a given sector may switch to domestic supplies if an import substituting industry is set up. Finally, it must always be kept in mind that the technical coefficients for a given sector can change considerably if the expansion of the output of the sector results in significant changes in the internal structure of the sector itself.

The main reasons for presenting imports as a column are two: first, from the point of view of presentation this makes it possible to see at a glance how large a proportion of the available supplies of products of a certain sector are imported. This suggests immediately the scope for import substitution, although it is of course necessary to examine in detail whether it is technically possible and economically justified to aim at replacing imports by domestic production. Second, from a purely statistical point of view it is far easier to distribute imports on sectors of origin than on sectors of destination.

The 'input-output Tables' as presented in this study have *not* been used as a basis for projections, but merely as a tool for *adjusting* certain projections. An input-output matrix is eminently well suited for short-term projections, on the assumption that the technical coefficients remain constant (or that changes in the coefficients can be predicted and introduced in the planning model). Some further assumption must also be made as regards the competitive position of domestic and foreign industries for items which either can be procured domestically or imported. In a developing country technical coefficients will not remain constant even during a short period. This has two reasons: (1) a few additional industrial units will in most cases change the input structure considerably in the industrial subsectors to which these units belong; and (2) introduction of modern techniques in traditional sectors will significantly modify their input structure. Furthermore, the relationship between domestic and imported sources of supplies will change very drastically, because of steps to promote import substitution. Detailed planning in a developing country must therefore be done on the basis of isolated projections for different sectors of the economy. Only in this manner can abrupt changes in the structure of demand and supply be taken into consideration. However, it is not possible to escape from the fact that a large proportion of demand for goods and services will consist of demand for 'inputs', and an input-output matrix is the most practical tool for estimating such intermediate demand.

The approach used in this study corresponds to the method suggested above — i. e. the growth of output in the different sectors was estimated separately, on the basis of firm assumptions as regards final demand and of provisional assumptions as regards intermediate demand. All output figures and the corresponding input figures were then organized in the form of input-output tables, and new figures for intermediate demand were obtained. At this stage it was fairly easy to adjust the provisional figures for demand for inputs to make them correspond to the 'true' demand for inputs.

The construction of the input-output Tables in this study was based on details which are not shown in the Tables.[3] The Table below suggests how the input-output Tables were built up:

	Main sectors	Sub-sectors	Specified goods and services; specified industries
All sectors	19	30	132
Main sectors broken down into subsectors	4	30	
Main sectors broken down into specified products or industries	5		19
Subsectors broken down into specified products or industries		25	113
'Basic' sectors	10	5	132

The ten main sectors which have not been broken down further into subsectors or specified industries, etc., are: Commercial construction; non-monetized construction; banking and insurance;

government; communications; housing; business premises for rent; trade; education; and health services. The five subsectors which have not been broken down further are: tobacco manufacturing; printing and publishing; misc. modern manufacturing industries; port services; and oil pipelines. Most of these 15 'basic' sectors amongst the main sectors and subsectors could have been broken down further, if it had been desirable. Thus, the sector education can easily be broken down into primary, secondary, higher, technical, and other specialized education.

For the 147 'basic' sectors listed above, projections of gross output (and of imports) are available, and in most cases attempts have been made to allocate the output (plus imports) between different uses. The input structure and the value added have only been calculated for a smaller number of 'basic' sectors. Thus while the subsector 'plant production' under agriculture was broken down into 15 different products or groups of products, the input structure and the value added were calculated on the basis of the global gross output of plant products. However, the input structure was calculated separately for all specified industries under modern and traditional manufacturing, for all subgroups under mining and for some other specified industries as well. In fact, the input structure has been calculated for 125 'basic' sectors. The figure may seem surprisingly high, but some subsectors under manufacturing were broken down into specific industries for the purpose of estimating the input structure and not for the purpose of distributing the output.

It follows from this approach that the input-structure in the various sectors and sub-sectors as shown in the reproduced tables changes considerably from one year to another. It would be presumptuous to claim that these figures for the changes could be utilized for planning purposes, as a means of predicting alterations in the input structure in Pakistan. Clearly, the changes as shown here depend on the structural changes in the various sectors and subsectors. If the structural changes are considerably different from those assumed in this study, the changes in the input structure will also be different. Furthermore, the basic data on the input structure are weak, and in many cases they do not amount to more than 'informed guesses'. Finally, over a period of 20 years, from 1965 to 1985, it would be surprising if technological developments did not lead to very marked changes in the input structure in many industries. However, the mere fact that the author has thought it worth while to go through the time-consuming exercise of constructing input-output tables so far ahead as for 1985 shows the belief that the changes in the 'technical coefficients' cannot become so fundamental that an

input-output table for 1985 made in 1965 becomes utterly meaningless and misleading. If the assumptions about the fundamental pattern of development in Pakistan prove to be reasonably
realistic, it is also likely that the projected pattern of uses of
goods and services for intermediate purposes will prove to be
reasonably close to reality.

The entries in the input-output Tables are, on the whole, identical with the figures in [0], Annex VI. The input-output Tables
include, however, far more details than those given in Annex VI.[4]

There are cases in whitch the figures in the input-output Tables
differ somewhat from those which can be found in [0], Annex
VI. First, there is a general case. The figures for value added in
modern manufacturing industries in Annex VI are, in general,
based on data from the Census of Manufacturing Industries 1959/
60.[5] The CMI does not, however, specify inputs of services, and
the value added is therefore somewhat too high. In the input-
output Tables, account has been taken of inputs of services, and
the value added is therefore somewhat lower than the original figures in Annex VI. Some of the revised Tables in Chapter 6 take
into account this change, but not all. Second, last-minute changes
in the input-output Tables to eliminate inconsistencies may not
always have been recorded in the Tables in Annex VI. All major
changes have been carried through in both places, however. Major
discrepancies should no longer occur — if they still do, they are
due to inadequate cross-checking.[6]

The entries in the input-output Tables which cannot be found in
Annex VI are partly some figures for the distribution of the total
domestic availabilities (gross domestic output plus imports) be-
tween different uses and almost all figures for the input structure.
Figures for imports and exports can be found in [0], Annex VIII,
Tables 1 and 3.

In Annex VI the distribution of total availabilities of products
of the different sectors has been shown in considerable detail;
but in making the rows of the input-output Tables, it was often
necessary to make a more detailed breakdown of the uses than the
one which is shown in Chapter 6.

Only in a few cases does Annex VI contain a discussion of the
input structure. (One example is agriculture.) For the purpose of
the input-output Tables further research had to be carried out.
Data were readily available only for most of the modern manufacturing industries (in the Census of Manufacturing Industries
1959/60). The CMI figures were checked against data from other
countries, and data for more industrially developed countries
were exploited to assess the impact on the input sturcture in Pakistan of a modernization of their industries.[7] For most of the other

sectors the input data represent 'informed guesses', based on scattered data from Pakistan (e. g. the accounts for the railways) and on data on input structure in similar sectors in other countries. In using data from other countries care has been taken to make adjustments for the lower wage level, less use of mechanical equipment, etc., in Pakistan. In some cases the input structure of specific industries, etc., was estimated on the basis of data contained in feasibility studies for new enterprises.

To make a complete picture of the inter-industry flow of goods and services it was necessary to include some auxiliary sectors. Two columns were added — non-specified intermediate uses and uses by non-specified manufacturing industries. The boxes in these two columns include, by definition, only figures in the upper halves (i. e. they represent the un-allocated parts of the total domestic availabilities). Four rows were added: non-specified inputs, non-specified inputs of manufactured goods, non-specified inputs of services, and 'invisible imports'. The last row includes only the expenditure of international shipping and air companies abroad. The figures for the four rows are entered in the lower halves of the boxes, i. e. they represent unallocated or crudely allocated inputs. It should be noted that these two columns and four rows have nothing in common in the input-output tables as they are presented in this study. (In a consolidated input-output Table non-specified intermediate deliveries must, per definition, equal non-specified inputs, but this is not the case here, since discrepancies also occur elsewhere: in the final uses, through the fact that deliveries are in producers' prices while purchases are in market prices; and finally because the output of trade services is not distributed between users.)

It should be noted that some non-specified final uses and availabilities have been entered as negative or positive non-specified intermediate uses in the upper halves of the relevant boxes. This is the case of investments in stocks, of exports of non-specified goods and of non-specified services, of imports of non-specified goods and services. Take the example of non-specified goods. Final demand is increased by investment in stocks plus non-specified exports of goods less non-specified imports of goods. The balance is entered as a negative availability of non-specified goods for intermediate purposes.

Note that in principle subtotals for main sectors should equal the sum of the figures for the subsectors in the respective sectors. This is not always the case because one figure or other has not been allocated between the subsectors (see, for example, the sector transport for which imports of transport services have not been allocated). These exceptions are few, but care should be taken not to conclude that a discrepancy is caused by a calculating mistake.

The reader will observe that there are some minor discrepancies between figures which in principle should be identical, or that figures which should add up, do not add up exactly. The first is notably the case for the row total output which should equal the column gross domestic output. For some sectors and subsectors slightly different figures have been used for two purposes, for the distribution of the output between different uses, and for the calculation of the value added. When these discrepancies were minor, it was not worth while to recalculate large parts of the tables in order to avoid insignificant discrepancies. The second is notably the case for the sum of the rows total intermediate purchases and value added which do not add up to the total output. These discrepancies are simply due to the effect of rounding the figures.

Appendix II: Notes on the Methodology for Projections in the Modern Manufacturing Sector

A. *The classification into modern and traditional industries*

In the national income estimates of Pakistan the output of manufacturing industry is broken down into two main sectors: 'large-scale' and 'small-scale' manufacturing. Large-scale manufacturing incldues those units which are covered by the Census of Manufacturing Industries, that is, factories which employed 20 or more persons on at least one day of the preceding year.[1] For other purposes an alternative dividing line is drawn between large-scale and small-scale industries. The Second Five Year Plan defines small-scale industries as follows: 'Industries engaged in the production of handicraft, consumer or produced goods,

(i) employing manual labour without the use of any motive power, or

(ii) using motive power but employing not more than 20 persons or using fixed assets valued at not more than Rs 100,000.[2]

The purpose of the definition in the Second Plan was to include all traditional industries (e. g. handloom weaving which is occasionally organized in factories employing hundreds of persons, or traditional industries which have been modernized to the extent of using some auxiliary equipment necessitating motive power) under small-scale industries which, as such, are entitled to benefit from various forms of government support.

For my purpose both classifications create unnecessary complications, and no attempt has been made to make separate projections for 'large' and 'small' industries. It is useful, however, to distinguish between 'traditional industries', manufacturing and handicrafts, and 'modern industries'. No sharp distinction can be made. The definition is based on an *existing situation* which permits me to list those economic activities, the *products* of which are *traditional* for the geographical region which I discuss or which, alternatively, use *traditional production methods*. Often the two criteria will coincide. In fact, sometimes the production of a traditional product seems to depend on the use of certain production methods (for example the preferred vegetable oil in East Pakistan is the one extracted by primitive methods in the villages).

I did not make any attempt to apply well-defined principles in classifying some industries as 'modern' and others as 'traditional', and in several cases the choice made will certainly be criticized, but such cases will in general be less important. Here I deal with most industrial activities which are normally included under manufacturing in an industrially highly developed country. The exceptions are, first of all, the handicrafts and also some industries, like boat building, the present products of which are so closely linked with the traditional economy that it is preferable to treat them as traditional industries even though they clearly will continue to exist also in a modern industrial society. The adjustments which are needed for the official statistical presentation (large versus small industries) are of minor importance. The 'modern' small-scale industries represent less than 2 per cent of the gross output and between 3 and 4 per cent of the value added of 'small-scale' industries, and only 2 per cent is added to the output of large-scale industries, by including the 'modern' small scale ones.

The traditional industries will certainly be modernized during the 25-year period I analyse. But the major characteristics have been assumed to remain: manual production methods, village industries, or production of traditional goods.

The so-called modern industries will undergo substantial changes. Not only will the structure change drastically, but many of the existing industries will be transformed as well. Labour productivity, the use of energy, and the use of capital will rise in many sectors in which the existing units use out-dated methods. In many industrial sectors, however, existing units are fully up-to-date.

B. *Methods of projecting output in manufacturing industries*

The output in the various sectors and subsectors of manufacturing will be estimated on the basis of three major determining factors: demand, the feasible rate of expansion of capacity, and other limiting factors (natural resources, minimum plant size).

Final demand

Estimates of a major part of final *domestic* demand (personal consumption, government consumption, and a significant part of investments) are presented in the main text. The basic assumption is that domestic demand will be covered by domestic production, if it is at all possible to increase manufacturing capacity fast enough and if there are no other limiting factors which prevent domestic demand from being covered by domestic production. Part of the demand for investment goods could not be estimated before the need for investments in manufacturing itself (and in transport facilities) was assessed. This was not very disturbing because (1) Pakistan will remain a net importer of capital equipment during the period under review since other factors than demand will limit the expansion of the engineering industries, and (2) a large proportion of the demand for building materials was included in the estimates in the preceding chapters. The provisional estimates of the remaing demand for these products did not deviate significantly from the final estimate.

Export demand is unpredictable. For some products it is feasible to assess the international market prospects, for others I assume that there will be a continued shift in sources of international supplies — away from the old industrialized countries to the new ones (e. g. textiles), but for other products a far more arbitrary method has to be used, i. e. that 'manufacturing industries' will be able to export an increasing part of their output.

Intermediate demand

A proper handling of the problem of intermediate demand requires a complete input-output Table. Over the twenty-five-year period the use of input-output analysis becomes highly questionable, because significant and unpredictable changes in the technical coefficients are bound to take place. Fortunately, the problem of intermediate demand is not quite as formidable as certain data might lead one to believe. (In the U.S.A., for example, the intermediate products accounted for 45 per cent of total production in 1947 —based on an input-output Table with 45 production sectors.) Very often the bulk of intermediate products from one sector is used by one single other sector — i. e. output in one sector may still be estimated easily on the basis of the final demand even though there may be one or two intermediary sectors in between. Also we find that some industries sell their *by-products* to a number of sectors, while the sale of the main product goes to one sector or to the final consumers. For some industries the sales of by-products may represent a major problem, i. e. it will not pay to produce the main product unless the by-products can be sold at a reasonable price. But in general the demand for the main product will be the determining factor.

(An example from Italy may illustrate these points: 97 per cent of the output of *cereals* goes to intermediate uses, of which 8 per cent is within the sector cereals, and another 19 per cent to the rest of the sector agriculture. Of the remaining 70 per cent, almost all (69 per cent) is delivered to the milling industry. The milling industry again delivers 46 per cent of its production for intermediate uses, of which the bulk — 37 per cent — goes to the food industries (mostly bakeries etc.) and of the remaining 9 per cent, almost all is used in animal husbandry. Thus we find that in spite of nominally high figures for intermediate uses, the demand for cereals is determined by the final consumer demand for flour and bread (and in Italy, macaroni) and by the demand for feeding livestock.)[3]

For some industrial sectors, the intermediate demand is both very important and very difficult to project. A review of available input-output data from Norway, Italy, Algeria, Morocco, and Tunisia — i. e. from countries with highly different economies — shows some striking similarities, in spite of differences in statistical presentation which would tend to magnify the picture of structural differences. The *chemical* industries are the ones which deliver the largest part of their output to the greatest number of other sectors. Even for the products of these industries there are some very important clients. Thus in both Italy and Norway more than half of the output used domestically is used within the chemical industries themselves. In both countries, agriculture buys more than half the output sold domestically to other sectors. Nevertheless, a projection of the output of the chemical industries has to take into account the expected demand from other industries. For *light* chemicals (including pharmaceutical products, soap, and many other consumer goods) final demand is important, but the significant demand for intermediate goods is characterized by the absence of any big purchasing sector.

The *rubber,* the *lumber,* and the *pulp and paper* industries all have numerous sectors as clients for their intermediate products. In the three North African countries the *metal product* industries have no single dominant customer. This is of interest for Pakistan, since in an early stage of her development the delivery of metal cans to the food-manufacturing industries can represent a large part of the demand for metal goods.

The most striking examples of 'single customer' industries are the basic metal industries (one large customer, metal products industries; one medium-sized customer, the construction industry) and the non-metallic mineral goods industries which deliver most of their output of intermediate goods to the construction industry. Data from all five countries show the same results. Differences in classification do not permit comparisons between the five countries for a number of important industries, such as the textile and leather industries. But where data are available, we find that most of the output of the textile industries goes to clothing (or directly to the consumers) and most of the output from the leather industry to the shoe industry.

In the present study, we estimate the output of most industries (for which demand is the decisive factor) on the basis of final demand, either directly or via the sector which consumes a significant part of the deliveries of intermediate goods. The only industry for which intermediate demand by a variety of other manufacturing industries is of the utmost importance is the chemical industry and consequently we have estimated the demand for chemical production on the basis of estimates of production and of inputs in a number of other sectors. Agriculture, with its demand for fertilizers, insecticides, etc., is the largest single customer.

For a number of industries, future output has been projected merely on the basis of one, or sometimes a combination of several, indicators. Thus I have used well-defined elements of demand as an index of the development of total demand. Total domestic demand has been adjusted by imports and exports to arrive at demand on domestic production. The advantage of this simplified approach is that it becomes unnecessary to establish a 'fictional' figure for total domestic demand on the output of a given industry at purchasers' prices, and the margin represented by trade and transport, in order to arrive at total demand at producers' prices. Statistics are inadequate to permit estimates of present demand to be made within a reasonable margin of error. For some industries it is nevertheless necessary to estimate total demand, as a lesser evil, because there are such obvious inconsistencies between available data on demand and on production. Total demand has also been estimated for industries which produce a variety of products with very different trends of demand so that the simple index approach becomes too arbitrary.

These remarks show that the demand projections are very crude. But projections over such a long period of time can merely serve as illustrations, and more refined methods of projections would add nothing to our knowledge.

The estimate of the total demand on the production of a given industry sets *the upper limit to the output of the industry*. The figure for total demand in the future is uncertain for a number of reasons: (1) the projected domestic demand is in itself a very uncertain figure, (2) the extent to which domestic production can replace imports cannot be defined in precise terms since it depends on a number of technical and economic factors (some of which will be discussed below), and (3) the projected export demand for many products will merely represent a working hypothesis.

It should be stressed, however, that the figures for domestic demand and for the degree of import replacement are estimates which cannot be changed in an arbitrary manner. They represent my best judgement of future trends. The estimates could be made more elaborate, additional sources of information could be taken into account or they could be improved and changed in other ways. But to change the projections merely because they do not 'fit into the picture' or correspond to one's prejudices would merely mean replacing one uncertain set of estimates by an even poorer one.

The figures for export demand, on the other hand, can be manipulated without harm, because of their highly hypothetical character. The assumptions on which the figures for exports are based are in a way more important than the figures themselves, because the range of 'reasonable assumptions' is so very wide. The assumptions I have adopted are, of course, open to serious dispute. For practical reasons I have used only one single figure for exports of each major category of goods and services. If I had used upper and lower limits for all major exports, it would have been necessary to calculate a series of alternative developments for the structure of the economy as a whole. Without going that far, however, it is possible to evaluate my estimates of exports as a whole and my estimates of exports from individual industries and so assess whether the figures seem too optimistic or too pessimistic.

C. *The feasible rate of expansion*

By a 'feasible rate of expansion' I mean the rate at which a given industrial subsector could expand, taking into account the need for capital, for skilled manpower and experienced management, and for 'external economies' in general. I do *not* under this heading discuss the feasibility of manufacturing specific products, i. e. the possibility of setting up specialized units within an industrial subsector. The feasible rate of expansion is important for industrial subsectors for which the upper limit of expansion set by demand is so far above the present level of production that it would require an extremely high rate of expansion if output is to catch up with demand.

If sufficient foreign aid is not forthcoming, *shortage of capital* will most certainly limit the rate of expansion of industries with a high capital/output ratio. My working hypothesis is, however, that *capital will not be the limiting factor*. My study will show how much foreign aid will be needed, without discussing whether this is likely to be available or not.

The major factor determining the feasible rate of expansion of each industrial subsector will therefore be the human resources — skilled manpower, university-trained technical staff, and experienced management. One additional limiting factor should be mentioned; there is an inadequate development for the industrial structure as such, which means that the possibilities of subcontracting are limited, and that repair and servicing facilities are inadequate.

These limiting factors apply particularly to industries which use relatively much manpower, of which a high proportion is skilled manpower, or which are particularly dependent on reliable access to supplies of semi-manufactured products, spare-parts, accessories, and servicing facilities. They apply very strongly to the engineering industries (including electrical engineering and transport equipment) and to many industries conventionally classified under miscellaneous industries (instruments, photographic and optical equipment, etc.). They also apply to industries which have complicated machinery requiring regular servicing, but which are too small to maintain their own servicing facilities.

The conclusion reached, which may seem surprising, is that the feasible rate of expansion in an underdeveloped country is extremely rapid for capital intensive industries consisting of large units, but far slower for more labour-intensive industries made up of medium-sized and smaller units.[4] For example, I find no reason why Pakistan should not be able to expand its fertilizer industry to meet domestic demand. The fertilizer factories need comparatively few engineers, scientists, and skilled workers (and they may still provide jobs for many unskilled workers on materials handling, etc.), and they are large enough to maintain their own servicing and purchasing organizations. Examples from Pakistan support this argument. The newsprint factory in Khulna in East Pakistan was set up in a region without any industrial traditions. A few months after it went into operation, it utilized its capacity fully, and the foreign management and technical staff was reduced rapidly. On the other hand, the larger engineering units which have been built in Pakistan, notably the shipyards, are remarkably unsuccessful ventures in the midst of a generally very successful industrial development programme.

D. *Other limitations to industrial growth*

Other limiting factors apply principally to enterprises producing certain products and not to entire industrial subsectors.

The most obvious limiting factor is the shortage of, or absence of, certain *natural resources,* notably suitable energy resources and necessary raw materials. I have concluded that Pakistan most probably can have an *ample supply of cheap energy,* notably in the form of natural gas, and that there are strong reasons to hope that the domestic supply of petroleum will also be adequate. Coke for metallurgical uses will probably remain the major bottleneck in the energy and related fields.

Raw material supplies will limit the expansion of several industries, either in the whole of Pakistan or in one of the provinces. (The most disturbing case is the uncertainty as regards the iron ore resources. On the regional level, the lack of limestone in East Pakistan limits the expansion of the cement industry in that province.) Industrial development in recent decades shows that poor access to raw materials is not such a definite barrier to industrial growth as was previously assumed. Striking examples are the growth of steel industries in certain ports in large consuming areas (Italy, Japan, most recently in French ports). Nevertheless, raw materials which lose greatly in weight or bulk through processing will probably not be imported to Pakistan, nor will particularly perishable raw materials. It must be expected that to some extent shortage of raw materials will limit the growth of some metallurgical industries (although probably not the steel industry) and some chemical industries. As regards industries based on perishable raw materials, Pakistan is in a comparatively favourable situation because its agriculture and fisheries will be able to supply enough raw materials to permit a rapid expansion of the food industries.

The *smallness of the domestic market* will remain a limiting factor throughout the period under review. The main considerations that are important in this respect are in general the following.

First, we must distinguish between *mass production* and *specialized production.*

If a country has special advantages which permit the mass production of certain goods for export, the domestic market will obviously not limit the expansion of industries producing such goods. In Pakistan there are many examples of such industries: processing of fruit and of fish, manufacturing of jute goods, industries based on natural gas, etc. The limits set by the domestic market are decisive when competitive advantages are absent and production, at least initially, has to be based on the domestic market only. In the long run industries which were initially set up to supply the domestic market may well develop into export industries. This is possible for all industries which do not operate under 'competitive disadvantages' of one kind or another. Future export opportunities are, in particular, present for industries in which industrial experience and traditions represent in themselves the main element of competitive advantages. The Japanese export performance is an excellent example of 'acquired competitive advantages'.

The optimum size of the market for mass-produced goods differs tremendously from industry to industry. Moreover, for many industries there is little variation in production costs as soon as a certain minimum scale of operations has been reached, i. e. there is a wide optimum *range* instead of a narrow optimum size of scale.[5] Furthermore, for many industries the optimum size is merely of theoretical interest, since the transport costs are so important that high-cost producers can compete against producers in other regions or countries. It should be noted, however, that in the case of small markets for goods which cannot be transported easily and cheaply, the two possibilities may be modern mass-production methods, or traditional small-scale methods. For example, modern bread factories will not replace the local baker in smaller towns, and the small primitive brick factory will continue to supply a narrow local market.

It is not possible to draw up a list of 'minimum market requirements' for individual industries engaged in mass production. Statistical studies cannot give us any firm guidance. For some industries the engineer and the business economist are able to tell how production costs vary with the size of the plant, and for these industries a minimum size (as well as an optimum size) can be determined; but such cases are relatively few, and mostly concern industries for which the entire plant has to be designed for a fairly inflexible production pattern. The minimum size of the plant will in such cases be determined by the minimum capacity of some costly parts of the plant. But even in such cases local factors, such as the cost of manual labour, will have considerable bearing on the layout of the plant. (Thus in Pakistan match boxes were filled by hand — the use of machinery to fill the boxes may have a significant influence on the choice of the size of the plant.) 'Process controlled' industries like the chemical industry, the cement industry, etc. will have their capacity more firmly determined by technical factors than 'product controlled' industries, in which the internal organization can be much more freely determined by the management on the basis of local factors.

This leads to another distinction which is of primary importance for countries with relatively small markets: the minimum profitable capacity of an *assembly* plant may be far smaller than the minimum profitable capacity of a plant producing certain *components*. Thus assembly of radio sets and even the production of certain components can be done on a small scale, whereas the production of valves and certain other components must be undertaken on a very much larger scale. Labour costs are of primary importance in the assembly plants, and this means that a country like Pakistan can envisage undertaking the assembly of automobiles, tractors, radios, etc. on a much smaller scale than the United States, or Western Europe.

There are fortunately relatively few mass-production industries which require such large markets that Pakistan cannot envisage establishing plants which at least reach the size needed to produce at reasonably low costs.[6] The characteristic feature of the development of mass-production industries in Pakistan will be the establishment of assembly plants where possible, and a gradual reduction of the imports of foreign-produced components. For industries in which integrated operations are indispensable, Pakistan will have to rely on imports of less commonly used products, but products in large demand like essential building materials, the most important basic chemicals, fertilizers, refined petroleum, steel, etc. can be produced at reasonably low cost in the country already at an early state of the industrial development. Because of its large population Pakistan is far better off than the many small underdeveloped countries, notably in Africa and in Central America, which can offer large enough markets for only a very narrow range of mass-produced goods.

How can these very general considerations be transformed into more precise projections of the future development of the mass production industries in Pakistan? In this study it is only possible to approach this problem in a very crude and approximate manner by assuming that imports in relation to total domestic demand can be reduced to a different degree in different industries — to practically zero for industries processing food or manufacturing building materials, somewhat less for the textile industry, and far less for the chemical industries. For the engineering industries the problem is first of all to determine to what extent it will be possible for Pakistan to reduce the imports of components.[7] To the extent that this is possible these assumptions are based on statistical evidence, which suggests either the import dependence of countries with relatively small markets for products of the different industries or the size of plants producing certain goods.

In some industries *specialization* is particularly important. Enterprises producing specialized products are not necessarily large — on the contrary, many of them will be so small that the capital, skilled manpower, and managerial talent which are needed will not in themselves prevent the creation of specialized enterprises in a country with a fairly small industrial sector. I am convinced that very specialized factories will be set up in Pakistan. Indeed, such factories already exist — such as the remarkable small-scale industries in Sialkot which produce surgical instruments, musical instruments, and sporting goods for the world market. Specialized industries depend on very large markets and the growth of such industries in Pakistan will depend on their ability to conquer foreign markets. But it is quite certain that during the rest of this century, Pakistan will remain an importer of a great majority of specialized products. Some specialized products are mass-produced and therefore belong to the group of mass-produced goods for which a fairly small domestic market is too small. It should be kept in mind, however, that such mass-produced specialized products are very often manufactured by a small number of producers in the entire world, and are to a high degree subject to international trade, even between highly industrialized and large countries. The same is true for specialized products which are made to order and which are produced by firms which, for example, concentrate their production on certain types of machinery or equipment. The superiority of such firms is not based on long production runs resulting in low production costs, but on their experience in producing and assembling certain types of products. It would be wasteful for Pakistan to aim at suppressing imports of all kinds of specialized products which are imported on a large scale by mature industrialized countries. Both in price and in quality indigenous products are bound to be far inferior to the imported product. This does not mean that Pakistan should neglect the development of specialized industries. The danger is that the uncontrolled import of all kinds of specialized products would kill any attempt to start producing such products in Pakistan. The right policy would probably be to encourage the production of specialized goods through government orders or other selective means of assistance. Existing entrepreneurial spirit in Pakistan suggests that this should be a fruitful approach. An example which can be mentioned is a small factory which took up the production of fairly large electric transformers some few years ago. Such efforts should be actively supported, even if it is likely to be years before the domestic products can compete in quality and price.

For this study it has to be assumed that during the period under review Pakistan will continue to depend heavily on imports of specialized products. In which industries will such products be significant? I believe that they will remain particularly important in the engineering industries, but will also occur in all industries (special food preparations, some textiles, certain glass and china ware, printing of maps, etc.).

Another factor which limits the drive for self-sufficiency is the *buyers' demand for variety*. In part, this is a rational attitude — an industrialist or farmer may wish to buy some equipment which can only be imported. For a long while yet the domestic industries in Pakistan will not be able to satisfy the demand for variety. The alternative is to force the buyer to choose between available indigenous products, but the legitimate right of the enterprise to select the most suitable means of production cannot be limited too severely without harmful effects on the growth of domestic production. The *consumers'* free choice can without harm be severely limited within the framework of an austerity policy. But it has to be realized that direct controls on imports will probably be needed to prevent the consumers from using large quantities of imported goods. Experience from almost any country shows that protective tariffs are not sufficient to prevent considerable 'luxury imports'. Thus the extent to which domestic production can cover domestic demand depends to a significant extent on the foreign trade policy which is followed. A country which follows a relatively liberal import policy must be prepared to import significant quantities of goods for which perfectly adequate domestic substitutes are available. This tendency in favour of imported products will, of course, be strongest in the case of products for which the domestic production can merely offer a limited choice compared with that of international suppliers (the most obvious example being automobiles).

Three factors — the minimum scale of mass production, the restricted scope for the manufacture of specialized products, and the buyers' demand for variety — all tend to widen the gap between domestic demand and domestic production. For each industrial subsector I have assessed the combined strength of these three factors; but even though I have based this assessment on available information, it can only be a working hypothesis. The limiting factors listed above will be of the greatest importance for the engineering, electrical engineering, transport equipment, and miscellaneous industries. In the case of Pakistan, progress in these industries will be held back by other factors which I have discussed under the heading of the feasible rate of expansion. In fact, the feasible rate of expansion of these industries will not be so rapid that the other limiting factors will make themselves strongly felt. In other words, I will assume that the expansion of these industries will be based on products for which there is sufficient scope for mass production or specialized production in Pakistan, and for which there will be a demand even if imported products should also be available. This eliminates an important factor of uncertainty in my projections. For some other industries, notably the chemical industries, the other limiting factors will have a very strong influence, and the chosen hypothesis on the effects of those factors will fundamentally influence the projections of the industrial pattern.

E. *The effects of regional trade arrangements*

The export possibilities have been assessed on the assumption that products will be exported to countries in which Pakistani exporters will enjoy no preferences over producers from highly industrialized countries. Therefore it will only be possible to export to the extent that industries in Pakistan are internationally fully competitive.

The effect of a regional common market on the industrial prospects of Pakistan would be to reduce the impact of the limiting factors implied in the relative smallness of the domestic market. The scope for industrial expansion would be widened.

The question remains, however, whether it is necessary to take into account the prospects of a regional common market in assessing the future industrial development trends in Pakistan. For two reasons I have decided *not* to project industrial production on the assumption of a regional common market:

1. A regional common market would almost inevitably include India. Recent developments not withstanding, there may be good reasons to believe that during the next couple of decades the political relations between the two large south-east Asian nations will be normalized. This is essential before serious negotiations on a regional trade area can start. These negotiations would in themselves become very complicated, because of India's industrial strength compared to its potential partners, and because of Pakistan's relative industrial strength compared to partners other than India. Furthermore, both India and Pakistan are large enough to be able to develop many industries inside the existing national markets, and there is therefore no overwhelming sense of urgency present in the Indian subcontinent as regards regional trade arrangements. Both nations are far more pre-occupied with the problem of gaining fair access for their export products in the large industrial countries in Western Europe and North America.

2. As explained above, in the essential engineering industries

as well as in many industries classified under 'miscellaneous industries', the limiting factor to growth is not the domestic market but first of all the shortage of trained manpower and management. Consequently, in my opinion, only for relatively few products, notably chemical products, would a larger market be a significant factor for the acceleration of industrial growth in Pakistan.

F. *Factors influencing the rate and pattern of industrialization*

I have discussed the importance of the size of the domestic market for future industrial growth, i. e. the output of one given product class must reach a certain minimum level before the production becomes profitable. This minimum level of output also implies, of course, a minimum size of the enterprise. But in most industries, this minimum size of the enterprise is fairly modest.[8] For example, in the United Kingdom in 1951, 35 per cent of the factory workers were employed in small or smallish plants (with less than 200 workers), 21 per cent in medium-sized plants (with between 200 and 500 workers) and 44 per cent only in larger plants with more than 500 workers. Another classification gives practically the same results: if the different industrial subsectors are classified according to the typical size of the plants, we find that industries which are characterized by small of smallish plants account for 23 per cent of the jobs in industry, industries with mainly medium-sized plants for 14 per cent, and industries with predominantly larger plants for 46 per cent. Industries with 17.5 per cent of the jobs have no prevalent plant size at all.[9]

Even if far-reaching conclusions cannot be drawn from the size distribution of firms in industrially highly developed countries, it is nevertheless evident that in most industries plants with less than 500 employed persons are large enough for profitable production. For an underdeveloped country this fact is encouraging because it seems to favour the decentralization of the manufacturing industries. Decentralization of industries will inevitably be one of the major objectives of the development policies in an underdeveloped country, in order to avoid serious internal imbalances. Unfortunately, the prospects for decentralization are not as promising as the data on the size distribution of industrial plants may suggest. There are two major reasons for this:

1. Industries with generally small units will frequently be located close to the consumers, or alternatively, close to the supplies of raw materials (examples of the consumer-oriented industries — bakeries, brick factories, mechanical repair shops; ex-

amples of raw material-oriented industries — food processing, sawmills). Such industries can therefore only be located to a limited extent in industrially less favoured areas.

2. An even more important factor is the marked tendency towards grouping many industries around centres where there is easy access to subcontractors, to repair shops, to complementary firms in general. Moreover, it is well known that enterprises which manufacture the same types of products, i. e. which belong to the same industrial subsectors, will seek to locate themselves in the same industrial towns, and there are tangible reasons for this, notably the easier access to skilled labour and qualified management in such towns.

The tendencies for industries to concentrate themselves in larger industrial centres or in specialized industrial towns will be even stronger in an industrially underdeveloped country than in a highly developed industrial country, in which industrial traditions and skills have gradually penetrated into almost all regions.

The tendency towards localization of many industries in larger industrial towns may have an influence on the industrial growth prospects if the government insists too strongly on a policy of industrial decentralization through restrictions against the establishment of new plants in the most favourable locations. In the past Pakistan has gone as far as to ban completely the setting up of new industries in Karachi and to restrict severely the right of establishment in certain other areas of West Pakistan. Such a policy may easily prevent the production of many goods domestically, because the entrepreneur will not set up the plant at all if he cannot set it up in the most favoured area. I have assumed that in the future Pakistan will *not* follow a restrictive policy of industrial location, and that consequently such measures will not limit the growth of domestic industries.[10]

Notes

1. Purpose and Background

1 A further discussion of this work is contained in Chapters 2 and 14.

2. Problems and Analytical Framework

1 Slower growth will not lead to the same results at a later stage as faster growth will do at an earlier stage because of changes in population, in technology, in the development of the rich countries, etc., in the intervening years.

2 Prominent examples of such studies are [38] and [39].

3 For a scholarly discussion of this problem, see [40].

4 The problem can be avoided by assuming constant prices. But this is not realistic since the prices of goods and, first of all, services which contain relatively high labour inputs will rise in relation to the prices of products of less labour-intensive industries. In many labour-intensive sectors – notably many service sectors – the scope for improved labour productivity is limited.

5 The alternative concepts of the national income or product used in national accounts are:

The *Gross Domestic Product* equals the sum of the value added in all sectors of the economy. The value added is defined as the compensation attributed to labour and capital in each sector. The compensation to capital includes the earnings of self-employed persons, the income of non-corporate enterprises, and also interest payments on debt. Depreciation allowances are also included in the value added. The GDP can be calculated at *factor cost* or at *market prices*. In the latter case the value added includes the indirect taxes paid by the sector while the subsidies received by the sector are excluded. The value added at market prices can be calculated as the difference between the sales value of the product (plus imputed value of the part of the product which is consumed by those employed in the sector itself) less the purchases of goods and services from other sectors. The value added at factor cost is obtained by deducting indirect taxes and adding subsidies.

The *Net Domestic Product* equals the Gross Domestic Product less depreciation of fixed capital. (Losses on inventories are implicitly taken into account in output and input figures which determine the GDP.)

The *National Product* (net or gross, at market prices or at factor cost) equals the Domestic Product plus the net factor income received from abroad. Factor income payments from abroad include investment income such as rent, interest, dividends, and profit of direct investments; in addition, earnings of residents working abroad and other income earned abroad by normal residents. A corresponding definition is used for factor income payments to abroad.

The *National Income* equals the Net National Product at factor cost. The contribution of each sector to the national income thus consists of the value added (at factor cost) less depreciation, payments of rent, interest, dividends, and other capital income abroad, and the payment of wages to foreigners abroad or to temporary foreign residents. In addition, the national income includes factor income payments from abroad less factor income payments to abroad not paid by one of the producing sectors of the economy (such as the general government or private households).

[6] The Gross Domestic Product at market prices can also be expressed as follows: Exports of goods and services (except factor income from abroad) + personal consumption expenditure + general government consumption expenditure + gross fixed investments (or capital formation) + increase in stocks = total final demand − imports of goods and services (except factor income to abroad) = Gross Domestic Product at market prices.

If total exports and imports are included in the formula above (i. e., if factor income to and from abroad is included), the total will add up to the Gross National Product at market prices. Note that total *final* demand + intermediate purchases of goods and services − imports of goods and services (except factor income payments to abroad) = total domestic output of goods and services. Total domestic output of goods and services − intermediate purchases of goods and services = Gross Domestic Product at market prices.

[7] [1], p. 2, para. 6.

[8] Source: [5], Table 1, p. 1.

[9] Recent estimates put the *birth* rate as high as 5.6 to 6 per cent [21], pages 70 and 78).

[10] See Table 4, p. 60, which shows that on our assumption the GDP will grow by 41.5 per cent during the Sixth Plan.

[11] The marginal rate of savings requires a more careful definition to make clear whether it refers to net or gross savings, to national or domestic savings, and similarly to net or gross, national or domestic product.

[12] This follows from the fact that if national income grows less than, at the same rate as, or only slightly faster than the population, a marginal rate of savings which is higher than the average rate of savings will mean a fall in consumption *per caput*. A more refined measure of the savings effort is the 'marginal rate of savings out of income *per caput*'. This figure is defined as:

$$\frac{\dfrac{S + \triangle S}{N + \triangle N} - \dfrac{S}{N}}{\dfrac{Y + \triangle Y}{N + \triangle N} - \dfrac{Y}{N}} = M_{SN}$$

where S is savings, Y national income, and N population, and the sign $\triangle$ denotes the respective increases in any one of these items over time. The relationship between the marginal rate of savings out of income *per caput* and other items can be expressed as follows:

$$M_{SN} = M_S + \cfrac{M_S - A_S}{\cfrac{\cfrac{\Delta Y}{Y}}{\cfrac{\Delta N}{N}} - 1}$$

where M_S is the marginal rate of savings $\left(\dfrac{\Delta S}{\Delta Y}\right)$,

and A_S the average rate of savings $\left(\dfrac{S}{Y}\right)$.

The concept is meaningless when the growth of population equals the growth of the national income. A negative figure shows that savings *per caput* and income *per caput* move in opposite directions. $M_{SN} = 1$ means that consumption per head (private and public) remains constant and that the entire increase in national income *per caput* is saved. This situation occurs when:

$$\cfrac{\cfrac{\Delta Y}{Y}}{\cfrac{\Delta N}{N}} = \frac{1 - A_S}{1 - M_S},$$

and depends therefore on both the absolute size of the average rate of savings and its relation to the marginal rate of savings and on the ratio between the growth in income and the growth of population (and thus *not* on the rate of growth of the national income *per caput* which can be identical under widely different rates of growth of income and population).

In the projections for Pakistan it has been assumed that the growth of national income will be considerably higher than the growth of population. As the average rate of savings is very low, the marginal rate of savings can be considerably above the average rate of savings without leading to a 'marginal rate of savings out of income *per caput*' which is close to one.

[13] pp. 232–233.

[14] In fact, domestic savings must eventually exceed domestic investments by the amount of interest payments, etc., on foreign investments in order to render additional net capital imports superfluous. In order to eliminate capital imports altogether, domestic savings must, in addition, be large enough to cover repayment of foreign debt.

[15] These assumptions are contained in unpublished staff papers produced by the Fiscal and Monetary Section of the Planning Commission. The head of that section, Dr. Mahbub-ul-Haq, was primarily responsible for these estimates. These very optimistic assumptions were, however, subsequently considerably modified by Dr. Haq himself, see [23], pp. 68–69.

[16] [5], p. 30, para. 31.

[17] Some very crude estimates are presented in Chapter 13.

3. *Methods of Projection*

[1] Note that in Pakistan the financial year runs from 1 July to 30 June the following year, and the 'plan years' are identical with the financial years. Throughout the study, plan years are referred to by the calendar year in which they end (i. e., 1960 for 1959/60, etc.). Whenever a figure refers to a calendar year, it is made clear.

[2] In some cases abrupt changes have been assumed from one five-year period to another; and when figures for individual years within a plan period were needed under these circumstances, they were frequently calculated on a basis other than an assumed constant rate of growth.

[3] The Pakistan Institute of Development Economics in Karachi has published the results of a series of interesting studies and enquiries; the Institute and the Planning Commission are collaborating in several fields and are preparing input-output Tables for the economy; existing official statistics have been improved and results of the censuses of population and of agriculture have been published; and the Central Bureau of Statistics has overhauled its national income estimates. Wherever possible such new data have been taken into account. It should be noted, however, that discrepancies between the data recently published in Pakistan and those used in this study do not always show that I have ignored or am unaware of the latest available material. In some cases I have deliberately stuck to my own figures which I believe are more in conformity with reality than other published data, official or non-official.

[4] Table 1 illustrates the rapid changes in figures for the Second and Third Plan period. In November, 1963, the growth of the GNP during the Second Plan was estimated at 22 per cent; in August, 1964, at 26 per cent, and in May, 1965, at 29 per cent. The target for the Third Plan was set at 30 per cent in 1963 and 1964, but was raised to 38 per cent in 1965.

[5] The incremental capital-output ratio is defined as the value of the fixed investments which are needed in order to increase the output by one value unit. The global capital-output ratio applies to the economy as a whole, and it is also possible to determine the capital-output ratios for individual sectors, subsectors, or industries of the economy. Sometimes estimates of the capital-output ratio include only investments in expansion and not investments which are needed to maintain the productivity of the existing stock of capital.

[6] Account has been taken of the fact that in some sectors the growth of the production capacity will necessarily be discontinuous whereas demand may increase smoothly. In such sectors there will normally be either some surplus capacity or a shortage of capacity. If the latter is to be avoided, there must always be surplus capacity; and this has been taken into account in estimating the capital-output ratio for such sectors which entail large investment projects.

[7] In fact, the breakdown must be even more specific. First, we are interested in the demand for products of different subsectors or even of different specialized industries for investment purposes. Second, whereas a large proportion of the demand for goods and services for fixed investments is for the services of the construction industry, we must know the breakdown of the construction work into different types of work in order

to determine the pattern of intermediate demand in the construction industry.

[8] This 'iterative' process was facilitated by the fact that much of the investment demand is for machinery and equipment, and Pakistan will, during the period under review, import a large proportion of its needs for such goods. The output of the engineering industries can therefore be calculated independently of demand, i. e., the expansion of the domestic capacity in those industries will be determined exclusively by the availability of skill, managerial talent, and the capacity of the training institutions. The output of the building and construction industry and the output of building material industries are, however, mostly determined by investment demand, and had to be adjusted several times.

[9] For some important intermediate goods, imports have been estimated. But, in general, imports by sectors of origin have been estimated as the difference between total final plus intermediate demand and total domestic output, or, if imports were estimated directly (such as in the case of imports of goods which cannot be produced at profitable terms in Pakistan), output equals total demand less imports. In neither case was it necessary to break down imports between intermediate and final goods in order to estimate the output of a given domestic sector.

[10] These details have not been reproduced in the present publication. The relevant statistics and comments to the estimates are available in stencilled documents which can be obtained on request from the Chr. Michelsen Institute ([0] and an earlier version).

[11] Note that exports and imports of goods and services exclude factor income payments from and to abroad. If these were included, Gross Domestic Product would have to be replaced by Gross National Product.

[12] The projected gross domestic savings can easily be calculated as a percentage of the Gross Domestic Product. This calculation shows that if the average 'global' incremental capital-output ratio turns out to be relatively low, i. e., barely above 3, savings will fall short of investments up to 1980, but may be close to investments in 1980 and 1985. However, the detailed calculations of investments led to a much higher average capital-output ratio and therefore to a 'savings deficit' and consequently also a balance of payments deficit throughout the period under review.

[13] *Gross* foreign aid includes the inflow of foreign capital needed to cover the current import surplus on goods and services (excluding net factor payments to abroad) plus servicing of 'foreign debt' (interest, dividends on direct investments, etc., plus contractual repayments of debt and expected withdrawals of private foreign investments).

[14] For a previous discussion of this problem, see pp. 47 and 48.

[15] Work on an input-output Table for Pakistan was started by the Planning Commission and the Pakistan Institute of Development Economics at the end of 1963. Preliminary results of this work are available, but for the present study only the estimates which are contained in the study itself have been used.

[16] Source: [18]. For many industries the Census gives a satisfactory breakdown of the purchases of *goods* from other firms, but no data are available on the purchases of *services*. In a number of cases the item 'others' is so large that the usefulness of the data is reduced considerably.

Moreover, there are unfortunately many obvious mistakes in the statistics, ome of which may be due to incorrect replies to the questionnaires, others which may have resulted from mistakes in the Central Statistical Office.

17 Sources: [41] and [42].

18 And imports. For the treatment of imports, see below.

19 It is not quite correct to say that each single entry in the input-output table for 1959/60 is unreliable. Some figures should, on the contrary, be as reliable as a statistical figure can be expected to be. But, unfortunately, there are examples of quite serious inconsistencies between two figures, each of which, when regarded in isolation, appears to be very reliable!

20 It was, for example, found that the implied producer price on sugar cane exceeded the price for sugar cane paid by the sugar factories which could be derived from the Census of Manufacturing Industries.

21 Can be obtained in stencilled version from Chr. Michelsen Institute, source [0].

22 Such data do exist in the form of allocations of imports to different users, under the system of import licensing. These data are not satisfactory, however. Part of the import licences are given to 'commercial importers', i. e., import merchants, and the end uses of this part of the imports are uncertain. Furthermore, not all licences are utilized; and finally, even in 1959/60, part of the imports was allowed under special arrangements.

23 Throughout this study the author has been faced with the choice between 'perfection' and 'expendiency'. If anything, the search for 'perfection' has been carried too far. Small adjustments entail a multitude of consequential adjustments in tables and text throughout the study. This is very time-consuming, and the 'gains' in internal consistency do not necessarily justify the delay in publication nor the use of manpower. The inconsistencies which persist between figures in text and tables and the figures in the input-output tables may disturb some readers, but they are too insignificant to call for an apology. Another matter is that inadvertently more serious errors can have slipped in. Such errors are unlikely in the input-output tables themselves or in tables which result from the combination of figures from several other tables. In such cases cross-checking prevents errors. But where cross-checking is not possible, errors are not excluded.

4. *Initial Assumptions and Subsequent Adjustments*

1 The assumption is that modern manufacturing will grow faster, and in fact considerably faster, than the national income.

2 [5], p. 1.

3 [22], p. 304.

4 This approach is sound in global terms, but in terms of individuals there will, of course, be many unemployed old-time residents of towns and cities, because their jobs have been taken by newcomers from rural areas.

5 At the beginning of the work on this study, I assumed that the urban population would grow by 5 per cent per year during the entire period

under review. The preliminary employment figures showed that this rate of growth was far too slow.

[6] The exodus of manpower from rural areas not only lowers the wage level in the towns, but the earnings of independent workers and small employers in trade, transport, services, handicrafts, and small industries are depressed for the same reason.

[7] Since output per head rather than income per head has been taken as a measure, it is possible that rural income can rise somewhat faster than urban income. As shown in Chapter 13 this possibility is quite likely, because relatively less rent for agricultural land may be transferred from rural to urban income earners in the future.

[8] Source: [5], Table 9, p. 29.

[9] Source: Table 10. If the output *per caput* in the rural and urban areas in the two provinces were the same as shown in my estimates, the distribution of the population between rural and urban areas being the same in East and West, we would obtain the following results for output *per caput:* if the ratio of urban population to total population were as in the East, output per head in West Pakistan would be Rs 262 or only 8 per cent higher than in East Pakistan; if the ratio of urban population to total population were as in West Pakistan, output per head in East Pakistan would be Rs 283, or output in West Pakistan 10 per cent higher than in East Pakistan. Both figures are far lower than the actual discrepancy of 29 per cent.

[10] Details can be found in Table 10 and [0], Annex II, Table 2. The ratio of urban to total population is projected to grow from 5 to 29 per cent in East Pakistan and from 22 to 47 per cent in West Pakistan. The total urban population will grow 10.5 times in East Pakistan and 4 times in West Pakistan.

[11] See [5], p. 28, para. 28.

[12] In [0], Annex X, see Table 7, I discuss the conditions under which the distribution of economic activities between urban and rural regions is realistic.

The conclusion shown in Table 7 is that rural income may lag slightly behind the figures assumed here, but the difference is small enough to justify that the assumed figures are retained.

[13] The rural population in West Pakistan is projected to grow by 32 per cent between 1960 and 1985, in East Pakistan by 45 per cent and the urban population by 460 per cent.

[14] Different absolute figures for the base year would, of course, influence the distribution of personal consumption between rural and urban areas. But the effects on personal consumption of various alternatives for the distribution of savings between towns and village would be fairly insignificant since the figures for personal consumption in any case are far larger than the figures for savings. It should be noted, however, that the implied figures for the marginal rate of savings out of income *per caput* are influenced by the level of savings in the base year (see formula in footnote 12, page 309).

[15] The hypothetical figure for higher savings in the rural rather than in the urban areas in 1960 is justified by the fact that a significant part of farm income is drained away to urban areas in the form of rent. As the

rural gross product is defined in the same way as the Gross Domestic Product, i. e., as the product which originates in the rural areas, not as the retained income in rural areas, this transfer of part of the income which corresponds to the product has to be treated as 'savings'. The alternative definition of rural savings is the difference between rural product and rural consumption; and as incomes transferred to urban areas automatically reduce rural consumption, they automatically increase rural 'savings'.

[16] The impact on the marginal rate of saving out of income *per caput* of an upward revision of the estimates of savings in the base year follows from the fact that if saving *per caput* is initially higher, a larger part of the increased total saving under constant rate of savings *per caput* is accounted for by the growth of the population.

[17] This is illustrated in [0], Annex II, Table 4. Both the marginal rate of monetized savings and the corresponding marginal rate of savings out of income *per caput* in rural areas are far lower than the rates for monetized and non-monetized savings together.

[18] See Chapter 13.

5. *The Changing Composition of Personal Consumption*

[1] The income elasticity is calculated as the percentage increase in expenditure on a given item divided by the percentage increase in consumers' disposable income. In calculating the expenditure elasticity we replace the increase in income by the increase in total consumer expenditure.

[2] The method can be further refined by studying changes in the observed elasticities over time and assuming that similar changes will also take place in the future.

[3] Expenditure elasticities have been used since no estimates are available of personal savings, and consequently not of the disposable consumer income. Note that elasticities calculated over a five year period differ slightly from elasticities calculated on a year to year basis.

[4] And in [0], Annex III, which gives implied elasticities for all products.

[5] One could have assumed that a deliberate policy to even out income distribution would be effectively implemented. But in actual fact income distribution is strongly influenced by structural changes in the economy. These latter could not be estimated in advance and, furthermore, their exact influence on the distribution of income is hard to assess.

[6] The figures which were used as a basis for the detailed projections of personal consumption are shown in [0], Annex III, Table 1.

[7] See [0], Annex X, Table 9.

[8] The sources for the estimates of the consumption pattern in this study were the 1959 National Sample Survey [13]. The results of the later surveys (1960 and 1961) have been studied; and since the results are not fundamentally different, no recalculation of the pattern on the basis of new evidence was made.

[9] [14].

[10] Annual data are published on the production of major agricultural crops. Monthly data are published on the production of cotton and art-silk, vegetable products, matches, and cigarettes, and on imports and exports, broken down in some detail in the Statistical Bulletin of the Central Statistical Office. There are various sources for annual data on other products; but for some important products, such as livestock products and fish, the data are based on surveys of doubtful value, and are extrapolated on an assumed trend basis. Nevertheless, these sources undoubtedly give an idea of the order of magnitude involved.

[11] Such studies have been published in recent years, e. g., [24] and [25]. The article on rural West Pakistan shows the surprising result that expenditure elasticity for food is close to 1 whereas for clothing and footwear the figure is only around 0.7, or the reverse of what would be expected on the basis of data from other countries. For rural East Pakistan the income elasticities are more in line with what would be expected: food, 0.67; clothing, 0.97; and other non-food items, 1.62. None of the articles give a specific figure for housing, and the article on West Pakistan does not list non-food items other than clothing and footwear.

[12] [46].

[13] Annex III gives details about the structure of personal consumption, broken down by rural areas in East and West Pakistan and by urban areas, based on the original assumptions in this report.

[14] In Pakistan, industrial firms are to some extent compelled to provide their staffs with housing.

[15] [0], Annex III, Table 8.

[16] [0], Annex III.

[17] Since this study is part of a wider research programme which analyzes the impact of fast economic growth in all developing countries, it would be illogical to assume that, for example, Pakistan could export large quantities of food to countries which cannot feed their people. Export demand is therefore bound to be small in relation to total agricultural output.

[18] [70].

[19] If the figures for food consumption and output in agriculture for the base pear 1959/60 were adjusted upward, the result would be higher national income and higher income *per caput* in that year and in all subsequent years; but since income in agriculture is projected to grow more slowly than the total national income, the growth rates should be lower than shown in this study.

[20] I. e., that calorie intake per head should have been 20 per cent higher in rural West Pakistan (i. e., 1,935 calories in 1960) and 10 per cent higher in rural East Pakistan (i. e., 1,685 calories in 1960). This underestimation is then assumed to be constant throughout the period under review.

6. Current Use of Goods and Services by General Government

[1] For a detailed explanation of the estimates, see [0], Annex IV.

[2] Note that social welfare expenditure which has the character of trans fers is not included here. But the administration of any type of social welfare programme will come under government consumption.

3 Government *investments* represent, of course, a very large part of total demand in the construction industry.

7. Investments in Consumption Capital, and Other Investments Classified as 'Autonomous'

1 Chapter 2, page 30.

2 See pages 42–48.

3 I. e., that output can be doubled each five-year period.

4 Investments in private roads will be included under investments in agriculture, forestry, mining, manufacturing, etc.

5 Investments in post, telegraph, telephone, broadcasting, and television include only investments in services available to the general public. In principle, the possibility that some of these services – telephone, broadcasting, television – may be provided by private enterprise is not excluded.

6 Subsequently the programme was also modified by the Planning Commission and our assumptions turned out to be fairly close to those used in the Third Five Year Plan.

7 There are many studies on the relationship between investments and economic growth, and all of them are subject to many qualifications. The following figures quoted by the *Economist* (London, January 16, 1965, page 234) illustrate well the orders of magnitude involved. During the period 1950 to 1956 the crude incremental capital-output ratio (i. e., the ratio between the percentage of the Gross National Product devoted to gross fixed capital formation and the percentage growth of the GNP) was merely 2.3 both in Germany and Japan, while it was 3.2 in Italy and between 3.9 and 5.9 in some other highly industrialized countries. During the period 1957–63 the ratio was higher in most countries.

8 Technological progress is also linked with investments. Investments in new types of equipment yield in general higher results than investments in old types of equipment. By definition the additional yield can be ascribed to technological progress, but in most cases this progress cannot take place without simultaneous investments. There are exeptions, such as when improvements in technology or organization allow higher output from the existing equipment.

9 [2], pp. 339–40.

10 The most recent targets are: For primary school education that 'universal primary education may be achieved as early as possible within the Perspective Plan Period' ([4], para 14, p. 162). The following intermediate targets are suggested: 45 per cent school attendance by 1965 and 70 per cent in 1970. Both figures are close to the figures used in Table 22. For education at 'the Junior High Stage consisting of Classes VI, VII and VIII', the target is that it 'is eventually to be made compulsory for all children during the perspective plan period' i. e., before 1985 ([4], para 20, p. 163).

11 See [0], Annex V-21.

12 This 25 per cent is an average figure which means that more (possibly 30 to 35 per cent) children at the age of 14 to 15 must enter the higher secondary schools.

[13] During his stay in Pakistan the author was surprised to discover how shocked his Pakistan friends were when he told them that many children in rural Norway still go to school only twice a week between the age of 7 and 10, and three times a week between the age of 10 and 14, and that he himself had spent the first seven years in school in that manner. It should be taken into account, however, that when children come from illiterate homes the need for more frequent school attendance is probably greater.

[14] This percentage is based on experience in other countries, see [0], Annex V, p. 40.

[15] [4], para 5, p. 200.

[16] [0], Annex V-24.

[17] [43], p. 309.

[18] *Ibid.*

[19] This is shown in [0], Annex VII–10, which indicates the breakdown of total investment costs by purpose.

[20] The value added in the health sector is projected to rise from Rs 400 million in 1960 to Rs 3,765 million in 1985. If the costs of the health programmes rose at the same rate, they would reach Rs 1,130 million in 1985.

[21] For details see [0], Annex V, Table 49.

[22] [12], Vol. B. No 8, August 1965, p. 2089, Table 28.

[23] 85 per cent of the projected urban population can live in 'pucka' houses in 1985 (on the assumption that the investments shown in Table 30 are implemented) if the average family dwelling costs Rs 3,650, of which Rs 2,450 is the value of the house itself.

[24] This statement, as it stands, needs qualification. The slow increase in the *average per caput* consumption standard in the urban areas may take the form that the standard of living of the urban proletariat will remain stable and that the standard of living of the middle classes will rise. If this were the case, the growing proletariat could only afford to live in shanty towns while the middle classes would get comfortable housing.

[25] There is also scope for non-monetized investments in the education and health sectors – through building of village schools or dispensaries, etc. No attempt has been made to estimate the volume of such investments, but they would represent only a small proportion of the total investments in health, education, and research.

[26] These figures can be found in [0], Annex V, Tables 73 to 75.

8. *The changing structure of the Gross Domestic Product*

[1] Total final use of resources equals GDP plus imports.

[2] Intermediate demand constituted about 34 per cent of total final and intermediate demand in 1960, and is estimated to rise to 39 per cent in 1985.

[3] The details of which can be found in [0], Annex VI.

[4] A summary of the assumptions which have been used for the different sectors is given in Chapter 2 (pages 30—40). These assumptions are particularly important for manufacturing, and they are described in Appendix II.

[5] Detailed figures for the different sectors of the economy can be found in [0], Annexes VI and VI A.

[6] Note that the figures for the output for forestry used in this study include imputed income, i. e., collection of firewood, etc.; whereas the CSO figures for the years preceding 1960 clearly include only commercial exploitation of statutory forests. This explains the higher growth figures during the period 1950–60 than in the following years.

[7] The average annual growth rate is the constant annual growth rate within a given period which will give as a result the total growth projected for that period. This rate of growth is sometimes referred to as the 'compound' growth rate.

[8] The pattern of growth in the sector 'rental income from business premises' is strongly influenced by the effects of the *ad hoc* method used to calculate the demand for such premises, and some manipulation of the figures ought to have been carried out. The item is too small, however, to have any influence on the overall growth pattern of the economy.

[9] The hypothetical figure for the growth of agriculture during the Second Plan (which was based on the Second Plan targets) places this sector close to the bottom of the scale during the plan period. In actual fact progress in agriculture was stronger than projected.

[10] Note that there is a global downward adjustment of 1.3 per cent in 1985 – this adjustment should mainly affect the goods-producing sectors.

[11] The projections for trade and transport are in any case uncertain. Very little is known about the contribution of wholesale and retail trade to the national income in 1959/60. The figures used in this study are considerably lower than those produced by the Central Statistical Office. (This study operates with a trade margin in 1960 of Rs 3,225 million, and value added of Rs 2,540 million – see the input-output table for 1960. The latest estimate by the CSO is Rs 3,665 million. Source: [14], Vol. 13, No. 8, August 1965, Table 28, page 2088.) In order to 'accommodate' a considerably higher value added in trade, which would entail a much higher total trade margin in 1960, it would be necessary to increase the trade margin on consumption goods and to increase personal consumption correspondingly. This is in all respects a logical approach since higher value added in trade entails higher national income; and since savings and government consumption are fairly firm items, the adjustment would have to be made to personal consumption.

The result of such an adjustment to the GDP, personal consumption, and trade would be to raise the share of trade in the GDP, but it would also mean that the share of trade in the GDP would fall over the period 1960 to 1985 since it would largely be determined by the growth of the demand for consumer goods which is considerably slower than that for the total GDP. Table 36 shows the share of trade as remaining the same during the period under review (it will first rise and then fall). The arbitrary character of this estimate is underlined by the remarks above which suggest the great importance of the choice of the base year figure.

As regards transport the initial figure is perhaps a little more reliable. In this case the figures used in this study and those produced by the CSO for 1960 are closer to each other (this study uses Rs 1,648 million for transport and communications – the CSO uses Rs 1,857 million). The figures for railway and air transport are reliable, but the figures for road transport are very uncertain and for traditional transport close to guesswork.

Both for trade and for transport the *projections* are bound to be very dubious. Attempts have been made to estimate the movement of goods, and its consequences on trade margins and transport costs. Another approach is to calculate trade and transport margins on the basis of expenditure on consumer goods, investment goods, goods which are exported and goods which are used for intermediate purposes. The different types of estimates are shown in [0] Annex VI, Sections L and N and in Annex IX at various places in connection with the final adjustments to the input-output tables. It is evident that the figures as ultimately calculated in [0] Annex IX are subject to a very wide margin of error, and consequently the figures for the contribution of trade and transport to Gross Domestic Product as shown in Table 36 are very vague.

[12] This already follows from the fact that health services and education both contribute directly to the consumption standard of the people. Since consumption (personal plus government) will rise less in absolute terms than the GDP, the contribution of increased output of health and education to the increase in consumption will be higher in relative terms than it is to the increase in the total GDP. Furthermore it would probably be justifiable to construct a 'welfare function' which valued health and education services higher than their costs, and this would raise the contribution of these services to increased welfare even further. No attempt is made in this study to embark upon the controversial issue of welfare functions, and the reference to welfare on this point is only made in order to underline the importance of not equalling the contribution of one sector to the GDP with its contribution to the general welfare of the people.

[13] This statement needs qualification. If consumers wish excellent services from retail trade, such as long opening hours and short waiting time which entail plenty of staff and pleasant, well-stocked shops, the trade margins must be far higher than if they satisfy themselves with primitive shops and poor services.

[14] 'Exports' of transport services include, *inter alia,* freight charges on the country's own imports and exports. This is a logical consequence of recording imports of merchandise at cif. prices and exports at fob. prices. Whatever method of accounting is used, the fact that an increasing part of the country's foreign trade is carried by its own ships represents a gain to the economy.

[15] In the case of non-monetized construction, its share in the overall growth fluctuates somewhat from period to period, but a clear downward tendency is present.

[16] Thus if the output in agriculture was 3 per cent higher than projected in 1985 whereas the demand for food was 3 per cent lower, the import surplus would disappear. Such small adjustments in the totals for 1985 would involve marginal adjustments to the assumptions regarding the increase in yield per acre in agriculture or the elasticity of demand for food under personal consumption. There is no reason whatsoever for trying to manipulate the figures in such a manner. Whatever manipulations are made, *total* imports will not be changed as long as no changes are made to the assumptions about exports, savings and investments. The figure for

imports of agricultural goods as it stands is consistent with the other import figures.

[17] It should be pointed out that in any case this measure is hypothetical. If no programme of import substitution took place, the growth of the value added in manufacturing industries would be much slower. If the GDP should still grow at the same rate as projected in this study, other sectors would have to grow much faster. Which sectors could grow, and what effects would a different pattern of growth have on imports?

[18] The 'import elasticity' we have defined as: $\dfrac{\triangle Z}{\triangle X} \cdot \dfrac{X}{Z}$

Here, however,

$\triangle Z = \triangle F + \triangle E + \triangle X - \triangle S$, which follows from the definitional equation.

$Z - X = F + E - S$.

Z = imports, X exports, F fixed gross investments, E increase in inventories, S gross domestic savings, and Y the Gross Domestic Product. $\triangle$ denotes the change which takes place over one year.

[19] Chapter 12 deals with the implications of economic growth on the employment pattern.

[20] The import of agricultural produce in 1985 is projected at Rs 2,467 million. To this should be added Rs 1,328 million of imports of manufactured foods (dairy products, vegetable oils), the raw materials for which, if they were produced in Pakistan, would represent a value of about Rs 900 million for agriculture. Thus in order to eliminate imports the output of agriculture could be increased by about Rs 3,400 million. The value added in agriculture would in consequence be increased by Rs 2,550 million (increased value added being 75 per cent of the gross output), personal consumption by about Rs 1,775 million (on the assumption that more than 30 per cent of the additional income was saved), and food consumption by about Rs. 1,150 million – this would represent a value of about Rs 865 million to agriculture. Thus another 25 per cent can be added to the effective demand for output from agriculture.

Even if it were assumed that all additional demand for goods resulting from higher output in agriculture (both demand for inputs in agriculture and for goods by the farmers as consumers) would have to be met by imports, additional income would be created in trade and transport and the service sectors, which in turn would lead to higher demand for agricultural goods. Taking all these indirect effects into account, the additional demand for products from agriculture will be at least 35 to 40 per cent higher than the initial deficit which is covered by imports. Applying this percentage to the initial deficit of Rs 3,400 million, the additional demand on the output from agriculture can be reckoned at Rs 4,750 million, or 12 per cent of the projected output in agriculture in 1985 (Rs 39,759 mill.).

[21] This figure is illustrative – more intense irrigation of smaller areas may be more advantageous.

[22] The scope for further irrigation in West Pakistan is a subject of considerable controversy, see the recent article in *Pakistan Development Review* which aslo includes valuable references to other sources [32].

[23] [0], Annex III, Table 4B.

[24] Indirectly, the textile industry will most probably contribute very much to the growth of other industries in the form of profits which will be re-invested in rapidly expanding industries and in the form of trained management which will gradually be able to face more complex industrial tasks than the spinning and weaving of cotton or jute.

[25] Production and repair of metal goods, machinery and equipment, electrical machinery and equipment, and transport equipment.

[26] There will always be some imports of special products from these industries. Imports of chemicals may continue to decline in relative importance as the domestic market becomes larger and permits profitable manufacturing of a broader range of chemicals.

[27] In 1960 the bulk of the output of the metal-working industries in Pakistan was either consumer goods or repair services.

[28] In the short run it can raise its demand by running down its savings or by accumulating debts.

[29] The assumption behind this reasoning is that imports are free. If they are not, increased demand will inevitably result in price increases.

9. Total Investments and Capital-Output Ratios

[1] Attention should be drawn to the phrase 'growth of output linked with the investments' which means allowance for a time lag between the period in which investments are undertaken and the moment when the productive capacity will be in use.

[2] Two other main reasons for the assumed fall in subsector capital-output ratios are: (1) expansion of existing units often requires lower investments per additional unit of output than the creation of new units; and (2) new units will be large in relation to the total domestic market during the early stages of industrialization, and will therefore for some time be under-utilized for marketing reasons, while at later stages full capacity utilization will occur much more quickly. The second reason does not, of course, apply to industries which can export their surplus production, but it applies very strongly to sectors like transport and electricity and gas supplies.

[3] In a free enterprise economy – and it is explicitly assumed that private enterprise will play an important role in the development of Pakistan – it is unavoidable that excess capacity will be created in some industries from time to time. This does not necessarily lead to waste, but it is likely that creation of surplus capacity will raise the capital-output ratios somewhat for sectors in which excess capacity occurs frequently. The effects of temporary excess capacity on the level of investments of the industry in question over a longer period of time depend strongly on the market structure inside the industry. If competition is lukewarm or non-existent, most units within the industry may operate below capacity, and the excess capacity may persist over a long period of time. This will most probably raise the capital-output ratio for the industry. If, however, competition is vigorous, little 'wasted' investment is likely to take place. Units with outdated equipment will be forced to close down, which merely means an acceleration of the scrapping of old equipment. Badly managed (or badly

planned) units with modern equipment may also have to close down, but it is likely that the equipment will be bought and utilized by better run units. Moreover, fierce competition will act as a disincentive to future investments, and excess capacity will disappear fairly fast. A third situation occurs when technical progress within an industry is rapid. Because new equipment is far more efficient than old equipment, capacity will increase faster than demand, but the end result is that the economic lifetime of the equipment is shortened and this can be taken into account by assuming high replacement investments in such industries.

4 For agriculture two examples illustrate this point. Costs of new irrigation in West Pakistan have been linked with the assumptions about increased irrigated areas in that province, which is used as the background for the projections of output of agricultural goods. Thus indirectly it is possible to link the increased output on irrigated land with the capital costs of irrigating the land. For East Pakistan, however, where flood control is extremely costly, the figures used in this study represent guesses of how much money will be used for that purpose in the future, and no consolidated attempt has been made to find out how much land will be improved as a result of this investment.

5 This percentage is the capital-output ratio divided by the fraction of the capital which is replaced in one year.

6 In practice the calculations for five-year periods were made on the basis of formulas built on the assumption that the annual rate of growth of output will remain constant during a five-year period (by subsector).

7 The reason for this is that the assumption of a two-year time lag is not necessarily consistent with the changes in investments from one five-year period to another.

8 Examples of falling capital-output ratios in modern manufacturing industries are (the first figures refer to the ratio during the Second Plan, the second to the Sixth Plan): Food 2.8 to 2.5, textiles 2.4 to 2.0, pulp and paper 4.3 to 3.5, non-metallic mineral products 3.1 to 2.3, metal-working 1.9 to 1.5, basic metals 5 to 2.5, and chemicals 4 to 2.3.

9 See [0]. Annex VII, Table 7–11.

10. The Balance of Foreign Payments

1 These adjustments are shown in [0], Annex IX, Tables 12 and 19.

2 If exports fall short of the target, and the targets for investments and imports are reached, savings *ex post* will fall short of the savings target.

3 This achievement would be entirely unlikely if it were not for the fact that there is still great scope for increased exports of manufactured jute goods, at the expense of the exports of raw jute.

4 Even jute baling is included in the manufacturing statistics of Pakistan.

5 See Chapter 3, Section D, pp. 50–51.

6 More detailed figures can be found in [0], Annex VIII, and a discussion of the assumptions is available in an earlier, stencilled version of this study, also available on request from the Chr. Michelsen Institute, Bergen.

7 'Soft loans' against repayment in local currency, or sale of foreign goods and services against local currency, may seem to be neither 'loans' nor 'grants'. In the long run, however, such a form of aid must either become a real loan or a grant. The intermediary position is only a short-term illusion.

8 Instead of the far more optimistic and in our view unrealistic assumptions contained in the section on perspective planning in the Outline of the Third Five Year Plan ([4], p. 20).

9 [4], p. 74.

10 [44], page 109. The 'DAC-countries' are twelve of the twenty-one member countries of the Organisation for Economic Co-operation and Development, including all the large capital exporting member countries.

11 In the 8 billion dollars are included large amounts of return capital transfers to the richer countries, transfers which do not affect Pakistan a great deal. Its share of the real aid therefore exceeds 7 per cent.

12 If the poor countries grow somewhat faster than the richer ones – say 6–7 per cent against 4–5 per cent – and their need for aid does not grow faster than their GDP, the demand for aid from the rich countries will rise only moderately from one year to another.

11. *The Gross National Product and Disposable National Savings*

1 At factor cost or at market prices, depending on whether Gross Domestic Product is expressed at factor cost or at market prices.

2 In 1985 the country will still be so poor that it must continue to aim at an annual growth rate of more than 7 per cent per year. Taking into account the time lag between investments and the result of the investments, the capital-output ratio may stay as high as 4.5, which implies that investments will have to reach 32 to 33 per cent of the GDP, or 33 to 34 per cent of the GNP under Alternative B. Gross national savings must be raised from 22.5 per cent in 1985 to, say, 33.5 per cent, or by another ten percentage points. In the meantime the interest on foreign loans will continue to increase, so that the gross *domestic* savings must be raised by more than ten percentage points. Against this background it can be stated that Pakistan will be far from being able to sustain an adequate rate of growth by its own means in 1985. Note that there is no reason to abstain from receiving an inflow of foreign capital even at the time when an adequate rate of growth can be reached on the basis of domestic savings alone. A developing country can always set herself even higher targets than those it can manage without help. The crucial point of time is nevertheless the stage at which it can be said that even without foreign assistance a satisfactory rate of growth will be possible. Which rate of growth is to be considered as 'satisfactory' is, of course, a subjective judgement. In the past an annual rate of growth of 4 to 5 per cent was frequently quite sufficient to ensure 'self-sustained' growth. In our days, when the income gap between rich and poor countries has become evident for the intelligent observer in the poorest and most isolated villages in the less-developed countries, the pressure for a rapid increase in the standard of living has become

so strong that only growth rates of 7 to 8 per cent may satisfy the 'revolution of rising expectations'.

[3] This follows from the assumption that the entire import surplus corresponds to domestic investments which otherwise would have been impossible. As the incremental capital-output ratio is around 4.5, the yield on investments is above 20 per cent, or far higher than the assumed 6 per cent interest on foreign capital. It may appear surprising that the actual yield on investments considerably exceeds interest rates. Investments which expand productive capacity and have very high yields are limited by other factors such as demand, supply of raw materials, or shortage of personnel. Customary 'normal profits' on investments (which, in general, will be higher than the prevailing interest rates due to the risk element involved) nevertheless largely determine the volume and composition of investments. Thus expected profit is fundamental when it comes to decisions to replace old machinery by new, or to replace labour by machines. Profit considerations will also determine the design of new factories and other expansions of capacity.

12. The Thorny Road towards Full Employment

[1] [15], p. vi.
[2] School holidays adapted to labour needs in agriculture are practised even in highly developed countries.

13. Income Flows, Savings, and Consumption

[1] Detailed descriptions of the methods used are contained in [0], Annex X.

[2] It can justifiably be objected that capital movements are by no means of secondary importance since poorly organized capital movements can prevent economic development from taking place. This is true, but it leads us nowhere to try to make a model for domestic capital movements. Such a model would be based on assumptions about the ownership of enterprises – privately owned non-corporate and corporate enterprises, co-operatives, collective ownership, state and other public and semi-public enterprises, foreign-owned enterprises, etc. Furthermore there is hardly any limit to the number of combinations of financial institutions which could be envisaged, and it is not difficult to construct a whole series of models which would ensure a smooth and efficient flow of capital.

[3] Depreciation of inventories is implicitly included in inputs or output. (Losses on stocks of raw materials or semi-manufactured goods are included in the current use of inputs, and losses on stocks of output of the sector are included as a reduction of the output. Depreciation of inventories due to price changes are irrelevant as constant prices have been assumed.)

[4] See [0], Annex VI, Tables for individual industries, and the section on employment at the end of Annex VI.

[5] An exception is made for retained capital income in agriculture (i. e. net of taxes and rent). It has been assumed that an increasing proportion of the increased capital income will be saved. Consumption out of capital income in agriculture is therefore treated as a residuum.

[6] Moreover, surplus savings in individual firms or subsectors inside the sector will not necessarily be invested in units within the sector.

[7] [0], Annex X, Table 4.

[8] Assumed and derived (from the income data) marginal savings rates can be shown to develop as follows:

	2nd Plan	3rd Plan	4th Plan	5th Plan	6th Plan
Assumed rates	18	26.5	26.5	30.5	32.5
Derived rates	26	30.5	25.5	28.5	30

[9] See [0], Annex X, Table 7. On the whole the rural product turns out to be lower than projected, although the discrepancy is not very serious.

[10] [0], Annex X, Table 9.

[11] [0], Annex X, Table 10.

14. Perspective Planning in Pakistan

[1] [5], pp. 17 to 30.

[2] [5], p. 17.

[3] [5], p. 18. para. 4. Resources may have to be used to create jobs, either in the form of public works programmes with little immediate effect on the national income (and which therefore contribute to raising the global capital-output ratio), or in labour-intensive industries. Contrary to the general belief, labour-intensive techniques will frequently entail a higher capital-output ratio than the most up-to-date capital-intensive techniques.

[4] Source of information on the implications of the policy objectives: [5], pp. 19–29.

[5] The number of equations was not given in the working paper. But it was clear that this model did not contain any complex system of equations to link income and demand with output of the different sectors. The demand on the different sectors was calculated on the basis of elasticities of sectoral growth to *per caput* income growth and population growth. These elasticities were based on two empirical studies, *viz.* Hollis B. Chenery, *Patterns of Industrial Growth*, American Economic Review, Vol. I, No. 4, Sept. 1960; and *A study of Industrial Growth*, prepared by the Division of Industrial Development, United Nations, New York, Feb. 1962 (mimeographed, provisional version). The empirical elasticities were adjusted in two important cases – for agriculture, to take into account the present low level of productivity, and for capital goods industries, which for balance of payments reasons must grow faster than suggested by empirical evidence.

[6] Result obtained by comparing figures in 1959/60 prices on page 2, and in 1964–65 prices on page 20 of [5].

[7] In the present study imports, excluding factor income payments abroad, are projected to grow from 14.8 per cent of the GNP in 1965 to 16.1 per cent in 1985.

8 The Third Five Year Plan does not include any figure for net factor income payments abroad, and it is therefore not possible to calculate 'marginal rate of savings B' for the Perspective Plan.

9 Alternatively, the rate of growth could be reduced to 6 per cent. To raise the marginal rate of savings is another possibility, but in that case the marginal rate of savings for the Perspective Plan period as a whole would have to be raised to 33, which implies a strictly controlled economy.

10 [5], p. 19.

11 This assumption is, of course, unrealistic. If the national income rose more rapidly due to a more rapid growth in agriculture, output in a number of other sectors would grow more rapidly as well. But this does not disturb the present argument provided that the additional growth in other sectors could be achieved with additional investment that did not significantly influence the average, global capital-output ratio. In fact, it is unlikely that the 'marginal' capital-output ratio related to this extra increase in national income will differ so much from the average capital-output ratio that it will alter it significantly.

12 Source of information in this paragraph, [33].

13 [35].

14 [5], p. 296.

15 Source: [34].

16 Source of information on East Pakistan: [34].

17 This is the rate which can be calculated on the basis of Table 2, p. 20, [5].

18 An internal document on prospects and policies for exports in the Perspective Plan, prepared by Mr. Just Faaland as consultant for the Planning Commission in 1964 [36]. At that time export requirements were estimated at Rs 11,900 million as against Rs 14,000 million in the Perspective Plan. Mr. Faaland projected food exports for Rs 1,180 million (rice, Rs 750 million; fish, Rs 250 million; fruit and vegetables, Rs 100 million; and oil cake, Rs 80 million). Some of these products would be processed (fruit, vegetables, fish, and oil cakes), and in any case the f.o.b. value would substantially exceed the farm value.

19 In the internal Planning Commission working paper of April, 1964, on the long term perspectives for the Pakistan economy 1965–85 [37], it was implicitly assumed that income per head in urban and rural areas would grow at the same rate. See Table 12, p. 58, on the basis of which figures for income *per caput* in rural and urban areas respectively in the whole of Pakistan can be calculated. Both incomes *per caput* are shown to increase by 81 per cent between 1965 and 1985.

20 The figures from the Third Plan referred to above can be found in [5], Table 8, p. 8.

There is one explanation for the high figure for foreign assistance used in the Third Plan for the year 1959–60. The figure may refer to foreign aid and other capital assistance received (including private investments). If this is the case, Pakistan will have increased its foreign-exchange reserves by an amount which corresponds to the difference between the inflow of foreign capital and the deficit on the current balance of payments. This increase in foreign-exchange holdings forms a part of domestic savings, and it is illogical to exclude it from savings. I have reason to believe that just such an illogical presentation has been used, since this has been done for 1965. [5], Table 1, 1. 19, shows that the import surplus amounted to Rs 3,940 million, and the use of external resources is shown as Rs 3,690 million. A footnote explains that imports worth Rs 250 million were financed by drawing upon foreign-exchange reserves. The figure for savings is estimated as the difference between investment and the use of external resources (excluding drawing upon foreign-exchange reserves). In other words, in 1965 domestic savings include the use of foreign-exchange reserves.

In several places the Tables in the Perspective Plan contain concepts which are not defined at all, or the definitions of which are obscure. Thus Table 1 referred to above uses the term 'gross *domestic* savings'. Since it corresponds to the difference between gross investment and external resources (which presumably cover the entire current balance of payments deficit, including factor income payments to abroad), it should have been referred to as gross *national* savings. This would also have been consistent with the use of the term 'Gross National Product' in the same Table. It is clear from [5], Table 4, p. 22, that the figure for consumption refers to the difference between Gross *National* Product and gross *domestic* savings as given in Table 1, which suggests that product and savings are either both national or both domestic.

[21] [5], Annex I, pp. 96–97, gives a detailed breakdown of imports of goods and services and debt servicing in 1964–65. It is not possible to find out how Table 6, p. 24, relates to this more detailed table. It has been assumed here that debt servicing is most probably classified as capital goods imports.

[22] If imports in 1985 were to be Rs 3,795 million lower, as implied in Part III of the Table, savings must be correspondingly higher. In fact, this is possible on the assumptions in the present study. More rapid growth of agriculture – at the rate shown in the Perspective Plan – means that the GNP in 1985 would be Rs 14,400 million higher than shown in the present study. If the marginal rate of savings was 25, savings would be Rs 3,600 million higher, or the reduction of the balance of payments deficit due to less food imports would be of about the same order of magnitude as the reduction of the savings deficit due to higher savings. Note that more adjustments would be needed than shown in Part III of Table 82. Factor income payments to abroad would be lower, because of a lower cumulative balance of payments deficit.

[23] *Mining:* In the present study it has been assumed that iron ore must be imported. However, it has also been assumed that petroleum will be found in sufficient quantities in Pakistan. It is more likely that Pakistan will have to import petroleum than that it can dispense with imports of iron ore, and the figure for imports of mining products used in the present study may therefore prove to be too low rather than the opposite. *Wood products:* Extensive use of domestic substitutes for wood has been assumed in this study. In the short run Pakistan cannot develop its forestry sufficiently to eliminate or drastically reduce imports of wood products. *Chemicals:* All imports of chemicals have been classified as intermediate products. A modern society needs a great variety of chemicals and it is unlikely that by 1985 Pakistan can satisfy more than 80 per cent of its needs.

Note also that for the sake of simplicity it has been assumed that Pakistan will not import petro-chemicals. Certain petro-chemical products, which cannot be produced economically in Pakistan by 1985, will therefore be included, under chemicals. *Products of the metal-working industries:* The domestic output of these industries has been projected to double each five-year period (or to grow by an annual compound rate of 14.8 per cent). Even at this rate these industries cannot meet all domestic requirements, and the projected growth of imports of products from these industries is a logical consequence of the overall domestic deficit of such products. *Invisible expenditure* by international shipping and air transport must grow in line with the projected rapid expansion of such activities. For the sake of simplicity, domestic purchases of petroleum products have been included under invisible expenditure abroad and exports of petroleum products.

24 [36].

25 It should be noted, however, that if, as has been done in various instances, the output in agriculture in the present study were recalculated on the basis of the projected growth rate in agriculture in the Perspective Plan, and if the assumption was maintained that value added per man year in agriculture should grow at the same rate as rural income per head, the implied rate of productivity growth in agriculture in the present study would become almost the same as in the Perspective Plan (3.2 per cent). Under this alternative, employment in agriculture would be raised to 29.3 million, and the unemployment figure, not counting imputed employment lowered to about 2.5 million, or 4 per cent of the labour force.

26 The following examples show the implications of the productivity assumptions as regards manufacturing in the present study and in the Perspective Plan:

Annual compound percentage increase in

	Value added	Employment	'Productivity'
The present study			
Modern manufacturing	11.3	7.8	3.25
Traditional manufacturing	1.75	0.05	1.70
Total manufacturing	9.6	3.1	6.3
The Perspective Plan			
Total manufacturing	10.2	4.7	5.2
Alternative I			
Modern manufacturing	11.0	10.1	0.75
Traditional manufacturing	2.2	0.5	1.7
Alternative II			
Modern manufacturing	10.5	7.0	3.25
Traditional manufacturing	5.45	3.7	1.7

Most of the value added and employment in the traditional industries originates in village industries such as grain milling, paddy husking, gur making, hand sawing, or hand-loom weaving. Value added per man year in traditional manufacturing is considerably lower than in agriculture, and in terms of employment the bulk of traditional manufacturing can be considered as an extension of farming activities rather than as a separate sector. As earnings in traditional manufacturing are very low, productivity will have to increase in order to ensure labour incomes which make it worthwhile to continue such activities. In the two alternative examples based on the figures in the Perspective Plan, the implied increase in productivity, obtained in the present study is applied to traditional manufacturing. Alternative I is based on a reasonably likely rate of growth in traditional manufacturing (somewhat higher than in the present study, in order to take into account the more rapid growth in output in agriculture projected in the Perspective Plan), and alternative II is calculated on the basis of the implied increase in productivity for both modern and traditional manufacturing in the present study. Alternative I shows that productivity in modern manufacturing could only increase by 0.75 per cent per year. It is highly unlikely that it will be that low. Alternative II shows that output in traditional manufacturing will have to grow by 5.5 per cent per year. This is also highly unlikely. Thus both alternatives, which in some respects represent extremes, appear unrealistic. And any combinations between these extremes imply an unlikely high rate of growth in output in traditional manufacturing and an unlikely low rate of growth in productivity in modern manufacturing.

[27] For coverage see footnote to Table 79.

[28] [5], para. 25, p. 27.

[29] *Sources:* Table 22, and [5], Annex, Table, p. 58.

[30] The working paper assumed that the urban population in East Pakistan would grow by 10.9 per cent per year, and by only 4.6 per cent in West Pakistan, whereas the present study assumes a corresponding increase of 10.3 per cent in East Pakistan and 5.8 per cent in West Pakistan.

[31] If this were the case, it would suffice if rural income per head increased by 2.9 per cent per year in East Pakistan as against 2.3 per cent in West Pakistan. On the other hand, the urban population in East Pakistan would have to grow by more than 12 per cent per year.

Appendix I

[1] [0], Annex IX, describes the adjustments which were needed in order to make the independent estimates of output, imports, and deliveries consistent with those of intermediate and final uses.

[2] [41].

[3] These details can be found in [0], Annex VI.

[4] In the following it has been necessary to make extensive reference to the background material contained in [0].

[5] [18].

[6] The figures have been cross-checked several times, but this is no guarantee since mistakes could still have slipped in.

[7] Notably [41], [42], and [61], but other sources were also used.

Appendix II

[1] [26], p. 85, and [18], 1954, p. 4.

[2] [2], Chap. 9, para. 30, p. 229.

3 [41].

4 This conclusion is not original. Cf. for example [67], Chap. 8, pp. 133 ff.

5 Cf. J. Jewkes: Are the Economies of Scale Unlimited? [68], p. 102.

6 By 'reasonably low costs', I mean a cost level which permits the domestic industry to compete with imported goods behind the shelter of transport costs and an acceptable tariff barrier that can be very high for luxury products and other dispensable consumer goods, but must be fairly low for means of production.

7 In unpublished working papers (available on request from the Chr. Michelsen Institute, Bergen, Norway) assumptions have been stated for each individual industry.

8 However, data from industrially high countries may be somewhat misleading. In such countries enterprises will be able to procure parts and semi-manufactured products from subcontractors, and thus the size of the plant producing the final product may be quite small. In an underdeveloped country the final producer may have to choose between importing parts and components, etc. (and even this may not always be possible, because of too slow delivery of imported goods) or manufacturing the parts himself. Thus the plant may become larger than a corresponding plant in a highly industrialized country.

9 [69], Appendix A, pp. 32–37.

10 This assumption does not imply an assumption that efforts to decentralize industries will be abandoned. But such efforts can take several forms, e. g. the location of self-contained large plants in industrially less favoured areas (thereby stimulating industrial development); the development of smaller industrial centres (by the creation of facilities, by organizing industrial estates, etc.); fiscal and credit incentives to firms choosing peripheral locations, etc.

Bibliography

This Bibliography contains only documents which in the text and in the Appendixes have been referred to by reference to the number given in the Bibliography. Occasional references to other sources referred to in only one place are annotated in the text.

Reference sources have been grouped together under five headings:

A. Earlier, more detailed version of the present study,
B. Documents published by the Planning Commission of the Government of Pakistan.
C. Other official publications, Pakistan,
D. Sources which mainly describe conditions in Pakistan, and
E. Other sources.

In the preparation of this study a large number of books and articles on economics in general and development economics in particular, on planning techniques, on econometric methods, etc., have been read and consulted. It would serve no purpose, however, to list such publications, since this literature is common knowledge to students of economic development. Also, it would be possible to trace adequately sources of inspiration for methods and ideas utilized in this study, This bibliography lists works which have been utilized explicitly.

A. Earlier, more detailed version of the present study

[0] *Development Prospects of Pakistan,* Ole David Koht Norbye, October 1965, Chr. Michelsen Institute, Bergen, Norway (mimeographed, 3 volumes).

B. Documents published by the Planning Commission (or before 1959 the Planning Board) of the Government of Pakistan

[1] *Outline of the Second Five Year Plan (1960–65),* Karachi, January 1960.
[2] *The Second Five Year Plan (1960–65),* Karachi, June 1960.
[3] *Guidelines for the Third Five Year Plan (1965–70),* Karachi, November 1963.
[4] *Outline of the Third Five Year Plan (1965–70),* Karachi, August 1964.

[5] *The Third Five Year Plan (1965–70)*, Karachi, May 1965.
[6] *Preliminary Evaluation of Progress during the Second Five Year Plan*, Karachi, March 1965.
[7] *The First Five Year Plan (1955–60)*, Karachi, December 1957.
[8] *The First Five Year Plan, Preliminary Evaluation Report*, Karachi, 1959.
[9] *A Survey of Leather Industries in Pakistan*, Karachi, 1958.
[10] *The Second Five Year Plan (Revised Estimates)*, Karachi, November 1961.

C. Other official publications, Pakistan

[11] *Pakistan Statistical Yearbook*, Central Statistical Office, Karachi.
[12] *Monthly Statistical Bulletin*, Central Statistical Office, Karachi.
[13] *National Sample Survey*, (First, Second, Third Round, 1959, 1960, 1961), Central Statistical Office, Karachi.
[14] *Family Budget Enquiry 1944, National Family Expenditure Survey 1955/56*, Central Statistical Office, Karachi, (see [12] November 1959).
[15] *Census Bulletin*, Population Census 1961, Karachi.
[16] *Livestock Wealth of Pakistan*, Ministry of Agriculture, Government of Pakistan, Karachi, 1949.
[17] *Report on Currency and Finance (1959/60)*, State Bank of Pakistan, Karachi, 1960.
[18] *Census of Manufacturing Industries*, Central Statistical Office, Karachi.
[19] *Monthly Summary of Jute Statistics*, Government of East Pakistan, Directorate of Jute, Narayanganj, Dacca.
[20] *Foreign Trade Statistics of Pakistan*, Central Statistical Office, Karachi.

D. Other sources which mainly describe conditions in Pakistan

[21] 'An Estimate of the Birth Rate in East and West Pakistan', Melvin Zelnik and Masihur Rahman Khan, *Pakistan Development Review*, Karachi, Vol. V, No. 1, Spring 1965.
[22] 'Population Size, Growth and Age Distribution: Fourth Release from the 1961 Census of Pakistan', Karol J. Krotki, *Pakistan Development Review*, Vol. III, No. 2, Summer 1963.
[23] *The Strategy of Economic Planning, A Case Study of Pakistan*, Mahbub ul Haq, Oxford University Press, Pakistan Branch, Karachi, Lahore, Dacca, 1962.
[24] 'Expenditure Elasticities in Rural West Pakistan', Azisur Rahman, *Pakistan Development Review*, Vol. III, No. 2, Summer 1963.
[25] 'Note on Consumption Patterns in the Rural Areas of East Pakistan', Mohamad Irshad Khan, *Pakistan Development Review*, Vol. III, No. 3, Autumn 1963.

[26] 'Estimation of National Income in Pakistan', prepared by the Central Statistical Office, Karachi, *Pakistan Development Review*, Vol. I, No. 3, Autumn 1961.

[27] *The Economy of Pakistan*, J. Russel Andrus and Azizali F. Mohammed, Oxford University Press, London, Karachi, Dacca, 1958.

[28] *Basic Data of the Economy of Pakistan*, W. P. Peach, M. Uzair, and G. W .Rucker, Oxford University Press, Karachi, 1959.

[29] *Yearbook of Information 1961*, Pakistan Western Railway, Lahore, and *Yearbook of Information 1961*, Pakistan Eastern Railway, Dacca.

[30] *Transportation Survey of East Pakistan 1961*, Department of the Army, Corps of Engineers, Washington, D.C., U. S. A., December 1961, and *Transportation Survey of West Pakistan 1962*, Department of the Army, Office of the Chief Engineer, Washington, D. C., 1962.

[31] 'Waterlogging and Salinity: An Analysis of the Revelle Report', Ghulam Mohammad and Christopher Beringer, *Pakistan Development Review*, Karachi, Vol. III, No. 2, Summer 1963.

[32] 'Waterlogging and Salinity in the Indus Plain: A Critical Analysis of the Major Conclusions of the Revelle Report', Ghulam Mohammad, *Pakistan Development Review*, Karachi, Vol. IV, No. 3, Autumn 1964.

[33] *Agriculture in West Pakistan: An Analysis of Past Progress and Future Prospects*, Walter Falcon and Carl Gotsch (Unpublished report to the Planning Commission, Karachi, December 1964).

[34] *An Analysis of East Pakistan's Agriculture during the Second and Third Plan Periods*, Walter Falcon and Carl Gotsch (Unpublished draft report to the Planning Commission, Karachi, March 1965).

[35] *Accelerated Wheat Improvement in West Pakistan and the Revolution in Agriculture*, Ignacio Narvaez and Norman E. Borlaug (Progress Report to the Secretary of Agriculture, Government of West Pakistan, Lahore, March 1966.

[36] *Prospects and Policies for Exports in the Perspective Plan*, Just Faaland (memorandum to the International Economics Section, the Planning Commission, Karachi, September 1964).

[37] *Long Term Perspectives for the Pakistan Economy 1965–1985. A First Approach* (draft memorandum to the Planning Commission, Karachi, April 1964).

E. *Other sources*

[38] *An International Comparison of National Products and the Purchasing Power of Currencies*, Milton Gilbert and Irving B. Kravis, Organisation for European Economic Co-operation (OEEC), Paris, 1954.

[39] *Comparative National Products and Price Levels*, Milton Gilbert and Associates, OEEC, Paris, 1958.

[40] 'National Income and Industrial Growth', *Economic Change, Selected Essays in Business Cycles, National Income and Economic*

Growth, Simon Kuznets, William Heineman Ltd., London, 1954, Essay No. 6.

[41] *The Structure and Growth of the Italian Economy*, U. S. Government, MSA, Rome, 1953.

[42] *Input-output Analysis of Norwegian Industries*, Central Bureau of Statistics, Oslo. 1960.

[43] *40 Years of Soviet Power*, Foreign Language Publishing House, Moscow, 1958.

[44] *Development Assistance Efforts and Policies*, Report 1964, Organisation for Economic Co-operation and Development, (OECD), Paris, 1965.

[45] *Plan Quinquennial 1960–64*, Royaume du Maroc, Ministère de l'Economie Nationale, Division de la Coordination Economique et du Plan, Rabat, Morocco, 1960.

[46] 'An International Comparison of Household Expenditure', Commemorating the Centenary of Engel's Law; Hendrik S. Houthakker. *Econometrica*, Vol. 25, No. 4, October 1957.

[47] *Statistical Yearbook of Norway*, (Annual), Central Bureau of Statistics, Oslo.

[48] *The Problems of Scientific and Technical Manpower*, OEEC, Paris (*ca.* 1958 – no date on the publication).

[49] *Europe's Needs and Resources*, prepared for the Twentieth Century Fund, Dewhurst and Associates, Macmillan Co., New York, 1961.

[50] *Statistical Yearbook*, (Annual), United Nations, New York.

[51] *Yearbook*, (Annual), International Labour Organization, Geneva.

[52] *Annual Bulletin of Transport Statistics for Europe*, United Nations, Geneva.

[53] *Basic Statistics of Food and Agriculture*, OEEC, Paris, 1954.

[54] *The Yearbook of Forest Products Statistics*, (Annual), FAO, Rome.

[55] *Towards a New Energy Pattern in Europe*, OEEC, Paris, January 1960.

[56] *Industrial Production Statistics, Annual Survey 1956*, Central Bureau of Statistics, Oslo. 1958.

[57] *The National Sample Survey*, The Cabinet Secretariat, Government of India, New Delhi.

[58] 'Basic Statistics of Energy 1950–60', *OECD Statistical Bulletins*, OECD, Paris, 1961.

[59] *Production Yearbook*, (Annual), FAO, Rome.

[60] *A Comparison of National Output and Productivity*, Deborah Paige and Gottfried Bombach, OEEC, Paris, 1959.

[61] *The Structure of the European Economy in 1953*, Etienne Kirschen and Associates, OEEC, Paris, 1958.

[62] *The Economics of Middle Eastern Oil*, S. Issawi and M. Yeganeh, Faber and Faber, London, 1962.

[63] *Long-term Trends and Problems of the European Steel Industry*, United Nations, Economic Commission for Europe, Geneva, 1959.

[64] *Investment for Food*, D. Groenveld, North Holland Publishing Company, Amsterdam, 1961.

[65] *The Development of the Indian Economy*, W. B. Reddaway, George Allen and Unwin Ltd., London, 1962.

[66] *Balance of Payments Yearbook,* published by the International Monetary Fund, (Annual), Washington D.C.
[67] *The Strategy of Economic Development,* Albert O. Hirschman, New Haven, Yale University Press, 1958.
[68] *The Economic Consequences of the Size of Nations,* ed. Austin Robinson, Macmillan & Co., London 1961.
[69] *Post-war Investment, Location and Size of Plant,* P. Sargent Florence, National Institute of Economic and Social Research, Cambridge University Press, 1962.
[70] 'Long-Term Trends in Food Consumption: A Multi-Country Study', L. Jureen, *Econometrica.* Vol. 24, No. 1. January 1956.

Note

Most, but not all, works listed in the Bibliography have been referred to in the present volume. Many of them, including those not referred to in the present volume, have been used for the preparation of the large number of estimates that support the present study. Additional references can be found throughout [0], and in unpublished notes available from the Chr. Michelsen Institute, Bergen, Norway.